STREET SCENES

STREET SCENES

Staging the Self in Immigrant New York, 1880–1924

ESTHER ROMEYN

UNIVERSITY OF MINNESOTA PRESS

MINNEAPOLIS • LONDON

An earlier version of chapter 4 was published as "Eros and Americanization: David Levinsky and the Etiquette of Race," in *Key Texts in American Jewish Culture*, ed. Jack Kugelmass (New Brunswick, N.J.: Rutgers University Press, 2003); reprinted with permission of Rutgers University Press. An earlier version of chapter 5 was published as "Judging Italian American Identities: Farfariello, King of the Character Clowns," *The Italian American Review* 9, no. 2 (Fall/Winter 2002): 95–128; reprinted with permission of The John D. Calandra Italian American Institute, Queens College (CUNY).

Excerpt from *Invisible Cities* by Italo Calvino copyright 1972 by Giulio editore s.p.a.; English translation by William Weaver copyright 1974 by Harcourt, Inc.; reprinted with permission of Harcourt, Inc.

Published by the University of Minnesota Press
111 Third Avenue South, Suite 290
Minneapolis, MN 55401-2520
http://www.upress.umn.edu

Library of Congress Cataloging-in-Publication Data

Romeyn, Esther.
    Street scenes : staging the self in immigrant New York, 1880–1924 / Esther Romeyn.
        p. cm.
    Includes bibliographical references and index.
    ISBN 978-0-8166-4521-3 (hardcover : alk. paper) —
    ISBN 978-0-8166-4522-0 (pbk. : alk. paper)
    1. New York (N.Y.)—Ethnic relations. 2. New York (N.Y.)—Intellectual life. 3. Minorities—New York (State)—New York—Social conditions. 4. Minorities—New York (State)—New York—Intellectual life. 5. Immigrants—New York (State)—New York—Social conditions. 6. Immigrants—New York (State)—New York—Intellectual life. 7. Performing arts—Social aspects—New York (State)—New York—History. 8. Self—New York (State)—New York—History. 9. Ethnicity—New York (State)—New York—History. 10. City and town life—New York (State)—New York—History. I. Title.
    F128.9.A1R66 2008
    305.8009747'10903—dc22
                                                        2008014710

CONTENTS

ACKNOWLEDGMENTS

I would like to express my gratitude to the following people and institutions. To the Memorial Foundation for Jewish Culture, the University of Minnesota and the Department of American Studies for their generous support of this project in its embryonic stage. To Rob Kroes, David Noble, Riv-Ellen Prell, Lary May, George Lipsitz, David Roediger, and Rudy Vecoli, who taught me to think beyond boundaries. To Jack Kugelmass, who first exposed me to "The World According to Jackie Mason" and with that set me on a journey of which this book turned out to be one destination. To Kathryn Milun, Charles Dellheim, Laura Gross, Randy Hanson, Elizabeth Anderson, David Goldberg, Judith Summerfield, Heleen van Rossum, and Maria Stoilkova for their support and friendship.

I would also like to express thanks to Doug Armato of the University of Minnesota Press for his patience; to Cherene Holland, my manuscript editor; and to Luc Sante for sharing Chuck Connors's book with me.

Special thanks also go to Eliahu Kugelmass, who recently introduced me as a professor of physics and made me think of this book in terms of the gravity and lightness of being; Tamar Kugelmass, whose laughter always pulls me toward lightness; Martin Romeijn, Jan Romeijn, and Onno Romeyn for brotherly hugs; and Mien Romeijn-Höweler for teaching me how to pull through.

This book is dedicated to the memory of my father, Jaap Romeijn, who, true to his character, read the manuscript full of compassion for the fate of Elsie Sigel, one of the book's protagonists.

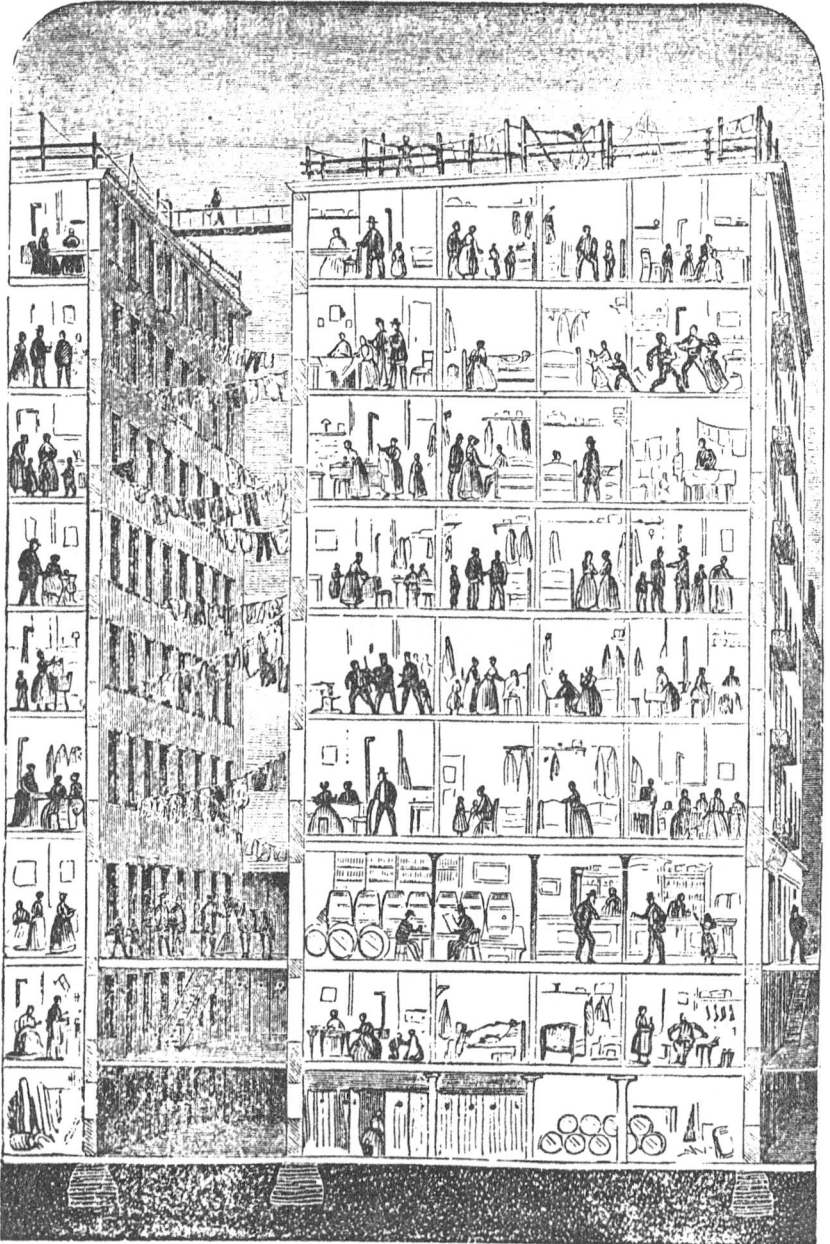

The city as stage: an inside view of a tenement house. From James D. McCabe Jr., *Lights and Shadows of New York Life* (Philadelphia: National Publishing Company, 1872), 688.

INTRODUCTION

In 1941, Claude Lévi-Strauss, living as a refugee in New York and developing the ideas that would lay the foundation for structural anthropology, found himself enchanted by his urban surroundings. The monumental modernist architecture that dominated the metropolis, he realized, imposed only a superficial layer of order on the landscape. Wandering down "miles of Manhattan avenues" and cross streets like a latter-day flâneur, he found the "physiognomy" of the urban landscape changing "from one block to the next: sometimes poverty-stricken, sometimes middle class or provincial, and most often chaotic." New York appeared an "immense vertical and horizontal disorder attributable to some spontaneous upheaval of the urban crust."[1]

Confronted with this apparent disorder, the anthropologist remained unbaffled. To him, these little islands of culture, cut off from their contexts and deposited as the debris of history on the shores of Manhattan, revealed their "secret affinities" with different times and places. "Whoever wanted to go hunting," he wrote about his New York experience later, needed only "a little culture, and flair, for doorways to open in the wall of industrial civilization and reveal other worlds and other times." New York was a collision of the old and the new, where, "in the disorder of a changing society, social strata were violently disrupted, sliding over one another and creating huge holes which engulfed styles and bodies of knowledge."[2]

A house in Greenwich Village recalled "Paris in Balzac's time." Harlem, Chinatown, the Puerto Rican district, Little Italy, Greek, Czech, Scandinavian, Finnish, and other neighborhoods seemed like time warps where along with "their restaurants and their places of worship and entertainment," "they had preserved customs and stories that had vanished without a trace in the old countries." With exhilaration, Lévi-Strauss remembers "the performances that we watched for hours at the Chinese opera under the first arch of the Brooklyn Bridge, where a company that had come long ago from China had a large following. . . . I felt myself going back in time no less when I went to work every morning in the American room of the New York Public Library. There . . . I sat near an Indian in a feather head-dress and a beaded buckskin jacket—who was taking notes with a Parker pen."[3]

But despite Lévi-Strauss's ambulant, almost wistful remembrance of ethnic things past, the visual order he himself imposes on this chaotic landscape, James Clifford has observed, is informed by a "unified perspective" that remains rooted in the notion of culture as organic unity, anchored in time, place, and language—even as New York, the embodiment of modernity, relegates that notion of culture to the past. Ethnic neighborhoods and Chinese opera appear as time capsules, specimens of genuine and authentic cultures about to face extinction in the "emerging uniformity" of mass culture.[4]

Indeed, the "one-dimensional fate" of modern culture announces itself most keenly in one key symptom: the "need to escape." This need, Lévi-Strauss remarks, is present in the tendency of American women to "disguise" themselves, "dressed as little sailors, Egyptian dancing girls, or pioneer women of the Far West." It appears in the "art of shopwindows," which "presented their collections on dummies acting out dramatic scenes—rapes, murders, kidnappings—settings, lightings and colors realized with a consummate skill that would have been the envy of the finest theaters." It also makes itself felt in the lives of Lévi-Strauss's American colleagues and friends, who exchange the comforts of East Side luxury for the rustic life of Long Island and the illusion of being homesteaders that goes with it.[5]

The tropes Lévi-Strauss employed in this cultural mapping of 1940s New York are familiar to the repertoire of the urban exploration narrative, which became exceedingly popular in Gilded Age America, when rapid industrial growth and immigration set the stage for an urban expansion that made its landscapes unrecognizable to its erstwhile inhabitants. These narratives responded to the visual chaos of the new metropolis with a scopic regime that uncovered its underlying semiotic codes and registers. They imposed an epistemological grid on the city that consistently mapped the congruence of place (neighborhood), class, labor, body and physiognomy, language, customs, and (ethnic) identity. At the same time, they were haunted by those instances in which this visual order broke down, and the slippages, improvisations, and incongruities of culture and identity became apparent. The resultant insecurity about the social perception and the nature of identity was captured in a discourse that pitted authenticity against theatricality and its trappings, impersonation, disguise, imposture, and illusion. Typically, these terms are given a topological correlative, with authenticity valorized as depth and interiority and theatricality dismissed as surface and shallowness.[6]

In Lévi-Strauss's mapping, authenticity is given a spatiotemporal dimension as well: embedded in the geological layers of the urban landscape, it is the time/space of the "Other," the ethnic, the folk, the lower classes. Once exposed, these successive layers lay bare their cultural "gems" at the same time that they unavoidably give themselves over to the corrosive forces of modernity, mass culture, and commodity capitalism—inaugurating the age of theatricality and "inauthenticity."

It is not surprising that Lévi-Strauss remains mute before the Native American taking notes in the Public Library with his Parker pen, a hybrid figure (in terms of time and space) he similarly relegates to the past as another vanishing point of history. It is not surprising either that it was New York City that spawned Lévi-Strauss's meditations on the relationship between culture, place, and language, or that it was in New York that he conceptualized a framework for understanding social organization that stood out for its excision of temporality.

Ever since its transformation into a modernist, immigrant metropolis, New York City has posed a challenge to interpretation. It defeats organicist, holistic interpretations of culture, identity, and continuity. New York exposes the fact that space and identities are never given and static, not "simply received from tradition, language or environment," that they imply "processes rather than essences," that such processes are relational and open-ended rather than predetermined, and that they involve "the interweaving of expression and imprint," and their difference.[7]

The modernity of New York, as of nineteenth-century Paris described by Walter Benjamin in his Arcades Project, "derives from the proposition that it is a place, not where the past is recalled by the present, but where 'what has been comes together in a flash with the now to form a constellation.'"[8] For that reason, Benjamin conceives of history as a physiognomy of space, an "infinitesimal analysis of the surface," designed to explode the "continuist abstractions" of historiography, which are merely "master narratives told over and over from the standpoint of the "victors."[9]

Physiognomy, as Benjamin understood it, "when displayed in the lines and traits, in the furrows and folds, of a face [. . .] is neither interiority or exteriority but the interweaving of expression and imprint as well as their irreducible difference." In that sense, his spatial physiognomy, in Rainer Nägele's words, "defines and delineates the forces of interaction through the determining quality of an *inter,* that is, through relations and differences rather than through self-identical substances." It "prepares the ground for the blasting of the metaphorical space of interiority that constitutes the bourgeois subject in its favorite social space: the private sphere as a cozy *intérieur.*" Space is conceived as a "scene," composed of "topological categories, as well as rhetorical and theatrical elements."[10]

Yet, as James Clifford has observed astutely, "People prefer order to disorder; they grasp at formulas rather than actuality; they prefer the guidebook to the confusion before them."[11] Lévi-Strauss's personal guidebook was informed by a "group-by-group" approach to identity and space that had little place for the "inter," the dialogic dimensions—cultural boundary crossings, borrowings, ventriloquisms, and impersonations—that "mark the moment of cultural production."[12] The chaos of the "constellation" of the urban landscape is placed within the overarching structure of modernization.

With his response to the modernist urban scene, Lévi-Strauss mobilizes two conceptualizations with which he takes his place in a long line of middle-class urban spectators. Like the spectators of the urban guidebooks of the Gilded Age, whose gaze transformed the slum into "theater" and its inhabitants into "types," his gaze is given to nostalgia, ordering, categorizing, and theatricalizing. Lévi-Strauss is libidinally drawn to the theatricality of the Other, encapsulated here in the image of the Chinese opera. In this performance, he recognizes culture in its most "authentic," crystallized, gemlike state. The theatricality of Chinese opera, even if displaced to the Brooklyn Bridge, is still the expression of the essence of Chinese culture. But apparently there is "good" (authentic) and "bad" (inauthentic) theatricality. Lévi-Strauss reserves the first perspective for foreign cultures, seemingly untouched by modernity.[13] When confronted with the dislocations, corrosions, and (perceived) homogenizations of capitalist modernity, his reaction is very different. At that moment, he betrays his "anti-theatrical prejudice."[14] For Lévi-Strauss, mass consumption, with its cultivation of surface and external appearances, renders culture inauthentic and transforms people into poseurs and frauds. With that judgment, he reverts back to the distinction between "reality" and "theater," corresponding to an (authentic) interiority (culture; being) and a (false) exteriority (commodity; appearance). This distinction, which runs through Victorian, modern, and postmodern responses to the order of commodity capitalism, was precisely what Benjamin's "physiognomy of place" hoped to explode.[15]

Urban Discontinuities

In his notes on the Arcades Project, Benjamin writes about the city as a "virtual" site: a "material place that becomes a medium of philosophical potential." It is in this context that Benjamin raises the "analogy between walking and reading," linked in his writing to the figure of the flâneur. Walking involves "reading the street," "in the now of its recognizability." The steps of the flâneur, which follow the street, make "possible an experience of Paris as communicative medium."[16] In them, teleology, the end-oriented conceptualization of time and history, gives way to the "mediacy" of experience.

Truthfully, however, most walkers and readers of the city actively attempt to preempt the experience of urban space as philosophical topos—as Benjamin very well recognized. In this book, I focus on the interpretations and performance of the urban space of New York City between 1880 and 1920, a period that predates Lévi-Strauss's wanderings and theories of culture, but one that evinces, in its texts, similar prejudices. The urban guidebooks, the murder of Elsie Sigel in New York's Chinatown, the dialect comedy performances, and the slumming tours I examine all participated in a widespread effort to establish solid grounds for interpretation and identity. The maps and physiologies that pervade these texts, events, and performances were informed by codes and norms of identity that were steeped in a bourgeois ideal of representation that hinged on the general rule of the "complete immanence of meaning," the "representation of an interiority in and through a homogeneous, adequate exteriority."[17] Their favorite strategy lay in what Samuel Weber, following Heidegger, identifies as "the reduction of language to *naming*," and "the locating of the named in an unequivocal *place*."[18]

In these readings and performances, the city as a philosophical topos and urban life in all its multiplicity disappear under an epistemology of grids, names, and types. Yet the confrontation of the remains of a Victorian worldview with the encroaching scenes of modernity reverberates in sudden caesuras in these narratives of continuity and holism. Frequently, such caesuras are expressed (and exorcised) in, and through, a discourse of authenticity and theatricality.

Inevitably, "inter"-pretations of turn-of-the-nineteenth-century New York are haunted by the performativity of language and culture, by the fact that

"acting" pervaded American culture, and by the realization that the grounds
for establishing authentic, "organic" identity were slippery, especially in a
modern, cultural borderland such as New York, where the production of
identity inevitably was infused by desire, ruptured by processes of immigration and social mobility, caught up in the system of commodity exchange
of an emerging consumer society, and taking place in "the border crossings
and transactions between Self and Other, in dialogic moments of intercultural 'lending' and 'borrowing.'"[19] What interests me in these cultural texts,
then, is the nature of the knowledge that is produced in these caesuras.

Historically, the period between 1880 and 1920 can be characterized by at
least three closely related structural transformations. As industrial capitalism unleashed its powers, it brought about the unmooring and restructur-
ing of identities, social structures, and urban space on an unprecedented
scale. These changes were accompanied by what Max Weber characterized
as the "Entzauberung der Welt," in which the processes of secularization,
rationalization, and bureaucratization of society and social relations combined to produce a "disenchanted" world devoid of transcendence, epito-
mized by the emergence of a new class of middle-class "professionals." The
introduction of consumer capitalism, meanwhile, reenchanted the world
with the promise of satisfaction and fullness of meaning through the "phantasmagoria of the world of commodities," inaugurating an economy structured on the basis of a "vicious circle of a desire," which thrived on perceived
lack, need, and dissatisfaction.[20]

It also stimulated the formulation of a new conception of personhood,
captured best by the transition, documented by the cultural historian Warren Susman, from the ideal of "character," with its cultivation of a moral
"interiority" congruent with producer values and an economy of accumulation, to the ideal of "personality," with its stress on the creation of a distinctive external persona (manners, proper clothes, good conversation, poise)
molded to impress and fascinate others in a society of strangers and momentary, fleeting impressions.[21]

As in Lévi-Strauss's reading of the urban landscape, the ambivalence
evoked by these processes was captured in discourses and performances
employing tropes of theatricality and authenticity. Not surprisingly, America's
social, ethnic, and racial Others were inscribed and encrypted in these discourses in particular ways, as the tropes of theatricality and authenticity intersected with discourses of class, race, and whiteness. Moreover, as power always
has a spatial component, and is about embodiment, these discourses were
deployed topologically, in relation to the urban spaces of New York City.[22]

The Place of the Stage

The association of the "cultivation of externality" with "theatricality," which is embedded in many modern and postmodern critiques of commodity capitalism and is reflected in Lévi-Strauss's prejudices, reaches back to classical debates that illuminate the extent to which the stage and (urban) space are linked, theoretically and experientially.

The question of the "place" of the stage in Western culture has preoccupied philosophers since Aristotle and Plato. Plato's deep suspicion of the theater, as Samuel Weber explains, was based on its presumed ability to undermine the authority of law and the social and political space structured by it, an ability that Plato attributed to the power of the theater to "move." In his analysis of a passage from Plato's *Laws*, in which the philosopher illustrates the degradation of Athens' political life with the example of the disruption of a ritual sacrifice (the inscription of communal values onto urban space) by groups of itinerant singers, Weber suggests that theatrical spectacle disrupts "the consecrated and institutionalized boundaries that structure political space: those, for instance, that separate the sacred from the profane, the 'altar' from the public." Theatricality becomes especially subversive when it ventures beyond the limits of the *theatron* (a word that, Weber explains, literally designates "the place from which one sees"), and "begins to wander: when, in short, it separates itself from *theater*. For in so doing it begins to escape control by the prevailing rules of representation, whether aesthetic, social, or political. . . . It breaks down the borders of propriety and restraint in others while itself remaining difficult to control and even identify."[23]

As this passage indicates, the "place of the stage" is highly ambiguous. It is the medium through which "space" becomes "place" or "topography" becomes "topology." Space, in other words, becomes a depository of meaning through ritual performances and ceremonies, which inscribe dominant social and cultural values and thus create the city as a space of community.[24]

At the same time, the "stage" has a tendency to become "dislodged" from its proper circumscribed space—a place ensuring a proper perspective conducive to social stability. By introducing a "multiplicity of perspectives and a cacophony of voices," the stage becomes disruptive.[25] As a consequence, Western culture has tended to view the stage with suspicion. It has set aside theater as a space of "unreality, debased imitation, and outright counterfeiting," separate and distinct from the world and other social practices, and has evinced a strong "anti-theatrical prejudice" in a more general sense.[26]

This prejudice found new fuel in the emergence of popular theater, which, in the Anglo-Saxon world, dates back to the late sixteenth and early seventeenth century. As Jean-Christophe Agnew and Steven Mullaney, among others, have argued, the popular stage as an institution and the protean, performative self as a concept made their appearances in conjunction with the onset of capitalism and modernity. The market, "gathering of strangers," driven by the illusion of value with which it imbued commodities and people, undermined stable identities and stimulated role-playing and self-fashioning. The expansion and intensification of mercantile exchange meanwhile inserted an unprecedented degree of mobility in society and transformed "conventional signposts of social and individual identity" into "mobile and manipulable reference points."[27]

The resulting preoccupation with "mobility and deceit" stimulated the emergence of a literature that aimed to counteract the fluidity and lack of transparency of the social world with "detailed social description." The inventories of social types and jargons found in sixteenth- and seventeenth-century character books, *"physiologies,"* rogue literature, and the "Ship of Fools" genre sought to impose fixity on a fluid social world. Yet in these efforts, these books presented society as "thoroughly staged," paradoxically providing a road map for social dissimulation.

Within this historical context, Agnew argues, the stage started to function as a metaphor for, and a register of, the protean nature of the self and the social world.[28] The disguise, masquerade, and self-conscious representation of theatricality suggested a "potential social fluidity" and hinted at the "protean capacities of individuals crossing class and cultural boundaries."[29] Located physically on the boundaries of the city, and metaphorically on the boundaries of society, the liminal space of the stage became a realm in which unfamiliar customs and cultures could be explored, exhibited, and reviewed with some license.[30]

At the same time, the "ground of 'theater'" is "opposed to 'reality,'" and the "common negative connotations of 'theatrical' are marked by a counterprojection of 'genuine' and 'true' actions and feelings."[31] This split is evident in the fact that, since as early as the seventeenth century, the Others of the bourgeois subject have tended to be constructed as the negative image of the real, authentic, truthful, stable, self-identical, self-contained bourgeois self, and represented as theatrical, inauthentic, exotic, flamboyant, slippery, and false.[32] In the "real" theaters, the mark of this split is in the separation of stage and audience, accomplished by the "abyss" of the orchestra pit.[33] Theater, then, Rainer Nägele concludes, has its "ground in a split," which is

"also the split of the self." It is the irreducible split of a human subject constituted and displaced by an Other.[34] And insofar as this split was projected
onto a split between interior essence and external appearance, which (imagined as a perfect correspondence) was constitutive of bourgeois identity,
theatricality continued to perform this splitting.[35]

But for all its efforts to represent this split as a perfect correspondence
between interiorized nature and an external expression, theater highlighted,
and thereby radicalized, exteriority. The theatrical body, Nägele argues, "is
the representation of a representation, representing the body that belongs
to the phenomenal world of appearance and representation." It is this aspect
of theater that links it closely to allegory. It plays itself out in the irreducible
split between interiority and exteriority, in the "abyss between pictorial being
and meaning," a split that allegory, unlike the Romantic symbol, does not
try to hide. It is also here that theater solidifies its link to urban space. Urban
space, by definition, functioned as the counterpoint of the cozy *intérieur*,
the metaphorical private space of interiorized bourgeois essence. [36] As such,
it is the space of theatricality. In Benjamin's writings, it is the flâneur, a
utopian figure, who externalizes bourgeois interiority and "inhabits the
streets as his living room," its "walls" his "writing desk," its "newspapers" his
"libraries," its "benches" his bedroom furniture. In his more modern incarnation, however, the flâneur as reporter or as detective probes the urban
surface for traces and meanings, haunted by the specter of a theatricality
that is profoundly Other and appears as treachery and disguise.[37]

The Stage, Theatricality, and Modern American Culture

In modern America, land of unbridled opportunities, self-transformation
has been at the core of the national mythology. Yet this belief in the mutability of the self has had a flipside, which has expressed itself in widespread
paranoia about "false" identities, a corresponding desire to locate the benchmark of "authentic" identities, and regulatory and disciplinary mechanisms
for policing boundaries of identity.[38]

Neil Harris has attributed the mid-nineteenth-century popularity of
P. T. Barnum, whose exhibits of freaks of nature thrived on trickery and
hoaxes, to Americans' need to meditate on, and contain their mistrust of,
appearances.[39] More recently, Karen Halttunen, John Kasson, and Shawn
Michelle Smith, in analyses more sensitive to issues of class, have interpreted the nineteenth-century panic over false identities and confidence
men as a middle-class paranoia that fed off the contradictions of bourgeois

ideology. The American bourgeoisie, Halttunen argues, suppressed its own recent social mobility and legitimated its social and cultural hegemony by claiming for itself a "superior morality." Taking outer appearance as an index of inner character, it subjected bourgeois conduct and appearance to a rigorous system of etiquette and rules of behavior, which made bourgeois morality visible as "complete self-restraint." It denied the performative aspects of "bourgeois status" through a sentimental "cult of sincerity," which constructed genteel behavior as the natural expression of innate character. Yet, at the same time, the codification of gentility in manuals of etiquette and manners made genteel status available for imitation, undermining the social boundary it supposedly made visible, and giving rise to a widespread anxiety about social impostures.[40]

Halttunen suggests that by 1870, increasing social mobility, the replacement of entrepreneurial with corporate capitalism, and the rise of consumer society and the "self-made man" prepared the way for a new concept of self that encouraged the "arts of the confidence man" and the "manipulation of outward appearance" as a key to success. With that shift, she suggests, the theatricality of the self and of social relations came to a new acceptance.[41]

Yet rather than exchanging the notion of "innate" character completely for one of fluid and performative "personality," and distrust of theatricality for its acceptance, as Warren Susman and Halttunen suggest, this new notion of the (middle-class) self was situated within a social matrix in which "authentic identities" were linked, ever more tightly, to the concept of race.

Self-fashioning—the ability to transform and transcend one's original identity—had always been considered to be limited by the existence of innate differences that were "stronger than human will and human creative potential" and constituted an effective limit to self-cultivation.[42] As Zygmunt Bauman argues, in the face of the Enlightenment belief in the potential of education and self-perfection, which undermined the "naturalness" of social differences by making it "hostage to human self-determination," race presented a "natural" limit to the protean self of modernity. Race locates difference at a level that is "stronger than the human powers of culture and self-determination." The essence of racism, then, lies in its charge of immutability. It claims that "man *is*, before he *acts*; nothing he does may change what he is."[43]

Precisely because of the American belief in the fluidity of social class, race came to carry the weight of social differentiation.[44] Indeed, Werner Sollors has observed that "the concepts of the self-made man and of Jim Crow had their origins in the same culture at about the same time, whereas aristocratic societies had no need for either. . . . It was not the hereditary privilege of aristocratic blue blood but the culturally constructed supposed liability of black blood that mattered most in the United States."[45]

With the development of "scientific racism" in the latter part of the nineteenth century, race came to be understood not in terms of "deep seated biological forces," but as occupying a nebulous terrain between biology and culture. As the neo-Lamarckian doctrine of the inheritance of acquired characteristics replaced the waning influence of Social Darwinism, American social science conceptualized race as the physical inheritance of complex cultural characteristics, which initially had been an adaptive response to environmental circumstances. In the course of centuries of adaptation, these cultural characteristics assumed a virtually instinctive quality.[46] This "unconscious inheritance" of "modes of thought, ideas, traditions and sentiments" encompassed such varied characteristics as propensity toward beauty, passion, business acumen, competitiveness, work ethos, civility, and manners.[47]

Moreover, despite a professed belief in the "self-made man," and the permeability of class boundaries, in an era of deepening social divisions and rising eugenicist concerns, the perception of the nation's working- and "under-class," spatially segregated in urban environments by class, ethnicity, and race, was increasingly filtered through racist and nativist lenses. Collectively seen as an "unknown race," the poor were thought to be subject to the hereditary transmission of character traits developed in response to the degrading slum environments, and thus doomed in a self-perpetuating devolutionary spiral.[48]

Nineteenth- and early twentieth-century notions of racial "type" and racial "character," then, racialized and naturalized social class and ethnicity, assuming the existence of an intimate, organic connection between body, physiognomy, occupation, class, language, manners, morals, and locale. The notion of race as embodied implied the intersection of nationality, race, and class. Moreover, the influence of neo-Lamarckian notions of environmental determinism meant that race, class, assimilation, and social mobility were, of necessity, configured in relation to, and enacted through and upon, the body and space.[49]

"Race traits" thus assumed center stage in discussions about the potential for, and limits of, the transformation of the "new" immigrants, who started to arrive at America's shores in the 1880s, into "Americans." Coming mostly from southern and eastern Europe, the new immigrants were legally considered "white persons" according to the racial categorizations of the naturalization law. They were therefore, unlike the Chinese, for instance, eligible for American citizenship.[50] Yet, racially different from and inferior to the "superior" Anglo-Saxon and Germanic races, they were also seen as unlikely candidates for the epic self-transformation that characterized the "true" American, who, in a climate shaped by eugenic concerns, was ever-more emphatically identified as Anglo-Saxon.

Social scientists generally regarded race as an independent and ulti-mately determining force in processes of cultural change in general and assimilation in particular. The question was to what degree this innate qual-ity was susceptible to change. Even those social scientists who diverged from the standard neo-Lamarckian environmentalism on this issue considered "race" to be a deeper "instinct" practically impermeable to "civilizing" influ-ences. Influenced by Gabriel Tarde's theory about the role of imitation in the transmission of culture, social scientists such as Jerome Dowd and Charles Ellwood, for instance, argued that assimilation was primarily the result of a process of suggestion and imitation and meant "acquiring the emotions, thoughts, and habits of another, by personal imitation and social imitation."[51]

Yet this partial nod to the place of "performance" in culture was offset by the fact that they considered the racial "habits" of many non-Caucasians (Jews and African Americans in particular) to be impermeable and their "imitation" of genteel etiquette a superficial layer masking deeper (racial) "instincts."[52] Assimilation, in the case of Jews and African Americans, was (per definition) bound to yield "false gentlemen."

The centrality of race in the debate about immigrant assimilation, then, meant that the dynamics of immigrant acculturation, social mobility, and self-transformation were embedded in a discourse of passing, "authentic-ity" and "imposture," and "true" and "false" identities. At the same time, however, acting, the successful manipulation of external appearance, was increasingly validated as a sign of white, middle-class professionalism. The acting and theatrical self, then, assumed a place within the social hierarchy, which was decidedly double.

Space and Race

In *Street Scenes,* I seek to uncover the cultural politics that lie embedded in the "inter"-pretation of urban space in the period between 1880 and 1920. In doing so, I suggest the extent to which the discourses of authenticity and theatricality construct space as well as race. This is not only because of the contemporary predominance of neo-Lamarckian ideas about the influence of the environment (space) on organisms. Race is made "visible" in the organization and distribution of social space. The fact that "racial politics are spatial politics" is most evident in the concept of the color line, which has operated as a spatial metaphor, but also has enabled and justified the social and spatial distribution of power, wealth, access, and privilege.[53] The apparently "innocent" spatial organization of social life inscribes structures of power and discipline into human geography. Spatial boundaries are the places where social divisions are at once most "self-evident" and most vulnerable to deconstruction, hence they tend to be heavily invested with symbolic meanings.[54]

Moreover, the construction of white bourgeois identity as transcendent, self-contained, mobile, and invisible, and its Other as "fixed," "embodied," and "localized," suggests that race is habitually linked to metaphors of space. Indeed, Richard Dyer and Patricia McKee have argued that such constructions are part and parcel of a symbolics of white identity, in which whiteness is "abstracted from physical attributes as well as from history and cultural practices," while others are represented as "material identities."[55] The symbolic codes of white identity therefore include an "escape" of "bodily identity" and a "mobility of vision" that is absent in "dark" characters. Consequently, McKee continues, "The most important difference between representations of white and nonwhite characters . . . is not a difference between abstract and embodied identities per se but between a theoretically open symbolics of white identity, and representations of limited, exclusive, embodied identity."[56]

Given the centrality of the concepts of "embodiedness" and "transcendence" in the conceptualization and symbolics of race and whiteness, it is not surprising that the American stage, and the popular stage in particular, has traditionally functioned as perhaps the most important symbolic staging grounds for these constructions. Theater, Sam Weber reminds us, has traditionally sanctified and consecrated the institutionalized boundaries that structure the public sphere. As such, the stage was central in the dissemination of concepts and distinctions that informed America's social and political space. Theater's own ground in the play with the mutability and protean nature of the self made it all the more pivotal in popularizing the notion of race as that what "man *is* before he *acts.*" Yet with its ability to signify the performativity of social practices and the mutability of all social identities, popular theater did retain its subversive potential.

These ambivalences have been most extensively examined in the case of blackface minstrelsy.[57] *Street Scenes* turns its attention to the popular genre of "racial comedy," of which blackface minstrelsy was but one component. "Racial" or "dialect" comedy, as it was popularly called, was a standard feature on the American vaudeville stage. It referred to comic acts that featured broadly caricatured and standardized "racial" types, whose popularity surged and waned in accordance with the nationality's positioning within the urban landscape and society more generally. My analysis of dialect comedy explores the ambivalences of these performances—as theatrical acts that "fix" as well as "wander," that inscribe as well as express—in relationship to urban space, the aesthetics of modernity, and the construction of race and class.

What emerges as central in my discussion, paradoxically perhaps for a discussion of racial comedy, is the widespread contemporary speculation about the place of the "real" and of realism—the artistic and literary conventions purporting to transcribe the "real"—within the genre of racial impersonation. The reification of the "real" has been a widely acknowledged by contemporary scholars of literary realism. The "real," valorized in turn-of-the-nineteenth-century realist fiction, is set off against the inauthentic, the superficial, the theatrical, the opaque. While "inauthenticity" rules the life of the middle classes, the privileged loci of the "authentic" are the ghetto and urban "low life." This dichotomy, which reversed earlier notions of bourgeois identity as "authentic" (which itself had been constructed in opposition to the mannerist self of the nobility), not surprisingly extended to contemporary interpretations of urban space, and was inflected by dominant notions of race and class. Moreover, it formed the basis of a hierarchy of cultural prestige and "distinction" that affected literary as well as theatrical production and consumption, and made its mark on racial comedy as well.

PERFORMATIVITY AND PERFORMANCE

The distinction between "reality" and "theatricality," to which these discourses of the city so feverishly return, has, over the last two decades, been upended by the notion of "performativity," a term that has become central in theoretical discussions of the place of the stage in culture and society. "Performativity," as it is being used in current scholarship, presents a concept that is deeply informed by poststructuralism, specifically J. L. Austin's idea of "performative speech" and Jacques Derrida's concept of "iterability." In the notion of performative speech, Austin interrogated the relation of "speech" to "act" and tried to capture the illocutionary and perlocutionary force or effect of an "utterance."[58] Performative speech acts are "utterances that accomplish, in their very enunciation, an action that generates effects."[59] As such, they cannot be characterized or evaluated by their relative truth ("authenticity") value. Austin considers performative speech on the theatrical stage a case apart from normal speech events, however, and rules such speech "*parasitic* on its normal use."[60]

Derrida interrogates precisely Austin's separation of the theater from the "norm," arguing for a generalized "iterability" or "citationality" that pervades both the stage and the social world, rendering both thoroughly "theatrical."[61] This notion has been the cornerstone of a critical discourse that seeks to blur the difference between the theater and the "real world" and, in particular, to "underscore the fictionality of an ontologically stable and coherent" (authentic, interior) identity.[62]

Seamlessly connecting insights derived from Foucault, Derrida, and psychoanalysis, Judith Butler further elaborates the notion of performativity in the context of the theory of gender identity. In her argument, gender is the "effect" and the "function" of normative (heterosexual) discourses that manufacture gender as an inner truth, through the inscription of "words, acts and gestures, articulated and enacted desires" *on* the body, which are then understood as the signs, the natural expression, of the illusory (gendered) interior essence they produce. Gender is performative in the sense that, in order to achieve the effect and semblance of stable, natural, identities, it has to be produced continuously, "through a *stylized repetition of acts*," in a "dramatic and contingent construction of meaning," in which both the actors and the social audience have come to believe.[63]

Far from being the natural expressions of an inner truth or interior essence, (gender) identities are the effects of performance. Performance, however, "does not refer to a voluntarist process" as much as a "'forced reiteration of norms' in the sense of a compulsory and constraining heterosexuality that impels and sustains gender identity."[64] Seeing performativity as a continuum, Butler follows Derrida's notion that "ordinary speech acts and theatrical performances are underpinned by the same citational practices."[65] While the staged performance is a "bounded act," theater also reiterates and recitates the same conventions that "precede, constrain and exceed the performer and in that sense cannot be taken as the fabrication of the performer's 'will' or 'choice.'"[66]

Performativity, for Butler, seems to act as a Foucauldian regimen of truth, as it is mobilized to uphold the notions of a natural gender and a voluntarist, coherent, self-determining subject. With its stress on determinacy, her model begs two interrelated questions. What happens, in this model, to the troubling aspects of theatricality? What is invested in maintaining the distinction between "performance" and the "real"—and what is at stake in losing that distinction?[67]

Responses to these questions of course differ according to theoretical orientations. According to Derrida, the irksome quality of the performative is inherent and resides in its ambivalent movement. Citation is never simply repetition and re-creation, it is "a reproduction that constitutes what it repeats *différance,* both difference and deferral, both altered and alterable."[68] From this perspective, it is the indeterminacy of the performative itself that creates the possibility for change. The excess of the theatrical cannot be contained.

For others, who seek to inject performativity with the possibility of agency, the subversiveness of the theatrical lies in the possibility of performative "resignification," which are particular modes of citation (parody, excess, hyperbole) and specific practices of iteration (conscious, self-reflective, transgressive), that cause the excluded "theatrical" to stage a "return of the repressed." Butler herself acknowledges the possibility of such a return, in which "the abiding gendered self will then be shown to be structured by repeated acts that seek to approximate the idea of a substantial ground of identity, but which, in their occasional *dis*continuity, reveal the temporal and contingent groundlessness of this 'ground.'"[69]

Elaborating this issue from a more dialogical principle, some scholars see the performative not as a seamless whole, but rather as a series of overlapping, disjunctive, contradictory, and possibly conflicting performative acts. The reproduction of the social world, Lois McNay suggests, involves "value clashes between groups, changes in consciousness, social protests, and repression based on force."[70] Thus, she argues that "the cultural necessity for a performative reiteration of these symbolic norms highlights the extent to which they are not natural or inevitable and are, therefore, potentially open to change."[71]

This necessity, however, raises the question whether such practices require an "autonomous" actor (a status Butler would deny the existence of, because there is no subject or identity prior to discourse or "cultural embeddedness"), and whether resignification is inherently or only conditionally subversive.[72] In response, Butler argues for a different model of agency. This model would free itself from "the unnecessary binary of free will and determinism," which accompanies an identity politics that takes identity categories to be "foundational and fixed." The fact that identities are constituted does not imply that there is no agency. Indeed, construction "is the necessary scene of agency, the very terms on which agency is articulated and becomes culturally intelligible."[73] The task of criticism then is to understand identity as an effect and a signifying practice, and, in particular, to interrogate what "constitutes a subversive repetition within signifying practices of gender." "What," Butler asks, "enables the exposure of the rift between the phantasmatic and the real, whereby the real admits itself as phantasmatic?"[74]

STREET SCENES

The starting point for *Street Scenes* is the perspective that the distinction between performance and performativity cannot easily be upheld. Consequently, I view all the "cultural texts" I analyze, which include guidebooks, slumming parties, "dialect" or "racial" comedy, the stage Hebrew, the performances of an Italian American clown, and a murder investigation in Chinatown, as performative acts. At the same time, it cannot be without significance that, as Steven Mullaney has remarked and Butler underscores, the boundary that power continuously speculates upon is precisely the demarcation separating the realm of "reality" from that of the "theatrical" and "appearance."[75] Therefore, I focus my attention precisely on the borders separating the "real" from the "theatrical." I examine the structures of authority, discourses of knowledge and power, and modes of "citation" that uphold these lines of demarcation, the authenticity "effects" these distinctions create, and the conditions under which they collapse.

Culture is not merely hegemonic and disciplinarian. It is the playground for what Cornelius Castoriadis calls the "radical imagination." As McNay argues, there is an imaginative aspect in all forms of behavior, even the most normative or disciplined. At the same time, even the most innovative practices carry the imprint of certain norms and values that structure the social. What Butler calls the performative, and Bourdieu characterizes as habitus, is central to this process of inculcation.[76]

Thus, it is possible to recognize the theatrical as a space with the capacity or power to reproduce, as well as "transcend, criticize, or at least self-consciously comment on the structure of those social conditions under which it is produced."[77] Guy Debord describes the theatrical dimension of the spectacle as consisting in the fact that the world it holds up to view is "at once *here* and *elsewhere*." As Samuel Weber comments, "This 'at once' constitutes the challenge of theatricality to every system of thought based on the priority of identity and self-presence."[78] *Street Scenes* seeks to uncover some of these challenges.

This book is divided in two parts. Part I, "The City as Theater," interprets the "theater" of New York City between 1880 and 1924 in the light of the "sharpening of physiognomic perception" that, according to Walter Benjamin, is necessitated by and accompanies shifts in power and the social hierarchy.[79] All inhabitants of the city, old, new, rich, poor, white, nonwhite, or in-between, were confronted with the need to make meaning out of an increasingly opaque landscape, and negotiate boundaries between self and Other, which, given the processes of social mobility and acculturation, were far from solid. Urban guidebooks and "Mystery and Misery" novels (written in English but also in Yiddish and Italian), slumming expeditions, urban sketches in such popular magazines as *McClure's*, and American and immigrant vaudeville were infused with the cognitive imperative to make sense of the fragmentation, discontinuity, and phantasmagoria of the modern metropolis.

Chapter 1, "The Epistemology of the City," explores American, Jewish American, and Italian American versions of the urban "Mystery and Misery" genre. It analyzes how, within the urban guidebook, the "mediacy" of the experience of urban space gives way to an epistemology laying bare the cultural and geographical grid of the city.[80] The social and racial typologies constructed by these "narratives of exposure" create distinctions between self and Other, mobility and localism, mutability and fixity, high and low, rich and poor, gentility and vulgarity, falseness and authenticity, which are mapped onto a spatial hierarchy of uptown and downtown, Broadway and the Bowery, East Side and West Side, Chinatown, Little Italy, Harlem, and Fifth Avenue.[81] At the same time, these guidebooks are haunted by a radical insecurity about social (mis)perception and the (performative) nature of identity itself.

Yiddish and Italian American versions of the "Mystery and Misery" novel make turn-of-the-century New York City the scene for dramas of mystification and unveiling. These texts, which retain a close affinity to the mid-nineteenth-century urban gothic novels that lay the foundations for the genre, construct the city as community, transforming the strange, unfamiliar, and dangerous into the familiar through the discovery of unknown or long-secret kinship, romantic, or friendship ties.

The growing social and racial divisions within the city, and the opacity of the urban landscape that was a result of social and cultural "mimicry" and social mobility, compelled a shift from the panoramic gaze of the spectator to an insider's experience of the "real life" of cultural and racial Others. Cultural knowledge came to depend crucially on the translation of go-betweens, individuals who could cross social and racial boundaries through the acts of passing, impersonation, and masquerade. The discourse of realism, which as critics have argued was strongly influenced by the notion of culture as "innate," provided these cultural go-betweens with an idiom of "truth" (and falsity) that served to naturalize race and class.

Chapter 2, "Detecting, Acting, and the Hierarchy of the Social Body," argues that the predilection for social and racial masquerade as methods of social (or criminal) investigation signals the shift from a culture of "character" toward a culture of "personality" as described by Warren Susman. This shift implied a change in the place of the stage in American society. Acting was no longer considered "imposture," but was regarded as a sign of the ability to project a convincing image to the outside world while keeping one's inner moral character intact. The far-reaching implications of this change, which coincided with the emergence of a new class of professionals whose status depended on the fictionality of their social roles, demanded that mutability of identity remain the preserve of the white middle classes. While mutability was constructed as the key aspect of white middle-class identity, whose identities are unmarked by class or race, the identities of racial Others were constructed as immutable, unable to transcend the "fixed" correspondence of physiognomy, class, innate characteristics, sentiments, and behaviors. For these groups, "acting" remained connected to the discourse of "imposture." This codification of the social body, then, hinged on differentiating between "acting" as the ability to negotiate a split between inner and outer self, which was constructed as the very essence of whiteness, and "acting" as the willful misrepresentation and dissimulation of a racially innate identity. Moreover, the construction of white middle-class identity as "mutable" was paired with a fetishization of urban low life as the "touchstone of the real." [82]

Literary realism, popular culture, and the urban tourist industry actively manufactured this codification of the social body by performing the "low life" of immigrant regions of the city such as Chinatown, the Lower East Side, Little Italy, and staging it as transparent, "real," and "inherently theatrical." This construction, however, contained complex cultural dangers that were linked to the deception inherent in "theater," and the desire for the Other that was embedded in the construction of the Other as theatrical, transparent, and "flamboyant." Chapter 3, "Crossing the Bowery: Female Slumming and the Theater of Urban Space," explores these dangers in the context of the murder of Elsie Sigel, a young woman of upper-class Wasp background devoted to missionary work among Chinese immigrants. Discourses surrounding the murder reveal the outlines of a moral panic that connected the female flâneuse, women's "love for the exotic," and the seduction techniques of commodity culture with the dangers inherent in the failure to recognize the theatricality and deceptiveness of the "Other," exemplified by Elsie Sigel's fatal boundary crossing.

The externalization of the self as actor, which accompanied the shift from a producer to a consumer economy, and its impact on immigrant subjectivity is explored in Chapter 4, "Eros and Americanization," which focuses on Abraham Cahan's novel *The Rise of David Levinsky*. In the novel, Cahan subjects the glorification of the ideal of self-transformation under the conditions of consumer capitalism to a radical critique. In its critique of the disjunction between David's inner and exterior selves, however, the novel interprets some of his postures and gestures as "mere show" and "emptiness," while valorizing others as signs of an interior racial (Jewish) authenticity. In that sense, Cahan's deconstruction of genteel status as a performative inscription on the body ends up naturalizing the notion of a Jewish racial essence that is physically irrepressible.

Part II, "Stages of Identity," examines the American popular stage as an arena in which the symbolic meanings of acting and impersonation as codes for mutability and fixity, transcendence and embodiment, Americanness and un-Americanness, whiteness and race, are exhibited, manipulated, negotiated, and disrupted. In the period between 1890 and 1924, the still relatively unadvanced state of mass media made the popular stage a primary means for the expression of, reflection on, and communication about the rapidly transforming social and cultural environment of the metropolis. At the same time, the analogy between immigrants' exploration of the boundaries of selfhood, its "realness" or "falsity," and the theater's play with the boundaries of reality, established the theater as a natural staging ground for the investigation of identity, change, and the potential for and limits of self-transformation. As John Higham has remarked, "Through their experience of displacement and assimilation, many second generation immigrants gained a special capability for the arts of the theater: for playing a role, for transforming the self, for projecting an instant identity, and for achieving these effects in an atmosphere of illusion and surprise."[83] These playful, performative approaches to identity, however, inevitably clashed with dominant constructions of immigrant identities, which were embedded in the representational conventions of American popular culture in general and the popular stage in particular.

Chapter 5, "Juggling Identities," examines the performances of "Farfariello,"

Italian American clown and master mimic of the Italian immigrant community of New York. The immigrant types of Eduardo Migliaccio, or
Farfariello, represent a carnivalesque, burlesque interpretation of Italian
immigrant life, mapped against the urban spaces of New York City. Taking
his models from the streets of Little Italy, Farfariello consistently limned
the boundaries between reality and the stage, producing a vision in which
the Italian immigrant finds his double in the clown. In doing so, he mocks the
promise of imitation as a trajectory to an "authentic" selfhood, articulating,
in his mimicry, the difference between "American" and "Americanized."

Farfariello's urban skits, like much of immigrant vaudeville, enact a "doubling" that mimics the doubling of the immigrant self. This doubling, however, retains a festive ambivalence, in contrast to the menace of the double
that pervades the urban mystery-and-misery genre, and is connected to the
tradition of grotesque realism and the carnivalesque, where the mask is not
(yet) the sign of deception.

This tension between the mask as sign of deception, alienation, and the
split of inner and outer selves, the mask as a topographical displacement of
an illusory interiority, and the mask as related to a festive celebration of
metamorphosis, is at the heart of the last three chapters, which focus on
racial impersonation on the American vaudeville stage. Chapter 6, "My
Other/My Self: Impersonation and the Rehearsal of Otherness," focuses on
the interpenetration of vaudeville and the experience of modern urban
culture, which is particularly pronounced in racial or dialect comedy, a staple of the vaudeville show. The fact that the theater, and vaudeville in particular, presented a cheap and viable career track meant that it often fell to
second-generation immigrants to interpret urban space and the immigrant
Other to American audiences in an idiom of racial types ("Hebrew," "Dago,"
Irish, blackface) that defined Otherness in terms of racial descent. The racial
impersonation of immigrants led to a complex play with the boundary between inside and outside, mutability and immutability, false and real, which
offered ample room for the manipulation of the codes of race and whiteness.
In addition, "realism," "impersonation," and "acting" presented sources not
only of cultural prestige but also functioned as codes for professionalism,
which ambitious entertainers such as the Hebrew comic David Warfield
and the playwright Edward Harrigan expertly exploited.

Chapter 7, "The Truth of Racial Signs: Civilizing the Jewish Comic," examines the controversy over so-called Hebrew comedy, which had come to
rival blackface comedy in popularity. At the beginning of the twentieth century, dialect humor started to encounter strong criticism from segments

within the ethnic population. Groups such as the Chicago-based "Anti-Stage Jew Ridicule Committee" campaigned to banish Hebrew comedy from the stage. Others, however, detected a paradox in this agitation, noting that frequently these impersonations appealed less to gentile audiences than to Jews themselves, and that nearly all "Hebrew" comics were of Jewish origin.

Responding to the desire for respectability among its audiences, Jewish comedians tried to rehabilitate the Hebrew comic and transform him from a lower-class, vulgar, backward, ghetto Jew to a middle-class, modern, uptown Jew. This effort culminated in the popular Jewish American play *Potash and Perlmutter,* which was advertised as the "Rehabilitation of the Stage Jew," but ultimately displaced the locus of "authentic" Jewish racial identity from ghetto "vulgarity" to an innate comic essence, which presumably had been fashioned as an adoptive response to centuries of oppression and was visible in the Jewish physiognomy.

It fell to a new generation of Jewish performers to successfully appropriate a model of identity on the stage that loosened the hold of racial character and its presumed connection between inside and outside. In the performances of Fanny Brice, Eddie Cantor, Al Jolson, and the Marx Brothers, the donning of the mask and the play with the mutability of self are simultaneously compatible with Jewish identity (now characterized by its "mutability") and a modern, urban, American self. In their acts, the "manipulation" of identity lost the aura of imposture. This development, I suggest, corresponds broadly to the social mobility experienced by segments of the Jewish American population and formed a preamble to the gradual inscription of erstwhile Slavs, Celts, Hebrews, and Mediterraneans as bona fide white and "Caucasian."

After 1924, when the restrictive immigration legislation contained in the Johnson-Reed Act marked the triumph of the eugenics movement and the protest against "over-inclusive whiteness," the characteristics of Jewishness, Italianness, or Irishness were gradually reinterpreted as a matter of ethnicity and culture rather than race, a reconceptualization to which the events of World War II lent added urgency.[84] But the social and racial mobility of white European immigrants, hard-won though it may have been, was predicated on their racial inclusion as "free white persons." It was played out against, and was facilitated by, the social, cultural, and political exclusion of certified racial Others.[85]

The final chapter, "Blackface, Jewface, Whiteface," examines Jewish and African American efforts to escape the strictures of racial comedy. While Jewish mutability for Randolph Bourne became a model for a "transnational

America," the restrictions that African American performers faced on the stage suggest the danger that was inherent in the suggestion of African American mutability. David Roediger rightly points out that "minstrels claimed the right to turn black as long as they desired and to reappear as white. They forcefully denied Blacks that right, parodying fancy dress, learned speech, temperance and religion among Blacks as ridiculous attempts to 'act' white."[86] On the stage, the most absurd consequence of these limitations, as George Walker, a famous African American blackface performer observed, was the fact that the "colored man" was forced to imitate white constructions of blackness, "making himself ridiculous in order to portray himself." These restrictions, then, were necessary in order to preserve the fiction of essential, immutable racial identity. They fit a racial logic whereby mutability and successful self-transformation was a property of whiteness, which, as Eric Sundquist points out, blacks could "*imitate* or parody but not . . . own."[87]

Part I

THE CITY AS THEATER

Performativity and Urban Space

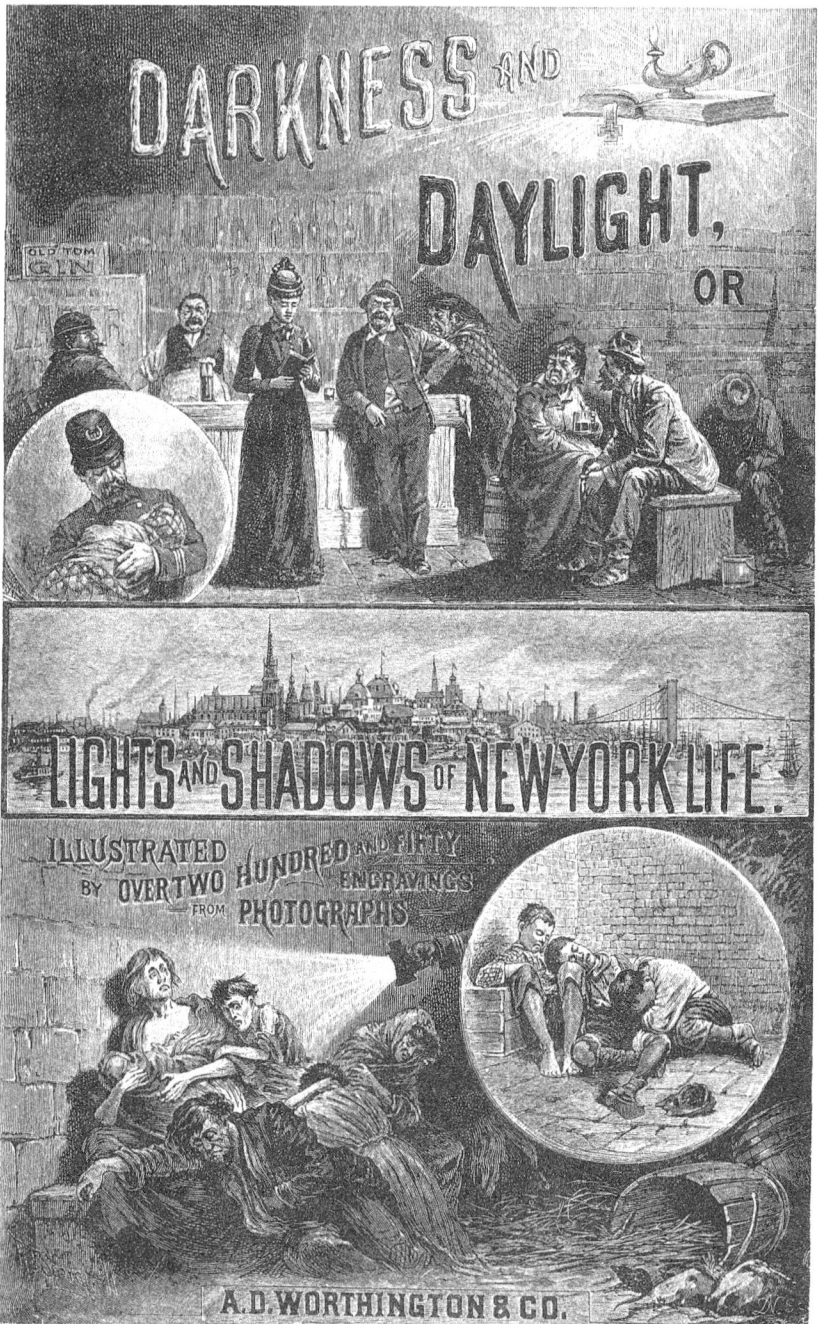

Dreaming the visible city: Helen Campbell's *Darkness and Daylight*. From Helen Campbell, *Darkness and Daylight, or Lights and Shadows of New York Life* (Hartford: A. D. Worthington, 1895), frontispiece.

Chapter 1

The Epistemology of the City

> With cities it is as with dreams: everything imaginable can be dreamed,
> but even the most unexpected dream is a rebus that conceals a desire or,
> its reverse, a fear. Cities, like dreams, are made of desires and fears, even
> if the thread of their discourse is secret, their rules are absurd, their
> perspective deceitful, and everything conceals something else.
>
> —ITALO CALVINO, *Invisible Cities* (1972)

NEW YORK CITY AT THE TURN OF THE NINETEENTH CENTURY was the visual embodiment of the contradictions of modernity. Within the span of the previous two decades, mechanization, improvements in transportation, and a general rise in the standard of living had stimulated a rapid industrial expansion. To cater to the demands of the expanding markets, factories gradually replaced the small-scale artisan workshops that up to that point had been the backbone of industrial production. The growth of the manufacturing system propelled New York City, and other urban centers such as Chicago, to the forefront of economic production. By the end of the century, the United States ranked as the leading industrial nation in the world.

The impact of this dramatic industrial take-off was felt in the social differentiation that marked the city. Millions of immigrants, predominantly from eastern and southern Europe, provided the unskilled, cheap labor force needed to fuel the unprecedented rate of economic growth. A growing middle class found a new economic niche in the managerial, office, and professional positions that accompanied the increasing bureaucratization of American society. At the top of the social hierarchy was a small but select group of "nouveaux riches" that had profited from the frantic pace of economic development by building corporate empires.[1]

These growing social divisions were replicated in the urban geography of New York City. The rapid rate of demographic growth and the general increase in wealth triggered a construction boom that in the span of a few decades reshaped the metropolis. The intimate and egalitarian "walking city" of the pre–Civil War years gave way to an urban landscape in which new, broad avenues crossed through neighborhoods marked by class and ethnic differences.[2] The construction of a rapid-transit system introduced an unprecedented degree of mobility and enabled the middle class to hide itself from the "contaminating touch" of the poor and withdraw, at the end of the workday, to their own "little islands of propriety," the suburbs.[3] Yet this freedom of mobility also brought a novel sense of the unity of this heterogeneous mix of people. So did the streetscape of such thoroughfares as Broadway, where, in the words of a contemporary observer, "clerks, millionaires, merchants of all kind and degree, speculators, idlers, countrymen, and here and there a thief or 'crook' make up the forms that fill the kaleidoscope to be seen any day."[4]

Rapid industrialization and capitalism injected its social effects into the very nervous system of the city, producing contradictions that no amount of planning or design could control. The more uniform, rationalized, and coherent the city, with its public spaces and broad avenues, physically became, "the more opaque and mysterious it came to seem socially, as governed by a contingent and chaotic play of forces, transactions and interests."[5] The city's public spaces, which, guided by principles of rational design, mapping, and order, allowed for the imagining of the almost theatrical unity of diverse urban populations, coexisted with a vision of a dangerous urban heterogeneity. Abandoned to the very rich and very poor, the city became a "mosaic of little worlds which touch but do not interpenetrate," in which rich and opulent neighborhoods alternated with the destitution and overcrowding of extensive slum areas.[6] This tension between self and Other, proximity and distance, individual and the masses, luxury and destitution, desire and control, that characterized life in the modern city was both intoxicating and unnerving.[7]

"What shall we do with our great cities? What will our great cities do with us?" queried the Reverend Lyman Abbott in his introduction to Helen Campbell's *Darkness and Daylight; or the Lights and Shadows of New York Life* (1892):

> [T]he city presents in microcosm all the contrasts of our modern life,—its worst and its best aspects. Here are the broad avenues, and here are the narrow lanes; here are the beautiful parks where landscape gardening has done its best, and here are the fetid streets whose pestering filth pollutes the atmosphere; here palaces on which selfish extravagance has lavished every artifice for luxury and display, and

here tenements where, in defiance of every law, moral and sanitary, men, women and children are crowded together like maggots in a cheese. . . . Here [are] the greatest churches and here the most garish saloons, nightly scenes of debauchery and vice, frequently of dreadful crime.[8]

In this heterogeneous cityscape, which escaped the imposition of a single vision, the gaze of the respectable middle classes was naturally drawn to the haunts of vice, the dark recesses of the slums. The slums became the emblems of the "leftovers, dirt, an excess of meaning, the ambivalence" that was the "inevitable underside" of the search for "order" with which the ruling classes responded to the paradoxes of the modern city.[9] Densely populated, inhabited by millions of diseased, poverty-ridden immigrants, the tenements and shanty towns of Lower Manhattan increasingly appeared a foreign country, uncivilized, overcrowded, dangerous, and, above all, unintelligible to the average American observer. Writing for *Munsey's Magazine* in 1900, Katherine Hoffmann commented: "Striking east from Broadway and crossing the dividing line of the Bowery, in the neighborhood of Grand Street, the average New Yorker comes upon a country of whose habits he probably knows less, and with whose inhabitants he certainly has less in common, than if he had crossed the Atlantic and found himself in Piccadilly or Pall Mall."[10]

This lack of transparency, coupled with the perceived explosive potential of the slums, especially in the hostile labor climate of the late nineteenth century, stimulated a widespread effort to survey these islands of foreignness. Sociological inquiries, detective novels, ghetto films such as *Romance of the Ghetto* or *The Musketeers of Pig Alley,* slumming tours, literary "ghetto" sketches in popular magazines such as *Harper's* and *Munsey's,* ghetto types on the popular vaudeville stage, slide lectures presenting the photographs of Jacob Riis and other "flashes from the slum"—all sought to penetrate the "secrets" of urban low life and bring "light" to its darkness.[11]

Perhaps the most concerted effort at mapping the city in transformation was represented by the genre of the metropolitan guidebook, which first began to appear in the late 1860s, and which, by the end of the century, counted at least thirty volumes.[12] These guidebooks, with such titles as *The Secrets of the Great City* (1868), *Lights and Shadows of New York Life* (1872), or *Mysteries and Miseries of America's Great Cities* (1883), recalled the antebellum gothic romances of Edward Zane Judson's (Ned Buntline's) *Mysteries and Miseries of New York* (1848) and George Foster's *Celio, or New York*

Above-Ground and Under-Ground (1850) and the urban sketches of George Foster's *New York by Gaslight* (1850) and *New York in Slices* (1854).[13]

Both the antebellum urban novels and sketches and the postbellum metropolitan guidebooks were informed by the trope of urban "mystery and misery," Victorian America's preferred phrase for the contrasts of the city. The antebellum mysteries, however, as Alan Trachtenberg has pointed out, expressed the aspirations of a rising middle class. While it offered readers voyeuristic glimpses of an urban "netherworld" made up of street gangs, gambling, prostitution, and crime, it simultaneously upheld the ideals of egalitarianism and the permeability of class boundaries.[14] Post–Civil War urban guidebooks such as James D. McCabe's *Lights and Shadows of New York Life* (1872) and Helen Campbell's *Darkness and Daylight, or the Lights and Shadows of New York Life* (1892) similarly set out to survey what lay beyond the borders of middle-class respectability. But in these versions of the genre, the trope of urban mystery became a sign of middle-class concern about deepening social divisions and the blurring of the boundaries of class, race, and culture.[15]

The Mystery and Misery of New York Life

Organized as a tour through the "lights and shadows of New York," the urban guidebook offered its reader an encyclopedic view of the cultures and subcultures of the city. Numerous chapters and subchapters introduced the reader to "Society," "Street Musicians," "Hotel Life," "The Tombs," "Wall Street," "The Bowery," "Fifth Avenue," "Broadway," "Lines of Travel," "Fallen Women," or "Roughs." In its discontinuity, the narrative of the guidebook mimicked the fragmented nature of the city and the fleeting quality of its interactions.[16] Yet the ambition of the guidebook was to defy the "radical incompleteness of the urban experience" by being all-encompassing.[17]

The urge to contain the explosive heterogeneity of the city is perhaps best illustrated by the fact that the most popular of the guidebooks saw numerous "updated" editions, in which the gradual expansion of the title mimicked the expansion of the city. McCabe, for instance, first published his guidebook, written under the pseudonym of E. W. Martin, in 1868 under the title *The Secrets of the Great City, A Work Descriptive of the Virtues and the Vices, the Mysteries, Miseries and Crimes of New York City.* It was reprinted twice, in 1872 and 1882. The bulky title of the 1882 edition was *New York by Sunlight and Gaslight: A Work descriptive of the great American metropolis (Its high and low life; its splendours and miseries; its virtues and vices; its gorgeous*

*places and dark homes of poverty and crime; its public men, politicians, adven-
turers; its charities, frauds, mysteries, etc., etc.).* Matthew Hale Smith's book,
published in 1868 as *Sunshine and Shadows of New York,* breached out in its
1887 edition as *Wonders of a Great City: or the Sights, Secrets and Sins of New
York: being a wonderful portrayal of the varied phases of life in the greatest
city in America. Giving Pen pictures of New York City—its Men and Women;
how and where they live; their manners and customs; how they speculate and
trade, cheat and get cheated; and in fact a photograph as true as can be made
of the Great Babel of the Western Continent, Where all sorts of things are done.
Giving a True Picture of New York's inner life, such as never before has been
published.*

Metropolitan guidebooks were structured as "narratives of exposure,"
designed to make "the grotesque *visible* whilst keeping it at an *untouchable*
distance."[18] The Reverend James D. McCabe, for instance, proposed his
guidebook as the perfect simulacrum of the heterogeneity of city life itself:

> It has been my effort to bring home to those who cannot see the city for them-
> selves, its pleasures and its dangers, and to enable them to enjoy the former with-
> out the fatigue or expense demanded of an active participant in them, and to
> appreciate the latter, without incurring the risks attending to an exploration of
> the shadowy side of the Great City. For the purposes of performing this task, the
> writer made visits, in company of the police officials of the city, to a number of
> places described in this work, and he is satisfied that no respectable person can
> visit them, unless provided with a similar protection. The curiosity of all persons
> concerning the darker side of city life can be fully satisfied by a perusal of the
> sketches presented in this volume.[19]

The guidebook introduced the middle-class reader to the "skating on thin
surfaces and a scrupulous study of style and manners" which, to use Robert
Park's phrase, constitutes the "art of life" in the city.[20] In a succession of urban
tableaus, it carefully laid out the rules of urban cognition. "To know New
York requires years of constant study and investigation. Strangers see only
the surface; they cannot penetrate into its inner life," James McCabe remarked on the opaqueness and illegibility of the urban landscape.[21] Nevertheless, he asserted, the city itself "is a good school for the study of human
nature, and its people are proficients in the art of discerning character."[22]

In the manner of earlier genres of urban survey literature, such as
seventeenth-century English rogue literature and the eighteenth-century
physiologies, the graphic and literary sketches of French street types, the

guidebook breaks down the chaos of the urban "mass" into an array of "types."[23] It infiltrates urban subcultures, scans the external appearance of strangers, and distributes otherwise anonymous individuals to particular racial, social, and moral categories.[24]

Guidebook authors are protected from the taint of these titillating glimpses of the urban underworld by the cloak of moral superiority. In the guidebooks of the 1870s and 1880s, ministers or reverends such as James McCabe are invested with the highest degree of interpretive authority, even when, for safety purposes, they are escorted by detectives on some of their more perilous excursions into sin.

In *Darkness and Daylight*, first published in 1892, however, such authority shifts to three urban "experts," possessing a "thorough practical knowledge of the subject": the female missionary and charity worker Helen Campbell, the journalist Thomas Knox, and the famous Chief Inspector of Police, Thomas Byrnes.[25] The "authenticity, incontrovertible facts, and startling revelations" of their writings are accompanied by two hundred and fifty realistic illustrations obtained with the help of modernity's "instrument of truth," the camera's "merciless and unfailing eye."[26]

This shift in authority is indicative of the increasing professionalization of the study of the poor in the late nineteenth century. New urban professionals, a group that included urban reformers, social workers, and sociologists, advocated for approaching the "labor question" from a scientific perspective, in order to replace earlier impressionistic observations of urban low life with facts, hard data, firm categorizations, and statistical analysis.[27] This, Allan Sekula has argued, resulted in the development of new technologies of surveillance, such as photography, the mug shot, and the fingerprint, along with such pseudosciences as physiognomy, phrenology, the Bertillon system of measurement, and Francis Galton's "composite" portraits of social and racial types. Given the ruling understanding of culture as innate and embodied, the focal point of these new "instruments of truth" was the body, from which the specialist could deduce information about "character," worthiness or unworthiness, and criminal tendencies.[28]

The urban guidebook applied these technologies to urban space. Its epistemology was informed by the notion of "type," which was supposed to represent a generic truth underlying the infinite variability of humankind, and assumed the existence of a correspondence between outside and inside, external appearance and inner character.[29] The typologies presented in the urban guidebook, which was guided by the fantasy of total surveillance, systematically mapped the correspondences between physiognomy, class, race, language, character, morality, and neighborhood. By doing so, it transformed the opaque surfaces of the city into an open book, whose meanings were understandable to those who knew its visual and linguistic codes.

DARKNESS AND DAYLIGHT, OR THE ART OF LIFE IN THE CITY

Travel writing, Howard Winant has noted, has been a particularly effective medium for the inscription of race, as "phenotypical signification," on the social body.[30] Urban guidebooks, which were typically written as travel narratives, are a case in point. "To place people where they belong," Detective Byrnes warns in *Darkness and Daylight,* requires "a long experience of men and their ways."[31] The first rule of urban cognition, according to the epistemology of the guidebook, is that streets and neighborhoods have their own racial and social morphology. The lower wards, explains Campbell, house "the strange foreign life that gives New York its title of 'cosmopolitan.'"[32] The Water Street area is inhabited by poor Irish, Mulberry Bend is home to Italian immigrants, and Mott and Pell streets form the center of Chinatown. Baxter, Grand, and Essex streets delineate the center of the Jewish quarter, the Bowery the German area, and Fifth Avenue the abode of the social elite.

These neighborhoods have their own moral character, imprinted on them by the virtues, vices, and habits of their inhabitants. In Chatham Street, famous for its "'old clo' shops run mostly by Israelites," for instance, the honest customer is likely to be "swindled, as the goods sold are of the cheapest sort, badly made and of wretched materials." According to detective Knox, the Jewish clothing dealers "have been known to convince a customer that a coat three or four sizes too large for him 'fits shplendid': they stand him before a mirror and as the customer observes the front of the garment the dealer gathers in a handful in the back. When the buyer is in a position to see the reflection of the back, the crafty swindler performs the same trick with the front and adds, 'Oh, mine frent, I vish you had eyes in de pack of your headt, shoost to see how shplendid dot gote fits betveen dose shoulders.'"[33]

Yet, according to Campbell, most are worthy poor, "hardly ever chronic charity seekers," and she adds, "whoever looks into their patient faces sees a type that under favorable conditions will do good service to the republic." Indeed, "they are far above the Irish in two cardinal virtues, thrift and abstemiousness. These virtues soon put them on their feet, and make them in time property owners and employers."[34]

The Italians, "from whatever part of Italy they come . . . bring the melancholy faces that are part of the Italian inheritance. They are fatalists. Long
oppression, unending hard work, and grinding poverty, have all left their
lines." Yet "they have proved efficient and patient workers at railroad construction and innumerable other forms of manual labor." And no matter
whether they are ragpickers, fruit sellers, organ-grinders, or construction
workers, the "New York passion for money is upon them, and they work
out of these noisome surroundings into something better in surprisingly
short spaces of time."[35]

In addition to the influence of racial "inheritance," the brutal environment of the city itself takes its toll on the inhabitants. Intemperance and
poverty have robbed the Irish of "the redeeming lightheartedness, the tender impulses, and strong affections of that most perplexing people," leaving nothing but the "most brutal characteristics of the Irish peasant." "Sullen,
malicious, conscienceless, with no capacity for enjoyment save in drink and
the lowest form of debauchery, they are filling our prisons and reformato-
ries." Indeed, according to Knox, the tenement-house districts in general
are cradles of poverty and crime. "In it are born and bred a class of beings
whose immediate ancestors were drunken, poverty-stricken, and vile, and
whose progeny must be paupers and criminals, pitiable as well as lawless."[36]

In the large thoroughfares, such as the Bowery and Broadway, filled by
anonymous strangers, social cognition poses more of a challenge. Nevertheless, Thomas Knox explains: "In shops, theatres, manners, customs, and
everything else, the Bowery and Broadway are wholly dissimilar." The Bowery is "intensely German in character," with the German beer saloons, German shops, German banks and German theaters and concert halls that
characterize it mostly ruled by the German sense of respectability. But "the
Bowery has its social divisions just as we find them in the aristocratic parts
of the city. There are race and class distinctions, and there is also the distinction of color no less marked than anywhere else in the land." The abodes
of crime and vice for which the Bowery is known are to be found in the
alleys and sideways running into the Bowery, where "lurk some of the worst
specimens of our foreign population."[37]

Broadway, by contrast, "mixes up the most dissimilar elements of nationality and condition."[38] But even there social identity is knowable by means
of the "involuntary signs" of the body.[39] On Broadway, Knox recognizes "the
thin featured shop-girl, or worker in a downtown factory" by her shawl,
"drawn around a shrinking form that tells plainly of low diet, hard work,
and bad lodgings." She is "jostled by a woman on whom fortune has smiled

if we judge her by her costly apparel and the absence of care on her face." There is "a merchant or banker whose fortune is counted in millions; near him is a clerk whose salary is too small for the comfortable support of his family, and whose head is prematurely whitened by the cares that have fallen upon it. The former walks with an easy, dignified pace, while the latter rushes along with his head bowed and his mind evidently in a state of perplexity."[40]

Campbell attributes the peculiar moral geography of these lower wards to the dialectic interaction between "innate capabilities" of various "nationalities" or "races" and the environment. This interpretation is informed by neo-Lamarckianism, which explained race as an adaptation to environment, which, in the course of centuries, becomes inherited. Much in vogue in the later decades of the nineteenth century, neo-Lamarckianism presented a theory of race that veered between biology and culture, or racial and environmental determinism, but left (limited) room for the possibility of racial "uplift."

In *Darkness and Daylight*, as in other turn-of-the century urban guidebooks, race (a term used interchangeably with nationality) and class are interpreted in terms of an organic connection between body, language, morals, manners, and locale. Through the systematic projection of racial, social, and moral categories of identity, the city in the guidebook emerges as "theatre, not spectacle merely but the potentially revelatory enactment of meaning."[41] This theater of identity is informed by what Mikhail Bakhtin has called the "'petty,' 'voyeuristic,' or 'alcove realism' of carefully observed types."[42]

This "petty" realism was standard in representations of the urban Other. It was replicated in the new journalistic genre of the urban sketch, reform tracts, the investigative reports of the *Police Gazette*, realist and naturalist novels, and on the stage of the contemporary vaudeville theater.[43] Part of its attractiveness, according to Walter Benjamin, was that it "opens up . . . a physiology of chatter." It mimicked voices, accents, speech patterns, slang, and specialized vocabularies as a means of "situating a person—establishing that person's class, métier, region."[44]

The urban guidebook staged its subjects with a sharp sense of the theatricality and the comic effect of the "realistic" representation of different dialects and sociolects. *Darkness and Daylight* is inhabited mostly by lower-class immigrants, whose broken English sets them apart from the correct, standard English of the urban professionals and officials, the missionary and charity workers, doctors, clergy, and detectives, who (ad)minister and

survey them. Campbell and Knox's representations of "Hebrew" pawnbro-
kers and clothing dealers, in their grotesquely accented speech, evoke the
comic routines of "Hebrew" impersonators on the contemporary vaudeville
stage.[45] Undercover, Knox presents himself as a "humble" customer trying
to pawn off his golden watch, bargaining for the best price he can get.

> "Loan me thirty," I begged, with all the pathos I could muster in voice and man-
> ners, "and I will try and get along."
>   "My frent, I vant to help you, and I would neffer sheat you, don't you pelieve
> it, and vot I tell you shall be sacred. I tell you vot I do. I gif you twenty tollars, and
> so sure as my name is Simon Levi dot is shoost vot dot vatch is vorth."[46]

Through such vocal mimicry, the metropolitan guidebook assures that
the different racial, social, and occupational idioms that constitute the "Great
Babel of the Western Continent," as Matthew Hale Smith's guide describes
New York, may require "Englishing" but do not escape translation.[47] Reduced
to linguistic oddities, social and racial differences appear as more theatrical
than threatening.[48]

But as Sekula and others have noted, the apparatus of social cognition
into which these texts instruct the reader actively constructs the social and
cultural categories it purports to observe.[49] In the pages of the urban guidebook, power is established through the position of the expert spectator.
Through his classifying and discriminating gaze, race and class are effectively inscribed on body and space. Racial Others and the working classes
have identities that are local, fixed, embodied, and innate. The white middle-
class "professional" by contrast has a "mobility" of body and vision that
other groups lack.[50] Indeed, the premise of the guidebook is based on the
contrast between the transparency of Others and the mobility and invisi-
bility of the middle class, which places itself outside the guidebook's field
of vision. This perspective established the conditions of middle-class anonymity, which, as Jean-Christophe Agnew has argued, provided the spectator, like the reader, "with the mask behind which its candid observations . . .
could continue undetected," while serving at the same time as a "voucher
of their authenticity and power."[51] In the act of observing, the middle-class
gaze "constitutes itself as respectable and superior."[52]

The guidebook projects these social and racial distinctions onto an urban
geography of uptown and downtown, the Bowery and Broadway, East Side
and West Side, Chinatown, Little Italy, and Fifth Avenue. Yet insofar as this
cultural grid of the city reflected the dominant social and cultural hierarchy,

and functioned to delineate these boundaries, it also laid out a compass for social and cultural mobility.

The City as Theater

In its "petty" realism, the urban guidebook displays the predilection for "recreated experience" which was characteristic of nineteenth-century Victorian middle-class culture.[53] Walter Benjamin aptly characterized its literary form, which presents the city in a succession of urban sketches enacting the "fleetingness of the urban encounter" by bringing "us in touch with the city without sustaining our involvement or resolving the questions these tantalizing glimpses often raise," as "dioramic literature."[54]

The predilection for the dramatic representation of Otherness based on the aesthetic modes of mimetic perfection and verisimilitude, according to various scholars, is inextricably linked to the history of colonialism. Indeed, the representational strategy of the guidebook mimics that of contemporary panoramas and dioramas, which simulated the experience of travel through "dark" and "exotic" landscapes such as panoramic scenes of Cairo or Mexico City, or the everyday life and rituals of "Caffre Life." The travel narrative and the trajectory of the panorama and the diorama combined to offer a "comprehensive" and "commanding" vantage point of "a world laid out conceptually in a Linnaean classification or evolutionary scheme, or experientially in a scenic effect." It permitted visitors the voyeuristic delight "to see without being seen, to penetrate interior recesses."[55]

The fact that the panoptic technologies of colonialism were also transferred to the urban ghetto should come as no surprise. The urban ghetto was, after all, inhabited by immigrants who were racially different, and inferior to, the Anglo-Saxon race, which, according to many Americans, had given America its culture and institutions. Various authors have pointed to the metaphorical link between the "dark" colonies and the "darkness" of urban slum life. But other terminologies were shared as well. Not only were slums often referred to as "colonies" and a "foreign country," but the lower classes were generically seen as a separate "race."[56] Not surprisingly, then, slum life called for similar explorations as the colonial hinterlands. As Walter Rauschenbusch wrote in *Christianity and Crisis*, "We have a new literature of exploration. Darkest Africa and the polar regions are becoming familiar; but we now have intrepid men and women who plunge for a time in the life of the lower classes and return to write books about this unknown race."[57]

The tendency of nineteenth-century popular culture "to enclose reality in manageable forms, to contain it within a theatrical space, an enclosed exposition or recreational space, or within the space of the picture frame," then, applied equally to "foreign countries" as well as the foreign quarters of street life.[58] This mode of seeing (and reading) reconfirmed the social and cultural distance between spectator/reader and his object. Its conceptual grid presented social and cultural Others as embodied and fixed, while it constructed white, middle-class identity as transcendent.

It also removed the sense of danger from the urban scene by creating a sense of emotional distance and by transforming every potentially disturbing image into a form of entertainment.[59] William Dean Howells pointedly analyzed these effects in one of his observations on urban poverty: "As soon as you cease to have the spectacle of poverty before your eyes,—even when you have it before your eyes—, you can hardly believe it, and that is perhaps why so many people deny that it exists. . . . When I go back to my own comfortable room, among my papers and my books, I remember it as something at the theater. It seems to be turned off, as Niagara does, when you come away."[60]

But this fantasy of directorial control was difficult to sustain. While the metaphor of the city as theater typically conveys a sense of confidence of the transparency of the urban scene, that same theatrical quality at other times tends toward a dangerous form of mimicry, a doubleness that cannot be controlled and that thoroughly subverts the distinction between reality and illusion, infecting even the position of spectatorial immunity.

Miles Orvell, Karen Halttunen, John Kasson, and others have observed that nineteenth-century middle-class culture betrayed a latent social anxiety in its preoccupation with deception, imposture, and false and mistaken identities.[61] Urban guidebooks are marked by similar slips of confidence. Houses that "command from ten to twelve thousand dollars rent" seem "palatial" in character, and are "always full of women competent to grace the best circles of social life," but turn out to conceal "houses of assignation."[62] Moreover, "There are scores of men and women whose appearance in the street gives no hint of their real character," Detective Thomas Byrnes warns. "Nearly all great criminals lead double lives. Strange as it may appear, it is a fact that some of the most unscrupulous rascals who ever cracked a safe or turned out a counterfeit were at home model husbands and fathers. . . . But all suggestion of the criminal's calling was left outside the front door."[63]

The city abounds not only with false gentlemen, but with false beggars as well. Thomas Knox betrays a barely concealed admiration for the mimetic "genius" of these confidence men:

At one time a fellow made a good revenue by a shrewd trick of putting a crust of
bread, the core of an apple, or some similar dainty on the sidewalk or a doorstep
. . . on some of the side streets leading out of Fifth Avenue. Then he would go a
hundred feet or so along the street, and when he saw a well-dressed person of
either sex he walked just a little in advance with his eyes eagerly scanning the sidewalk and doorsteps. Suddenly espying the crust or apple-core, he rushed to secure
it and crunched it between his teeth with the manner of a man nearly famished.
His movements were sure to attract attention, and if the spectator was at all
benevolent and unsuspecting the performance was sure to be rewarded. . . . He
was always dressed in clothing too small for him, the trousers being fully two
inches too short for his nether limbs, and the coat buttoned so closely that it threatened to burst. The garments were threadbare, but always clean, and altogether his
make-up was well adapted to his scheme, and his acting was admirable.[64]

The late nineteenth-century preoccupation with the "mechanics of representation and misrepresentation" was rooted in a deep-seated ambivalence toward the effects of the rapid industrialization of American society.
In the context of urban anonymity and the increasing competitiveness of
the workplace, success increasingly depended on the ability to master the
codes of a new professional, middle-class identity and project a convincing
impression to the outside world.[65]

This provoked what Richard Terdiman, writing about nineteenth-century
France, has described as a "widespread crisis of socialization" in which the
social and cultural knowledge needed to move within the cultural system
was found to be seriously inadequate. The proliferation of etiquette books
and urban guidebooks during this period indicates the expansive market
that existed for "how-to" books that provided guidance in the details of genteel self-representation and the correct reading of social signs.[66]

The effort to map social relations systematically, however, provoked an
increased awareness of the "coded nature of social life," which resulted in a
twofold crisis of representation.[67] The "performativity" of genteel status
undermined the basic belief underlying middle-class self-identity that gentility, made visible through an elaborate system of manners and etiquette,
was the sincere and "natural" outward expression of an innately superior
morality.[68] In the guidebook, this erupts in what Philip Fisher describes
as moments of "reperception," which subliminally register "the process of
contamination by which the very stance of the distanced observer is acknowledged as a danger."[69] Instead of a window onto Otherness, the city becomes
a mirror to the bourgeois self, reflecting the repressed knowledge that in

the management of appearance and emotions, and in the doctrine of self-control, the distinction between the bourgeois and the actor was very hard to draw.[70] Thomas Knox indeed acknowledged as much in his remark that the false beggars execute their schemes with "a genius that would secure a comfortable existence in respectable callings, and, not unlikely would bring a fortune to its possessors."[71]

The antitheatrical prejudice of the late nineteenth century not only indicated a severe crisis in bourgeois self-representation, but it simultaneously signaled a profound crisis in the representation of social difference. By making the body an index of social relations, the rules of etiquette aestheticized and naturalized social distance. But in a period of increasing social mobility, this codification, rather than serving as a class barrier, further threatened to blur class boundaries. The imitability (or "reiterability") of social codes made bourgeois identity available to the skillful actor.

The anxiety over the "false gentleman," then, was informed by the realization that ultimately in bourgeois culture the "appearance of elevated status" served just as well as the "real thing."[72] According to Audrey Jaffe, the source for this moral panic must be found in the mechanization of production, which gradually removed the "stamp of labor" not only from the commodity itself but also from the bodies that produced them. The gradual transition from a producer society to a consumer society, and from a labor theory of value to an exchange theory of value, realigned the relationship between "labor, value, and identity." If "value" consisted in the production of identity, the distinction between "worthy" and "unworthy" poor—which is based on the differentiation between "productive" and "unproductive" bodies, is obscured as well.

Ultimately then, Jaffe argues, the "scandal" of the false beggar and the false gentleman lies in the fact that they "exchange" identity for "coin." In that sense, the "labor" of the false beggar/gentleman is not unlike that of the middle class, for whom the cultivation of bourgeois character was a similar "investment": marking trustworthiness, it was meant to further business by inviting confidence.[73] The changing conceptions of the nature of work and productivity, then, also profoundly undermined the moral geography of the city. Detached from its connection to work, the body lost its ability to serve as an index of social (and moral) identity.[74] Moreover, the spread of consumer culture potentially extended the dress and behavioral codes of the gentleman and the lady to groups for whom that status had previously been out of reach.

The period spanned by the publication of the metropolitan guidebooks witnessed the rise of the cult of the self-made man and marked the transition from what Warren Susman has described as a "culture of character" to a "culture of personality." In the increasingly socially dynamic and commodity oriented society of the later decades of the nineteenth century, Susman has argued: "The social role demanded of all . . . was that of a performer. Every American was to become a performing self."[75] The guidebooks registered the fear that, within this changing cultural context, the opposition between being and acting, between "authentic self-representation" and deception, breaks down.

Urban Mysteries: The Immigrant Version

For the millions of foreign newcomers to the metropolis, the experience of immigration presented a profound challenge to moral codes, social structures, cultural mores, and previously held notions of self. Coming mostly from poor, rural areas and small towns in southern and eastern Europe, immigrants, like the rising middle class of post–Civil War America, frequently felt hopelessly inept at deciphering social relations within the city. In the shtetl and the village, John Berger has written, people "do not play roles as urban characters do . . . because the space between what is unknown about a person and what is generally known . . . is too small." The American metropolis, however, demanded an extension of the boundaries of selves and the experimentation with new roles and identities.[76] The lesson that, within the context of the anonymity of urban life, "the fleeting impressions made by surface appearance become of great importance" was as well heeded by immigrants as it was by the middle class.[77]

Buoyed by the American belief in social mobility and the fluidity of class identity, many immigrants anticipated their own social rise by acquiring the tastes and manners and, above all, those habits of speech widely regarded as "the surest sign of a gentleman."[78] Indeed, the dread of being mistaken for a *"greener,"* a greenhorn, someone clinging to retrograde old-country customs, made many adopt the emblems of American middle-class identity such as the starched collar and necktie, which alone seemed to suggest a new self-identity.[79] To master the more minute details of the "urban art of 'skating on thin surfaces' of styles and manners," they turned to etiquette books, newspapers, the vaudeville theaters, and urban guidebooks.[80]

Bernardino Ciambelli's *I Misteri di Mulberry Stritto* (The Mysteries of Mulberry Street, 1893) and *Il Mistero di Bleecker Street* (The Mystery of

Bleecker Street, 1899), and John Paley's *Di Shvartse Khevre* (*The Black Gang,* 1900), represent immigrant versions of the "mystery-and-misery" genre. These immigrant "mysteries and miseries" resemble the middle-class guidebooks in their attention to the minute social details marking social and cultural hierarchies in the city. Ciambelli's mysteries offer glimpses of the depravity reigning behind the facades of respectability. "A house of the most honest and modest appearance" turns out to be a well-known hangout for "libertines," while apparent gentlemen are revealed as swindlers or pimps. The novels also instruct the reader in notorious swindles and con acts such as the "luggage switch," describing it as "a trick which the notorious Italian criminal organization the 'Black Hand' pulls on unsuspecting immigrants."[81] In *The Black Gang*, chewing gum and too much rouge and jewelry betray a "false" lady, and a "false" gentleman is too familiar with women, too generous with money, and prone to visiting disreputable locales.

But these crash courses in the "mysterious world of social signs" are provided not from the vantage point of a detached, professional urban spectator, who subjects the entire city to his incriminating, cold panoptic gaze.[82] These gothic novels, closer in style to the romances of Eugène Sue, which precipitated the popularity of the genre in the 1830s, feature either (American and Italian) detectives whose sympathies lie solidly with the victimized immigrants or immigrant protagonists who are deeply implicated in the unfolding of the novels' capture, escape, and rescue plots. The superior ability of these immigrant heroes to penetrate the mysteries of the urban underworld is informed not by the power of the detached gaze, suggesting professional knowledge, but by a "knowing" vision that is street smart yet quintessentially moral. And while Ciambelli's novels do take the reader, by foot, carriage, and elevated tram, on a tour of the highs and lows of New York life (the trajectories of both novels include opulent villas on Long Island, humble abodes of Italian workers on Bleecker Street, the hustle and bustle of a department store with its indecently made-up girls at the cash register, the pandemonium of Ellis Island, the cheerfulness within an Italian-owned factory manufacturing artificial flowers, and the desolation of the Tombs), both Ciambelli and Paley center their "mysteries" on the Italian and the Jewish quarters of New York, respectively.

THE MYSTERIES OF BLEECKER AND MULBERRY STREETS

Ciambelli's *The Mysteries of Mulberry Street,* published in 1893, features the famous police inspector Byrnes as its hero, as does Helen Campbell's *Darkness and Daylight, or the Lights and Shadows of New York Life.* In Campbell's version, however, Byrnes catalogues the skills of urban cognition and his stance is one of professional detachment. *I Misteri,* part melodrama, part mystery novel, steeped in murder, love, the white slave trade, and corruption, shows Byrnes in action in the Italian quarter, which Ciambelli vividly describes as

> cheerful, noisy, always crowded with people born in the beautiful home country . . . , everyone minding their own business, with decent hotels, stores full of Italian products, bars stocked with wines made of grapes matured on the blessed vineyards of Chianti, of Asti, of Modena, and of Sicily. Italians do not lose their habits in America. They stop on the sidewalks, engage in arguments, shout, gesticulate, and discuss everything and everyone. They stop in groups, pour into breweries, crowd the stores, asking and answering questions, and create a cheerful racket which surprises Americans who are used to quiet neighborhoods, with a continuous silence the like of which in Italy one only finds in church. (11–12)

Byrnes's decision to explore the mysteries of the Italian colony is based on solid reasoning: as the colony becomes more numerous, its importance increases. "It's important to find out who these people are, if they are serious workers," Byrnes declares, in a nod to the contemporary concern with the distinction between the "worthy" and the "unworthy" poor. According to Ciambelli, Byrnes "reads the mind of delinquents like a god." Moreover, he is a great masquerader. Undercover, he "hears a word here, a sentence there." He puts these fragments of information "together with great patience," and thus gains "the keys to the most impenetrable mysteries" (193). But unlike in Campbell's guidebook, where Byrnes's allegiances are clearly middle class, in *I Misteri* he uses his skills on behalf of immigrants, whose naiveté makes them easy victims of urban depravity. The simple moral economy of these novels is one of just deserts, in which evil is exposed and punished (by acts of providence and the police, including the famous Italian American detective Petrosino and the American detective Byrnes), and honest work, moral behavior, modesty, and courage rewarded.

The Mysteries of Mulberry Street begins with the author's rectification of the impression that his novels, with their exposure of the dark side of Little Italy, seek to dishonor the Italian colony (19). His promise that his narrative will rehabilitate the Italian immigrant neighborhood is borne out in the novel by Byrnes's objections to the prejudices of his colleague Dikens, "who because of his Irishness was of the opinion that all Italians pull the wool over everyone's eyes," and according to whom Italians all "belong to the mafia" (193).

The opening scene of *The Mysteries of Mulberry Street* introduces the reader to the pandemonium of immigrants arriving in Castle Garden, and the array of types that make up the metropolis. "[Jews] with frightened faces, cloaked in long flowering robes adorned with fur, formed a group apart as if they were frightened to mix with the crowd that pushed against them. The Germans, serious but satisfied, like people arriving in a conquered land, stood alongside one another, like soldiers moving to attack an enemy. The Italians, joyous, . . . noisy, brought in the gay note, with their observations made in a loud voice in the diverse dialects of the mediterranean provinces" (222).

The scene also introduces Vittoria, on the run from a criminal husband, and her son Enrico. Vittoria's eyes register the lure of the nightly city, whose lights and lit-up shop windows "make the night seem transparent." She is so mesmerized that she fails to hear her companion's warning to "be careful, because in New York anything can happen." True enough, the transparency of New York is a dangerous illusion. Soon after Vittoria arrives in Mulberry Street, which reminds her of her hometown Naples, she falls into the hands of the white slave trade. Her first client is her husband, who attacks her, leaves her in a state of insanity, and goes on to kidnap little Enrico. A male friend, Righetti, is arrested for the crime and thrown into the Tombs.

A second plot involves the rich Fanny Spencer, daughter of a Broadway merchant, who has developed a passion for Italy after spending time in Florence learning Italian from the young Enrico Leonardi. Fanny harbors a misguided romantic interest in Renato Ruizzi, who is the head of a criminal organization headquartered at the Banco Centrale in Little Italy.

The two plots come together in the detective work of Inspector Byrnes, who is called in on the job by his colleague, Inspector Boni. Byrnes goes to Little Italy in the disguise of a "tramp" or "loafer," assuming the physiognomy, speech, and mannerisms of the type. He visits a "Bar Room" on Mulberry Street, buys drinks for two suspicious Italians, and continues to make fun of the police and of "Inspector Byrnes." Having won their confidence, he retrieves the information he needs to recover little Enrico, reveal the head of the criminal organization, and destroy the white slavery ring. Vittoria gets her sanity back and marries Righetti, whose innocence is proven, while Fanny Spencer marries her Italian teacher, Enrico Leonardi. Byrnes is saluted for saving the city from evil and is honored during the Festa di San

Rocco with a parade in which all the nationalities of the city—Irish, German, Italian, Polish, and French—stand side by side.

The narrative of *The Mystery of Bleecker Street* similarly works its way through a series of highly improbable incidents. These include multiple abductions and murder attempts on Ada Rains, daughter of a famous Anglo-Saxon general and his Italian-born spouse, by her depraved half-sister, and Ada's subsequent miraculous rescue by the Italian American working-class family of Enrico Arnoldi, and later by a band of gypsies, whose leader turns out to be the father of her half-sister. Attacks by Native Americans and pirates and battle scenes of the Spanish-American War provide this novel with an American flavor.

In *The Mystery of Bleecker Street*, leading upper-class Anglo-Saxon characters are also forced to reconsider their prejudices against Italians. General Rains, who "as many Americans, had a fairly bad conception of the Italians," becomes "convinced that the prejudice of his compatriots was wrong" after he encounters the rich Pia, who becomes his wife and the mother of Ada (12). Moreover, Enrico Arnoldi, who in his despair over the presumed death of Ada has joined Roosevelt's Roughriders, distinguishes himself during the Battle of San Juan. It earns him Ada's love, the admiration and friendship of Roosevelt, soon to become governor of New York, and the adulation of the population of Little Italy.

Both novels unite America and Italy, and the upper and lower classes, through a love that transcends these social and cultural divisions. In *The Mysteries of Mulberry Street*, the genteel Fanny Spencer falls in love with the sophisticated Enrico Leonardi. In *The Mystery of Bleecker Street*, marriage bonds join the upper-class family of general William Rains and the lower-class Italian Arnoldi family. In these resolutions, Ciambelli projects an image of America as a country where boundaries of class and nationality are permeable. His narratives uphold the prospect of social and cultural reconciliation in the face of the urban threat of social fragmentation and disintegration, replicating the narrative structure that informed the antebellum versions of the mystery-and-misery genre.[83] Above all, it is the detective who consolidates the fragmented social urban landscape. Personified in the American Inspector Byrnes and the Italian American detective Petrosino, the detective, in Ciambelli's imagination, retains the allegiance to the collective that marks the flâneur, his historic predecessor.[84] But it is the detective's penetrating gaze and his masquerades, and not the flâneur's mode of perception, dwelling on the surface, that is critical to the art of living in the city. The model modern city dweller knows the arts of deception and dissimulation from the inside out.

DI SHVARTSE KHEVRE, OR THE BLACK GANG

John Paley's Yiddish version of the mystery-and-misery genre was published in 1900 under the title *Di Shvartse Khevre, oder Nuyork bay tog un nakht: an origineler roman fun der Nuyork geto (The Black Gang, or New York By Day and Night: an Original Novel from the New York Ghetto)*. Like Ciambelli's novels, *The Black Gang* combines crime, adventure, and sentimental romance, and is set almost exclusively within an immigrant milieu. The actions of the novel are confined to the Jewish area of lower Manhattan known as the East Side, covering locales in Allen Street, Hester Street, and Christie Street. Unlike Ciambelli, however, Paley hardly ventures out of those locations. Moreover, the novel betrays none of the social and cultural aspirations of Ciambelli's novels, with their projected fusion of Italy and genteel America. The Jewish taboo on intermarriage precludes this kind of interethnic romance as a viable trajectory of social and cultural mobility. Instead, those aspirations have to draw on the inner forces of the community itself.

The Black Gang is concerned mostly with the moral economy of the self-contained Jewish immigrant community, in which urban anonymity, individualism, and social ambition threaten to erode family loyalties and moral precepts. It counters the pressures of disintegration with a network of connections, based on the family and the culture of the shtetl. These links extend across the Atlantic Ocean and enable Jewish immigrants to establish a social, economic, and emotional foothold in America.

In the prologue, the novel prides itself on representing the world "as it is." Instead of being a work of fantasy, it reveals what happens "nekst dor" (next door) in the "streets and the houses in which we live."[85] This realism offers the pretext for a narrative of exposure. Sin in New York, the novel explains, is a world unto itself. Operating under the cover of deceiving appearances and false pretenses, it lures unsuspecting greenhorns and naive virgins into the clutches of gambling, drinking, and prostitution. It is aided and abetted by corrupt police, the shady actions of immigrants who sacrifice moral principles to the lure of money, and the misguided notion that in a democracy all individual opinions, no matter how insane, should be considered equal, which makes decisive communal action impossible.

The story begins with the arrival of Rachel, an innocent girl, in Castle

Garden. Unbeknown to her, the "gentleman" she followed to America on the promise of marriage and respectability, is a procurer for the white slave trade. Willy intends to sell Rachel off to a brothel as soon as her bondage to him is sealed by marriage. To that end he enlists the help of a down-and-out rabbi, who performs an orthodox wedding ceremony, unaware that the hotel where the wedding is held is really a brothel, the guests are whores and their clientele, and that his blessings seal the fate of the poor Rachel.

When his son discloses the real meaning of the red lamp outside the hotel's window, the rabbi, who disowned his own daughter after her elopement with her teacher, an erstwhile yeshiva student turned worldly, vows to save this unknown woman from a similar fate. They turn for help to the police, only to be thrown in prison by a corrupt police chief. In jail they meet Yankel, nicknamed "Yankel shmates," or "Yankel of the rags," an acquaintance from their Old World shtetl. Yankel's newfound fortune in the New World is matched by his lack of street smarts, which has led him to be defrauded by a gentleman named "Brown," who had promised to show him the sights of the city.

At the rabbi's court appearance, the rabbi recognizes in the "street corner" lawyer who is to defend him none other than Levi, his daughter's seducer. A scene ensues, in which the rabbi accuses Levi of ruining his daughter. The judge orders the rabbi to be transported to Belleview, the hospital for the insane. His son Max and Yankel vow to prove the rabbi's sound mental state and innocence, save the girl from the clutches of crime, and have the fraudulent gentleman Brown and the dishonorable lawyer Levi proven guilty.

They discover Rachel, who has tried to escape and is determined to defend her chastity until death, in one of the neighborhood's seediest brothels, from which girls leave only in a casket. Max falls instantly in love with her and helps to save her. His own sister, however, is less fortunate. After her downfall, she has turned to prostitution. In fact, she works in the same brothel where her father performed Rachel's wedding ceremony, and she recognizes him as she dances her famous "dance of the seven veils." She tries to secure a respectable occupation, but the lady placing maids in families tells her that her expensive taste and ladylike appearance disqualify her as maid. She belongs in "Allen Street," and from that past there can be no escape. Even a marriage proposal by Yankel, who discovers that she is from the same shtetl and is too naive to realize her real profession, cannot save her. She is ruined by her loss of innocence and commits suicide. Rachel, however, is freed from the bond of marriage to pursue her romance with Max when Willy, Rachel's husband, is murdered at a card game. The rabbi is proven

innocent, the lawyer, guilty, and Max sets up a (Shabbat-observing) diamond business with Yankel's financial backing. Max decides never to reveal
the fate of his sister to his father.

As in Ciambelli's mysteries, in *The Black Gang* real ladies and gentlemen
are marked by inner distinction, modesty, honest work, and the observance
of (Jewish) religious and moral precepts. Misplaced trust in a depraved city
can result in the loss of "innocence" and ultimately, death. Even though the
city in general, and the Jewish and Italian quarters in particular, in Paley's
and Ciambelli's mysteries is marked by crime, seductions, and dangers, it
ultimately is bound together by moral convictions, shared traditions, last-
ing loyalties, and, most important, blood ties. Chance encounters, attractions, and friendships between strangers are ultimately revealed as "organic"
connections: origins in the same shtetl, blood relationships between distant
cousins, long-lost brothers and sisters, patrons and servants, benefactors
and their clients. It is this "web of connections," rather than the epistemology of types characteristic of the middle-class urban guidebooks, that transforms the "city of strangers" into a "knowable community."[86]

Paley's *Di Shvartse Khevre*, Ciambelli's *I Misteri di Mulberry Stritto* and
Il Mistero di Bleecker Street challenge American middle-class efforts to cast
immigrants as innately different, lower-class, rude, criminal, boorish, unin-
telligent, ill-mannered, and defined by labor and physique rather than
morality and intelligence. As such, they confirm the social anxieties evident
in the middle-class urban guidebooks. Not only were the codes of gentility
indeed imitable, but the boundaries of middle-class identity were open to
erosion. The very notion of the existence of immutable, innate identities
itself was under assault by groups who defiantly staked their claims on an
identity still in the making.

The intertextuality of the middle-class metropolitan guidebooks, and
Ciambelli's Italian American and Paley's Jewish American urban mysteries,
points to a central site of cultural struggle in turn-of-the-century American society. Modernity introduced itself within the cityscapes of America
by transforming and violently disrupting the linkage between "place, the past,
memory and identity." The increasing mechanization of production, the
gradual transition to a consumer society, and the replacement of a labor
theory of value by an exchange theory of value combined to produce the
sense of a radical split "between the visible city and the work or productive
aspect of city life" and of a loosening of the organic tie between external
appearance and inner reality.[87]

According to Ciambelli, the real mystery of the city in his "dramas of emigration" lies in the lure of gold, and in the question why it tempts some to crime, some into becoming parvenus by profiting from workers, while others continue an honest but often miserable working life. But in framing that question in terms of "mystery," the trope of urban "mystery," as Karl Marx argued in his analysis of Eugène Sue's *Mystères de Paris*, itself functions as a "form of mystification," which replicates the mystification that attaches itself to the commodity under the conditions of consumer capitalism.[88]

Yet in these novels, the relentless desire to dispel the city's mystery by uncovering a "mechanics of representation and misrepresentation" stumbles upon something about the city that may be irreducible to containment, naming, and cataloguing. Jean-Paul Sartre described the paradox at the heart of the urban mysteries: "A city is a material and social organization which derives its reality from the ubiquity of its absence. It is present in each of its streets *insofar as* it is always elsewhere, and the myth of the capital with its *mysteries* demonstrates well that the opaqueness of direct human relations comes from this fact, that they are always conditioned by all others."[89]

The paradox of the city is thus fundamentally one of an excess of meaning and an absence. Jean-Christophe Bailly considers the history of the modern city one of "a permanent combat between the production of a constantly displaced excess of meaning and the control of all social forms which produce this excess by those in society who exercise or maintain their power by naturalizing these forms."[90] From this perspective, the middle-class versions of the mystery-and-misery genre are exercises in bourgeois boundary drawing, informed by a vision of the city, its bodies, and its social order as transparent, coherent, and ordered by supposedly natural hierarchies. The immigrant mysteries, with their utopian vision of an organic social order, natural identities, and communal solidarities, bound by love and respect, articulate an alternative that, despite its premodern overtones, has informed the construction of ethnic communal identities within the city.

That, in these texts, the fear of the excess of the irreducible pluralism and heterogeneity of the modern city would be expressed in terms of a vehement "anti-theatricality" should come as no surprise. Theatricality implies the impossibility of (self) containment. Indeed, as Weber argues, "Theatricality emerges where space and place can no longer be taken for granted or regarded as self-contained." Theatricality—like the city—points to that which is simultaneous, present, and elsewhere.[91]

" He sung, sitting beside the widow, on her bed, with Mollie Williams nigh, perched on the wooden excuse for a chair."

Acting and detecting: McParlan/McKenna sings himself into popularity. From Allan Pinkerton, *The Mollie Maguires*, 373.

Chapter 2

Detecting, Acting, and the Hierarchy of the Social Body

*D*ARKNESS AND *D*AYLIGHT CAN BE CONSIDERED INDICATIVE OF a paradigm shift that started to overtake dominant bourgeois attitudes toward the "problem" of the inner city and the poor in the late nineteenth century. The explosive growth of late nineteenth-century New York City and other major cities lent a new urgency to the efforts to lay bare the inner workings of the city, and bridge a social chasm that was widely perceived as a source of social and political unrest. Moreover, the teeming populations of the inner city, made up of racially inferior Jews, Italians, Negroes, Slavs, and Orientals, also seemed to lend support to eugenicist claims about the impending dangers these degenerate ghetto inhabitants posed to Anglo-Saxon racial supremacy.

Within this context, the amateurism and detachment characteristic of the urban spectator of earlier metropolitan guidebooks no longer sufficed. Penetrating into the recesses of urban life called for a professional, whose specialized knowledge, based on hard data, firm categorizations, and statistical analysis, was needed to replace earlier impressionistic observations.[1] Moreover, these facts gleaned from the "outside" needed to be complemented with knowledge based on close observation and detailed study. *Darkness and Daylight*'s triumvirate—the journalist, the detective, the social worker—points toward the various fields of forces that intersected in the reinvigorated mapping of the late nineteenth-century social body.

Allan Sekula, in his influential essay "The Body and the Archive," has described these forces as the emergence of a "bureaucratic-clerical-statistical system of intelligence." The epistemological underpinning of this intelligence was based on the sciences of physiognomy and phrenology. Physiognomy and phrenology exemplified the contemporary belief that the external surface

27

of the body carried the sign of inner "character." Physiognomy isolated different parts of the body (especially the head, but also more general features, such as posture), to which it attributed specific characterological value, while phrenology linked the shape of the skull to specific mental faculties. Both sciences analyzed individual cases in relationship to "type," a generalized form or "gestalt" based on the aggregate data collected by physiognomists, phrenologists, and statisticians. In the late nineteenth century, as the middle classes frenetically sought to distinguish its white, respectable, law-abiding bodies from those of their deviant, cultural others, the collection of such data was increasingly framed by criminologist and eugenicist concerns.[2]

Against the threat of theatricality and the dissimulation of identity so characteristic of deviance, the middle class guarded itself with a new instrument of truth, the camera, and new technologies of surveillance, such as the mug shot, the Bertillon system of identification, and the Rogues' Gallery, a collection of mug shots of known criminals published by Police Inspector Thomas Byrnes in his *Professional Criminals of America* (1886). Yet the professional knowledge of deviant types contained in the Rogues' Gallery was useless unless circulated among, and assimilated by, the population at large. Typologies of the poor, the criminal, and the racial Other found their way into realist fiction, urban journalism, vaudeville sketches, documentary photography, and early film, composing an ever-expanding "archive" of the social body.[3] According to Walter Benjamin, in physiognomic knowledge, which is built on a view of the human being as "creature," "a machinery of affects that can be controlled to the degree that it is calculable," the Enlightenment, with its emphasis on rationality and will, shows its sinister side.[4]

The techniques of (self) surveillance were popularized first and foremost in the figure of the detective, who by the late nineteenth century had become an increasingly familiar institution in the city. "At his work . . . everywhere throughout a great city, in the horse cars, in Wall Street, in all the great stores, at the churches on Sundays, in the lager-beer gardens on the steamboats at the wharves, throughout the large manufactories, around various dens of iniquity, at the theatres," the detective exemplified the fantasy of total surveillance that permeated the discourse of the inner city.[5] Moreover, as an expert in de/coding the social body, the detective also served as a model (self) surveilling urban subject.

His techniques were popularized in the dime novel and in the memoirs of actual detectives. Nick Carter, Frank Merriwell, and Sherlock Holmes relied on their knowledge of physiognomy, their skills of disguise, and their familiarity with the Rogues' Gallery to detect the "criminal character" and recognize fraud. Memoirs of actual detectives such as Allen Pinkerton, George McWatters, George Walling, and New York Chief Inspector Byrnes similarly instructed the city dweller in the tricks of their trade. Introducing the reader to the hidden worlds of crime and depravity and to the skills needed to navigate them, such memoirs claimed to enable, as the subtitle of Phil Farley's *Criminals of America; or; Tales of the Lives of Thieves* (1876) suggested, "Every One to Be His Own Detective."[6]

Crucial to the position of the detective as model subject of the city was his ability to transcend the "radical incompleteness" of urban experience through a comprehensive understanding of the system of urban signs. Detectives not only trained their readers in de/coding their environments, but also enabled them to share in the fantasy of temporarily overcoming the "deep atomization of experience," which, according to Walter Benjamin, lies at the heart of the perception of the city as mystery, by engaging in an intellectual exercise of association and connection.[7] Detectives, investigative reporter Knox pontificated, "oftentimes from insignificant signs that occasionally surround the most mysterious of crimes . . . are able to construct a complete and correct theory of the motive and the operations of the criminal. They acquire a wonderful memory and seldom fail to recognize a face they have once seen, however altered or disguised it may be. It becomes second nature to them to unravel plots, unmask falsehoods, and extort the truth."[8]

The skills of the detective combined, and professionalized, the two prevalent epistemological models that, as Peter Stallybrass has argued, guided the middle class in its encounter with the city. The first of these models sought to gain command of the theatrical heterogeneity of the city through the cataloguing and collection of urban types and speech modes. The second model, impersonation, employed theatricality against itself and involved the dissimulation and splitting of the bourgeois subject.[9]

"The greatest essential," Pinkerton, from the famous Pinkerton Detective Agency, wrote about the requirements of the detective, "is to prevent his identity from becoming known, even among his associates of respectable character." In order to do so, the detective needs to possess "an ability to adapt himself to every association in which he may find himself" and "acquire all the information possible" by "assimilating, as far as possible, with the individuals" with whom he interacts in the course of his investigation.[10] As the detective adjusts his personality according to the demands of the job, detective George McWatters explained, "to-day he perhaps personates one character; tomorrow, another."[11]

In the view of some, the detective's investigative strategies and his close association with the underworld presented the potential danger of contamination. "The word 'detective,'" Crapsey wrote, "taken by itself, implies one who must descend to questionable shifts to attain justifiable ends."[12] As such, the figure of the detective exposed the repressed knowledge that the dividing line between the law-abiding body and the criminal body, which the bourgeoisie was at pains to establish as "hard fact," was more porous than it liked to acknowledge. The law-abiding citizen recognized in the criminal "his own acquisitive and aggressive impulses unchecked." The respectable (self) surveilling subject, who faked appearances and concealed the signs of his true identity, was as much an actor, trading on falsehoods for profit, as the criminal.[13]

Indeed, in an era that sentimentally embraced the qualities of authenticity, honesty, and trust, the detective frequently faced the same antitheatrical prejudice as the confidence men and impostors who were his suspects, and whose techniques of dissimulation and impersonation he copied.[14] In McWatters's opinion, "The detective is a thief . . . and steals into men's confidences to ruin them. He makes friends in order to reap the profits of betraying them."[15]

The detective operates in the space of radical exteriority. It is a space that is marked by a fundamental distrust in hermeneutics and communicative signs, a space that focuses attention instead on "traces that must be deciphered and read." It is also the space of theatricality. But where some interpreted the theatricality of the detective as the dissimulation and concealment of identity, others saw a sign of true mastery and professionalism. Pinkerton himself was given to boasting about his acting talents, and claimed that "nine-tenths of the actors on the stage . . . would do well to take lessons in their own profession" from the detective.[16] Jacob Riis, when he was still a police reporter, wrote of the famous Chief Inspector Byrnes: "The boys called him a great faker, but they were hardly justified in that. I should rather call him a great actor, and without being that no man can be a great detective."[17]

The ambivalence toward the professional methods of the detective can serve to illuminate the repercussions of the transformation of conceptions of work and productivity that accompanied the shift from a producer society to a consumer society in the late nineteenth century. This transformation had a profound impact not only on theories of identity and the place of theatricality in self-presentation, but it also served as the basis of a new social and cultural hierarchy in which radical externality—theatricality— was transformed into a mark of white, professional identity.

The Undercover Professional

The contours of this realignment and the controversies it engendered sur-
faced most markedly in the case of McParlan, an Irish immigrant recruited
by Allen Pinkerton to infiltrate the orders of the Mollie Maguires, an Irish
secret society devoted to organizing America's coal industry and suspected
of a series of murders committed in the heart of Pennsylvania mining country in the 1870s. Confronted with widespread criticism of McParlan's testimony, which resulted in the death penalty for a number of the suspects and
provoked the defense to accuse McParlan of being an agent provocateur,
Pinkerton defended the use of an undercover detective on the basis of the
menace that the Mollies presented to the social order. Successful elimination
of this secret order required unconventional methods, Pinkerton explained
in *The Mollie Maguires and the Detectives,* his own self-serving account of
the case, published in 1877, shortly after the execution of the first suspects.
"What we want . . . is to get within this apparently impenetrable ring; turn
to light the hidden side of this dark and cruel body, to probe to its core this
festering sore upon the body politic."[18]

The case, for which Pinkerton was recruited by Mr. Gowen, the eloquent
and gentlemanly president of the Philadelphia and Reading Railway Company and the Philadelphia and Reading Coal and Iron Company, called for
an operative who was Irish and a Catholic, as "only this class of people can
find admission to the Mollie Maguires." The recruit would have to possess
the ability to "become, really and truly, a Mollie of the hardest character,
attend their meetings, and possibly be charged with direct participation in
certain of their crimes." More crucially, however, in order to fulfill his mission to destroy the Mollies, this undercover agent would have to be able to
"go against his life-long habits, early impressions, education, and his inherited as well as acquired prejudices." "Was there one who held sufficiently
broad and deep-grounded notions of the real duty of a true Irishman to his
country and his fellow countrymen to entrust with this mission?"[19]

McParlan, a "fine specimen of the better class of immigrants," fit the description. He had become a low-level operative in Pinkerton's Detective
Agency a few years earlier, after having tried his hand at a variety of low-
paying clerking and selling jobs. A man with "a clear hazel eye; hair of
auburn color . . . ; a forehead high, full and well-rounded forward; florid
complexion [and] regular features," he had earned "a reputation for honesty, a peculiar tact and shrewdness, skill and perseverance." He came to
Pinkerton's attention while working undercover as a streetcar conductor.

Pinkerton called him for an interview, during which he was impressed by "his peculiar Irish accomplishments to ingratiate himself with those to whom he was sent" and his professed readiness to "start at the word of command."[20]

As preparation for his new identity, McParlan's "ordinary but cleanly citizen's attire" was replaced by a tramp outfit:

> His head [was] covered by an old and dilapidated slouch hat, with plentiful space for his cutty-pipe in its narrow, faded band. . . . The pantaloons, of brown woollen stuff, were whole, but too large for him in the body, and worn strapped tight at the waist with a leather belt, which, from its yellowish and broken condition, might have been a former bell-thong off the neck of some farmer's cow. . . . With face unshaven for a week or ten days, and hair quite dry and straggling from want of proper attention, it is probable that McParlan's mother, had she been present, would have refused him recognition.[21]

With this disguise, Pinkerton writes, the detective was ready to be dispatched "to perform his difficult *role*, under my directions." In Pinkerton's version, McParlan's subsequent undercover experience, in which he posed as an itinerant laborer, provided him not only with the evidence necessary to convict the suspected criminals but also with an insider's view of the mysterious world of the Pennsylvania coal mines and its "habits and customs," "mostly novel to the American reader," which included Irish wakes, Polish weddings, dog and cock fights, violence, drinking, secret codes and passwords, and lots of "foreign idiom and native eccentricities."[22]

McParlan's basic detecting technique is captured most succinctly by the title of one subchapter, "The Detective Sings, Fights and Dances Himself into Popularity." For the sake of establishing a convincing persona, McParlan/McKenna gets embroiled in fights, drinking parties, murders, and shootouts, and even develops something of a romance with the sister-in-law of one of the primary suspects. According to Pinkerton, this was a ruse designed to enable McParlan to spend time in the suspect's immediate environment. True to his role, he exhibits a healthy taste for strong liquor, and he frequently adopts the "appearance of intoxication, staggering about." "With an assumption of unlimited assurance, and pretending to be more than half way under the influence of liquor [he] broke out with such a roaring, rollicking ditty as he supposed might please those about him, or, if he felt in the mood, began a spirited Irish jig, performed with much agility and many comical contortions of countenance and body."[23]

In real life speaking a slightly accented English, the undercover character of McParlan/McKenna speaks a heavy Irish brogue. This gives Pinkerton the opportunity to entertain those readers with a "keen sense of the humorous" with the comic possibilities of dialect. In Pinkerton's version, McKenna executes his role with all the ruddy finesses of the contemporary stage Irishman: "An' what is it I'm here fur? What should a dacent Irish lad want whose stomach is full of emptiness and ne'er a morsel of bread or mate in the wallet. What I want is worruk, and somethin' to relave my hunger."[24]

As a result of his winning persona, "he never failed, with those in whose company he cared, for the purposes of his undertaking, to be received, in immediately placing himself upon a secure and friendly footing." His everyday companions included "Ferguson, alias Fergus . . . of dark complexion . . . as full of genuine wit as he could be," and McNulty, of "swarthy complexion, black hair, dark grey eyes," who "could steal like a born thief."[25]

Two and a half years "underground," however, took their toll on the zealous McParlan. Owing to environmental influences, such as exposure to bad weather, late hours, and an overabundant supply of bad liquor, "he grew thin, cadaverous, and his strength perceptibly and rapidly failed." An illness made him lose his hair, which he replaced with a reddish wig "about the color of his former natural growth, which, as he was not a barber, seldom received proper dressing, and gave its wearer a very uncouth and shabby appearance." His external transformation was so complete that his "friends flattered him by saying that he was the wickedest and toughest, as well as the roughest-looking vagabond seen at the county fair." One author commented that "seeing him with a slouch hat on a bald pate, with green spectacles, rough shirt, and an old linen coat, swaggering along the streets, the last idea likely to present itself was that through his exertions a new era of peace, of law, and of order was about to dawn on the anthracite coal-mines."[26]

Indeed, McParlan's role as a Mollie was so successful that it stirred suspicions about the detective's moral character and his true allegiances. Some suggested that, under the influence of his environment, he truly had become "the wildest Irishman of the mountains, and the most unprincipled Mollie in the whole country."[27] Just such a threat had lurked for the police detectives of Springfield, Massachusetts, who had joined the ranks of the New England "tramp" army during the national railroad strike of 1877. According to Chief Detective Stephenson, after just a month on the road these detectives were "ready for pillage and destruction" and fully qualified as candidates for incarceration in the workhouses that were the reformers' answer to the tramp problem.[28] McParlan's increasingly "wild" appearance and behavior resulted at the trial in the defense's accusation that it had been the detective himself who had instigated the most violent crimes the Mollies were charged with.

Pinkerton refuted these claims by explaining McParlan's "wild Irishman" as the sign of a professional's zealotry and dedication to his job. It was this professionalism that inured McParlan to environmental influences, according to Pinkerton. Even though McParlan seemed, outwardly, "the most eccentric and savage appearing Mollie Maguire in the whole seven hundred," "his deeds were not criminal, however unseemly he appeared, and his duty was ever uppermost in his thoughts."[29] Even in his alcohol consumption McParlan, being the dutiful professional that he was, remained in control of himself. As Pinkerton asserted, "considered the dangerous company he was in, and the extra-hazardous duty he was performing, his mind was so unduly excited, his brain so highly stimulated and alert, the liquor he swallowed produced no more effect upon his organization than so much water."[30]

Upon his disclosure as a detective, one acquaintance, baffled by the variety of identities sported by McParlan/McKenna, commented: "It's a mystery to me, anyhow! . . . He's a counterfeiter, a thief, a gentleman, a singer of songs and dancer of jigs, an' be gorra, now they say he's a detective!" But as Pinkerton insisted, underneath all these impersonations lay McParlan's professional identity as a detective, and it was in "true character as a detective" that McParlan prepared to "come out" on the witness stand to testify against his erstwhile friends and companions in crime. As a professional who completed his job, McParlan provided names and details of crimes without flinching: "He told the story in slow, measured sentences, without any manifestation of feeling or attempt at display. . . . Upon the witness stand, his evidence is entirely devoid of passion, and although feeling proper pride in professional success, he never, for the sake of making a point, seeks to stretch the truth or give a false color to his recital of facts."[31]

Pinkerton's appeal to the rhetoric of "professionalism" as a way to deflect attacks on the detective's methods or political and social allegiance points to a significant transformation of the middle-class notion of character, toward an acceptance of the "performing" aspect of the self. In what Warren Susman has called the new culture of personality, what counted was not sincere self-expression but "the production of a profitable identity," whether those profits lay in assuming the appearance of a Mollie in order to restore social order or of a gentleman while selling commodities in a new downtown department store.[32] In representing McParlan as someone uniquely able to ingratiate himself with his various consorts and cultivate a "winning persona" while maintaining an "authentic" inner self, uncorrupted by his environment and by the various roles he assumed in the course of his assignment, Pinkerton makes McParlan into a model for an urban professional middle-class identity, which reconciles the idea of identity as the "imagined manifestation of interiority" with the possibility of "the multiplicity of expression" through the performance of self.[33]

In the transformation of a "culture of character" to a "culture of personality," the detective and the impostor, then, emerged as the twin images of the middle-class professional. McParlan and the "unscrupulous rascals" described by Inspector Byrnes, who left "all suggestion of [their] calling . . . outside the front door at home" to be "model husbands and fathers," successfully negotiate the public/private split that constitutes middle-class professional identity. Their primary mission is to perform their various public personae without investing too heavily in their roles or corrupting their inner self.[34]

Paradoxically, Pinkerton's portrayal of McParlan suggests the possibility that the "very anchor of middle-class identity, its split configuration, might be used by others to undermine the boundaries of middle-class exclusivity."[35] It hints at the importance of professionalization for different immigrant groups as a potential trajectory not only of social but also cultural mobility. Professionalization, the mark of which is absence of signs of labor on the body and the successful performance of a variety of social roles, provided the possibility of mythic self-transformation, of becoming the prototypical American "new man." Moreover, as Pinkerton would have it, professionalism enabled one to overcome the degenerative effects of one's environment, transcend the marks of race and class, and thus outwardly enter the promised land of middle-class whiteness. At the same time, this new identity did not demand the erasure of McParlan's Irishness. Indeed, it was McParlan's "peculiar Irish accomplishments to ingratiate himself with those to whom he was sent" that made him especially well suited for the job.

Allen Pinkerton himself laid out the trajectory for such mobility when he described the requirements for the Mollie Maguires investigation. The right man for the job, according to Pinkerton, was "a man who, once inside this, I supposed, oath-bound brotherhood, would yet remain true to me; who would almost make a new man of himself, take his life in his hands, and enter upon a work which was apparently against those bound to him by close ties of nationality, if not blood and kindred." Indeed, the true professional distinguished himself by his ability to "go against his life long habits, early impressions, education, and his inherited as well as acquired prejudices."[36] The fact that Pinkerton trumps the accusations of imposture that trailed McParlan's disjunction of inner and outer identity with claims about his detective's status as a professional suggests that professionalization, for white non-Anglo-Saxon Europeans at least, might have enabled a loosening of the hold of "racial character" and its presumed link between physiognomy and behavior.

Matthew Frye Jacobson has stressed the fact that the "contest over whiteness—its definition, its internal hierarchies, its proper boundaries, and its rightful claimants" was "an untidy affair," which resulted in "conflicting or overlapping racial designations such as white, Caucasian, and Celt" that could "operate in popular perceptions and discussion simultaneously."[37] Catherine Eagan, however, points out that Jacobson's focus on the "glacial" movements in the racial ascription of European immigrants, in which he discerns a series of shifts toward the consolidation of a bona fide "Caucasian" identity in the period after 1924, leaves many questions unanswered. Is it really possible to discuss "class and race apart from each other," she asks, when analyzing the field of force affecting white racial formation (and transformation)? In particular, "To what degree were racist depictions of national groups . . . fueled by differences in class and the level of assimilation?" The Mollie Maguires trial, according to Jacobson, indicates the degree to which the Irish, as a race, were still regarded as inferior in the 1870s. But Eagan points to the class dimensions of this conflict, in particular the ways in which middle-class and professional Irish regarded the Mollies as a disgrace to the race.[38]

The trial of the Mollies was precisely about making Irishness white and respectable. At its heart, this struggle was about the intersection of race and class, or, more accurately, about the unlinking of race and class. The Mollies, prosecutor Gowen charged, presented themselves as the true representatives of "Irishness," claiming, "in addition to the criminal and political motives . . . national characteristics." For Gowen, a self-described "son of an Irishman, proud of my ancestry, and proud of my race, and never ashamed of it, except when I see that Ireland has given birth to wretches such as these," this presented an insult to the Irish race and the Catholic religion. "Does an Irishman wonder why it is sometimes difficult to get a job in this county? Does he wonder why the boss of a colliery hesitates to employ him, when these people have been allowed to arrogate themselves the Irish character and have been permitted to represent themselves to the people of this county as the proper representatives of Ireland?" According to Gowen, in Pennsylvania the Irish race as a whole stood accused.[39]

According to Gowen and Pinkerton, McParlan's "performance of a professional duty" "succeeded in having both nationality and religion . . . gloriously and successfully vindicated." In yoking together Irishness and professional role-playing, then, Pinkerton formulated a model for an Irish middle-class white identity that was based on the possibility of maintaining a dual self, in which "race" (or nationality) does not determine external (American) identity but may constitute an authentic inner core, which is uncorrupted by, and uncorrupting to, the various roles one plays in public. In his self-serving advocacy of spying as middle-class professionalism, then, Pinkerton moved toward the undoing of the systematic linkage between internal and external identity, which was the foundation of contemporary theories of race.[40]

IMPERSONATION AND THE SEARCH FOR "EXPERIENCE"

The masquerades of the detective and the undercover experiences of McParlan, directed initially toward the investigation of crime and labor activism, were soon to become accepted as an alternative strategy of social investigation. In the context of an increasingly explosive social climate, which confronted many with the harsh reality of the existence of radically different experiences and social views, impersonation offered a perspective of low life from the "inside."[41]

Nelly Bly's *Ten Days in a Mad-House,* published in 1887 in Joseph Pulitzer's *World,* marked a significant shift from the urban spectator's positioning on the "outside" to a new "stance within the city."[42] It was one of the first accounts of an experimental total immersion in the world of the low and the marginal, and as such it signaled the adoption of the methods of the detective by young urban professionals, such as the neophyte journalist Bly.

In this report of her sojourn in a New York asylum, Bly not only disguises her own identity and goes undercover, but she effectively transgresses the boundary separating self and Other by assuming the identity of the insane. Widely acclaimed, not in the least for the vicarious thrill of providing an "interior" perspective, Bly's account set a standard for veracity in the representation of low life for the following decades. In order to "get at" the reality of working- and under-class life, it was considered necessary to get beyond the narrow confines of one's own limited point of view.[43]

This active pursuit of reality through firsthand knowledge, according to Walter Benjamin, Amy Kaplan, Miles Orvell, T. J. Jackson Lears, and others, was characteristic of turn-of-the-century middle-class culture. Cushioned by a life of comforts and commodities, and accustomed to living life vicariously, through newspaper reports, dioramas, and panoramas, many members of the middle class felt more and more alienated from "experience."[44] In addition, the growing regimentation and specialization of tasks within the professional urban workplace led to an increasingly diminished sense of self. This sentiment was articulated by Basil March, the protagonist of William D. Howells's *Hazard of New Fortunes,* when he compared "life in the metropolis" to a "solvent" bringing out "the deeply underlying nobody" in everyone.[45]

To counterbalance the sense of the unreality of respectable bourgeois life and what some considered the emasculating effects of modern metropolitan existence, late nineteenth-century middle-class culture embraced a cult of raw and authentic "experience" that sought revitalization through the shock of encounters with "real life."[46] While some, like Theodore Roosevelt, found rejuvenation in hunting expeditions in the African jungle and the strenuous life of the outdoors, for many others "real life" was synonymous with the simple, savage, atavistic life of the working classes. "How unreal, and consequently how uninteresting, the ordinary sheltered, well-to-do-man or woman of so-called refinement is!" Hutchins Hapgood lamented in his indictment of middle-class culture. "His words . . . lack a sense of conviction as to what is 'the real thing.' How can he know, in his Cook's tour-like voyage through life, what the necessary and fundamental things are?" By contrast, Hapgood asserts, "The very lowest people, like the very highest on the social scale, come very close to the facts of life. They are, through poverty, through toughness, through crime, brought up against the 'limit.' Like the highest, they are often cultivated, in a real way, through real experience."[47]

Crossing the boundaries of class and trying out "real" life on the other side of the social divide became the new fad. In London, Charles Booth combined a positivist confidence in statistics with impersonation for his multivolume study of lower-class life in London, *Life and Labour of the People in London,* which was published between 1887 and 1903.[48] In the United States, between the 1890s and 1910, dozens of reporters, sociologists, writers, and reformers, motivated by a Progressive confidence in the ability of data—acquired through experience—to mediate between the social classes, set out to follow Bly's example.[49]

Walter Wyckoff, a graduate of the University of Chicago School of Sociology, impersonated an unskilled laborer to get at the "truth" of the labor question. Lillian Pettengill became a domestic servant to discover "the conditions of industrial life"; Josiah Flynt dressed up as a tramp to examine the reality of life as an itinerant laborer; and Alvan Sanborn acted out the role of a beggar to experience the lodging house from the inside.[50] Even the Reverend Parkhurst, in his crusade against the moral depravity of slum life, did not eschew impersonation in order to observe vice unnoticed.

In their quest for intimate knowledge of the Other, social masqueraders were inspired by the basic tenets of physiognomy, which held that "as we look, so we feel, so we act, and so we are."[51] Accordingly, the impersonation of someone's physiognomy, posture, speech, and manner of walking could put one "en rapport" with the character of the type thus imitated. As Samuel Wells, author of an authoritative book on the principles of physiognomy, explained:

> Fall upon his trail, observe his motions when yourself unobserved; take on his manner and step, and by following him a short distance, you will feel as he feels, and soon become *en rapport* with him. If he puts on airs and attempts to show off in the character of a "swell," you will do the same, and for the moment lose your own individuality or identity, and be swallowed up by him; but your second thought will make you heartily disgusted with this false or assumed character, and you will then return to yourself. . . . If he be a rogue, fleeing from justice, and you closely watch his movements, you will soon get into the same spirit, and feel like the wicked who "flees when no man pursueth." If on the contrary you are seeking the rogue for the purpose of dealing out justice to him, being actuated by a different motive, your walk will be different. But inasmuch as "it takes a rogue to catch a rogue," or rather, we should say, one who appreciates the language of secretiveness and understands setting traps, the pursuer may, to a certain extent, exhibit the same general traits in his manner and his walk that are exhibited by the rogue himself.[52]

Social class, according to the common belief of the period, was expressed not only in dress but also inscribed in posture and features. Signs of social difference such as crooked legs, or Sanborn's beggar's shambling gait and drooping head, according to Wells's *New Physiognomy*, were engraved upon the body by persistent exercise and pressure. Differences in appearance, ultimately, were the outward signs of the social division of labor, which itself was seen as the result of differences in "natural calling." As the chapter "The Physiognomy of Classes" explains, "Each profession and occupation has a tendency to impress its peculiar lines upon the physical system of those habitually exercising it; so that we may generally know a man's trade by the cut of his features."[53]

This line of reasoning was perfectly molded to naturalize class difference, since it presumed that class was innate. In Wells, a neo-Lamarckian nod to the modifying influences of the environment allowed for a measure of class mobility. Neo-Lamarckianism, which steered a middle course between the

relative influence of inheritance and the environment, held that modifica-
tions in class status would result in changes in body and physiognomy,
which in due course would become inherited. Following that principle,
Wells argues, the "general law" of physiognomy could be modified through
the "law" of "special development," namely, exercise.[54] As Wells explains,

> a person whom nature has set apart as it were for a certain calling, by giving him
> the organization best fitted for it, will have the impress of that calling stamped
> upon him from the beginning; though if he disregard the indication of nature and
> devote himself, or be devoted, to some other pursuit, he may partially obliterate
> the original signs and acquire those of his actual calling. . . . We may *direct* and
> *control* even our *thoughts,* our *feelings,* and our *acts,* and thus, to some extent—
> by the aid of grace—become what we will. We are free to choose what course we
> will pursue, and our bodies, our brains, and our features readily adapt themselves
> and clearly indicate the lives we lead and the characters we form.[55]

Social masqueraders modeled their own undercover personas on what
they perceived as the characteristic physiognomy of generic social "types."
Alvan Sanborn, for instance, treats the individual details of his beggar's outfit with utmost seriousness: "I began by sacrificing most of the hair on my
head—to prevent insect ambuscades—and mustache, and by going unshaven
for about ten days. When the time for going out came, I thoroughly grimed
face, hands, and neck, donned several suits of worn, soiled underclothes
(several for warmth and armor), a pair of disreputable pantaloons, a jacket
out at the elbows, clumsy, discolored shoes, and a hat that was almost a disguise in itself." The "finishing touches" of Sanborn's disguise, in which he
professes "a genuine artistic pride," included "a dingy red flannel handker-
chief fastened around my neck with a safety-pin, a clay pipe filled with vile
smelling tobacco, a cheap whiskey breath, a shambling gait, and a drooping
head."[56]

Bessie Van Vorst assumed her "disguise," that of a Pittsburgh factory girl,
shortly before she left the comforts of her upper-class New York existence.
"In the Parisian clothes I am accustomed to wear I present the familiar outline of any woman of the world," she assessed self-appreciatively. "With the
aid of coarse woolen garments, a shabby felt sailor hat, a cheap piece of fur,
a knitted shawl and gloves I am transformed into a working girl of the ordinary type." As soon as she reaches the train depot, she realizes, from observing the gateman's reaction, that "I had divested myself of a certain authority
along with my good clothes, and I had become one of a class which . . . as I

found out later myself, are devoid of all knowledge of the world and, aside from their manual training, ignorant on all subjects."[57]

Others interpreted their mission in an altogether more artistic manner. In Stephen Crane's *Experiment in Misery,* it is an "artist friend" with a flair for "types" who prepares the narrator for his experiment as a tramp. Bessie Van Vorst, by contrast, approached her masquerade first and foremost as an exercise in comparative shopping. Her account priced her transformation as one from designer's hat ($40) to small felt hat (25 cents); sealskin coat ($200) to gray serge ($3); black cloth dress ($150) to flannel shirtwaist ($1.95); silk undershirt ($25) and underwear ($30) to underwear ($1.00). Total value of the transformation: discarded clothes, $447; new clothes, $9.45. "No sooner had I taken my place in my plain attire than my former personality slipped away as absolutely as did the garments I had discarded," the author claimed. "I was Bell Ballard."[58]

Crossing the boundaries of class required the divesting of an old identity and the adoption of a new one. Despite the customary claims of a spontaneous identity shift that accompanied drastic changes in outside "style," the almost innate quality of social difference meant that social impersonation required some genuine acting skills. Apprehensive of her ability to successfully pass for "insane," Nelly Bly thought it cautious to rehearse her role in private before making a public appearance.

> Could I assume the character of insanity to such a degree that I could pass the doctors . . . ? I said I believed I could. I had some faith in my ability as an actress. . . . I began to practice the role in which I was to make my debut on the morrow. What a difficult task, I thought, to appear before a crowd of people and convince them that I was insane. . . . I feared that they could not be deceived. . . . So I flew to the mirror and examined my face. I remembered all the doings of crazy people, how first of all they must have staring eyes, and so I opened mine as wide as possible and stared unblinkingly at my own reflection.[59]

Bly's training for her new social role closely resembles the exercise of bodily control that defined middle-class identity. Indeed, as Maude Cook (herself an accomplished actress) counseled young women in her *Social Etiquette* (1896), being a lady required a daily acting lesson: "Practice talking without moving the facial muscles but slightly. Do this before the mirror daily, if necessary, and before the same faithful mentor learn to open the eyes less widely, parting the lids only just so far as to show the colored iris without a glimpse of the white portion, or cornea, of the eye above or below it."[60]

Being well trained in middle-class etiquette, it is no surprise that Bly expressed her confidence in "her ability as an actress." But while self-discipline and control of appearance signifies middle-class identity, it is the lack of self-discipline and control of facial expressions that signify the insane as well as the lower classes. It is this lack of control that Bly and other impersonators try to master.

Consequently, Rheta Childe Dorr, a social worker, masked the fact that she lacked the "short, stocky build and thick ankles of the 'average peasant type'" by mimicking a "hang-dog position of the head" and "a sort of swinging drawl of a gait."[61] She also adopted a "monosyllabic" style of talking, which she considered characteristic of the uneducated and unrefined. Other investigators armed themselves with "book-learned slang," pipes, and tobacco chewing. Cornelia Stratton Parker picked up another supposedly indispensable accouterment of low life, gum-chewing, in her effort to pass as a New York working girl. After purchasing the gum from a newsstand, Cornelia "there and then got out a stick and chewed it, and chewed it on the Subway and chewed it on the streets of New York."[62]

Judith Walkowitz has suggested that the "comprehensive knowledge of the Other" that could be acquired through masquerade would enable middle-class progressives not only to report objectively on their conditions but also to advocate more effectively for urban and social reform on the basis of their intimate exposure to the "facts" of low life. Yet the primary goal of such experiments, she argues, was not the reformation of the poor but a self-transformation of the middle-class investigator.[63]

But what was the nature of this "self-transformation"? Social impersonators typically dramatized the extent of their self-transformation by emphasizing their social distance from the existence they were about to assume. Wyckoff coyly evokes socialist theory to deny the reality of his act of social boundary crossing, stating that "I am so far familiar with Socialist writings as to know that, from their point of view, I have not gone from one economic class into another. I belong to the proletariat, and from being one of the intellectual proletarians, I am simply become a manual proletaire."[64] But the fact that he furtively "sneaks" out of his own house in his old fish and hunt outfit, and encounters his disapproving butler along the way, underscores his distance from lower-class life. In a similar strategy, Sanborn's use of French terms to describe his initial trepidation—"Plainly enough, I did not possess the *savoir-faire* the occasion demanded"—classify him as "overbred" rather than, as his self-description would have it, "hopelessly underbred" for his lodging-house experience.[65]

Not surprisingly, it was in the gaze of (former) social equals, and not in their acceptance by (former) social inferiors, that the social impersonator found his or her new identity confirmed. Initially, the social impersonator's transformation was completed as a result of a change in self-consciousness in response to the realization that the new appearance marked one as belonging to the other side of the social divide. Wyckoff, for instance, began his slide into a lower-class being under the gaze of his butler, which caused him "to feel conscious of change in unexpected ways. There was no money in my pocket, and a most subtle and unmanning insecurity laid hold of me as a result of that. The world had curiously changed in its attitude, or rather I saw it at a new angle, and I felt the change most keenly in the bearing of people. My good-morning was not infrequently met by a vacant stare."[66]

Upon meeting an old acquaintance, and realizing the inappropriateness of approaching her in his present garb, Wyckoff at once "knew I was a trespassing vagrant. . . . I grew painfully aware of my work stained clothes, and my faded flannel shirt, and the holes in my old felt hat, and of how all of these marked me as belonging to another world. And so I quietly stole away and returned to 'mine own people.'" To his self-professed chagrin, Wyckoff's social masquerade removed all traces of his "real" identity: "I have been mistaken for a drunkard, and a detective, and a disreputable double of myself . . . but not once, so far as I know, have I been mistaken for a gentleman."[67]

As Mark Pittenger has suggested, such claims about the veracity of these new social identities were bolstered by a neo-Lamarckian perception of poverty. Common notions of lower-class life held that poverty- and disease-stricken environments and "mind-dulling jobs" automatically muted the moral and intellectual senses, degenerative conditions that, in the course of multiple generations, resulted in profound genetic mutations and a biologically determined "under-class."[68] According to this line of reasoning, immersion in lower-class life itself turned what initially was external "play" into an interior reality. In Sanborn's words, "The lodging house makes over the outward man in a single night, and thereafter no dramatic effort need be made. The lodging-house odor never lies. A parched and itchy skin, a foul-tasting mouth, smarting eyes, a 'big head,' and a raging thirst make a man look seedy and wretched, and make him talk and act as he looks, nolens volens. Life does away with the necessity of play at living."[69]

Not surprisingly, social masqueraders found themselves hardly immune to such environmental pressures. Amy Tanner, who had become a restaurant worker, suffered bruises, exhaustion, swollen and blistered feet, and a lame back as a result of her thirteen-hour days. This bodily condition caused a perceptible shift in temperament. She internalized her new social role to the degree that she, in her own words, became a "typical shiftless servant." Her senses became "dulled," she became careless about personal cleanliness and ceased to bathe regularly, supplied herself with desserts meant for guests, lost most of her other inhibitions, and found that her "ethical tone" had deteriorated. With this "background of ache and lassitude," thoughts of "outside interests, my friends, my books, even my family" lost their interest and she "became a creature ruled chiefly by sensations."[70] Frederick C. Mills, who impersonated a hobo in the course of an investigation of rural labor conditions for the California Commission of Immigration and Housing, reported after a lunch of stolen oranges: "The virus must be getting into my veins, as I felt absolutely no compunctions."[71]

After one day of work in a pickling factory, Bessie Van Vorst said that her assumed name seemed to her "the only one I had ever had." As to her coiffed hair and manicured hands, marking her as a lady, "a half-day's work suffices for their undoing. And my disguise is so successful that I have deceived not only others but myself."[72]

In the final analysis, however, social impersonators were protected against environmental pressures and full-fledged social degeneration by their social prejudices and their professionalism. Regardless of their political orientations, their sympathies or antipathies toward the laboring classes or the poor, social impersonators ultimately tended to construct the lower classes as wholly and innately Other, a primitive but vital "race" inhabiting a "Dark Continent." Placing her coworkers low on the evolutionary scale, Bessie Van Vorst observed that knitting-mill workers exhibited a "primitive love of ornament," while Frances Donovan insisted that her fellow waitresses shared the "vulgarity and robustness of primitive life everywhere."[73]

Not only did social impersonators dutifully categorize their coworkers as "primitive," but they also produced taxonomies of different "types" of tramps, steelworkers, lumberjacks, or lodging-house dwellers, complete with lexicons of typical slang words and expressions. Thus, Bessie Van Vorst explains the face of a southern millhand as "unique—a fearful type, whose perusal is not pleasant or cheerful to the character-reader." She typifies her fellow boarder Maurice, "one of the absolutely real creatures I have ever seen," as "Labour—its Symbol—its Epitome," and describes him in obsessive detail as "tall, lank, loosely hung together, made for muscular effort," with a collarless flannel shirt thick with grease and oil stains and redolent with tobacco, a strong neck, bullet head, sunken dark eyes, black hair, sensual mouth, and clean hands with fingers forever darkened by toil.[74]

While this physiognomic proficiency establishes their social superiority, it was the act of writing that most firmly reestablished the boundary between Self and Other that social impersonators transgressed (so they claimed) through corporeal labor. After a hard day's work, they would withdraw to a little corner of a logging camp (as in Wyckoff's case) or to their room, as Lillian Pettengill did, to note their experiences of the day. Writing itself, in these narratives, functions as a sign of class difference.

Walter Wyckoff, for instance, recounts that he is about to lose his job as a logger because of his physical unfitness for hard labor, which already marks his elevated position in the hierarchy of labor. Then, the foreman discovers his bookkeeping skills and cuts him some slack: "Say, Major, this is pretty hard work for you; you suit yourself about this work and help me with the accounts."[75] The fact that Lillian Pettengill "writes" her own identity as a domestic servant by falsifying her own reference distinguishes her from her lower-class companions from the very beginning. Indeed, Pettengill justifies her escapades by referring to the inability of lower-class subjects to record their own experiences: "How else am I to learn what I would know. Gretchen cannot tell me, and I am likely to wait long before one of her class pictures to the public the conditions of industrial life. Neither pen nor brush, scrub-brush excepted, has so far been effective in their hands."[76]

Amy Kaplan has suggested that this "playing" at a social slide was one way to control anxiety about the possibility of real downward mobility that haunted many writers struggling to find publishers and audiences in an increasingly commercial, competitive publishing climate. As she argues, social masquerades provided these writers with an opportunity to explore and reaffirm the boundaries of their own, newly invented professional identities as writers, journalists, or academics.[77]

Most important, it was the act of impersonation itself that confirmed these social boundaries. Social impersonation lifted the writer's or journalist's professional status because it tapped into the growing cultural prestige of representational "veritism." Moreover, the very fact that these reporters were unmarked by the physical signs of labor, and in some cases unequipped for the demands of labor, identified them as being "of the mind" rather than "of the body." It also meant that they were not locked into "character," "type," or "environment," but could project a series of convincing personas to the outside world, passing back and forth between a public and a private identity in confirmation of their status as white middle-class professionals.

The same codification of the social body structures Theodore Dreiser's account of his "failed" experience as an "amateur laborer." From the outset, Dreiser emphatically distinguishes his transgression of social boundaries from other "experiments in reality" by fellow writers and journalists. Instead of impersonating a laborer, Dreiser is forced to become one after a nervous breakdown leaves him unable to write. Partly out of necessity, partly in order to regain his health, ruined by the overexertion of mind over body, Dreiser decides to earn a living by his hands: "Once I read an account of the labor struggles of another writer who dressed himself to look the part of a laborer and I always wondered how he would have fared if he had gone in his own natural garb. Now I was determined or rather compelled to find out for myself and I had no heart for it. I realized instinctively that there was a far cry between doing anything in disguise as an experiment and doing it as a grim necessity."[78]

While this preface extends the promise of a truly authentic labor experience, Dreiser's account, as Kaplan has pointed out, is structured around his inability to pass.[79] Having fallen between the cracks, his masquerade consists of desperately clinging to his "true" identity as a gentleman while being a laborer. He is profoundly disturbed when he loses his hat and is forced to purchase a cheap one that makes him look like a beggar, which Dreiser characterizes as a "self-misrepresentation." His "distinguished appearance," Dreiser fears, makes him circumspect not only in the eyes of his fellow workers, whom, as he imagines, view him as an "interloper, perhaps a spy," but in those of his employers as well. This fear is affirmed when Dreiser joins a line of job applicants outside a factory: "When I came in he looked at me with so much consideration that I felt he mistook me for someone who had important business with him. When I finally explained that I wished to know where applications for positions were made his face changed immediately and he told me in brusque tones where to go. I felt like an impostor slinking out for it seemed to me that I had in some indefinable way misrepresented myself to him. I had not turned out to be what he took me for."[80]

For Dreiser, language, character, dress, appearance, demeanor and, above all, physical prowess set apart the different classes. A remark of one of his fellow workers that "yere not the kind of a man that'ud be doin' labor. I sh'd think ye'd be in a store or office now," causes him to "ponder over this for sometime. . . . [I]t set me thinking about the innate difference that exists between the mental and the physical types. These men given to facing the world with their physical skill only could detect at once the mental interloper."[81]

Dreiser's "failed" experience as an amateur laborer, like the more "successful" acts of social passing from which he distances himself, codify the social body by distinguishing those whose bodies are marked by labor, and whose social identities therefore are inscribed from the inside out, from those whose bodies are essentially unmarked. These "experiments" naturalize social difference by falling back on the well-worn dichotomy that opposed head versus body, mental versus manual labor, the ability to "act" versus the inability to transcend the marks of race, class, and environment on the physical body.

Mark Pittenger has suggested that, amid mounting anxiety about the instability of class identities in a society where everyone seemed to be either rising or falling in social status, social masquerades confirmed the perception that, despite the chaotic industrial changes that seemed to undermine social boundaries, a "world of difference," of "darkness" and "daylight," continued to separate the middle class and the poor—a view the middle-class urban guidebooks strived to uphold as well.[82]

But the gradual acceptance of impersonation as the ideal strategy for surveilling the city also can be seen as an expression of a more comprehensive change in the place of the stage within late nineteenth-century American society. Implicitly, what was constructed in the boundary crossings of middle-class professionals was a "new hierarchy of work," which, as Philip Fisher has argued, determined social status on the basis of the presence or absence of signs of labor on the body. This hierarchy of work, according to Fisher, involves "selling the self while at the same time providing a sanctuary for the self within the more clearly acknowledged fictionality of its role." The further one was removed from the mark of labor on the body and the production of commodities, and the greater the fictionality of one's role, the higher one's status within the ranking of labor. For those on the lower end of the economic scale, the body is consumed by work, one's identity determined by labor. On the high end, the body is freed from the mark of work and identity is detached from productive labor. In that sense, Fisher has argued, the actor/actress represented the perfect model for the new corporate self: producing nothing except their own fictionality, the actor/actress is nevertheless able to maintain a clear boundary between an inner character and an outer role. Because of the clearly articulated fictionality of their roles, the self remains intact and sheltered. With a total mastery and manipulation of social codes, they stand at the top of the hierarchy of labor.[83]

In this new hierarchy, acting was no longer considered a "counterfeiting" of one's identity. Instead, it drew "moral meaning . . . from a dynamic society in which all are rising and falling." The successful masquerades of Bly, Wyckoff, Pettengill, and others dramatized their ability to negotiate the split between a private self and a public self, without experiencing the corrosive effects of work (or the demands of the market) on one's private identity, an effect of identifying too closely with one's social role, or being subject to the determining influence of one's social and cultural environment. In doing so, they projected a perfect model for a new, professional identity, which depended on the successful projection of a convincing outer image while preserving the integrity of one's inner self.[84]

But in this hierarchy, social class was conflated with race. According to racial doctrine, the white races were characterized by their intellectual capabilities. Accordingly, those who could transcend the innateness of class through exercise, willpower, and intellect were by definition white. Not only, then, did such a codification construct a lower class whose position in society was fixed and racially determined, but it constructed whiteness as in essence middle class and identified it as the very ability to take on other identities in public while keeping one's inner identity intact.[85]

The "Real" Thing

The discourse of professionalism, then, provided a model of split identity, in which one could be "everyman" in the public workplace while expressing one's essential (racial) "core" identity in the private sanctuary of the home.[86] The potentially unsettling consequences of the valorization of acting and "fictional" identity within this new hierarchy of labor come to the fore in Henry James's story "The Real Thing."[87]

James's story takes place in an artist's studio, which becomes the scene of fierce competition between two sets of models. Mrs. Churm is "only a freckled cockney" who "couldn't spell, loved beer" and had "not an ounce of respect, especially for the *h.*" Mrs. Monarch and her husband, by contrast, are "real" aristocrats who, having fallen on hard times, offer their services as models to the artist. Being the "real thing," they expect to generously outbid their competition. Mrs. Monarch, however, turns out to be so much consumed by her own "fullness" that she dominates the artistic representation. She "has no sense of variety"—her being is one of complete (social) immanence, which also expresses itself in her reluctance to model in "costumes" that are in "*general* use" (52, 47).

Mrs. Churm's qualities as a model/actress, by contrast, are predicated on the fact that she has "no positive stamp" other than a "curious and inexplicable talent for imitation." "Being so little in herself, she could be so much in others," the artist explains. Possessing a "kind of whimsical sensibility, and a love of theatre," Mrs. Churm could "represent everything, from a fine lady to a shepherdess" (48). Her "usual appearance was like a curtain which she could draw up at request for a capital performance." Though "plain" herself, her performance is "suggestive" and transformative: when she models, she becomes "pretty" and "graceful" (53).

Major Monarch, as a model even more irrepressible than his wife, in his turn finds himself displaced by a bankrupt "Italian orange-monger." This man, who turns up one day on the artist's doorstep, has "the making of a servant, as well as of a model," and consequently is hired in that double capacity. Happening upon this "scrap of lazzarone" outfitted in some of the artist's old clothes, the Major cannot suppress his reaction and blurts out: "Is *he* your idea of an English gentleman?" (63). But Oronte, the servant/model, turns out to be the artist's real "treasure."

"The Real Thing" is typically read as James's refutation of a bourgeois aesthetics that concerned itself with the relation of the beautiful to the true, and that regarded truth as immanent in subject matter—an idea expressed not only in aesthetics but also in the bourgeois idea of subjectivity. To this James opposes the "irreducibly illusory character of all art" and the "seem to be" of appearance, "an innate preference for the represented subject over the real one," which the artist himself describes as a "perversity" (46).[88]

In her analysis of the story, Shawn Michelle Smith comments on the social and racial context to which James attaches this "perversity." It is precisely the "lack" in his lower-class, non-Anglo-Saxon models, a lack that James juxtaposes to the "fullness" of aristocratic Anglo-Saxon identity, that fuels Mrs. Churm's "knack for imitation" and her ability as an actress. But the implications of this perspective of identity as "performative" are kept firmly contained. In the story, it is only in the artist's studio that such boundary-crossing desires are expressed and the boundary between appearance and "reality" subverted. If Mrs. Churm's "labor" is the exchange of identity for coin, it is only in the artist's studio that it receives its reward. Only in the province of art are social hierarchies temporarily reversed. In real life, Mrs. Churm remains the essential "freckled cockney."[89]

The portrayal of Major and Mrs. Monarch, meanwhile, naturalizes the aura of upper-class subjectivity as fullness. The performativity of gentility is transfigured into an interior essence, expressed "in and through a homogenous and adequate appearance," which even economic hardship and want cannot bend out of shape. The Major might profess that "I'd be *anything*— I'm strong; a messenger or a coal-heaver. I'd put on a gold-laced cap and open carriage-doors in front of the haberdasher's; I'd hang about a station,

to carry portmanteaus; I'd be a postman" (48). But his inner fullness prevents him from convincingly playing other social roles even in the face of
desperate need. He cannot assume any distance from his genteel self. When
Mr. and Mrs. Monarch exchange roles with the "servant" Oronte in the desperate attempt to obtain some value as "workers," they are abominable fail-
ures because, as Smith observes, they are "unnatural" at it. The gentleman
can only be immanently himself—even if, in the new hierarchy of labor
under commodity capitalism, this identity holds no intrinsic value.[90]

Meanwhile, the flexible, performed identities of Mrs. Churm and Oronte,
even if rewarded with coin by the artist, do not imply social or racial
mobility. They remain "false" externalized appearances, without affecting
their ontological "core" identities, which are determined by class and race.
And if their protean capabilities as models are predicated on something
lacking, this lack does not translate into desire for self-transformation in
any space other than the artist's studio and is harnassed by the artist for his
profit. It is the artist who maintains directorial control over the performances of his models. He is the producer of their alternate identities. When
the Major asks with "lurking alarm" if the artist thinks Mrs. Churm "looks
like a Russian princess?" the artist responds: "When I make her, yes" (49).

Thus, James effectively neutralizes the social danger that the "performativity" of professionalism, the disjunction of inner and outer in the service
of the market economy, might pose to the social positioning and the "auratic
interiority" of the middle and upper-middle class.[91] In the social masquerades of Pinkerton's detectives, the undercover social investigators, and James's
models, the play with the distinction between appearance and being, and
the subliminal desire for and fear of the Other that such play expressed, remained safely contained. It took a more deadly turn in the case of Elsie Sigel.

Crossing the Bowery: "The Real Yellow Peril." Illustration by Robert Carter, *New York World*, June 21, 1909.

Chapter 3

Crossing the Bowery

Female Slumming and the Theater of Urban Space

IN 1897, IN AN ARTICLE IN *HARPER'S WEEKLY* ENTITLED "EAST SIDE Considerations," E. S. Martin described the difference between the Lower East and the Upper East Side. For Martin, as for many middle-class observers, what distinguished the lower classes from gentility was the absence of a distinction between private and public domains:

> The East Side is especially convenient for the observation of people because there are such shoals of them in sight, and because their habits of life are frank, and favorable to a certain degree of intimacy at sight. Where each family has a whole house to itself and lives inside of it, and the members never sally out except in full street dress—hats, gloves, and manners—it is hopeless to become intimately acquainted with them as you pass on the sidewalk. You may walk up and down Fifth Avenue for ten years and never see a Fifth Avenue mother nursing her latest born on the doorstep, but in Mott or Mulberry or Cherry Street that is a common sight.[1]

If middle- and upper-middle-class culture had increasingly become defined by the separation of a public and private self, and an intense self-monitoring with regard to public appearance and conduct, low life was perceived in terms of the opposite. In its supposed lack of self-discipline, low life for Martin evokes associations with lower and more primitive species of being. Comparing the outings of Fifth Avenue children "under such restraint as good clothes and even the kindest of nurses involve" with the behavior of East Side children, who "tumble about on the sidewalk and pavement hour after hour," she comments: "The most natural behavior we are used to see obtains in a cage of monkeys. The East Side children are nearly as untrammeled as the monkeys, but they are a great deal kinder to each other" (856).

For Martin, the absence of the distinction between the public and the private also implied a perfect correspondence between the inner and outer self. Unlike in the upper parts of town, people in the lower wards do not pretend to be other than who they are, nor do they dissimulate the self as the genteel convention regarding public behavior would dictate. As Martin observes, "There are coarse people here, but they wear cheap clothes and work hard. There is no such disconcerting contrast between their outside and what one reads in their faces as afflicts the observer in more opulent parts of the town." Unlike genteel culture, generally "overfed, overstimulated, overamused," the lower classes are concerned with life's basics, such as "paying rent for a tenement-house apartment and buying bread and simple food for a working man's family" (856–57).

In her preoccupation with the supposed transparency of low life, Martin voiced a conception that was consistently emphasized in turn-of-the-century writing about the life of the lower classes, from the literary realists to the popular magazines. Amy Kaplan has argued that in a period when middle-class culture, in its pursuit of consumption and status, increasingly came to be regarded as artificial and removed from reality, low life emerged as the "touchstone of the real."[2] In his *Types from City Streets*, Hutchins Hapgood attributes this "realness" of low life to the daily confrontation with the "facts of life."

> They have lived intensely, if not broadly, have suffered keenly, and when they talk, they talk not of trivialities, as your sheltered comfortable person, but of fundamental and universal things. . . . [I]f you can get very close to experience , and not have your nervous system shocked by so doing, you have acquired culture and implicit literature. . . . There is, as is well known, much vigorous beauty in the language of the commonest people. Bowery slang is full of force and of the figurative quality; and so is the dialect of thieves. . . . The middle-class person, on the other hand, striving constantly to rise, to get where he is not, is comparatively vulgar, graceless, and unformed. He is admirable in a moral sense, but his words lack literature, for they are confused and pointless, over-abundant and reveal a lack of conviction as to what is the "real thing." How can he know, in his Cook's-tour-like voyage through life, what the necessary and fundamental things are . . . ? When a man seeks his stuff for writing from low life he is at least sure of one thing; namely, that what he sees is genuine. He will not be deceived.[3]

The conception of low life as "real" and transparent constitutes the background for the emergence of the slum as a tourist destination. There, the "desensitized" urbanite could hope to recuperate the sense of experience and shock that, as Walter Benjamin has argued, mechanized life had conditioned out of him.[4] Contemporary observations leave little doubt that, around the turn of the century, when new habits of consumption and leisure started infiltrating every aspect of urban life, the slum was on a par with the department stores and theaters as the newfangled attractions of the city. Abraham Cahan wrote of the young women who came to New York, "either to make it their home or to do the shops and the matinees for a week," that they were possessed by a "great yearning to 'go slumming'; to see with her own eyes those hopeless undercurrents of the huge city that dragged men and women hopelessly beneath their sodden depths; to go into the hidden places where the slaves of opium dreamed away their lives in Gustave Doré attitudes."[5]

The Bowery emerged as one of the favorite destinations of these slumming parties. With its intersecting Mott and Pell streets, where, as one account described it, "Chinatown and the Irish Bowery come in close contact and result in a milieu probably without parallel in any other part of the world," the Bowery had the reputation for being "the most unhealthy section in New York." "The Bowery," *Harper's Weekly* concluded,

> is supposed to be the seat of certain high classes of criminals; of certain kinds of merchants shrewder than any other kind and less scrupulous; of a Bowery boy and a Bowery girl. So widespread is this impression that the Bowery is inspected daily in summer by crowds of tourists. . . . Some of them walk its streets with eyes looking right and left for signs of danger, with coats tightly buttoned, and money hidden in deep-lying pockets. Others,—and they, for the most part, have their families with them, observe it open-mouthed from the safety of a hired hack.[6]

The area exerted such fascination that D. W. Griffith decided to shoot the ghetto scenes for his *Musketeers of Pig Alley* (1908) on location. Other directors took the act of slumming itself as their theme. *Lifting the Lid* (Biograph, 1905), for example, features a group of respectable, middle-class out-of-towners who "travel from their mid-town hotel in a large touring-car advertising 'Chinatown Trips.'" Their itinerary includes a Bowery "dive," a Chinese restaurant, and an opium den filled with white women and Chinese men. At the final stop of the slumming tour, a concert saloon, they get drunk and are thrown out for joining the dancers on the stage."[7]

The transformation of the Bowery and Chinatown into a tourist hot spot had been ongoing ever since the plays of Edward Harrigan, with its latter-day

"Bowery-b'hoys" and "tough girls," had made the area, its types, and its
Bowery dialect fashionable. With the publication of Stephen Crane's *Maggie*
in 1893 and Edward T. Townsend's *Chimmie Fadden* in 1895, the ghetto craze
spread to literature, and Bowery culture became a fixture of the national
imagination. The "dese, dem and dose" of "New York gutter dialect" developed into the newest fad. As Alvin Harlow records in his guidebook, "Conversation everywhere was punctuated with the supposed Bowery gesture, a
lateral slicing motion with the hand held flat, palm down and almost at a
right angle to the arm; and spiced with 'youse guys,' 'dead game sport,'
'Hully Chee!' 'Chase yerself!' 'Wot t'ell!' 'See?' and the underworld technology, 'Come-on,' 'come-back,' 'easy mark,' and 'he run a scare into him.'"[8]

Yet these "low types," whose supposed authenticity was the object of the
middle-class gaze, were not the passive prototypes and objects of representation that these tourists and writers took them for. Indeed, some of them
were quite actively engaged in shaping and manipulating the reality that so
fascinated middle-class observers. An anecdote told by the photographer
Jacob Riis illuminates the fact that the representation of low life was embedded in relationships of power and exchange. On one of his visits to the
"Bend," Riis becomes outraged by a "particularly ragged and disreputable
tramp," whom he has offered ten cents for sitting for a picture. As Riis gets
ready for work, the tramp takes his pipe out of his mouth, puts it in his
pocket, and calmly declares that "it was not included in the contract, and
that it was worth a quarter to have it go in the picture. . . . The man, scarcely
ten seconds employed at honest labor, even at sitting down, at which he was
an undoubted expert, had gone on strike. He knew his rights and the value
of 'work' and was not to be cheated out of either."[9]

What piques Riis is not just the tramp's act of defiance (quite different
from Mrs. Churm's docility in Henry James's story), but his appropriation
of the "reality" Riis wants to represent. By charging extra for the inclusion
of the pipe, the tramp indicates his awareness of being constructed by Riis
as a type, and as such he is incomplete without his props. It is the tramp
who defines his posing, the "production" of identity as labor, and who puts
a price on its value, breaking the illusion of a free transcription of reality by
claiming ownership of the prototype. The tramp's act of sabotage reveals
that in the commodification of low life, a development that informed the
vogue of realism as much as the fashion of "slumming parties," reality and
the theater were hopelessly intertwined. What Jacob Riis photographed, and
what urban slummers were presented with, was not "transparent reality"
but a performance, made to fit preconceived notions of the ghetto and its

"types," and often staged with the active participation (or in this case, sabotage) of ghetto dwellers themselves. The public sphere created in these performances was definitely one whose control was actively contested.

Perhaps most influential in shaping and popularizing the late nineteenth-century Bowery image were the local guides and self-styled Bowery celebrities Steve Brodie and Chuck Connors. Well connected with a group of newspaper reporters, for whom they held court in local bars, "Chuck" and Brodie were the source and often the main character of many Chinatown tales. Both had their exploits and anecdotes published in book form, complete with Bowery dialect and slang. Both acted as "lobbygows" to groups of well-known celebrities and tourists.

Steve Brodie earned his fame by jumping from the Brooklyn Bridge, a feat whose veracity itself was under dispute. The jump landed him a job at Alexander's Museum on the Bowery and the starring role in the hugely successful 1894 play *On the Bowery,* in which he chatted in Bowery dialect and reenacted his famous jump. Brodie was considered such a crowd pleaser that one brewery set him up with a saloon, which Brodie transformed into a "mecca for sports and slumming parties."[10] According to one anecdote, Brodie, known for his practical jokes, once invited General Booth Tucker, head of the Salvation Army, for a slumming trip to a joss house and a Chinese restaurant on Mott Street. After inviting the general in with the words, "Come in an' I'll fix yer fer de trip," Brodie, obviously playing on the fad of roaming the slums and observing depravity in disguise, outfitted Tucker "with a pair of huge false whiskers and a wig similar to that worn by Svengali."[11] Well aware of the value of publicity—any kind of publicity—Brodie would beg reporters "whose beat was the Bowery" to "say something about me. . . . Say I'm a crook, a faker, that I never jumped off a curbstone; anything, so you print my name," for every time they did so, "the hayseeds and suckers came in hordes."[12]

Chuck Connors, a famous wit and raconteur of dialect stories in German, Yiddish, Chinese, Cockney, and Irish, who was said to be the prototype for Edward Townsend's Chimmie Fadden, tirelessly promoted himself as an expert on the life of the Bowery, or "de Lane," as he called it.[13] Known as the "Mayor of Chinatown," he acted as tour guide for the likes of Israel Zangwill, actress Anna Held, Prince William of Sweden, Prince Henry of Battenberg, and the German Admiral Diederichs, whom he regaled with frightful stories, pointing out "inoffensive Chinese merchants . . . as desperate hatchet men, and any feminine face looking from an upper window [as] a 'slave wife,' white or yellow."[14] He supplied reporters from the *World* and the *Sun* with an endless range of stories, or, as some believed, "would stand for anything they put into his mouth," scanning the morning papers to adjust his own stories to match the ones he was credited with.

"Chuck Connors and Company" also represented Bowery life in a play, in which Chuck and his associates "enacted themselves, talked Bowery slang, gave Bowery songs and dances, and reproduced the life with great fidelity."[15] According to Hapgood, the play, which ran for a few weeks at a Bowery vaudeville theater, was "a genuine slice of life—no 'fake' about it," "admirably true and admirably indicative of that intense if ragged culture always attending the uncompromising living out of any set of conditions." But judging from descriptions, the play comes across more as an ingenious publicity stunt that self-consciously exploits the contemporary fascination with low life. Chuck himself promoted it by reiterating its authenticity: "It's de real t'ing. We don't act, we just play ourselves—see? . . . Dere ain't no plot in me play, fer it's de real t'ing. Dere ain't no plot in life, is dere? . . . De rest of de bunch has been rehearsed every day. But I never rehearse. I go on stage and talk what I want to—see? I do me best, I do meself. . . . It's de real t'ing we play, see? What's de good of acting when we play de real t'ing?" (34–36).

Attuned to the tourist value of representing the "real thing," local guides and entrepreneurs such as Connors even found it profitable to equip opium dens and joss houses "for display purposes." In order to satisfy the slummers' expectations, popular sites along the slummers' trajectory were literally turned into theater. Alvin Harlow reports:

> In one synthetic opium-den . . . a half-caste Chinese, Georgie Eye, and a woman known as Lulu regularly posed as addicts for the tourist trade. To be able to stand the daily grind, they smoked a much weakened grade of opium. Georgie Yee, pretending to be crazed by it, would dance around and sing in broken English, "Sweet Sixteen" and "Alee Samee Jimmie Doyle." "This ex-ibish -n cannot reely be called immoral," the guide would drone. "These poor people are slaves to the opium habit, and whether you come here to see them or not, they would've spent the night smoking opium just as you see them now.[16]

An expert "amateur slumologist" in one of Abraham Cahan's stories explains that, "Sham burglar dens and opium dives—as much like the real ones as the scenery in Ten Nights in a Barroom—were arranged, with property burglars and fiends, and New York's 'beauty and chivalry' was lured there and went home shuddering and delighted." The "amateur slumologist" explains the attraction of the slum by linking it to a more general commodification of visual culture: "Why, slumming is—or was until the novelty wore off, the most conventional thing we did. People went to the slums in quite the same way they went to picture galleries or the shops."[17]

The commodification of the ghetto as tourist site and "touchstone of the real" compelled its subjects to play out their allotted "low" identities roles for gain.[18] The self-stagings of Brodie, Connors, and Riis's tramp, as well as the museumification of burglar dens and opium joints, betray an acute awareness of being constructed as an image on the slummers' stage and a keen sense on how to turn this image into "aesthetic/commercial value."[19]

But such obvious manipulation of visual codes also contained a danger, which was humorously touched on in the film *The Deceived Slumming Party* (Biograph, 1908). In the film, according to the *Biograph Bulletin*, "A plain-clothes cop, in cahoots with the guide and some 'Chinese' friends, black-mails the tourists by threatening to arrest them after a fake suicide in a phony opium den; the Chinese restaurant serves up ground up cats and dogs; and a dandy has his pocket picked during a sham murder in a salon."[20] The tourists in the slumming party are duped by the confusion of the boundaries of reality and fiction. The dangers of mistaking theater for reality and, even more important, reality for theater indeed pervaded the discourse on the city more generally. But it was particularly pronounced in writings about Chinatown.

Chinatown

Descriptions of Chinatown typically located Chinese difference tightly within the boundaries of a self-contained urban ghetto. "There it lies, unfathomed and unknown," William Brown Meloney wrote, "contemptuous, blandly mysterious, serene, foul-smelling, Oriental, and implacable behind that inde-finable barrier which has kept the West and the East apart since the cen-turies began. Within the boundaries of the three acres which it occupies, five thousand slant-eyed children of cathay . . . order their existence like rabbits in a warren."[21]

The representation of Chinatown as untouched by Western influences gave rise to a romanticized notion of the Chinese American as "never assim-ilable, always alien to modern American life."[22] But it also fostered the notion of Chinese duplicity, a deeply ingrained anti-Chinese prejudice. The trope of "urban secrets," when used in reference to Chinatown, was typically asso-ciated with the stereotypical notion of Chinese secretiveness, leading Jacob Riis in 1890 to complain about the quality of Chinatown as "spectacle." In comparison to the "Bend," with its "outdoor stir and life" and its "gaily-colored rags or picturesque filth and poverty," Riis judged it lacking. "Stealth and secretiveness are as much part of the Chinaman in New York as the cat-like tread of his felt shoes," Riis observed. "His business, as his domestic life, shuns the light, less because there is anything to conceal than because that is the way of the man. . . . The very doorways of his offices and shops are fenced off by queer, forbidding partitions suggestive of a continual state of siege. The stranger who enters through the crooked approach is received with a sudden silence, a sullen stare, and an angry 'Vat you vant?' that breathes annoyance and distrust."[23]

Projected onto a circumscribed and limited physical space, the mystery of Chinese culture was both heightened and safely contained. But the "indefinable barrier" that for Meloney contained Chinese difference was less watertight than these descriptions would lead one to expect. This was suggested already by Meloney's observation that for "three or four hundred whites," Chinatown and its population held such appeal that they would "cast their lot with them." Moreover, missionary efforts in Chinatown seemed to suggest at least the possibility of supplanting what Riis described as the Chinese "pagan worship of idols" with Christian teachings and induct the Chinese American into Western civilization.[24]

The perception of a breakdown of the barrier between "East" and "West" took on more ominous overtones in the immediate aftermath of the murder of Elsie Sigel, a white upper-class missionary worker. Indeed, the Sigel case provoked a moral panic that mobilized and exposed contemporary anxieties about race, female desire, and the boundary between reality and theater.

The Murder of Elsie Sigel

On June 19, 1909, the headlines of the *New York World* read, in bold letters:

> "Elsie Sigel slain, hidden in a trunk in Chinese Resort"
>   "Murdered woman, a Granddaughter of Gen. Franz Sigel, of Civil War Fame, Had Been Strangled to Death at No. 782 Eighth Avenue. Letters of Endearment Found From her Oriental Waiter"

The article below provided preliminary details of the murder of a young woman that would grip the entire nation. On the morning of June 19, police were summoned by the owner of a chop-suey restaurant on Eighth Avenue.

They were asked to break the lock of an apartment above the premises, after patrons of the restaurant had complained of ill smells. In one room of the apartment, which had been rented by the restaurant owner to Leong Lee Lin and Li Chung, two of his Chinese waiters, they discovered a trunk containing the body of a white woman, in partial state of undress and hair undone. Further investigation of the apartment yielded several letters written "in terms of endearment" and signed "Elsie," a letter in "pidgin English" threatening the addressee of the letter to cease his attentions to a girl the police declined to name, and textbooks with "scrawlings of the name 'Elsie' such as would be made by a person learning to write," as well as a New Testament and various religious tracts.[25]

The elderly Mrs. Sigel identified jewelry found on the body as belonging to her daughter, who had been missing for a week. Other members of the Sigel family, however, in an apparent attempt to save the family from imminent scandal, dissociated themselves from the victim. Mr. Sigel claimed not to recognize the lock of hair he was shown, and, after being taken to the morgue, issued a public statement in which he asserted, "I do not know her." The next day, while Mrs. Sigel was taken to an insane asylum after an apparent nervous breakdown, the family declared in another statement: "Elsie Sigel is not dead. We are convinced she has wandered away in a temporary fit of mental aberration and is now alive either roaming about aimlessly in the lower parts of the city, where she carried out her missionary work, or in some other city where she has strayed without knowing where she was going." According to the family, the strain and confining life of caring for her mother, "who had been an invalid for three years," had caused Elsie to "break down mentally."[26]

In the meantime, details of the close relationship between Elsie and Leong, one of the waiters at the chop-suey shop, had leaked to the public. According to reports, Elsie Sigel had for a number of months, "if not years," "taken a deep interest in the welfare of William L. Leon, the Americanized name of Leong Lee Lin, a Chinese waiter who professed great belief in Christianity, and was one of the notable converts of the Chinese mission."[27]

Apparently, as letters found in the lodgings of Leon indicated, the relationship had not ended there. Although publication of the letters was suppressed because it would bring "an uncalled for amount of additional humiliation on Miss Sigel's relatives and also on some persons, presumably women, who had also corresponded with the Chinese convert," one police inspector divulged the following information:

Altogether we have found thirty-five letters written to Leon and signed Elsie. They were all what I would call clean love letters, but the endearing terms she called the Chinaman were revolting to me. . . . Every one of them read as if the Chinaman had been a white man and decently engaged to the Sigel girl. . . . Of peculiar significance is the fact that not once in these thirty-five letters does Elsie so much as mention her missionary work. There is nothing in them to indicate that either she or Leon regarded each other in the light of pupil and teacher in the missionary sense. They were simply the ingenious love notes of a girl madly in love with a man she respected and evidently considered her equal in every way.[28]

Adding to the scandal was the fact that apparently the entire Sigel family had known about the affair. Greatly enamored with Chinese and Japanese culture, Elsie and her mother purportedly had visited the Chinese theater accompanied by Leon. According to neighbors of the Sigel family, "In the ten or fifteen years that the family had lived in the neighborhood, they were constantly entertaining Japanese and Chinese visitors," among them Leon, who, it was rumored, had actually lived in the Sigel residence for several months. Not only had Elsie's father and mother known all about their daughter's relations with Leon, but Elsie's mother had championed a marriage between Elsie and Leon.

"Mrs. Sigel knew all about the affair," "Mother" Todd, head of the Christian mission through whose services Elsie and Leon apparently had made their acquaintance, declared, "but did not seek to break the intimacies. Scores of Chinamen knew her as 'Mother Sigel,' and she seems to be as deeply interested in the Orientals as her daughter was."[29] But according to the police, the romance between Elsie and Leon had been the source of a deep rift in the family. "We know that the father was bitterly opposed to the continuance of these relations and that the mother was Elsie's champion in all these family rows," a police source stated. "The father was down on the whole missionary game. He threatened a long time ago to break up the whole family if his wife and daughter did not give up their trips to Chinatown and stop having Chinese visitors at home."[30]

Inevitably, the discourse surrounding the case evoked a panoply of Chinese stereotypes. Oriental or Chinese cunning, clannishness, secretiveness, "the stone wall of Chinese stolidity," and their "shield of sullen indifference," according to the press, seriously hampered the detectives in their investigation: "Chinatown sunned itself in languid ease yesterday and blinked stolidly at the detectives and reporters. . . . Aside from their clannishness, there was not one Chinaman who would dare to betray the hiding place of

Leon and his companion, Chung. Both the missing men were high in Chinese secret society circles and the betrayal of a brother, those who have spent years among them say, would mean the certain death of the betrayer."[31]

Elsie's presumed lover, and the main suspect in her murder, fit preexisting stereotypes less easily. Leong Lee was described as "a very good-looking Chinaman," "very dark complexioned and smooth faced, with black hair and eyes," but "with the Chinese characteristics not very strongly stamped."[32] An "American in appearance," he wore American clothes and had his hair cut short. In an attempt to reinscribe the boundaries that Leon's (or Leong's) apparent adjustment to American life seemed to have subverted, the press took his outward appearance as evidence of Chinese cunning. Leon was a false gentleman, who used American clothes, genteel mannerisms, and a false interest in Christianity as a mask for perverted and criminal intentions.

The effort to convert the Chinese was a controversial issue, precisely because it questioned the image of the Chinese "heathen" as radically Other. It therefore did not fail to evoke strong emotions. Jacob Riis stated his opinion on the matter in *How the Other Half Lives*, pontificating:

> I state it in advance as my opinion, based on the steady observation of years, that all efforts to make an effective Christian of John Chinaman will remain abortive in this generation; of the next I have, if anything, less hope. Ages of senseless idolatry, a mere grub-worship, have left him without the essential qualities for appreciating the gentle teachings of a faith whose motive and unselfish spirit are alike beyond his grasp.... I am convinced that he adopts Christianity, when he adopts it at all, as he puts on American clothes, with what the politicians would call an ulterior motive, some sort of gain in the near prospect—washing, a Christian wife perhaps.[33]

Moreover, the fact that missionary work in America's Chinatowns put the main agents for conversion, white Anglo-Saxon women of good families, in close contact with predominantly Chinese men proved to be a deep source of unease. In a culture preoccupied with "white slavery," rumored alliances between Sunday school teachers and their Chinese pupils were enough incentive for the formation of the Chicago-based anti-Chinese Sunday School Society in 1894.

It was therefore not surprising that Captain Carey, in charge of the homicide bureau, ruled the case an outcome of the "missionary game," a term designating "Chinamen who consent in being tutored by attractive, young missionary women for the otherwise unobtainable privilege of gaining their good graces." Moreover, Captain Carey asserted, Leon was an old hand in the business. In support of this theory, he "produced a copy of the New Testament on the fly leaf of which was written in feminine hand: Leung H. Kim, from his teacher Elise M. Oakford, 1905," and suggested that "Kim" and "Leon" were one and the same man. Other evidence gathered at the scene of the crime supposedly pointed in the same direction. According to Carey, "Beside the murdered girl's letters we found ten others addressed presumably to Leon, but of that we can't be sure until we find out how many aliases he traveled under." Photographs of white women, "some of them very good looking and well dressed" and some with "loving messages inscribed on the back," showed that, as the police captain put it, "Leon was doing a land office business with women's affections."[34]

Leon's friends in Chinatown (where, according to reports, he was known as a gambler and "confidence man") had known of his amorous "dual life" but had kept that information from Miss Sigel, who had regarded him as "a young man of steady habits and a devout worshiper of Christianity."[35] His apartment, in which objects suggesting erotic interests, such as pictures, cheap novels, and rouge, were juxtaposed with paraphernalia of the Christian faith, Chinese objects of worship, and a "false queue," bore similar marks of deception: "Everywhere were pictures and all the pictures were of women. . . . Women, women, women, nearly all of the Caucasian race, and of every age! . . . Over on the window sill was a little box of rouge powder in a Chinese box with a little mirror over it. Contrasted with it the picture of the Virgin and Child hanging over the dresser in the room where the trunk was found told an equally legible story of cant and imposture."[36]

Slowly, however, from a focus on the deceit of "Chinese masquerading as Christian converts," attention turned to the role of Elsie Sigel in her own seduction.

THE FEMALE *FLÂNEUSE*

The nineteenth-century city, with its illicit pleasures, diversions, and encounters with strangers, was regarded as the perfect environment for the wandering eye of the male flâneur. For women, however, as many scholars have argued, the city was deemed an immoral domain, a place antithetical to the domestic space in which women found their natural calling. For women to venture unaccompanied into public space amounted to an act of transgression, which implied pollution and the loss of virtue, and seriously jeopardized a woman's reputation.[37]

Nevertheless, by the 1880s new female activities such as shopping, phi-
lanthropy, and other forms of civic participation contributed significantly
to the creation of a legitimate public space for women. The emergence of
department stores, tea shops, and kiosks allowed women independent access
to some urban spaces.[38] This participation of women in urban space did
not go without a significant public outcry. Some foresaw a moral degradation of women as a result of their immersion in city culture, a fear focused
on the possibility of unwanted male attention—a real possibility when the
time that the only women frequenting public spaces unaccompanied would
be women of questionable moral stature was only just around the corner.
Others attacked what they saw as the disintegrating effects of consumer culture itself: seduced by the new fantasy world, women would give up "the
self-sacrifice of traditional reproductive womanhood in favor of the selfish
pursuit of pleasure and self-display."[39]

Missionary and charity work, however, were one of the few activities in
which the motivations of middle-class women making unchaperoned trips
into even the most disreputable parts of town were unquestioned. In missionary work, "typically female" attributes such as emotionality, religiosity,
and maternal feelings, were considered assets rather than weaknesses, because success in the job depended on an appeal to the heart. Under the cloak
of work, religious zeal, and maternal feelings, many middle- and upper-class
women were able to enjoy a significant amount of personal freedom, search-
ing for excitement and self-fulfillment and participating in the same kind
of "slumming" expeditions that had traditionally been reserved for men.[40]

That the thrill of venturing into forbidden and dangerous places, at least
for some women, constituted part of the attraction of charity and missionary work is made clear in the journalistic account of an "under-cover" Salvation Army "lassy," published on the heels of the Sigel murder. Armed with a
Salvation Army bonnet and a bundle of Salvationist newspapers, the undercover lassy accompanies a young but experienced salvationist on a journey
of "discoveries" of "perfectly dreadful places," which include "saloon visits"
and a trip to "every penetrable place on Pell and Doyers streets" in Chinatown. Besides glimpses of the underworld, the trip offered valuable experience in the art of fending off the unwanted advances of men—an art that
women, as newcomers to urban public space, were well advised to master:
"You must watch everywhere . . . especially the man behind you," the experienced guide advises the undercover journalist. "One time I forgot—I was
talking to one poor fellow—and I just happened to turn my head, and another man almost had his arm around me. I barely managed to slip away."

"But what do you do," the undercover lassy asks, "if some day one of them should actually do it—kiss you, put his arms around you?" "I should push him away," she answers, "no, not strike him, just push him away."[41]

But according to some skeptics, it was not the art of warding off unwanted advances that women mastered in charity work. In the aftermath of the Sigel murder, stories of liaisons and even marriages between former missionary workers and their pupils flooded the press. A letter of a former missionary brought to ruin by her close and "long intimacy with the Chinese" detailed the steps of seduction by which the missionary worker would be brought to moral ruin:

> Every Chinaman tried to get his teacher into some corner of the room as far away from the other groups as possible. . . . The pupil is learning to read from a primer. As the lesson goes on their chairs are moved until their faces are so close together the girl can feel the breath of the Chinaman on her face. Their glances meet many times during the "lesson." His eyes are always fastened on her face. After that it's only a question of months when she gets to be the same kind of opium fiend as I am.

The newspaper report detailed the story of a husband who claimed that his wife, a Sunday school teacher, had been lured away from him and her fourteen-year-old son by a Chinese laundryman, a former pupil. A police official told the story of a Chinaman arrested for embezzlement, who, within two hours of his arrest, received a visit from a white missionary woman. The woman "was well dressed and showed every evidence of being a lady. I accompanied her to the Chinaman's cell. She flung her arms around his neck, kissed him repeatedly, called him endearing names, and begged him to tell her what she might send him."

In response to such press reports, one court magistrate was quoted as asking: "Is it the soul or the heart of the Chinaman that interests women missionaries?" Providing the answer himself, he continued, "If you want to know what is the real yellow curse, here it is: It is the mawkish sentimentality on the part of Sunday School teachers which expresses itself, in this court, by the presents of flowers and cigarettes to accused Chinamen awaiting trial."[42]

Headlines proclaiming "Chinese Sunday Schools Source of Great Scandal—Marriages of White Teachers and Yellow Pupils Cause All the Trouble," and cartoons of a missionary worker wearing a cross and cutting of a Chinese pupil's pigtail, accompanied by a caption stating, "The Real Chinese Peril," implicated the missions in creating an atmosphere that not only condoned but actively stimulated racial boundary crossing and sexual transgression.

This accusation, of course, predated the murder case. In 1904, Biograph released a feature film entitled *The Heathen Chinese and the Sunday School Teachers,* which presented a similar scenario of moral degradation and sexual license. In the film, several Sunday School Teachers visit a Chinese laundry and persuade a number of workers to attend Sunday School. After their session, the Chinese politely invite the teachers back to the laundry, which turns out to conceal an opium den. The women are seduced into sharing a pipe with the workers, and are caught in the act during a surprise police raid. After the men are arrested, the teachers visit them in prison to present flowers.[43]

After Elsie's death, the critique that Sunday Schools actively "promoted intermarriage" and offered "John Chinaman" the opportunity to "become intimately acquainted with women of a race which, hitherto, had held up an impassible barrier against him" gathered force. Even as it became apparent that Elsie herself was never engaged in "legitimate" mission work, that she had made Leon's acquaintance at the chop-suey restaurant on 191st Street—which was close to the Sigel family home on 188th Street—and not in Chinatown, and that the murder was committed on the premises of Leon's Eighth Avenue apartment, the aftermath of the murder saw a heavy crackdown on the Chinese quarter.[44]

According to the police, as many as four hundred plainclothesmen were dispatched into the neighborhood, where "they are hanging about everywhere, drinking, gambling, occasionally fighting, mixing in the crowds that they may overhear odds bits of conversation." In addition, it recruited fifty Chinese "informers," hoping for tips about Leon's whereabouts.[45] Police incursions on Chinese businesses, combined with an intense anti-Chinese sentiment (specifically directed at businesses supposedly "courting" a white female clientele), caused a significant disruption in the economic life of the neighborhood.

In addition, many of the "supposed" missions of Chinatown, as they were continually referred to in the press, were closed for an indefinite period. Increased police surveillance, in particular of the movements of white women, resulted "in the arrest of four Chinese laundry men and three white girls, charged with disorderly conduct after going to four different laundries consecutively." In another raid on a laundry, detectives "discovered a trap door underneath the counter. Opening this, Captain Post and his men slipped down into what they said was an elaborately fitted opium den hung with dragon flags. In the little room were two bunks and a complete layout of pipes, bowls and needles. Grace Hudson was asleep on one of the bunks with an opium lay out beside her." Besides Grace Hudson, police arrested the owner, Louis Suey, as well as his "white wife," Josie Suey, twenty-three years old, formerly said to have been a "missionary worker with Elsie Sigel."[46]

The uncovering of supposedly widespread erotic alliances between well-bred American women and Chinese men continued to fire the public imagination. This was even more the case after it was established that in the weeks before her death, Elise seemed to have transferred her affections to Chu Gain, owner of the Port Arthur Restaurant, making the motive for the murder jealousy on the part of Leon, the spurned lover. "This Chu Gain," one newspaper wrote, "is even more of a Chinese Don Juan than Leon. Not only was Elsie Sigel infatuated with him, as her letters clearly indicate, but numerous other women openly confessed their love for him. . . . According to 'Mother' Todd and intimates of Gain, he is so well provided with American women adorers that one more or less makes little difference to him."[47]

The confiscation on the premises of Chu Gain of a number of love letters written by white women focused renewed attention on the state of mind of the young women in question. As *Munsey's Magazine* formulated it, "The women who write these missives evidently were young women of some education and of decent training. Yet they had thrust themselves into the haunts of these low creatures, and the letters found by the police showed that they had become infatuated with them. How could young girls, whose upbringing had been so different, descend so easily to such a level?"[48]

WOMEN'S INNATE LOVE FOR THE EXOTIC

Elsie's ill-fated romance stimulated an extensive search for the underlying causes of the moral downfall of these white, young, genteel women. Some attributed such racial boundary crossings to women's maternal inclination to pity the disadvantaged, in this case Chinese men despised by American society; or to their failure to "realize that these strangers from the East are really men like other men, so different are they in looks, manner and apparent submissiveness."[49]

Others were more inclined to focus on women's religiosity and attributed the liaisons that flowered in the context of missionary work to "the closeness of religious emotion to physical emotion." A German newspaper described the crime as the result of the "religio-sexual atmosphere in America." "Religious ardor and sexual passion are bound deeply and abidingly," the paper conjectured. "But in puritanical America, conventional morality [is] strung so high a pitch [that] it results in religious practices practically unhealthy in character."[50]

For others, the source of such transgressions lay in some deep and innate aspect of women's character. Elsie's Sigel's death, according to the author of an article in *Munsey's Magazine,* forces "the question . . . whether women have not somewhere lurking in them a strong love of the exotic, a willingness to overstep race lines, and whether they do not even feel a peculiar and inexplicable pleasure in doing so."[51] The author found the explanation for women's attraction to the "Oriental personality" and its "insidious ways and fawning manners" in women's atavistic passion for objects, colors, and adornments. In the course of the civilizing process, the author explained, Western men had shed the passion for the conspicuous and had steadily simplified their tastes. Women, however, had not. Despite their claims for equality, women remained chained to the "primitive" taste for the effects of color and ornaments, which, for all intents and purposes, placed them in the company of non-Western races on the scale of civilization.[52]

The linkage between makeup, ornamentation, and femininity, implied by the article in *Munsey's Magazine,* is part of a long-standing tradition in Western culture that regarded makeup as indicative of the problematic of femininity. As Jacqueline Lichtenstein explains, ornamentation and makeup were, in a sense, the stigmata of a "dissolute femininity," signifying not only excess, seduction, and vulgarity but also an inherent feminine "falseness" and treachery.[53] In the nineteenth and early twentieth centuries, these same associations were applied to the opposition between the West and the East. "Oriental" cultures were typically described in terms of their theatricality, femininity, and their abundance of objects and ornamentation. They provoked a similar "aesthetic-moral" condemnation due to their association with sexuality, illicit pleasures, and the masking of truth.[54]

The *Munsey's Magazine* article linked this long-standing discourse on women's "ontologically deficient" nature with a notion of a hierarchy of civilizations, which was similarly deeply informed by notions of race. Indeed, the author of "Women's Love for the Exotic" argues, the primitive and perverse nature of this infatuation with ornamentation expresses itself in women's fascination with other low and repulsive creatures. "Not a few women in high stations have appeared in ballrooms with live lizards wringing in their hair," he claims. "Other women, like Judith Gautier and Sarah Bernhardt . . . exhibit what seems an unnatural fondness for snakes."

Ultimately, this perverse passion, which "shades off from the slightest whim or preference to a sort of mad degeneracy," manifests itself in a sexual fascination with cultural Others. "A man, almost instinctively, distrusts a foreigner, or, at any rate, he has a feeling he must know the foreigner and mentally appraise him before regarding him as a person to be cultivated," he writes. "With women, the very fact of a person's being foreign seems to be a passport in their favor." "No white man, if he be above the very lowest level, would ever dream of marrying a Hindu woman or a negress." American heiresses, however, not only tended to marry foreign men, but they also married across racial lines, as the example of English women marrying Hindu men or even "full-blooded negroes" showed.[55]

Women's love of the exotic, then, demonstrated the innate feminine predilection for effect and appearance, rather than substance and reality. As the author concludes, "It is part of their sensitiveness to color-effects, to strangeness, to the unknown, and to all those subtle sensations which are evoked by lights and shades and perfumes and dainty differences."[56] Paradoxically, while this sensibility supposedly made women particularly susceptible to their seduction by cultural Others, it was exactly this fascination with things foreign and exotic that a newly emerging consumer culture was trying to cultivate.

COMMODITY CULTURE AND ORIENTALISM

The emergence of elaborate shopping arcades and lavish department stores in the wake of the late nineteenth-century retail revolution made shopping a central function of urban culture. The success of the new businesses, however, depended on their ability to develop constant new markets for their goods. In that effort, they had to contend with a deeply ingrained Puritanical value system that emphasized the restraint of appetites and desires and inculcated a spirit of repression of wants and needs. According to this value system, the "consumption of luxuries and indulgence in them" was considered morally suspect or sinful.[57] One crucial step in the introduction of consumer culture involved the cultivation of a new set of moral guidelines that would be conducive to the consumerist ideology. In that context, the Oriental theme, with its connotations of luxury, indulgence, desire, impulse, and immediate self-gratification, became the most popular marketing concept before World War I.

As William Leach argues, "For selling and consumption, [American business] opened the door to waste, indulgence, impulse, irresponsibility, dreaming, or qualities thought of as non-Western."[58] In the very period in which the federal government enacted legislation that all but barred the immigration of Chinese and Japanese to the United States, movies and theaters were "Orientalized" with Persian rugs, Arabic drapes, Chinese vases, and

Persian fountains. At the lavish costume balls of the turn of the century, New York's elite dressed up as "pashas and rajahs, harem dancers, and Persian princesses."[59]

The Oriental theme was explored in novels (most notably by authors such as Rider Haggard and J. K. Huysmans) as well as in theater and movies. Some of these representations claimed a scrupulous realism. David Belasco, one of the first Broadway producers to espouse theatrical realism, reproduced San Francisco's Chinatown "down to its very smells" for the 1897 production of Francis Powers's "Chinese" play *The First Born,* causing the reviewer of *The New York Journal* to complain that "the entertainment last night began with small whiffs of sickening, nauseating odor that was burned for atmospheric and not for seweristic reasons. The theatre was bathed in this hideous tinkative odor of incense, and during the long overture, you sat there getting fainter and fainter."[60]

Other versions of theatrical Orientalism were more melodramatic. The 1905 play *A Night in Chinatown,* by Walter Campbell, explicitly linked the Oriental theme with its threat to female morality to Chinatown and its dangers. The struggling heroine of the play, Mildred Claire, owns a flower stand on Chinatown's Mott Street. She is pursued by a depraved villain, Antonio Gonzalez, a Spaniard, who has learned that Mildred is the sole heir to a family fortune and plots to seduce and marry her. Rejected offhand by Mildred, who has lost her heart to Jack Rivers, an honest sailor, Gonzalez enlists his Chinese business partner, Moy Kee, to kidnap Mildred, bring her to his opium den, and adorn her in a Chinese silk dress, hoping that surrounded by Oriental luxuries and opium she will loose her moral judgment and inhibitions and yield to his advances. Fortunately for Mildred, the plot is foiled by the joint efforts of Mamie, a white opium addict and Chinatown resident, Brogan, an Irish policeman (who redeems Mamie by proposing marriage), and Jack Rivers (who marries Mildred).[61]

While the moral and sexual connotations of the Oriental theme were, by contemporary standards, contemptible, its benefits for department stores seeking to draw customers into the dreamworld of commodity culture were obvious. As Rosalind Williams has suggested, department stores are places "where consumers are an audience to be entertained by commodities, where selling is mingled with amusement, where arousal of free-floating desire is as important as immediate purchase of particular items."[62] The cultivation of Orientalism was a powerful tool in the stimulation of such desires because it eroticized commodities and linked goods and environments with the fantasy of a lifestyle of luxury, sensuality, and abandon. Moreover, the entertainment potential of the Oriental theme was virtually limitless. As a blanket term for a wide range of regional cultures, the "Orient" could provide fashion themes for different seasons. In order to market the fashion of the season, department stores decorated their interiors as mosques or a desert oasis, complete with "sheiks, tents, and exotically dressed women." They presented lavish fashion shows in store theaters or actual theaters that were organized around an "Islamic, Indian, Japanese, or Chinese" theme and often had all the trappings of a theatrical production.[63]

A favorite was the "Garden of Allah theme," which was based on a popular novel about a woman, who, disenchanted with the repressed regime of bourgeois life and Western rationalist thought, seeks to reconnect with "elemental forces" and "raw passion" in the North African desert. A huge bestseller, the novel was adapted to the stage and released in a number of screen versions. Seeking to capitalize on its success, numerous department stores picked up the theme. In 1912, Chicago's Marshall Field's, the Boston Store, and the Fair staged "troupes of Arabic men," which they had temporarily borrowed from the cast of the Chicago production of the play based on the novel, to "parade in sham Islamic dress around the main floor and theatre during the fashion shows."[64]

This intertwining of display and spectatorship, Chantal Georgel has argued for nineteenth-century France, was characteristic of the explosive early phase of commodity culture. By adopting the visual strategies of the museum, the world's fair, the tableaux vivant, and the theater, the department stores imbued their mass-produced copies with an aura of authenticity and prestige.[65] Moreover, the stores cleverly obscured the "literal character of merchandising space" by severing "its bond with commerce and business." People bought not the commodity but the stage "effect," along with all that it suggested.[66] Indeed, this strategy perfectly emulated the makeup of the commodity itself, which hides its own "mark of labor" in order to create its surplus value. In these dreamscapes of commodity culture, the boundaries between reality and theater were deliberately blurred. Female shoppers were thought to be particularly susceptible to the illusions created by such stage effects.

But the gradual erosion of the distinctions among commerce, theater, and museum was evident outside the confines of the department store as well. The construction of Chinatown as a major tourist attraction cannot be understood without considering the vogue of Orientalism that overtook American commercial culture around the turn of the century. Indeed, what strikes one in descriptions of slumming expeditions to the "strange, compressed, swarming little Mongolian world" is this same intertwining of discourses of spectacle, novelty, and shopping that informed the politics of display in department stores.[67]

Accounts of visits to the Italian quarter around Mulberry Bend or the Jewish area of Orchard Street customarily refer to strange customs, the hustle and bustle of markets, the untamed presence of children, and "picturesque" filth and poverty. But it was the Chinese quarter, with its endless attractions for the eye, the palate, and the purse, that presented the most coveted stop on the slummer's shopping trajectory. Even New Yorkers, *Theatre Magazine* wrote,

> to whom Broadway is a twice-told tale, and whose jaded appetites a Delmonico, a Sherry, or a Martin scarce can tempt, surprise themselves with new sensations when they saunter through this populous but clean and orderly Chinatown, peering into its weird shops and stores, buying souvenirs from the rich and gorgeous stock of its bazaars, and dining on mo goey chop suey with snow-like rice and tea that is a blissful revelation, in the "Chinese Delmonico's" or the "Celestial Sherry's."[68]

In Chinatown, the female slummer is seduced by the wealth of quaint stores with their dazzling display of Oriental goods, which create an effect not unlike that of the department store. But whereas in the department store the passions aroused by such environments were safely directed toward commodities, on the streets of Chinatown this "free-floating desire" was less easily contained.[69] It was precisely this linkage between Orientalism, slumming, and the transgressive potential of the (female) desires mobilized by the marketing strategies of commodity culture that emerged as a leading theme in the debate following Elsie Sigel's death.

MERCHANDISE AND MISCEGENATION

"Mother" Todd, head of the settlement house at 10 Mott Street, publicly attributed "Elsie Sigel's fatal infatuation for the clever young Americanized Chinaman" to an Orientalism gone awry. In that regard, she considered female slumming tours in Chinatown as dangerous as female missionary activities among the Chinese community. "There seems to be a sort of fascination in the Oriental character that appeals to young American girls, and for that reason I have always believed it to be unwise for young women to teach Chinese," she was quoted as saying. "I am equally opposed to these slumming parties of young people who visit Chinatown. You would be surprised to know how many young girls of respectable families get their first ideas of wrong doings from these sight-seeing trips and return by themselves one day to see more of this Chinatown life and then comes their ruin."[70]

The perception of Mrs. Todd, which was widely shared in press reports, was that the act of female sightseeing itself evoked illicit fantasies that ultimately would be enacted. *Munsey's Magazine* traced the various stages in this process of seduction by following "a typical party of slummers, eager, curious, prurient even, to know the worst that lies hidden within," into the quarter.[71] On the sightseeing tour, all of Chinatown is transformed into a diorama. Indeed, the commentary of the guide incorporates even the murder of Elsie Sigel as a source of tourist excitement, exclaiming: "Now, ladies and gents, followin' th' point of me finger, yer can behold th' famous Port Arthur. It was right in there that Elsie Sigel useter go with her little prayer-book an' eat chop suey. But more a-non!" The party of tourists is guided through narrow alleys, past the Mott Street settlement house, from where, according to the guide, Elsie carried out her missionary activities, and then conducted into the dark corridor of a dilapidated building reeking of "peanut odor." In the basement, they discover a hidden opium joint:

> [A] Chinaman is lying to the left of the sputtering lights, and to the right is a shell of a white woman, with hollow cheeks and bare, bony arms. The eyes of the Chinaman and the woman—she is his wife—seem to burst from their heads. The pair go through the motions of opium-smoking—the twisting of a wire in a tiny box made of horn, the twirling of the molasses-like stuff, which the wire catches on its point, over the flame at their side until it sputters greasily; the manipulation of the "cooked" opium into a pill, the placing of the pill over a needle opening in the bowl of the pipe, the holding of the canted bowl against the flame; and then the long guttural inhalations; and a burst of smoke from the nostrils.

The elaborate ritual turns out to be a staged exhibition of the horrors of opium smoking, complete with a drawing on the wall showing all the implements of an opium layout. The moral of the exhibition was stated on a placard on the opposite wall, which read, "One half of the world doesn't know how the other half lives." This "theater of the real" was performed by the two addicts "anywhere from ten to twenty times a night, for pay. It is their 'turn' on the slummers' stage."[72]

Inducted into a fantasy world in which every danger is turned into theater, the slummers, slightly "drugged by poisonous atmosphere," lose their inhibitions and fears. Their eyes "are brilliant, dancing, excited, eager. The women have lost their timidity. They talk loudly, they laugh without occasion." In their excitement, they forget the basic rules of public etiquette and lose their guard. Most of them "fail to pull in their skirts now as the Chinese go jostling by them on the narrow sidewalks" and "no longer turn their eyes away from the impudent glances of the slant-eyed yellow men staring at them from the shop doors and the dark openings of the noisome tenements. They give back stare for stare."

The next stop is the Chinese theater, which the slummers leave with "ears buzzing from the crash of gongs and cymbals of brass, the squeaking of nine-stringed fiddles, and the falsetto voices of the actors." Then follows a mission "for white wrecks" where they are treated to a hymn; and a joss house, where "taloned fingers . . . seek to trace the fortunes which slant eyes pretend to see in the clean, white hands of the women."

At the Port Arthur Restaurant, the final destination of the tour, the slummers order chop suey. Here "the women are in ecstasies over the heavily carved ebony tables, with their inset tops of dull onyx marble; the carved unbacked stools, the dainty teacups and brewing pots, the rice-bowls and dinner plates. The banners of rich embroideries, with always a dragon rampant dominating the scheme of decoration, hold their eyes."

In the scenario proposed by the article, the slumming tour stimulates a mode of seeing that erodes the boundaries between reality and theater and turns the outside world into a phantasmagoria of amusements and displays of commodities, not unlike the department store. The group is completely taken in by the decor of this "picturesque Oriental world" and is oblivious to its duplicity: "They do not notice the floor, covered with linoleum or sawdust; the cheap wall-paper, against which the embroideries are hanging; the thinness and staginess of it all."

Finally, it is the temptation of a bargain that sets the women in the party up for disaster. Two young women fall behind the group while looking in a shop window at a display of lingerie. "A sleek Chinaman, smiling and deferential, is inviting them within. They return his smile, declining but not resenting the invitation. . . . How muchee? asks one of the girls, pointing unashamed at an article of feminine finery, and unconsciously using 'pidgin English' to which, half an hour ago, her ears were alien. The Chinaman's answer is a repetition of his invitation, and the naming of a ridiculously low price." Seeing themselves behind the rest of the group, the girls decline with a "No can buy now, John. . . . Bimeby. Maybe tomorrow." But to the plainclothes detective watching the group of slummers, the girls' use of "pidgin English" and the allusion to eroticism implied by the feminine finery already intimates transgression. Even if the women do not fall into the trap this time, the bait of luxury items for low prices will bring them back to the quarter, this time unchaperoned. "That's the way and that's the kind," the detective predicts. "There's always a tomorrow for one or two of every slumming party, who have not seen enough the night before."[73]

Seduced by mercantile Orientalism, women are at risk of conflating the Orientalist dreamscape promoted by commodity culture with the culture itself. Looking at the world through a shopper's gaze, they are taken in by facades and effects. Just as they confuse appearance and value in the commodities to which they are attracted, they are confused by the blurring of boundaries between the real and illusion in Chinatown and do not perceive the falseness of it all.

A similar conflation of commodity culture, eroticism, and Orientalism converging on Chinatown suffuses the accounts sketching the background setting for Elsie Sigel's murder. Significantly, the major scenes of Elsie's seduction include the Chinese theater, to which Leon introduced Elsie and her mother, as well as the Port Arthur Restaurant, which was situated "directly opposite the Chinatown and Bowery settlement for girls." According to the press, it was in the restaurant that Elsie made her fateful acquaintances: "Mrs. Sigel and her daughters, both Elsie and Mabel, often dropped into the Port Arthur after they had visited Mother' Todd's mission across the way. The tea and quaint oriental dishes seem to have had a fascination for the women, and they were soon recognized as habitués of the place. Followed soon after an acquaintance with Gain, who was invited to call at the Sigel home; then an acquaintance with Leon, who was also asked to call."[74]

The direct cause for the rivalry between the two lovers of Elsie, which was seen as the motive for the murder, reportedly lay in Elsie's favoritism of the lover who could better cater to her material needs. As one article explained, "Leon could offer the girl but the tawdriest, cheapest sort of a 'good time' while Gain, when he wished to, could spend money liberally to create an effect. That he did use his money lavishly in this way, entertaining white women on whom his fancy had fallen, is well known to the denizens of Chinatown."[75]

In the aftermath of Elsie Sigel's death, Chinatown became a symbol of the seductions of commodity culture and the effects of the confusion between the boundaries of fantasy and reality that it intentionally created. Ultimately, the discourse was about the dangers of the "free-floating desire" evoked in the new public spaces of the city, which opened up the possibility of women pursuing (sexual) pleasure outside the confines of the home and the surveillance of middle-class men.

With the passing of time, hopes of apprehending Leon Ling, initially high, grew dim.[76] Hundreds of Leong Lin "look-alikes" (Asian-looking men with Americanized appearances) were spotted and apprehended all over the United States and as far away as England. The "real" Leong Lin, however, vanished into thin air.

A renewed outbreak of violence between the On Leong Tong and the Hip Song Tong (said to control the gambling industry in the quarter), however, coupled with complaints that white women going to Chinatown in slumming parties were making more frequent visits, led Deputy Police Commissioner Driscoll to order another police raid on the quarter. The investigation, this time around, was not "in search of Chinese." Its target was precisely the "picturesqueness [that] has so much accelerated to make [Chinatown] a productive tourist center." Driscoll, resolved to "abolish Chinatown as a show center," marched his policemen right to "the things which draw tourists": "a fraudulent opium joint," "where tourists were taken to be shown a white woman rolling opium pills with a decrepit Chinese" and "a 'chop suey' restaurant, where white girls ate in company with Chinese residents of the neighborhood." These establishments, according to Driscoll, "show white women the way into dens from which they often fail to return to their former companions." White women found in "opium dens arranged for exhibition purposes" and in chop-suey restaurants were notified that "Chinatown would harbor them no longer." Situations in which white women and Chinese were found quartered in the same house were turned over to tenement-house inspectors and would be handled through tenement-house law.[77] In addition, Driscoll asked the five sightseeing automobile companies operating sightseeing trips to Chinatown to remove their midnight excursions from their schedules.[78] "In a few weeks there will be no alliance between Chinatown and vice, and Chinatown . . . will be strictly Chinese," the police commissioner claimed confidently.

But, as one commentator remarked, the effort to contain the boundaries of the quarter and secure it for "Chinese only" by closing the "make-belief Chinatown on the lower east side," seemed an exercise in futility. "It is, to tell the truth, as difficult to find 'the Chinese quarter' in New York as it is to find 'the Judenstrasse' in Amsterdam," he observed. "The Chinese are pretty well scattered now all over the city. Laundries and chop suey restaurants are everywhere. . . . The neighborhood called Chinatown has been preserved as a show place for sightseers of questionable taste. . . . Mr. Driscoll proposes to abolish the 'sights.' Good luck to him."[79]

Driscoll's police action, designed to maintain the illusion that there is "a meaningful distinction in modern society between illusion and reality, fact and fantasy, fake and genuine images of the self," was bound to fail as well.[80] So were the efforts of four Chinese students from Columbia University, who petitioned Mayor William Jay Gaynor to ban the performance of "The Chinese Trunk Mystery," a play about the Sigel murder that was first shown in the Lipein Theater on the Bowery in August 1910, because "the malicious layering of the plot of the show and the inflammatory language used . . . is calculated to stir up racial animosity between the Chinese and the American people." The mayor's office found nothing "indecent" in the play.[81]

Eros and Americanization: David Levinsky and the forbidden fruit. From Abraham Cahan, "The Autobiography of an American Jew: The Rise of David Levinsky," *McClure's Magazine* 41 (July 1913), 118.

Chapter 4

Eros and Americanization

The Rise of David Levinsky, *or the Etiquette of Race and Sex*

B Y THE TURN OF THE NINETEENTH CENTURY, HEAVY JEWISH immigration from eastern Europe had transformed the neighborhood from the Bowery to the East River and from Market Street to Fourteenth Street (and pressing east of Second Avenue) into a center of Jewish life. In the nation's popular press, the Lower East Side, overcrowded, foreign, predominantly working class, yielded images of a "foreign country of whose habits [the average New Yorker] probably knows less, and with whose inhabitants he certainly has much less in common, than if he had crossed the Atlantic and found himself in Piccadilly or Pall Mall. . . . Its feasts and its fasts, its great personages and its common folk, its markets, its restaurants, its ceremonies, the very language it uses, are as strange to him as if the Bowery, with the shadow of the elevated forever darkening it, were some impassable stream."[1]

In the course of the next decade, the "picturesque" ghetto, with its bustling streets and markets, its "hawk visaged and bearded" men and its women with their "ugly wigs," its malodorous tenements, synagogues, and cheders full of "young ragamuffins," and its ghetto "types" such as the wedding broker or "shadchen," the peddler, and the labor agitator, became a familiar institution in magazines like *Harper's Weekly* or *Munsey's Magazine*.[2] Genteel readers even became accustomed to the sound of the quarter's "queer mongrel dialect." For their convenience, the "guttural, mongrel tongue, half German, half Hebrew" was usually transcribed according to the contemporary conventions of stage "Yiddish" or the "English of Cracow," yielding such tidbits of amusing banter as this exchange between a street vendor and his customer, who complains that the pitcher he has sold her has a crack in it:

"Vat you vants? Be-auttiful *chinay* for dwenty-five cents? I never say wunst you put vine in dat bitcher, but artefishjul fe-lowers, even if you hat to vate undil your dochter she gets a pridegroom; and she must be past dirty dis day, begause she was so ugly. . . .

"Zo! . . . My tear young mans, you is as much gracked as your chinay."[3]

Despite the favorite image of the Lower East Side as predominantly (and vulgarly) lower class, by 1910 the area was beginning to see the rise of a small immigrant bourgeoisie. The gradual social ascent of Jews of recent immigrant origin, which in 1930 would result in the classification of 71 percent of Russian Jews as middle class, was fueled primarily by manufacturing and commerce. The garment industry, which by 1900 was all but completely dominated by Jews, and in which eastern European Jews were slowly outcompeting their German cousins, was booming. A sizable proportion of the Jewish workforce moved from working as "hands" in small factories to becoming proprietors of wholesale and retail businesses and commercial enterprises. Others joined the emerging white-collar class as employees in clerical or sales jobs.[4] Some even grew rich. Samuel Silverman, who began as a sweatshop worker, became a cloak manufacturer worth half a million dollars. Harris Mandelbaum, erstwhile peddler, became a millionaire through his investment in tenement houses. Harry Fischel, broke on arrival in New York, became a real estate and building magnate whose mansion on Fifth Avenue, a block away from Andrew Carnegie's, was worth sixty thousand dollars. Israel Leibowitz worked himself up from peddler to one of the largest shirt manufacturers in New York.[5]

Genteel America responded to these slow but steady social advances, which went hand in hand with the gradual integration of eastern European Jewish immigrants and their offspring in the commodity and leisure-driven culture of America, and, in some cases, with their move out of the ghetto and into the suburbs of Bronxville and Harlem, or even the Upper West Side, with measured concern. In the eyes of some, Jewish social and geographical mobility was not a measure of acculturation or "Americanization" and thus a part of the American success story but a "Hebrew Conquest" designed to turn New York into a "city of Asiatics."[6]

This ominous reading of Jewish mobility permeated a sudden flush of articles about "Jewish success stories" in the popular media after 1910. In 1913, *McClure's* published an article by Burton J. Hendrick, one of its editors and a populist muckraker of some repute who would take up the cause of immigration restriction in the 1920s. Entitled "The Jewish Invasion of America," it surveyed what Hendrick called the penetration of a "distinctive type—the successful and aggressive Jew" in key sectors of the American economy.[7] The economic landscape it sketched, in subchapters titled "The Conquest of the Clothing Trades," "Intensity of Jewish Competition," "Jews the Greatest Owners of Land," "Business Completely Transformed by the Jews," or "The Most Perfect Trust in the Country," was one in which Jews were rapidly overtaking other immigrating "races." The writer concluded his article with the introduction of *McClure's* next foray into the phenomenon of "successful Jews":[8]

> Th[is] writer has contented himself chiefly with recording facts, and has only incidentally touched upon the racial traits and training that have made possible this success. In succeeding articles in this magazine a well known writer, himself a distinguished Jew, Mr. Cahan, editor of the Forwaerts . . . will show this phase of the subject. Mr. Cahan will show, by concrete example, the minute workings of that wonderful machine, the Jewish brain. His articles will make clear why it is the Jews so easily surpass or crowd out, at least in business and finance, the other great immigrating races—Irish, German, Scandinavians, and Italians, and why, in the next hundred years, the Semitic influence appears likely to be preponderating in the United States.[9]

The dubious honor of Hendrick's introduction of *The Rise of David Levinsky,* the serialized novel Abraham Cahan wrote in response to a request by the editors of *McClure's Magazine* for a series of pieces on Jews in business, illustrates the precariousness of the position of a crossover author such as Cahan, a Russian immigrant, socialist, prolific journalist, editor, essayist, critic, polemicist, and writer of feuilletons in the Yiddish press.

Cahan first ventured into writing fiction in English in 1895. His commitment to realism (he was familiar with the conventions of Russian and European literary realism, and his American models were realists such as William Dean Howells and Henry James) led him to confine his literary explorations mostly to the world he knew intimately, that of New York's East Side. Cahan's depictions of Jewish immigrant life brought him to the attention of William Dean Howells, who secured a publisher for Cahan's novella, *Yekl: A Tale of the New York Ghetto* (1896), and promoted the author as "a new star of realism."[10]

Cahan's early English novellas, *Yekl* and *The Imported Bridegroom and Other Stories of the New York Ghetto* (1898), bear the mark of the type of journalistic realism prevalent at Lincoln Steffens's *Commercial Advertiser,* where Cahan briefly had found employment. This realism, which found its supreme expression in the genre of the urban sketch, as well in the investigative reporting of the *Police Gazette,* mimics "voices, accents, dialects, and specialized vocabularies" as a means of "situating a person—establishing that person's class, métier, region."[11] *Yekl,* in particular, inscribes Jewish difference externally, through the *couleur locale* of the Lower East Side, and the lower-class status, the comic peculiarities of speech, the stumbling English, and the "uncouth" manners of its characters.[12] Indeed, the Americanizing ambitions of the lower-class Jake/Yekl are encapsulated in his use of a bungled English *("Dot'sh a' kin' a man I am"),* the aberrance of which is visually rendered in the text through the use of italics. Moreover, Cahan comments explicitly on Jake's features, which he describes as "strongly Semitic naturally," but even more so when brightened up by his "Semitic smile," which makes "Jake's very nose" seem "to join the Mosaic faith."[13]

But it was exactly with the use of such conventions that Cahan found a place in the culture industry that had made "low life" its focus. Cahan's "stories of Yiddish life," which Howells lauded as "so entirely of our time and place, and so foreign to our race and civilization," found a ready readership among genteel audiences eager for a glimpse into the "poor, workworn, ambitious, blundering grotesque lives" that Cahan described with such humorous detail.[14]

Not surprisingly, upper-class Jewish readers did not cherish this conflation of Jewishness, the Lower East Side, lower-classness, and "uncouthness," and complained "that there were more admirable Jewish characters than the central figure in *Yekl.*"[15] Cahan's socialist convictions, however, made him highly critical of what he regarded as the corrupting influences of capitalism. Cahan had no patience for the *"allrightnik,"* his self-invented term for pretentious Jewish immigrants whose sudden wealth had given them access to lifestyles and luxuries to which they not only were unaccustomed but also were ill-suited. Confronted with the ostentatious lifestyles that a proportion of immigrant manufacturers had begun to adopt, he wrote some slightly ironic sketches about the topic in 1906 and 1907, and was ready for more when approached by the editors of *McClure's.*

In 1913, *The Rise of David Levinsky* appeared in four richly illustrated installments. An abbreviated version of the novel Cahan would publish four years later, it detailed the transformation of David Levinsky, a penniless and motherless Russian Talmud student, into an Americanized and successful, but spiritually and emotionally unmoored, clothing manufacturer, worth two million dollars.[16]

In the manner of other American realists, most notably Theodore Dreiser, Cahan wrote his quintessential *American*, Horatio Alger–like story of social climbing and self-transformation as a simultaneous moral demise. Yet, as Burton Hendrick's introduction demonstrates, Cahan's indictment of the bourgeois aspirations of his fellow Jews easily collapsed into a racialized discourse. Some American and Jewish readers interpreted the story not as one about Jewish transformation—from immigrant to American, poor to wealthy—but about racial sameness, an illustration of such proverbial Jewish traits as ambitiousness, competitiveness, shrewdness, lasciviousness, lechery, vulgarity, and uncivilized behavior.[17]

In an intellectual climate that habitually understood culture in terms of race and biological immutability, the (supposedly "quintessentially American") discourse of self-invention was inevitably filtered through the prism of racial difference. Consequently, even a highly sympathetic review of *The Rise of David Levinsky* in *The Dial*, which astutely picked up on the novel's Spencerian themes and interpreted David's moral decline in terms of "nurture" and the corrupting influence of the environment (that is, American capitalism), ultimately reverted back to "nature" in its assessment of David's moral downfall. "Swept into business by circumstances which he hardly understands himself, and against which he is powerless," the author suggested, Levinsky's "wealth forces him to associate with all that is vulgar and acquisitive in Jewry and isolates him from all that is idealistic."[18]

Kate Holladay Claghorn, writing in *Survey*, was even more appalled:

> Told in the first person, [the novel] reveals with crude and unashamed realism the growing ascendancy of the sensual over the spiritual, the material over the ideal. . . . The people we are introduced to are in varying combinations crude, selfish, sensual and tasteless—above all, tasteless!—foolish, ignorant, ambitious and egotistical. Had the book been published anonymously, we might have taken it for a cruel caricature of a hated race by some anti-Semite. But the author is Abraham Cahan and the caricature is all the more cruel for the thousand little touches of realism which could have been given only from the inside. . . . Unfortunately this campaign poster will be taken by an already critical outer world as a picture of Jewish life in general. It really is not.[19]

Writing a novel that dealt (critically) with Jewish social and cultural mobility, Abraham Cahan was forced to confront the multiple contradictions of the discourses on race and rise, nature and nurture. Indeed, the inner logic of the narrative of *David Levinsky* itself propelled Cahan toward an exploration of Jewish difference. David, the millionaire, is no longer confined to that "touchstone of the real," the East Side, his lower-class background, dialect, or his vulgar manners.[20] Indeed, it is David Levinsky's fundamental ambition to excise the external signs of Jewishness—located precisely in his poverty, lower-class status, religiosity, speech, physiognomy, manners, and mannerisms—and supplant them, first, with the signs of Americanness, and second, of gentility.

But what, then, exactly was the makeup of David's "inner identity" that, as David himself professed in the novel's famous opening paragraph ("Sometimes . . . the metamorphosis I have gone through strikes me as nothing short of a miracle. . . . And yet, my inner identity . . . impresses me as being exactly the same as it was thirty or forty years ago") had remained unchanged in the course of David's otherwise radical self-transformation? What was the source of David's demise? What was it that capitalism threatened to corrupt in David Levinsky?[21]

RAISING DAVID LEVINSKY

On one level, *The Rise of David Levinsky* reads as a bildungsroman—in this case a cross between an etiquette book and Andrew Dale Carnegie's *How to Make Friends and Influence People*—in which David progressively deciphers and masters the tools of his own self-fashioning. Indeed, the fact that David's Jewishness, in what parades as David's own account of his self-transformation, is stylistically "unmarked" (David writes in a highly literary and flawless English), serves as a testimony of David's (and Cahan's) social and cultural achievements.

The most important lesson David learns almost as soon as he steps off the boat is that in America, radical self-transformation is not only possible, but it drives the culture itself. In contrast to the Old World, where identities are fixed and transparent—through the correspondence of occupation, neighborhood, physiognomy, and character—in America, one can transcend the marks of labor and nationality on the body. America is the land of the "unsmiling smile" (130) and the "credit face" (202). Policemen look like noblemen (90), and a good Jew can walk around without sidelocks (101). As David observes a butcher who appears to be the perfect gentleman, he is especially struck by the disjunction between labor and manners: "He was the most refined looking man . . . and his vocabulary matched his appearance and manner. I could not help thinking of raw beef, bones, and congealed blood. I said to myself, 'It takes a country like America to produce butchers who look and speak like noblemen'" (330).[22]

Identity in America, then, is a question of performance. As David con-cludes, after his first successful impersonation of a businessman with a healthy "capital" has persuaded the designer Chaikin and his wife to lend their services to his business, "We are all actors, more or less. The question is only what our aim is, and whether we are capable of a 'convincing imper-sonation'" (194).

David quickly learns that in America, the cultivation of the exterior deter-mines success. Early in his business career, Mr. Nodelman, David's model in business, quickly corrects him when David considers his "honest heart" to be one of his business assets: "Your heart I can't get into, so I don't know. . . . Maybe there's a rogue hiding there and maybe there isn't. But your face and your talk certainly are all right. They ought to be able to get you some more cash" (222).

David's self-transformation, then, is at once material and immaterial. His pursuit of capital is paralleled by his pursuit of cultural capital, the building blocks for his "convincing impersonations." His "rise" is predi-cated on erasure (of his sidelocks, beard, Talmudic singsong and gestures—the marks of race and class) and accumulation. First, David masters the ele-mentary signs of Americanness, consisting of language, gestures, dress codes, manners, mannerisms, expressions, pieces of jargon, and an "affected Yan-kee twang" (323), which David considers distinctively American. His next task is to appropriate the signs of education, the English literary "canon," and the intricacies of grammar. Finally, he moves to conquer the character-istics of a "gentleman," such as the "four-in-hand cravat" (260) and "the dif-ference between Rocquefort and Liederkranz cheese, or between consommé Celestine and consommé princesse" (292–93).

David demonstrates his social mobility by employing his former "supe-riors," Bender, his English teacher, and Loeb, his German Jewish competitor in the clothing business. He shows off his increasing linguistic proficiency through his snotty corrections of the grammatical errors of Dora, with whom he conducts an illicit affair. His biting observations of the gaudy style of the Kaplans, to whose daughter Fanny he is briefly engaged, and their circle of parvenu friends, are an indication of his growing aptitude in matters of taste and mark the rising stock of his cultural capital.

Indeed, David's mordant critique of the ostentation of bourgeois Jewry evokes pages from Tashrak's *Etikete*, a Yiddish etiquette book published in 1908, which instructs a prospective "Yiddishe Lord Chesterfield" and his wife in the intricacies of "respectable behavior."[23] The women David encounters at dinner parties and in Catskills hotels are decked up like a "veritable jewelry store" (367), a habit that, according to Tashrak, designates the wearer as "undeveloped, at a far remove from culture, a parvenue, and a woman without intelligence."[24] Fanny's habit of eating "voraciously, biting lustily and chewing with gusto" (397), the sight of which jars David, is a glaring transgression of Tashrak's fundamental rule not to "gulp, eat overeagerly, or make any noise" when eating soup or chewing.[25] The habit of parading children's talents in front of guests, which grates on David's nerves and tests his endurance ("a nauctournn by Chopin, her mother whispered" [366]), is classified by Tashrak as an extremely bad habit, which places a heavy burden on a guest and causes children to overestimate themselves.[26]

In these observations, we discern echoes of Cahan's own social prejudices. Cahan once stated that "not the literary and socialist Jews but the vulgar upstart parvenues" encountered anti-Semitism, an assessment that brought him some strange bedfellows, such as the racist University of Wisconsin sociologist Edward A. Ross, who quoted Cahan to support his contention that "what is disliked in the Jews is not their religion but certain ways and manners" and that "the gentile resents being obliged to engage in a humiliating and undignified scramble in order to keep his trade or his clients against the Jewish invader."[27]

But in his opinion, Cahan was by no means alone. According the *Menorah Journal*, "The boisterous, ill-mannered, pushing Jew is disliked much more heartily . . . by the highbred Jew than by any other man."[28] Walter Lippmann advocated socialism not as a means to redistribute wealth but as a means to curb the "blatant vulgarity" of "the rich and pretentious Jews of our big city."[29] Abraham Cahan may well have shared Lippmann's disdain for the ostentation of Jewish parvenus. Yet his socialism had a much deeper ideological foundation. And if Cahan, in *The Rise of David Levinsky*, was committed to a "civilizing" project that bore superficial resemblance to that of Tashrak and upper-class German American Jewry, his civilizing mission ultimately had a very different social orientation.

The contours of Cahan's ideal "Jewish gentleman" emerge clearly in his 1903 *Forverts* editorial entitled *Derekh Eretz Beim Esen,* or "Proper Table Manners." In the article, Cahan takes an anonymous German Jewish lady to task for misunderstanding the proper meaning of *"Bildung."* In her opinion, many Russian and Polish inhabitants of the lower East Side may be described as "educated" in the sense of "learned," but they do not qualify as "cultured" in the sense of *"Bildung."* They lack the proper etiquette, and, for all their education, continue to drink coffee with the spoon in the cup, instead of placed on the saucer.

Cahan rejects the notion of etiquette as the touchstone of *"Bildung."* He cites the example of gentiles and Jewish Americans whose entire education has focused on the cultivation of the external being, but who lack the inner cultivation stemming from education and intelligence. This inner deficiency cannot easily be remedied. By contrast, those who possess inner nobility, but eat soup from the tip of the spoon rather than from the side, can very easily master the outward signs of being "cultured." Nevertheless, Cahan argues, etiquette is not, as some socialists would have it, merely a "monkey ceremony." It is a sign: the inner cultivation of a Jewish student or self-educated worker will go unacknowledged if it is not accompanied by a style of self-presentation that signifies "culture."[30]

Cahan's assertion that etiquette and manners can be learned and are devoid of any moral meaning in their own right subverts the dominant discourse of "taste," which naturalized the cultural hegemony of "gentility" through the linkage of external appearance and inner "character." Cahan empties the "gentleman," a synecdoche of white, upper-class, "superior" America, of its surplus value.[31] With this move, Cahan transforms gentility from a figure of class as well as racial exclusivity into an expandable category. Social identity is performative rather than innate and can be appropriated by Jews. Ultimately, external signs of identity are superficial and deceptive, and authenticity and "gentility" reside in an interior space, deep within the inner self.

The Rise of David Levinsky is an extended exploration of the implications of this perspective. David has been seduced into a life ruled by appearances. His practice in role-playing has served him well in his business: David becomes a multimillionaire by embodying and trading in exteriors. He sells the "air" of distinction that a good suit evokes (291) and develops "into an excellent salesman," whose forte lies in his ability to sell make-believe for the "real thing." The single greatest contribution to his "success on the road," David explains, was "the enthusiasm with which I usually spoke of my merchandise." And in his characteristic double voice, he adds: "It was genuine, and it was contagious: retailers could not help believing that I believed in my goods" (329).

Committed to the mastery of the symbolic order of America, David assimilates into a world he himself recognizes as "honeycombed with what Max Nordau called conventional lies, with sham ecstasy, sham sympathy, sham smiles, sham laughter" (380). David has mastered the art of "whiteness" but finds that its signifier, the wealthy gentleman, is ultimately empty. Yet what is the internal register that makes David aware of this emptiness in the first place?

Desire and Jewish Difference

Throughout his autobiography, David's persona is characterized by a curious distance from the self that is taking shape in its pages. This distance is persistently expressed in the self-conscious phraseology of such sentences as "I said, feelingly" (276); "I rejoined, fervently" (476); "I answered, with filial docility" (396); or "I said, ardently" (396), which insert a metacommentary on the performativity of their own "bogus emotions."[32] Indeed, this duality frames the narrative from its beginning to the famous last paragraph:

> I don't seem to be able to get accustomed to my luxurious life. I am always more
> or less conscious of my good clothes, of the high quality of my office furniture,
> of the power I wield over the men in my pay. . . . I can never forget the days of my
> misery. I cannot escape from my former self. My past and present do not com-
> port well. David, the poor lad swinging over a Talmud volume at the Preacher's
> synagogue, seems to have more in common with my inner identity than David
> Levinsky, the well-known cloak manufacturer. (530)

Of course, as a literary device, this self-estrangement conveniently provides Cahan with a register for his social critique. But more critically, commentators have consistently taken this duality as the core of David's character, and have structured their interpretations around the question of its provenance.

In the most conventional readings, David's duality reflects the social reality of the Americanization process and the inevitable sense of loss and inner division that continued to trail immigrants.[33] Some consider this inner division, coupled with the novel's "lonely millionaire" motif, fundamentally "American." Others universalize David's duality as reflecting the "discrepancies of the modern." Alternatively, the novel is seen as utterly "parochial" in its concern with the futility of David's attempt to escape Jewishness.[34] These interpretations share the perception of David's duality as fraught with tension and conflict: between universalism and particularism, gain and inevitable loss.

In a brilliant essay published in *Commentary* in 1952, Isaac Rosenfeld suggests an alternative reading. Paradoxically, Rosenfeld suggests, the two Davids, David the capitalist and American millionaire and David the *yeshiva bokher,* whom David regards as irreconcilable, are also fundamentally compatible. They exhibit a deep, structural correspondence. Both are predicated on the maintenance of yearning rather than the striving for fulfillment.[35]

Rosenfeld's argument, in its casting of the Jew as the paradigmatic (capitalist) American (and the alter ego of the Anglo-Saxon Protestant), ignores the social critique Cahan embedded in *The Rise of David Levinsky*. Indeed, the novel seems to suggest precisely the incompatibility of Jewish spirituality and capitalism. Nevertheless, it has the distinction of pointing beyond the discrepancies—dualities—that superficially rule the novel, to the underlying psychological and narrative unity—desire—in which they are subsumed. Rosenfeld counts David's disjointed linking of business, religion, and sex (David describes his broken engagement in "less than twenty lines," to continue with "Our rush season has passed") as his major literary shortcoming. But the extreme mobility of David's erotic desire begs to be inserted in the logic of what Rosenfeld calls the "reflexive desire" of the Diaspora Man, whose endless movement between yearning, accumulation, dissatisfaction, and ascesis accounts for the compatibility of the Jewish yeshiva boy and the Jewish capitalist American.[36] Rosenfeld does not fully explore the implications of this insight. His explanation ignores the significance of the centrality in the novel of the language of desire and its various adjectives in the novel, such as rapture, yearning, passion, love, and ardor.

Indeed, it was the centrality of desire that many Jewish and non-Jewish critics objected to when the novel appeared. With its frank discussion of David's sexuality, the novel certainly did not conform to bourgeois standards of respectability. Moreover, the graphic details of David Levinsky's economic rise and moral decline dovetailed with the worst anti-Semitic stereotypes of the usurious, lustful, conniving, ruthless, and sexually depraved Jew. Indeed, a number of the illustrations with which *McClure's* chose to accompany Cahan's text seemed to invite such a reading. One showed a racially distinctive, cigar-smoking wealthy Jewish type spying on a woman's figure from behind. The highly suggestive caption, "Many a time, when I see a well-dressed American woman in the street, I follow her for blocks," quoted only part of Cahan's sentence (which continued, "I never weary of studying the trend of the American woman's taste").[37]

It is hardly likely that Cahan, in describing David's life as one ruled by desire for sex, love, money, and status, would not have been aware of this possible interpretive angle. His authorial decision to face this danger nonetheless can be attributed to his commitment to realism, his socialist ideals, and a desire to shock. But the centrality of desire is not just a sign of an ideological commitment or realism. It is a structural conceit. It is desire that accounts for David's dual self, and that brings coherence to an otherwise disjointed narrative. Moreover, it is in desire that Cahan locates the engine as well as the limits of David's self-fashioning. It is desire that delivers David to the clutches of capitalism. But it is a desire that is predicated on a lack that is integral to his being. It is in the structure of David's desire that Cahan inscribes Jewish difference.

Looking back on his life, David is aware that he has been driven by the desire to conquer "thousands of things" that were "forbidden fruit," and to claim ownership of a world from which he felt debarred (525). Nevertheless, for all his current "sense of success and ease," David's self-transformation is ultimately conditioned by its very impossibility. He can never become, as he desires, "to the manner born" (291). It is in this observation, in which culture ambiguously collapses into descent (and race), that the limits of David's self-fashioning emerge.

The internal boundaries that thwart David's complete self-transformation manifest themselves physically, in David's inability to deactivate his Talmudic singsong, his propensity to "talk too much," and his gesticulations, a "habit" that he likens to a "physical defect" (327). But they are as much psychological as they are bodily inscribed. David likens the fact that "I was not born in America" to a "physical defect that asserted itself in many disagreeable ways—a physical defect which, alas! no surgeon in the world was capable of removing" (291).

To all external appearances, David is no longer "a kike" but has become "David Levinsky, the cloak manufacturer," a highly valuable object of female desire (407). Yet, as Phillip Barrish has pointed out, insofar as David will never be able to master completely the minute details of distinction, his goal is bound to recede before him, causing the tenuousness in such statements as "The difference between taste and ostentation was coming slowly, but surely, I hope (260)."[38] Even when David no longer needs his notebooks listing bits of business slang, names of dishes served in the better restaurants, and the composition of macaroni au gratin, at the bottom of his heart he continues to "cow before waiters," whose "white shirt-fronts, reticence, and pompous bows" make him feel "as if my expensive clothes and ways ill became me" (515).

David's self-difference, then, is based on a cultural lack—which is simultaneously a racial mark. Paradoxically, it is this experience of lack that sets David's desire in motion and causes its most intense expression in the urge for self-transformation. This mechanism is made explicit in a number of mirroring scenes (both literal and metaphorical) that bracket the novel.[39]

One of the first, and perhaps the best, examples is his relationship with Matilda, the sophisticated, Russianized, radical daughter of a wealthy benefactress who houses the penniless David after his mother has been killed in a pogrom. In a bout of teasing, Matilda imagines David's transformation from shy and asexual Talmud student into sophisticated secular college student: "She proceed[ed] to put my sidelocks behind my ears. . . . She then smoothed them down, the touch of her fingers thrilling me through and through. Then she brought me a hand-glass and made me look at myself. 'So you see the difference?' she demanded. 'If you were not rigged out like the savage that you are you wouldn't be a bad-looking fellow, after all. Why, girls might even fall in love with you'" (75).

This incident causes David to fall head over heels in love with Matilda. His desire is, as all desire, fundamentally narcissistic: he is in love with the image of himself, which she projects. The "more" than himself, which Matilda sees in him, and with which David develops an identification, is his Ego Ideal, that place in the Symbolic Order from which he would like to see himself.[40] Matilda's consequent snub of his advances ("You forget your place, young man!" [80]), however, indicates his lack.

When, in David's imagination, the stern image of Matilda mutates into the hostile glamour of America (87), the outlines of the structure of his desire are in place. He will continue to identify with himself from the position of an Ego Ideal, in the form of various love objects, which occupy a place of authority within the Symbolic Order. In the specular gazes of Gitelson, his steerage brother; Mr. Ewen, the benefactor who pays for his "American" haircut; Mr. Bender, his English teacher; Jake Mindels, the refined, effeminate Yiddish theater fan; Dora, the wife of his friend Max with whom he has an affair, and Anna Tevkin, the socialist daughter of a Hebrew poet, he discerns his Ideal self.

It is this Ego Ideal that David internalizes and to which he submits himself. It will make him aware of his lack (of education, status, language, sophistication, money, love) and incite intense feelings of love, envy, rivalry, or a combination of all. It informs the self-transformations David undertakes to erase his defaults and invests his successive projects of Americanization and secularization, social and cultural mobility, and his intellectual and economic pursuits with a libidinal charge.

The structure of this desire dictates that it cannot be fulfilled in his private life. As he complains, it causes him to profile himself in terms of lack and makes him, in love, "apt to put my least attractive wares in the show window" (515). David's investment in unattainable love objects indicates that they serve primarily as conduits for a revision of the self that is never-ending, as David himself acknowledges in such statements as: "I found that in 1893 my judgment of men and things had been immature and puerile. I was convinced that now at last my insight was a thoroughly reliable instrument, only a year later to look back on my opinions of 1894 with contempt" (350). David craves an object that sets his desire in motion, but he avoids unification and its fulfillment, and with it, keeps open the possibility that there is always something "more" in himself. In that sense, his desire serves the logic of accumulation of capital and cultural capital: his rise needs a "rise" of a more intimate nature.

The same logic of desire, in business, accounts for David's success. There he has a handle on "how to show my goods to their best advantage" (515) because he knows the specular logic of narcissistic desire inside out. He knows "how women want to be seen" because he is an expert in self-Othering. He knows that women are driven by the same desire to recognize, in the other's desire for them, their own Ego Ideal, the "more than oneself," which they themselves long to be.

Indeed, the first time he can put this experience to his advantage also serves as the first sure sign of his "oisgrinen": the seduction of his landladies Mrs. Levinsky and Mrs. Dienstog, for whom he feels no physical attraction, is primarily an exercise in the mechanics of desire. He continues to reap the harvest of this expertise in role-playing and the mechanics of desire in his subsequent career in the clothing business, which is, ultimately, all about appearances and narcissistic desire. In that sense, David's career is, more than he is willing to concede, his life.

David, in that sense, resembles Carrie, the heroine of Theodore Dreiser's *Sister Carrie*. The one constant of Carrie's character, Walter Benn Michaels argues, is perpetual desire. Carrie's ceaseless urge to erase "the distinction between what one is and what one wants" is the manifestation of the unrestrained capitalism of the late nineteenth and early twentieth centuries, which introduced an "economy of excess" in which desire "in principle is never satisfied" because it "outstrips any possible object." In such an economy, Michaels argues, character itself becomes "speculative": "What you are is what you want, in other words, what you aren't." Satisfaction, on the other hand, spells death.[41] Carrie's ultimate triumph as an actress suggests the nexus between lack, desire, self-transformation, and the production of speculative identities—suppressed in Henry James's portrayal of Mrs. Churm—which was symptomatic of a new hierarchy of labor that attributed "value" on the basis of the relative fictionality of social roles and the degree of distance from the process of production.

The Rise of David Levinsky portrays such distance as a sign of "false consciousness," of which David is the supreme incarnation. Having submitted himself to a life of acting, make-believe, and illusion, he has become the "narcissistic consumer-actor" who is the perfect subject for the new order of commodity capitalism. In this order, which replaces an economy based on production, scarcity, and moral restraint, "the stage is the epitome of reality, and imitation the model for individuation."[42]

Imitation had also made its appearance in American sociology and psychology, as a theory explaining the process of assimilation. Formulated first by the Frenchman M. Gabriel Tarde, this theory argued against the influence of "organic heredity" as the basis for human action and activity, insisting instead on a "suggestion-imitation process" as informing "all changes and movements in society."[43] American critics of the theory of imitation countered that "it takes no sufficient account of those deeper characteristics of species and race which come to light in the psychical life of the individual and in the psychical processes of society." Charles Ellwood, for instance, argued that it is "race heredity" that determines "personal and social development . . . to take one direction rather than another." "If the process of growth by imitation were not limited and modified by innate tendencies, we should expect children of different races, when reared in the same cultural environment, to develop the same general and moral characteristics," he concluded.[44]

Jerome Dowd thought it necessary to distinguish between social and personal imitation. Personal imitation, in which "one individual assimilates the emotions, thoughts, and habits of another by more or less long contact and association," he considered crucial to the "acquisition of higher culture." Members of "an ostracized race or one that does not intermarry," however, are barred from this "elevation . . . to a higher moral plane." By default, they become "extraordinarily susceptible to social imitation." "But unfortunately," Dowd argued, "social imitation alone does not enhance personality, but on the contrary, unless restrained by personal imitation, either results in the degeneration of the ostracized race or leaves it on the same moral level. To dress and eat in the fashion, to catch on to native industrial methods and technique, to patronize American public amusements, and to acquire something of the current knowledge of the time does not carry a race very far in the direction of assimilation."[45] This "arrested process of assimilation to the American type," according to Dowd, explained "the moral retrogression of the Negro since emancipation, the backward trend of many of our Indian population, and the moral peculiarities of the Jew."[46]

Cahan's critique of David's "sham existence" has an awkward resonance with the arguments of Dowd and Ellwood. Despite David's repeated insistence that there is a more "wholesome" core to his persona, his behavior continues to cast doubt on the truthfulness of that claim. His belief in the power of image continues to dictate his behavior even in the most intimate moments in his life. Even when he faces the crushing defeat of being rejected by Anna Tevkin, whom he considers the love of his life, he resorts to the "posture" of what he believes to be the manner of "a man of firm purpose," declaring , "I won't give you up. . . . I am resolved to win you" (497).

The better self that David wants Anna to see in him to her has no basis in reality. No matter how hard he tries to talk up his "wares" and convince her that "her image of me is, spiritually speaking, not a good likeness," to Anna there is no "more than" the David who is a "money-bag" (468). To all appearances, there is no other David than the persona he performs on a daily basis. Ultimately, what David's failed romantic pursuit of Anna drives home to him is that he has, indeed, become a prisoner of his own performance. Regretfully, he observes that "whatever good there may be in me eludes the eye of a superficial acquaintance" (468). But the truth is that the only inner "reality" that David himself has access to, after the fiasco of his affair with Anna Tevkin, are "the real conditions of my affairs," and the only illusions he is willing to confront, his disastrous speculations in real estate (501). David may long for a "heart-to-heart talk" (529), but he has long since given up his "honest heart" (the "primary metaphor of interiority") and has cashed in on his face and his talk.[47] In a (capitalist) society believing in the power of appearances, the performed self *is* the "real" self.

Cahan's critique of the theory of imitation, however, is curiously double-faced and can be seen as Cahan's response to what he perceived as the utopian and distopian dimensions of the American creed of self-fashioning. His deconstruction of the "gentleman" as an external effect of the imitation and performance of the "codes" of gentility rather than an innate cause suggests that social identity and "character" are not determined by (racial) descent, but rather are adaptable to new circumstances. If racism claims that "man *is*, before he *acts*; nothing he does may change what he is," Cahan seems to suggest that in America, that distinction being "being" and "acting" has been utterly confounded.[48]

But this perspective also opens up the possibility that underneath this performed identity, there may be no authentic, essential self. And in the final analysis, it is this possibility that makes Cahan back away from fully embracing a concept of culture as imitative, performative, and constitutive of identity. It is consumer capitalism that confounds the distinction between the stage and everyday life. But this split, which capitalism exploits, is based on a lack. It is precisely this lack that is authentic to David's character. David's interior authenticity lies in the short-circuit of lack and desire and registers both in David's body (his sexual eagerness, the uncooperativeness of its speech and gestures) and his soul (his endless yearning).[49]

The same experience of desire and lack that drives his success but causes him to be suspended in an endless becoming, "everlastingly revising my views of people, including myself" (350), also prevents him from collapsing into (hegemonic, genteel, bourgeois) sameness. He will never mistake his "personation" for the "real thing," even if others do. The "fullness" of the gentile Mr. Eaton, with his confidence-inspiring reticence, or even the self-satisfied mien of Fanny and her family (for which he expresses his scorn) will never be his.

David's success is based on the opposite of the "distance from necessity" that, according to Pierre Bourdieu, certifies "real distinction": his nervousness, his enthusiasm, his exuberance, the "emphasis rather than dignity" in his appeal.[50] Indeed, in that sense, the same signs of excess that David, and along with him a generation of American Jews, seeks to eliminate are the most authentic aspects of his being. The very fact that he cannot attain bourgeois self-sufficiency, that he is in-between, and split, is the mark of his authenticity, and at the same time it constitutes his drive.

Cahan's version of an "authentic" Jewish identity, then, is only superficially characterized by a split between inner and outer self, between external appearance and interior character. Careful examination of the surface yields an underlying, deeper structural correspondence of inner and outer identity that belies the apparent disjunctions to which the novel ceaselessly calls attention. Yet this correspondence does not invoke the fixity and immutability of other constructions of Jewish racial identity, precisely because it is rooted in lack and desire. Desire is by definition transitive—it links the Self to the Other and the Symbolic Order. In that sense, it is compatible with transformation and refuses the language of "authenticity," or the dichotomy of "inner" and "outer" selves. It subsumes change.

Yet there is a (natural/racial) limit to David's desire—and to Cahan's ironic perspective on it. David's final confessions are devoted to his relationship with a Gentile woman—who is not named—who David might have married were it not for the "chasm of race between us" and the "medieval prejudices against our people which makes so many marriages between Jew and Gentile a failure" (527–28). David's desire for self-transformation founders naturally at the taboo on intermarriage.

David's final words, too, are not to be read ironically: "I can never forget the days of my misery. I cannot escape from my old self. My past and my present do not comport well. David, the poor lad swinging over a Talmud volume at the Preacher's Synagogue, seems to have more in common with my inner identity than David Levinsky, the well-known cloak-manufacturer" (528). David's lack and desire are deeply rooted in the experiences that shape his childhood.

On the one hand, the image of David as a young Talmud scholar evokes the same vindictiveness and one-upmanship that will characterize his later years. But, on the other hand, it also locates the source of David's yearning in the realization of man's imperfection in relation with God—a God, David acknowledges, "I loved . . . as one does a woman" (38)—and in the trauma of his mother's murder during the pogroms of 1881–82. This one core aspect of David's identity remains constant and unchanged. Moreover, it inextricably links David to what he recognizes as the "streak of sadness in the blood of my race (4)."

Once detached from the Sacred Book, this desire has become mobile.[51] But even if David has directed the energy mobilized by hunger and desire toward ends that are ultimately egotistic, materialistic, and futile, at the root of it lies an element of deep spiritual, messianic longing. It is the same root that Walter Benjamin recognized as the utopian foundation of commodity capitalism. It is the same root that, as Jules Chametzky argues, informed Cahan's own early conversion to socialism. And it is toward the higher ideals of socialism, whose calling David Levinsky consistently spurns, that Cahan wished to channel the lack and desire of his fellow American Jews.[52]

Part II

STAGES OF IDENTITY

Performing Ethnic Subjects

The immigrant as clown: Eduardo Migliaccio, alias "Farfariello." Eduardo Migliaccio Papers, IHRC 1540, Immigration History Research Center, University of Minnesota.

Chapter 5

Juggling Identities

The Case of an Italian American Clown

I N 1919, CARL VAN VECHTEN, JOURNALIST AND EXPERT SLUMMER, visited the Old Bowery Theatre to attend a performance of Eduardo Migliaccio, or "Farfariello," one of the most popular and successful Italian American entertainers of the early decades of the twentieth century. He found the theater "filled with all sorts and conditions of men and women, working men in their shirt-sleeves . . . women with their oval olive faces suckling their babies, or with half-nude infants lying over their knees."

When the orchestra strikes up a tune, Farfariello appears in evening clothes and announces his first song, *Femmene-Fe,* a trifle about women. The song over, he leaves the stage. A few minutes later, Farfariello returns, this time as "a French singer of the type familiar at Coney Island. He has transfigured his eyes, his nose is new; gesture, voice, all his powers, physical and mental, are molded in this new metal. He shrieks his vapid ditty in raucous falsetto; he flicks his spangled shirt; he winks at the orchestra leader and shakes his buttocks; his bosom has become an enormous jelly."[1]

As the evening continues, Farfariello goes on singing, acting, and impersonating. To thunderous applause and shouts of "Bravo," he passes "from one character to the next," exchanging his "aristocratic top hat for a Sicilian cap, his impeccable tails for the vest of the working man, the magnificent décolleté of the chanteuse in the beer hall for the torn skirt of the talkative folk woman."[2]

By the time of Van Vechten's visit, Farfariello had reigned as Little Italy's *"Re Dei Macchiettisti,"* or "king of the character clowns," for nearly two decades. As the resident physiognomist of Mulberry Street, his repertoire of more than four hundred stock characters ranged from Italian American *prominenti* (bankers, doctors, or presidents of benevolent societies, in

sketches such as "L'Ondertecco" (The Undertaker) or "Il Presidente del Club
F.F.," to the underworld, in such acts as "L'Imbroglione" (The Swindler) or
"Il Mafioso." He covered the world of show business as "Il Vecchio Corista"
(The Old Chorus Singer), "Il Filodrammatico" (The Amateur Actor), and
"Il Divo, Commendatore Enrico Caruso," a parody of the opera star Enrico
Caruso, in which "Il Divo" is all but smothered by a heavy-set female admirer.
He spoofed radical politics and feminism in "Il Rosso" (The Red One).
Occasionally he impersonated American types that Italian immigrants were
likely to encounter, such as "The Judge," "The Cop," or "Un Todesco" (a
German). But mostly he found his subjects in the neighborhood, in such
topics as "Scul-gherl" (School Girl) or "A Talianella" (The Wop Girl). His
favorite character was the "little man" on the street, whom he portrayed in
various incarnations as "The Night Watchman," "Il Signor Colonno" (Mr.
Colonist), "'O Pressatore" (The Presser), "The Ragpicker," "'O Spazzino"
(The Street Cleaner), "'O Scupatore Policante" (The Sweeper Politician),
"Il Venditore Ambulante" (The Street Peddler), "The Pick-and-Shovel Man,"
"'O Sarto" (The Tailor), "'O Scarparo" (The Shoemaker), or the "Iceman,"
who regales his customers with Neapolitan street songs.

Intensely place-bound, Farfariello's impersonations offer an illuminating
parallel to the epistemology of urban space prevalent in the urban guidebooks and on the American vaudeville stage. In his performances, place
becomes what Benjamin has called a "human language," a "'virtual site' in
the sense of a material place that becomes a medium of philosophical potential."[3] But what does this language communicate?

Farfariello's immigrant types, presented as visually grotesque and excessive in physiognomy, language, dress, and mannerisms, present a catalogue
of a community in transition, whose cultural lag often creates a comic effect.
Oscillating between Neapolitan dialect, American colloquialism, and a mon-
grelized vocabulary of Italian American makeshift words, such as "stritto,"
"naise ghella," "carro," and "Cunailando," the language of these types captures the heterogeneity and multiplicity of this Italian immigrant world.

Farfariello operates in the interstices of two cultures, in the confrontation between the mores and values of the Old World and the New. His
"intelligent satire," according to one reviewer, "exploited the customs, the
manners, the sometimes exaggerated liberties, of this country which has
adopted him. . . . In this satire appears always, continuously, the confrontation with the customs and manners in his other country, his home country."[4] Farfariello's acts project this confrontation onto the dichotomy not only

between Italy and America, but onto urban space itself. In the juxtaposition of specific localities, such as "Brodue" (Broadway), "Cunailando" (Coney Island), "Mulberry Stritto," and "la casa" (home), Farfariello maps a moral ecology in conflict. His typology of urban space unveils an immigrant community beset by contradictory notions of self and self-worth and conflicting moral and social codes. As such, his acts provide a unique perspective on the inner experience of Italian immigration. But the starting point of thought in Farfariello's performances is laughter.[5]

The comic urban characters that Migliaccio created were inspired by a repertoire of folk humor and a native Italian clown tradition, which also lay at the base of commedia dell'arte, with its exaggerated and parodic stock characters: *Il Dottore* (the charlatan doctor), *Pulcinella* (the servant), *Pantalone* (the old greedy Venetian merchant), and the clowns *Pierrotto, Scaramouche,* and *Arlecchino* (Harlequin).[6] In the spirit of "campanilismo," the extreme regionalism or localism that characterized Italian culture for centuries, Italian regions or villages used to have not only their own specific saints, but their distinct clown types as well. Vernacular clowns such as the Neapolitan *Pulcinello,* the Sicilian *Pasquino,* the Milanese *Menaghino,* and the Florentine *Stenterello* wore characteristic local costumes and spoke the local dialect. Traditionally, these clowns had a cultural license to mock local personalities, satirize political or social events, or make vulgar remarks. As simpletons, country bumpkins, gluttonous servants, or shiftless drunkards, they would intrude upon town plays with indecent remarks or gestures, parodying the gestures of the heroes and heroines and satirizing local *prominenti.* Representing the mocking of the official, hegemonic "high-brow" culture by the popular "low-brow," they offered an important vent for social and cultural critique and moral censure.[7]

Transplanted to America, these regional clowns reemerged in their original forms in the Italian American theater, which quickly became a dominant social institution in Italian enclaves. Initially, their familiarity, idiomatic expressions, and slang served as visible symbols of a continuous moral and social world that now stretched across the Atlantic Ocean. But over time, their conventional jokes and mannerisms offered little relief to immigrants facing the confusion and frustrations of adjusting to life in a modern metropolis, and they could hardly compete with the entertainment provided by vaudeville halls and nickelodeons.[8]

Eduardo Migliaccio was born in 1882 in the province of Salerno, near Naples, to an upper-class Neapolitan family. He developed his interest in the

stage in Naples, where he studied at the local art institute and briefly appren-
ticed with the leading comic actor or "macchiettista," Niccolò Maldacea,
who would become a direct source of inspiration for his later acts. In 1897,
Migliaccio emigrated to the United States, initially to become a clerk in a
bank his father owned in the mining town of Hazleton, Pennsylvania. Dissatisfied with his position, which consisted mostly of writing letters accompanying money orders for the bank's mostly illiterate clientele of miners
and laborers, he soon left for New York, where he obtained a similar post at
a bank on Mulberry Street, which would sustain him throughout his acting career.[9]

After some largely unsuccessful attempts at serious theater, including a
short engagement as an act in a marionette performance, Migliaccio took
the stage in a small café-chantant, which at the turn of the century was
filled with singers, musicians, and mimics, and performed some of his own
songs and sketches. One was about a character named "Farfariello." Literally meaning "little butterfly," the name made an oblique reference to Far-
farello, the clown-devil in Dante's *Divina Commedia,* but it also provided
an apt metaphor for the transformations that would become the hallmark
of Farfariello's career.[10]

In his acts, Farfariello assimilated the Italian clown tradition to a modern American urban environment. Thus he created a cultural space for the
expression of, as one reviewer described it, *"la storia viva della nostra emi-
grazione,"* the living story of our emigration.[11] With what another described
as his "reflexive imagination," Farfariello became the comic chronicler of the
lives and histories of the millions of Italians who found themselves washed
ashore in metropolitan America.[12] His multiple impersonations presented
a shorthand of the Italian immigrant community. As one correspondent for
L'Italo-Americano de Los Angeles wrote:

> If I wanted to acquaint a foreigner with the psychology, somewhat grotesque yet
> full of common sense . . . good-natured, gay and rugged, of the cafone in America
> . . . I would have to speak two hours and have the eloquence of a Demosthenes, or
> massacre the reader with two columns of prose. But if I led him to see "The Cafone
> Who Reasons," recited by Eduardo Migliaccio, or Farfariello, all this little world,
> somewhat distorted, somewhat sullied by local speech and customs, but full of
> an indestructible Italianità, would reveal itself with a marvelous, limpid, livid
> truth. . . . He has written the true story of the Italian colony in America, and has
> carved in these very images this process of continual transformation with a very
> subtle and facile art."[13]

THE TYPOLOGY OF IMMIGRANT SPACE:
"A DISTORTED LITTLE WORLD"

On an imaginary level, America, for Italian immigrants as for many others, constituted a dreamworld composed of utopian visions. It was a land of plenty, a counterspace to the scarcity and poverty that characterized the lives of the majority of Italians. In contrast to the strict hierarchical order of Italian society, where social rank was determined by birth, in America one could pursue ambitions and social mobility. But inevitably, this space had its dark side as well. Immigrants often found their hopes dashed in the daily grind of underpaid work and living conditions harsh enough to earn a "Little Sicily" slum in Chicago the nickname "Little Hell."

In order to escape rural poverty, which characterized the experience of the majority of Italian immigrants, most headed for urban areas and industrial jobs. By taking up urban professions, Italian immigrants performed a "vicarious act of defiance against their former superiors."[14] But as Rudy Vecoli writes, "Diggers in the earth they had been, and diggers in the earth they remained; only in America they duck with the pick and shovel rather than the mattock."[15] Largely illiterate and unequipped with industrial skills, more than 53 percent of the Italian immigrants who entered the United States in 1880 were obliged to take up unskilled jobs. As organ-grinders, ragpickers, or common laborers in the mines and on the wharves and construction sites, they were employed at the lowest, most repulsive jobs.[16] Skilled blue-collar workers usually worked as shoemakers, masons, and tailors, while in the service industry many established themselves as barbers and restaurateurs. The few professionals and intellectuals who decided to emigrate found their rank among the *prominenti* and businessmen within the Italian colonies.

In their desire for *pane e lavoro,* bread and work, in order to support their families in Italy or in America, Italian workers were often vulnerable to exploitation by bosses or *padroni.* The main function of the *padroni,* in the early decades of Italian immigration, was to secure manpower for the burgeoning railroad and construction industries at the cheapest price. Italian workers often found themselves exploited as contract laborers or employed as strikebreakers in return for an advance payment for their passage to America.

This collision of social ambitions, fueled by a mythical image of America as the "Golden Land," with the reality of relentless work and poverty constitutes one of the paradoxes of Italian immigrant life that Farfariello continuously explores. In his acts, the middle-class tropes of the "darkness" and "daylight," or "mysteries" and "miseries," of urban life are reconfigured in the alternating "Dream" and "Nightmare" worlds his characters experience. Indeed, in his performances, Migliaccio returns the grotesque imagery of the urban gothic, in which the mask hides and deceives—an expression of the subjective, individualized world invented by Romanticism—back to its original source, the folk carnival and its aesthetic of grotesque realism. Whereas the "petty realism" of the urban guidebooks constructs its types as "mere mask" and signifies a view of life as "alien," in grotesque realism the mask is connected to "transition, metamorphoses, the violation of natural boundaries." Grotesque realism is, as Mikhail Bakhtin writes, based on a "peculiar interrelation of reality and image, characteristic of the most ancient rituals and practices," and expresses a world in which the *"interior infinite"* of the individual, with its suggestion of depth and complexity, is as yet unknown. Whereas the Romantic grotesque in the urban gothic views reality as "nocturnal and frightening," grotesque realism is characterized by a celebratory double vision, which connects life and death, destruction and renewal, in an ongoing process of regeneration and creation.[17]

In Migliaccio's performances, this double vision emerges in the twinned image of heaven/hell. In one sketch, Farfariello, as Pagliaccio, a traditional Italian "fool" figure, recounts his arrival in New York, where his encounter with a construction site, a typical job for Italian immigrants, turns a vision of paradise into one of inferno: "What a big city, New York. When I saw the palaces rising up to the sky I told myself I must have gone to Paradise, without having noticed. But then I saw men who were working in a deep pit, between water and dynamite and all sorts of pipes, and although I first thought that they were in Paradise, it dawned upon me that they must have been summoned to hell."[18]

In another sketch, entitled "Il Mio Compare" (My Friend), Farfariello voices his anger at his "compare," who has told him fairy tales about "Neviorca" (New York):

This imbecile friend of mine told me that in America
You can scoop up the money from the street . . .
And this imbecile also told me: "Friend, Neviorca is truly a paradise . . ."
But here if you walk and don't pay attention,
You will meet a sudden death in an accident.
The houses are higher than a thousand feet,
And seem about to fall on your neck.
Trains run as fast as the wind,

In the sky, on the ground, under the palaces,
Machines, cars, dogs, fools.[19]

Texts such as these evoke the sense of sensory bombardment and shock stimulated by the lights, noise, traffic, and crowds of the burgeoning metropolis. But the Paradise of the New World also disintegrates under the pressure of linguistic confusion. "I flew, and I flew," Farfariello tells about a dream he had, in the skit "Che Suonno!" ("What a Dream!") "And suddenly I found myself in a new world, but it was not paradise anymore, it was the Tower of Babel, a sort of Nueva Yorca (New York), they talked all kinds of languages. . . . I did not understand a word."[20]

Farfariello's characters, moreover, exteriorize a double vision that results from the experience of immigration itself. His humor plays with the dilemmas of what constitutes a viable identity in the New World, publicly confronting questions that immigrants had to face privately: which traditional cultural patterns and moral prescriptions they could, or should, retain and pass on to the next generation. Through Farfariello, we enter the ambivalent moral universe of these immigrants.

One source of conflict was the degree to which immigrants should transfer their allegiance to their new country. Immigrants often perceived the pressure to Americanize, exerted by immigration officials, social workers, and certain *prominenti* or public personas within the Italian community, as a threat to their central values and identity. At the same time, the efforts on the part of mostly middle-class Italian Americans to replace regional allegiances with a communal identity based on the concept of "Italianità" were viewed with suspicion as well.

In the skit "Il Presidente del Club F.F.," Farfariello appears in the guise of a well-known type in Italian immigrant communities: the "president" of an immigrant reform club, which aims to introduce Italian immigrants to American customs and values. The "Presidente" takes a condescending attitude toward the Italian language and Old World customs and slavishly espouses everything "American." Farfariello ridicules his pretensions of being "Americanized," which consist mostly of a keen awareness of the value of "profit":

I have been the first to profit
From my compatriots by forming this club.
And I waste my time by playing the maestro over them
And turning them into fools like myself . . .

In our "clubbo" a man, for $50 per month,
Learns to speak the mother tongue, "ingrese,"
Because I present them every week,
With a bit of American parlance.
This club is not like American clubs,
Which are for diversion only.
Our club is to teach our "paesani"
To accustom to this society.
Because every member of our clubbo,
Must make it out of here as a gentleman.

After this refrain, the president starts instructing his pupils in a stream of nonsensical phrases, emphasizing that "Dis club coste moni ed evri bari moste givve moni . . . allraite!"—a command that is received by his students by applause and "Bravos."[21] In "Il Cafone Patriota," Farfariello reverses the situation and portrays a "cafone" (peasant or "boor"), who displays an exaggerated allegiance to Italy, chastises his friend who never speaks Italian because he perceives that as humiliating, and interrupts his speech with shouts of "Viva L'Italia."[22]

But perhaps even more profound was the conflict over moral values and ethical prescriptions that the confrontation with American culture engendered within the Italian immigrant community, and particularly between first-generation immigrants and their children. America was perceived as a place of license and transgression of traditional moral and ethical codes. As such, it evoked deeply ambivalent responses. On the one hand, defiance of the traditional Italian social and moral order often was an implicit, if not explicit, motivation for the act of immigration itself. On the other, it contained a threat of moral and social disintegration.[23]

This ambivalence is registered in much of Farfariello's repertoire. In his sketches, American society is mapped by contrasting a topography of transgressive spaces, such as "Drimilando" (Dreamland) at "Cunailando" (Coney Island) or "Brode" (Broadway), with spaces representing traditional values, social stability, and security, such as Italy, Mulberry Street, and "la casa," home and domain of the family. Farfariello's oscillation between these different spaces corresponds to the reality of his Italian immigrant audiences, a reality that, according to Robert Orsi, was made up of "numerous interrelated levels of conflict, ambivalence, and desire."[24]

The Italian American community was, as Orsi calls it, a "domus-centered society," in which standards of self-worth and success were defined according to the values and moral standards of the extended family. Individuals were supposed to submit their personal wishes and decisions to the authority and scrutiny of the family and respect and defer to the family hierarchy in social and moral decisions.[25] The "domus" was, in many ways, what defined the boundaries of Italian American culture. It was strongly contrasted with America, a place of "loose morals," where the values of the family and its very existence were felt to be endangered. Many immigrants feared that the lure of going "the American Way," which meant discarding traditional values and placing individual self-interest before the interests of the family, would result in the collapse of their entire social order.[26]

The second generation experienced the conflict between the Italian American and the American world much more directly than their parents. American born or raised, they often derived their conceptions of prestige, success, and romance from American society, while their deepest values and sensibilities were shaped, and mostly remained loyal to, traditional Italian American values. At home, family loyalty and obligations were the cultural resources that were used to navigate everyday life. Outside the home, the environment demanded a more malleable self, one that was sensitive to the power of surface impressions and the importance of style in a world of strangers and fleeting impressions. While at home, the expression of selfhood was curbed by the demands of the family; outside, the modern metropolis seduced the second generation to explore individuality, independence, and personal distinction. The two generations clashed above all over matters that concerned the continuity of the family: relations between the sexes, including dating, courtship, sexuality, and marriage. Although Italian custom dictated that such family affairs needed to be closely monitored, the modern American perspective on romance held that this was where one's individuality was most vividly expressed.[27]

Parks, subways, social clubs, the beaches and Luna Park of Coney Island, and city streets like Broadway were to some extent removed from the surveillance of the family. These spaces became registers of the desires that had to be repressed in the sphere of the home. It is exactly this "geography of rebellion" that Farfariello replicates in his performances.[28] In his moral ecology, these American public spaces are emblematic of transgression, and as such they are typically contrasted with "home," the base of traditional Italian norms and values.

Farfariello captures the intoxicating atmosphere of Broadway, a dreamscape of modernity, in an early song:

Broadway
Dream of all, celebrated street
Most luminous trail of New York
O, variegated crowd which does not know
how to find the way home, and comes and goes.
Broadway . . .
Dream of the entire world,
of living, enjoying
all the happiness
all the perversity
you are the source
that will never extinguish.[29]

But Broadway also seduces one to get drunk with excitement and lose one's head. In his song "Portame 'a casa mia" ("Bring Me Home") Farfariello plays with the dark side of the phantasmagoria of Broadway:

I don't know why I ever thought
of going to Brodue.
I had never been there.
I wanted to go and see
the thousands of lights
turn here and there
making your head spin.
At home, it seemed to me,
that I wanted some fun.
But now I'm broke.
I don't know anymore where I am.
It hasn't become me well, I think,
that last glass.
Who can tell me, please,
the way to my home."[30]

Another favorite setting is Coney Island, a carnivalesque place of license. In "Le Donne a Cunailando" ("The Women at Coney Island"), Farfariello, the physiognomist, reads the bodies of the female bathers, contrasting the erotically suggestive behavior of women of various ethnic backgrounds with the prudishness of the "Italiana":

It's a great pleasure to go to Cunailando,
between all those beautiful signorine,
there are things to see, that heat the blood,
when these beautiful daughters, go to take a bath.
Courageous the "Americana,"
moves away from the beach,
not minding certain impertinent fish,
that like the taste of human flesh.
The Jewish women, after their swim,
drape themselves on the sand,
in their sticky costumes,
and show what they have to everyone.
L'Italiana prefers to take her bath at home . . .[31]

Coney Island is also the favorite setting for young couples to carry out their clandestine affairs, risking the wrath of the family. In "Iammo a Cunailando" ("Let's Go to Coney Island"), Mamie's boyfriend tries to persuade her to escape from her family's control:

Hey Mamie, this is a beautiful day,
You go and close yourself up in a shop?
Don't listen, let's go away,
Afterwards, we'll have a drink. . . .
Let's go, your mother went out shopping . . . and your father
I saw him,—no offense Mamie—
Standing on a street corner shining shoes. . . .
I want to show you Luna Park,
Everything is electricity! . . .
What do you say, are you coming or not? . . .
Your brother the shoemaker doesn't count:
Right now he's already drunk on whiskey! . . .
I'll take you to the Loop the Loop and then to a dance. . . .
If your mother complains,
Tell her: Hey mama,
When you were in the old country . . . even you enjoyed
Being with papa![32]

In another sketch, described in the *Corriere della Sera* of 1918 as "a story about a slightly intoxicated person recounting his sensations of an outing to Coney Island," "Nik" takes "Meri" to Coney Island, where they both have never been before, to see "all those American tricks," which otherwise you can experience only during "Mardi Gras."

"Orioppo!" ["Hurry Up!"], Nik tells Meri. "Come nda!" ["Come down."]
"Mai matera no uante." ["My mother does want it."]
"Ezze natingo, Iu' come giuste seme." ["That's nothing, you come just the same."]

At Coney Island, Nik recounts, they are completely bewildered by the crowds, "tu mocce piple de gente" ("too much people of persons"), the many lights ("quanta lumere"), and the entertainments of Luna Park. They marvel at the attractions: spots where lovers are supposed to embrace ("Meri said to me, 'Nik lok, lok!' ['Look, look!'] and we did the same"); a woman weighing 600 pounds; another with four legs; the "Stipleacciso" (Steeplechase) with the wind machine that blows up Meri's skirt. When they return home, Meri, fearing her mother, is on the verge of crying. "No be freddo, Meri" ("Don't be afraid, Mary"), Toni tells her. "Gecco" ("Jack"), Mary's brother, is already waiting for the couple, ready to defend his sister's honor with his fists. The police interfere in the fight, and would almost have arrested them, if not for Meri's pleading: "Misto police ezze nating" ("Mister police, it's nothing").[33]

America invited men and women to pursue their ambitions and desires and transform themselves. In doing so, it often utterly estranged the familiar. America, according to one of the characters in Garibaldi Lapolla's novels, was "a strange land . . . where things are topsy-turvy."[34] In the United States, social orders could be reversed: the first could be the last, and the last could be the first. Farfariello pokes fun at this reordering of hierarchies, which was a staple of carnival and other popular festive forms. In a sketch entitled "Il Barone Cameriere" ("The Baron Waiter"), the grotesque subject is an Italian "barone" who has squandered all his money on women, and now, in the United States, is forced to earn his living as a waiter, a job at which he proves himself utterly incompetent. Still, the baron waiter keeps boasting to his customers of his illustrious forbears and his family tree going back to the Medici. His absurdity consists of his failure to perceive that in America, noble descent is of no value whatsoever. In the reversible world of America, he is exposed for what he is—a weak, whiny, pretentious failure:

I am reduced to the level of waiter,
Cruel destiny, malediction . . .

Who would ever have dared to utter the prediction,
That there would be a day,
when I would be reduced to play,
at being a waiter.[35]

A similar theme informs "'O Bloffo," or "The Bluffer," a sketch about a marquis who thinks he can still cash in his Old World social prerogatives, but whose real situation is revealed by the last line, a request for a cigarette:

More than one who knows me, asks me:
"Marquis, you're here?"... with surprise....
This country doesn't impress me
with these big buildings with banners....
My castles are taller.
Half the city of Naples is mine...
I used to light cigars with bills of a thousand lire
and I still wear suits that everyone admires...
Who has a cigarette?[36]

But in the paradoxical world of Italian immigrants, the desire for achievement and material success and an admiration for those who had "made America" coexisted with a deep-seated fear that success would turn one into a "cafone." "Cafone," literally meaning "peasant," carried the negative connotation of "boor." A cafone displayed a behavior that contravened the traditional values of the family and the community. He was a person without "any sense of dignity, ill-mannered, shiftless, with no interest in life."[37] In the words of one immigrant, a cafone was "rough, ill mannered. He showed no interest for the traditions of the family and the society. When he could get away with it he did not consider the rights or feelings of other people. He had no ideal to rise to. He was an unfeeling clod, too dull to think of the finer things in life. He was engrossed merely in material pursuits. Nothing was sacred to him. A man with no soul."[38]

Farfariello portrays the cafone in a variety of social situations, in which he is always out of place, and slightly ridiculous as a result. In "'O Cafone c'a Sciammeria" (The Country Bumpkin in Tuxedo), Farfariello portrays an opportunistic social upstart, who proclaims that he likes America because here everybody is equal, no one is better than him, one can do away with morals, one can trade in one's wife and get another, and one can go to Cunailando.

Dezze bicose Franci' ("That's why, Franky")
Me laiche dis contri. ("I like this country")[39]

If the cafone in "'O Cafone c'a Sciammeria" embraces his new country because of the "equality" (and moral license) it offers, the "Cafone Patriota"
(The Patriotic Cafone) remains so dedicated to his mother country and
language, that he ruins his interview for his citizenship by refusing to learn
a word of English and by constantly interjecting the phrase "Viva L'Italia!"

The cafone, as someone from a lower-class background, is often very
human, if laughable in his desire for a change of fortune. In "'O Spuorto 'e
Mulberry Stritto," Farfariello portrays a bouncer who stands on Mulberry
Street all day long while daydreaming of being upgraded to a position as
bouncer on "Brodue." There, as he imagines himself among the luxurious
life of furs and sports cars, it is appearance and style—and his distinguished
doorman costume—that counts, not his origins as a "cafone":

> But what a fool I am. . . . Here I stand,
> on Mulberry Stritto day and night,
> As if there existed in Nuovo Yorca,
> only this street and nothing more. . . .
> At Brodue they value you,
> when you walk with a stick, like I did, a *bastone,*
> But here they look down on me,
> Because I am, and remain still, a *cafone.*[40]

In the reversible world of Farfariello's America, where ambition creates
the winners, it is the cafone who rises to the top, as the song "La Sciabola"
indicates. The humor of the song, Emelise Aleandri and Maxine Schwartz-
Seller point out, lies in the pun on the word "sciabola," which means "sabre"
and thus has upper-class connotations, but that had come to mean "shovel"
in America, reflecting the predominance of Italian immigrants in the construction business.

> This new world is upside down
> And the cafone here can smile
> For the coat of arms has no renown
> And callouses are in style
> There the signore raises his sabre ["sciabola"]

when his sacred honor's hurt
But here the shovel ["sciabola"] is used in labor
And raises mostly dirt.[41]

In many sketches, the cafone is the social upstart whose behavior continues to betray his lowly origins. In "Il Cafone Arrichito" (The Italian American Banker, or the Greenhorn Who Got Rich), Farfariello, according to one account, "staggers onto the miniature stage in a half-tipsy condition, as though he were just leaving one of those innumerable Italian banquets. In reality he is an ignorant peasant, but fortune has smiled upon him here, opening a new world prosperity which has gone to his head quite as much as the wine. . . . Having become rich, he is full of conceit but faithful to his ignorance and his linguistic blunders."[42]

In a similar vein, "Il Cafone Presidente della Società e della Festa a Sant'Antonio" (The Greenhorn President of the Social Club and of the Festival of Saint Anthony), presents "a typical conceited colonial show off [who] got drunk to the disgrace of the many insignias, badges, buttons, sashes and cockades that cover his inflated chest," after having pocketed the profits of the refreshments and entertainments provided at the *festa*.[43]

But in his grotesqueness, the cafone also often speaks a fool's truth, as in the case of "Lu Cafone c'a Ragione" (The Cafone Who Is Right), who takes issue with Americans' prejudice against Italian immigrants:

Today in this land here the American man
is in charge, and he can do anything he wants to you;
therefore when he sees an Italian,
even if he were a King, he would call him a dago
I say, for what reason
do you offend Italians? . . .
What Americans do here
not even pigs do where I come from:
they blow their noses with their hands,
right in the street . . . and we are ghinnys?!
With tobacco in their mouths,
they eat lunch! . . .
They say, we are sons of macaroni!
. . . They fill their bellies with potatoes
And then they throw up in your face! . . .
We are sons of macaroni?!

So then the Americans
are a bunch of sons of . . . potatoes.[44]

Regardless of the role, the cafone in Farfariello's acts is always more
grotesque than despicable. This is either because his version of the American Dream is extremely absurd or because he has not yet quite mastered
the new social and cultural codes to match his newly acquired status in
society. Despite the airs he puts on, he remains a "cafone" in the core of his
being.

In Farfariello's vision, it is the history of dislocation and the paradoxes
of Italian immigrant life that produce this disjunction and enables him to
create the grotesque subjects he preferably portrays. His humor, according
to a review in *Il Popolo* on January 20, 1924, "always takes as its basis the
grotesqueness of life itself."[45] It is in this affinity between Farfariello's impersonations on the stage and the grotesque reality of immigrant life that we
must look for the deeper meanings of Farfariello's performances.

GROTESQUE REALITY

Reviewers tended to attribute Farfariello's popularity among Italian American audiences to the "true-to-life" aspect of his acts and the verisimilitude
of his impersonations.[46] This apparent "realism" may be one clue to Farfariello's fame. His sketches and jokes were intensely context-bound, expressing the social and cultural situation in which they occurred and were
performed. They can best be described as a kind of microsocial analysis of
the conflicting realities in which Italian immigrants found themselves.

Migliaccio, like the flâneur, found the raw material for his acts on the
streets of Little Italy, in its social relations, moral codes, and collective fantasies. Sitting at his corner table at the Caffe Ronca, he "would sip his black
coffee with anisette [and] studied the types and characters that some days
later had new life on the stage."[47] As the chronicler, or "cronaca," of "everyday life in the Italian American immigrant community," Farfariello, in his
continuously expanding catalogue of Italian immigrant types, externalized
and mediated their hopes, ambitions, and anxieties.[48]

But for all its referential exactness, Farfariello's comedy refused a drama
of interiority and depth. His typologies of immigrant types are caricatures,
their reality inflected with hyperbole, exaggeration, and parody. He even
ridiculed the physiognomic disposition itself in his portrayal of "'O Scarparo" (The Shoemaker), who considers himself an expert in "scarpalogia"

or the "physiognomy of the shoe" (a knowledge "inbred" because of the boot-like shape of Italy), and reads the owner's character from the way the shoe has worn.[49] His' was the language of what Mikhail Bakhtin has termed "grotesque realism," the language of the carnivalesque. As a "comical interpreter" of the Italian immigrant community, to use the description of the *Progresso Italiano*, he "interprets [it] with a grain of salt, revealing its caricatural level."[50] It is this observation that brings us to a second level of meaning upon which Farfariello operates, the level of metacommentary and self-reflexivity.

Farfariello presented his audience with a cultural performance, which John MacAloon has described as "occasions in which we as a culture or society reflect upon and define ourselves, dramatize our collective myths and history, and present ourselves with alternatives, and eventually change in some ways while remaining the same in others."[51] The privileged languages of this form of metacommentary are irony, parody, travesty, mockery, and paradox: the languages of the joker, the trickster, and the clown, who comment critically on what they represent literally.

Caricature, parody, and irony are the languages of heterodoxy, which reveal that which is contradictory and ambiguous, and overflow the conventional boundaries of the "real." These metalanguages of humor highlight gaps of meaning rather than continuities, offering, in the words of Edmund Burke, a "perspective by incongruity." In transitional periods in particular, what is defined as "reality" turns into a grotesque version of itself, and the cultural need to scrutinize and evaluate the changing nature of what is understood as reality increases. Paradox, reversibility, and indeterminacy of meaning are in themselves consequences and expressions of a discontinuous world.[52]

The experience of social and cultural alienation that tends to accompany the act of (im)migration produces an acute sense of incongruity and paradox and fosters a particular form of humor. Characteristic of ethnic humor is a "constant double vision," which juxtaposes two or more cultural contexts. Another feature of ethnic humor is the interplay between the "minor" and the "major" language, the language of the country of origin and that of the adopted country, which itself encodes social and cultural differences. Ethnic humor, moreover, tends to be preoccupied with social roles and status categories, often in a decidedly self-deprecating form. This preoccupation might be attributed to what Michael Fischer has characterized as "ethnic anxiety," which is fueled by the alienation from a former self, and a strong apprehension about the proper and competent performance of new or transformed social roles.[53]

In each society, what is understood as the self is to a large extent a performative effect. Acts, gestures, and enactments, Judith Butler argues, repetitively manufacture and sustain the illusion of an authentic, interior reality, an "essence," of which they purportedly are the corporeal expression. The acts and gestures that institute "the integrity of the subject" are a "function of a decidedly public and social discourse, the public regulation of fantasy through the surface politics of the body."[54] Every culture proscribes the conventions of behavior appropriate to, as well as techniques for adequately performing, specific social roles. Mimetic behavior, Benjamin reminds us, is a central mechanism in the process of perceiving and learning these role patterns.[55] In times of rapid social and cultural transformation, however, individuals tend to become increasingly sensitive to the disjunction between their private and public selves. This creates an intuitive awareness about the performative nature of social identities and of the signifying system that forms the basis of identities and structures of social distinction.

The prevalence of "types" on the ethnic stage, in Farfariello's performances and in ethnic humor more generally, owes much to this increased sensitivity to the coded nature of social roles. By condensing and hyperbolizing familiar aspects of real behavior, such as dress, gestures, and speech mannerisms, Farfariello's humor constructs types as symbolic indexes of the immigrant world. Not only does it offer ethnic audiences visual clues to help decipher a chaotic and opaque environment, but the combination of mimesis and hyperbole in his impersonations provides a means of instructing audiences in the "proper" execution of these roles, as it were by default—through the example of clumsiness and incompetence. In that sense, Farfariello's performances functioned in ways not dissimilar to the mid- and late nineteenth-century etiquette books and urban guidebooks that defined the codes and boundaries of middle-class identity.

Farfariello's routines also instructed immigrants in street smarts, as the urban guidebooks did as well. In one sketch, "Pasquale Passaguai" (Pasquale the Troublemaker), Farfariello described "the ordeal of an immigrant who wants to return to Italy after having saved through hard labor a hoard of money, which two swindlers steal from him with the familiar trick of the valise and the substitution of the package of money with a package of foreign paper."[56] According to one anecdote, the sketch had its unexpected result in a visit to Migliaccio by two crooks warning him to cut the act, explaining that it interfered with their business: while they were in the middle of pulling the valise trick on a naive immigrant returning to Naples with his savings, the immigrant suddenly realized that he was the target of two confidence

men, yelling, "Madonna santa, questa è la macchietta di Farfariello, di Pasquale Passaquai!" ("Holy Mother Mary, this is Farfariello's sketch, Pasquale
Passaguai!").[57]

The Italian American press frequently celebrated Migliaccio for his mor-
alizing achievements. "Castigat ridendo mores," or "satire educates," is the
expression widely used by the middle-class Italian reviewers of Migliaccio's
performances.[58] "Farfariello educates, morally as well as socially," was the
opinion of the *Progresso Italo-Americano*, "poiche anche il grottesco educa,"
because the grotesque educates as well.[59] Apocryphal stories detailed how
corrupt mafiosi or community leaders came to repent and then reformed
after seeing themselves parodied on the stage.

The "educating" role attributed to Farfariello's humor undoubtedly owes
much to the social biases of Italian American journalists. Farfariello never
tired of lampooning the languages of "official" knowledge or status. Nevertheless, by ridiculing excesses and extremes in Italian immigrant behavior,
Migliaccio implicitly projected a middle ground. His performances articulated a very specific "moral economy," to use James Scott's term, an agenda
of moral and cultural values he deemed absolutely essential to a viable Italian American notion of selfhood and community.[60]

Indeed, in that sense, Migliacio's performances may have helped to transform his audience, immigrants who identified primarily with regional or
local Italian cultures, into a community sharing a common Italian American identity. This process of ethnogenesis might have operated on three
levels. In his own morphological genesis, Farfariello merged different clown
traditions into a generic "Italian American" clown, whose kaleidoscopic
consciousness could interpret a wide range of Italian immigrant experiences. In his burlesque use of "Italian Americanese," Farfariello gave official
status to an ethnic language invented in communications with Americans
but also with fellow Italians, who, speaking their own regional dialects,
were often unintelligible to one another. But Farfariello's role as a cultural
broker was not only the result of the content of his humor. To a significant
extent, it was an effect of his status as a clown.

Clowns, Liminality, and Self-Transformation

The clown, according to Don Handelman, is one of the ritual figures to
emerge in the liminal phase of rituals of transformation. Clowns are profoundly ambivalent figures, which arise in situations of incongruity, when
regular norms and role patterns disintegrate and fail to provide coherent

explanations of reality and adequate paradigms for social action. In their attributes, clowns reflect the context out of which they emerge.[61]

The humorous effect of clowns is caused by their deviation from "normal" roles and social norms; their incoherence follows their oscillation between different systems of meaning and their inability to maintain one steady point of view. Playing with inconsistencies of meaning, misunderstandings between people, and misinterpretations of reality, they deconstruct a culture's key categories of meaning and invoke a deep sense of reflexivity.

But ritual clowns do not only reflect their context. As a result of their attributes, they play a key role in moving a ritual of transformation from a liminal state toward its resolution. Rites of transformation involve the reordering and translation of one context or structure of meaning, in terms of another, in such a way that the new, transformed ordering connects the two contexts in a coherent way and resolves the inherent contradictions between the two states, roles, or cultures.

Clowns come adequately prepared for their roles as mediators between different contexts. Internally, they are able to hold, and shift between, various worlds and orders of existence. They typically juxtapose different systems of meaning and role patterns. By letting these contexts reflect upon each other, they ultimately prepare for a resolution of the contradictions and conflicts of the in-between state. They do this by establishing a relationship of analogy between themselves and those undergoing the ritual transformation, imbuing those participating in the ritual with their attributes of ambivalence and contradiction, and creating a liminal "communitas," which they then guide toward a return from disorder to order.[62]

Farfariello performs a similar mediating role. Oscillating between his different immigrant types, in his (grotesque) body and language he reflected, and reflected on, the various contexts fracturing the Italian immigrant experience. As reviewers never tired to emphasize, the universe that Farfariello created in his acts found its analogy in the "piccolo mondo un po' deformata," the "slightly deformed world" that these immigrants, with their "psicologia un po' grottesca," their "slightly grotesque psychology," inhabited.[63] Given this relationship of analogy, the nature of the identification and symbolic interaction between Italian immigrant audiences and the clown Farfariello comes into clearer relief.

In their state of being in-between-worlds, Italian immigrants found a figurative analogue for their experience of social and cultural alienation in the humor of Farfariello, who, in his parodies, reframed reality as grotesque and absurd. Just as immigrants became others, strangers, to themselves, so did Farfariello's impersonations and parodies estrange the familiar—the broad range of characters and personalities that served as his prototypes. By replicating and magnifying, through irony and parody, the inner experience of these immigrants on the stage, Farfariello functioned as an extension and externalization of these immigrants' selves. His impersonations, mixing the familiar and, through his grotesque inflections, the strange, presented an ambiguous image that, on a subconscious level, must have resonated with a double and ambiguous sense of self on the part of his audience.

In the reflexive surface of Farfariello's mirror, Italian immigrants became both subject and objects to themselves, became their own inner audience, looking at their own split selves, the roles they played in everyday life, as it were through the eyes of an Other. Farfariello's mimicry, then, mimicked and enacted what Steven Mullaney has called the "art of alienation": the power to project an image upon the Other, which causes the Other to see himself through the eyes of the majority culture. But these eyes were simultaneously the laughing eyes of a clown. By way of Farfariello, their Other but yet their self, these immigrants could conduct a dialogue with themselves about their experiences.[64]

The most important juxtaposition that Farfariello played with, and rendered ambiguous, was the one that divides the "real" from the "theatrical." By impersonating immigrant types that were often recognizably modeled after well-known personalities, Farfariello limned the boundary between theater and reality. It is between these lines, at the site of mimicry, that his most troubling double vision emerges.[65]

Farfariello's mimicry mocks the promise of "imitation" as the trajectory to "authentic" selfhood. Such a promise was held out by social theorists such as Gabriel Tarde, who argued in his *Laws of Imitation* (1890) that assimilation proceeds "from the inner to the outer man, and starts with the "imitation of beliefs" and "imitation of desires" of one class or group of people by another, followed by the "imitation of tastes." Commodity culture offered the same promise: the desire for self-transformation and social mobility through the cultivation of external appearance (style and manners), which the machine would make available to the masses.[66]

The mimicry of Farfariello rearticulates, and in doing so exposes, the difference between "American" and "Americanized." It reveals the concealed knowledge of the "lack" that informs and structures the desire for the Ideal (American) self and enacts, in the form of Farfariello's continuous transmogrification, the repetition compulsion that lies at the base of the desire for self-transformation. It enacts *and* parodies the "knowledge" of sociologists like Jerome Dows and Charles Ellwood, who doubt the validity of Tarde's theories on the basis of the "innate instincts" of different races that cannot be transformed by "superficial" imitation.[67]

But while this subterranean knowledge, in David Levinsky, produces a split self that is experienced as inauthentic, tragic, and estranged, in Farfariello's grotesque realism it produces laughter. In his double vision, self-estrangement, the result of immigration and the exigencies of consumer culture, produces not *actors,* but *clowns.* Farfariello enacted this transformation in his performances. By assuming the roles of well-known types within the Italian immigrant community, he contaminated these figures with his clown virus. As a result, Farfariello spilled over into the context of his performance, imbuing reality with his own grotesque qualities. Under the weight of his lampooning, everyman was transformed into a clown. Through this leveling effect, Farfariello transformed his audience into a community bound together by a shared immigrant experience, cemented by a comic language, and sharing the alternative reality of the carnivalesque.[68]

DAVID WARFIELD.

13 and 15 WEST 24TH ST. N.Y.
MADISON SQUARE

Impersonating the ghetto Jew: David Warfield as Simon Levi. "David Warfield," 1897. Photograph by B. J. Falk, Museum of the City of New York, Theater Collection.

Chapter 6

My Other/My Self

Impersonation and the Rehearsal of Otherness

"THE VAUDEVILLE THEATRE," EDWARD ROYLE OBSERVED IN 1899, "belongs to the era of the department store and the short story. It may be a kind of lunch-counter art, but then the art is so vague and the lunch is so real."[1] With the department store and the short story, vaudeville was perhaps the most eloquent expression of the complexities of turn-of-the-nineteenth-century American metropolitan culture. Vaudeville's roots in urban life were reflected in the term "vaudeville," which originally derived from the French expression *voix de ville*, or voice of the city, the term for urban folk songs.[2] But city culture also structured vaudeville's morphology and aesthetic.

The consensus of contemporary writers who studied the impact of the experience of the modern, industrial metropolis on the mental and social organization of the city dweller was that it produced a profound disturbance in the individual's nervous system and energy level. Writing about the transformation of Berlin from big city to world city, Georg Simmel, in his famous lecture "The Metropolis and Mental Life" (1903) pointed to the urban "intensification of nervous life, which proceeds from the rapid and uninterrupted fluctuation of external and internal impressions" as the source of a profound alteration in "the psychological foundation" of the self in the city. The sensory barrage that accompanied "every walk across the street," combined "with the tempo and multiplicity of economic, professional and social life," caused human nervousness to respond so violently and brutally that nervous exhaustion, a jaded reaction to any impulse, and a need for ever-more extreme excitement were the net results. Consumption and amusements such as variety, that "growing concatenation of heterogeneous impressions" and "increasingly hasty and motley fluctuation of stimulations," catered to nerves that were overstimulated but underfed by an increasing monotony in the realm of labor.[3]

In a similar vein, Walter Benjamin wrote of modern (metropolitan) man as a "man cheated out of his experience." Here too, shock, the norm of everyday life in the city, is the culprit, and the mechanical conditioning of man is its correlate. Taking his cues from Marxist and psychoanalytic theory, Benjamin argued that human consciousness, like a bumper, parries the shocks experienced by the walker in the crowd and the assembly-line worker, and gradually becomes desensitized. It engages impressions and sensations that are experienced as shocking on the level of reflex, rather than letting them penetrate into conscious experience as a traumatic effect.[4]

Modern technology continues to recapture the moment of shock. Technological innovations are at the same time new "innervations" that respond to the city-rooted need for strong stimulation. Where photography "delivers a posthumous shock to the moment," film "makes shock the formal principle of perception."[5] Although these new technologies participate in the ongoing training and inoculation of the human sensorium, Benjamin detected in the new media a utopian potential. In film, photography, and recording, technological reproduction reverses the contraction of time and the fragmentation of space brought about by technological production.[6] Writes Benjamin: "Our taverns and our metropolitan streets, our offices and furnished rooms, our railroad stations and our factories appeared to have us locked up hopelessly. Then came the film and burst this prison-world asunder by the dynamite of the tenth of a second, so that now, in the midst of its fur-flung ruins and debris, we calmly and adventurously go traveling."[7]

Innovations such as photography, film, and impressionist painting reflect the degree of sophistication of the urban eye, trained for decades on the "daily sight of a moving crowd." They are a testament to the power of mimicry as "cognitive apparatus." Benjamin specifically attributed an educational if not revolutionary potential to film's capacity for constructing a new "time-space" through the process of montage, which at once mimics the fragmentation of experience and redeems it.[8]

It is not surprising that many modernists saw in vaudeville an intense expression of modernity's fragmented consciousness, and celebrated its vitality. While in eighteenth-century France, "vaudeville" signified a combination of comedy and music, by the turn of the nineteenth century it had evolved into a form of entertainment that in its rhythm, polyphony, heterogeneity and its reliance on quickness, gags, and punch lines dramatized the diversity, tempo, and intensity of modern urban life.[9] Structured as the "unfolding" of urban space in "temporal succession," it was designed to showcase as much variety and spectacle as possible: a typical vaudeville bill featured magic tricks, ventriloquists, pet tricks, tramp impersonations, song-and-dance routines, transvestite acts, minstrelsy, and dialect comedy acts.[10]

Sergei Eisenstein regarded vaudeville's aesthetic fragmentation and emotional intensity as a source of inspiration for his own filmic concept of a "montage of attractions." The futurist Filippo Marinetti called vaudeville, or "variety," "the crucible in which the elements of an emergent new sensibility are seething." Variety was everything that bourgeois, realist theater was not. It could boast of "no tradition, no masters, no dogma," other than "swift actuality." Where realist theater "vacillates stupidly between historical reconstruction . . . and photographic reproduction of our daily life," variety, "born as we are from electricity," offered speed and "astonishment."[11]

For the Bavarian playwright Oskar Panizza, modern urban culture itself was infused with the spirit of the variety show. This spirit, which he designated as the "poetry of the people," with its complete absence of respect for moral or aesthetic norms and its total lack of social consciousness, happily destroyed the "aura of classicism." In its "absolute naïveté in the use of artistic media," its "crudest (because unselfconscious) use of make up and powder, of lipstick and eyelash black, of tutus and tights," the art of vaudeville was one of "sparkling joy, childish enthusiasm, and purest delight in the result."[12]

Vaudeville was indeed a product of the machine age, in its notion of theatrical production as well as its aesthetics. Celebrating "infinite diversity in infinite combinations," individual vaudeville acts were interchangeable, and their juxtaposition within a vaudeville bill was geared toward delivering the greatest shock, punch, and climax. The lack of direction in vaudeville production made the individual performer the creative force as well as the manager of his own act. Facing intense competition to grab the footlights, performers honed their acts to showcase their individual "specialties."[13]

"A comedian in vaudeville," Eddie Cantor explained in 1924, "is like a salesman who has only fifteen minutes in which to make a sale."[14] This brutal economy of time pointed performers toward adopting conventionalized, broadly delineated, instantly recognizable social types. While naturalistic drama, invested in the notion of psychological "immanence" and interiority, required actors to blend into their characters and mask their own peculiarities, vaudeville rewarded actors for showmanship and "their ability to project a unique personality that transcended stock roles." "Conventionality of character" was accepted, but "conventionality of performance" was to be avoided at all costs.[15] "Originality," James J. Morton explained in 1906, was "the first step to recognition. Personality next and an indomitable nerve to withstand criticism last."[16]

VAUDEVILLE AS CULTURAL MIDDLE GROUND

As a form of mass entertainment, American vaudeville drew inspiration from a number of different popular amusements that flourished in the mid-nineteenth century. It combined elements from blackface minstrelsy, Bowery melodrama, and the dime museum with its array of freaks, variety acts, and curiosities.[17] Its immediate predecessor, however, was the concert saloon, which, in the 1850s, dotted the Bowery and Broadway. A smoke-filled tavern, which besides whiskey and beer offered entertainment of a rather questionable allure to its exclusively male, working-class patrons, the concert saloon belonged to what guidebooks referred to as the "shadows" and the "lower depths" of metropolitan life.[18] As such, it was, as Sophie Tucker, nicknamed "last of the red hot mama's" for her spicy songs, explained, "almost forbidden fruit in polite circles where it was regarded as a sort of slumming which must be viewed from behind drawn curtains."[19]

In its very existence, the concert saloon marked the ways in which the growing social and cultural divisions within the city were reinforced by an increasingly stratified cultural life.[20] The diversification of audiences by class, gender, race, and nationality was matched by the diversification of urban space: upper Broadway, with its lavish theaters and opera houses offering entertainment to the rich; the cheap Bowery theaters catering to the working classes and the poor; the foreign-language theaters of the Lower East Side attracting the patronage of the "foreign elements."[21]

The potential economic advantages of reversing this cultural fragmentation were not lost on theatrical managers and entrepreneurs. In the 1870s, the actor-entrepreneur Tony Pastor advertised his shows as being "free of vulgarity," and offered special matinees for women and children and free entrance on Friday night for ladies accompanying gentlemen in an effort to attract the patronage of women and middle-class families. But Pastor's metamorphosis of the concert saloon was far from complete as the theater continued to offer the "best qualities of ales, wines, liquors and cigars, to be had at the saloon inside the theatre."[22]

As Robert Snyder explains, it was left to a following generation of entrepreneurs to carry vaudeville into the age of mass entertainment. In the late 1880s, B. F. Keith and Edward F. Albee hit upon a formula that transformed

what had been mostly a small, localized industry into big business: continuous shows, characterized by an aura of cultural refinement that would
attract a middle-class and female clientele hitherto repelled by the disreputable aspects of the concert saloon, burlesque halls, and the variety theater.

Keith and Albee learned their lessons from the techniques of mass production that laid the groundwork for the evolution of America into a consumer society. Their introduction of the "continuous performance," which
lined up interchangeable acts without logical connection, conformed to the
principle of the "assembly line." Their next move, which was copied by
other theatrical entrepreneurs, such as Proctor, A. L. Erlanger, Sylvester
Poli, Marcus Klaw, and Williams, reflected the empire building of John D.
Rockefeller's Standard Oil and Carnegie's United Steel, which augured the
age of corporate capitalism. The institution of a centralized booking agency,
which maintained a monopoly over booking by regulating the access of theaters to performers and of performers to theaters, combined with the consolidation of a circuit of theaters across the city and the continent, transformed
what had been "small, proprietary and largely itinerant amusements" into
a corporate bureaucracy.[23]

Keith and Albee also borrowed from the idiom of exoticism that accompanied the construction of a consumer-subject. The Orientalist dreamscape of the department store with its intertwining of spectatorship and
display was extended to the vaudeville theater, which was refurbished with
lavishly decorated interiors, stained-glass exteriors, and ushers dressed in
Turkish costume, as if to underscore the fact that in commodity culture
"the stage, with all its paraphernalia of things and clothes and newspaper
celebrity, . . . consists of all the same elements that, in the world outside, go
to the making (up) of a successful individual."[24]

To expand vaudeville's audience, Keith introduced various disciplining
measures. In the refurbished vaudeville houses, one observer remarked in
1899, employees carried around printed placards requesting that "Gentlemen
will kindly avoid the stamping of feet and pounding of canes on the floor,
and greatly oblige the Management. All applause is best shown by clapping
of hands," or that "Gentlemen will kindly avoid carrying cigars or cigarettes
in their mouths while in the building, and greatly oblige The Management."
Another sign read, "Please don't talk during acts, as it annoys those about you,
and prevents a perfect hearing of the entertainment. The Management."[25]

Other measures focused on bowdlerizing the language and contents of
acts themselves, warning performers to refrain from "all vulgarity and sug-
gestiveness in words, action, and costume . . . and all vulgar, double-meaning

and profane words." "Such words as Liar, Slob, Son-of-a-Gun, Devil, Sucker, Damn and all other words unfit for the ears of ladies and children, also any reference to questionable streets, resorts, localities, and bar-rooms, are prohibited under fine of instant discharge."[26]

The success of this strategy of cultural upgrading was reflected in vaudeville's geographical mobility: from disreputable streets and areas on the margins of genteel society, vaudeville theaters moved to the center of the new business districts for shopping and entertainment that were emerging in metropolitan areas. In New York, its center of gravity shifted from Fourteenth Street and Union Square in the 1880s and early 1890s, first to Twenty-third Street, and ultimately to Times Square, which, with the opening of New York's City first subway line in 1904, soon became an urban hotspot.[27]

Secondary vaudeville centers emerged in the Bronx and Brooklyn following the expansion of mass transit and the subsequent migration to the outlying boroughs. From the high-priced Keith-Albee theaters and the roof-gardens frequented by a middle-class clientele to the lower-priced Loew's Theatres on the Lower East Side, catering to Jewish immigrants, "there was a vaudeville theater for practically every type of New Yorker."[28]

The crowning glory of vaudeville, however, Charles R. Sherlock explained in 1901, was the growth of the "roof-garden." The roof-garden, which took the vaudeville spectator, through an elevator shaft, away "from the blistering pavements of a city in a bake-oven to aerial heights," played on the suggestion that this "ascent heavenward" lifted you "above the little conventionalities of everyday life." "Until the stage went up with the elevators, vaudeville may be said to have stood on the ragged edge of theatrical society," Sherlock continued. Now, "with the generous recognition that roof-gardens have given to vaudeville talent," "the patronage of these establishments is not likely to be distinguished from the audiences that uphold grand opera."[29]

Courting a mass audience with a form of entertainment that had something to offer to everyone, vaudeville entrepreneurs created a cultural "middle ground."[30] They were forced to recognize the different aesthetic sensibilities and interests of its various audiences. To its middle-class clientele, it had to appear respectable without losing its illicit edge for those chafing against the constraints of Victorian society. Indeed, for middle-class audiences, a trip to a vaudeville house or roof-garden, Sherlock suggested, evoked "the notion that you are taking a furtive peek in forbidden places. It is something bohemian that you are doing. You are in fascinating propinquity to the gilded sin of a great city. Whether you live in Oshkosh or 'on the Avenue,' you must not mount to a roof-garden without feeling a trifle wicked, or you are sure to miss half the fun."[31]

But vaudeville also had to accommodate the preferences of working-class and immigrant audiences that did not conform to the "canons of gentility" and contain sufficient references to their experiences.[32] This, Edwin Royle explained, could account for the fact that in vaudeville "there is a sameness even about its infinite variety.... Everyone's taste is consulted."[33] In addition, different vaudeville establishments nurtured very different social environments. A performer working for Keith and Albee might encounter middle- and working-class, native and immigrant, male and female audiences, sometimes in the same theater, sometimes in different theaters situated a block away from one another.[34] As Norman Hapgood observed in 1901, "There are two continuous houses on a certain street in New York, within a block of each other.... Sometimes the same person will appear in both places but in general the whole personnel is unlike, the superiority of the performances in tone and ability at one house corresponding to the superior quality of the patrons."[35]

The different levels of vaudeville offered performers, many of whom came from immigrant backgrounds and were attracted by a booming industry requiring little start-up capital or education, a veritable ladder for social mobility. But the possibility to "move up," or even to attain star status by getting top billing at one of the famous vaudeville circuits, required performers to juggle the different linguistic, cultural, and aesthetic sensibilities of the patrons. As a result, vaudeville's texts were flexible and open to revision, often on the instant cue of the audience. Seasoned performers became adept at pitching their acts by "reading" their audiences.[36] They often learned the pitfalls of the trade the hard way. Eddie Cantor, for instance, recalled flopping onstage when he presented an English-language act before an audience of mostly Yiddish speakers. Realizing his mistake, he switched languages and scored:

> We had simply talked to them in the wrong language, and this in a way is every actor's problem in adapting himself to his audience. Drifting as I did into every conceivable crowd, I trained myself to the fact that "the audience is never wrong," and if a performance failed to go across it was either the fault of the material or the manner of presentation. By carefully correcting the one or the other or both with an eye to the peculiarities of the audience I could never fail a second time. I proved this to myself on many occasions later on, when in the same night I'd perform at the Vanderbilt home and then rush down to Loew's Avenue B and be a hit in both places.[37]

As a cultural middle ground, then, vaudeville was intersected by competing and often contradictory, interests. Inevitably, these interests left their traces in the performances themselves.

VOICES OF THE CITY

Vaudeville, according to Gunther Barth, "dramatized the spectrum of humanity in the city and the diversity of its subject matter and variety." Indeed it proposed "models for everyday behavior and guides for living in the modern city." But the relation between the middle class and the city, as we have seen, differed radically from that of the working-class and immigrant groups. As a "guide for living in the modern city," vaudeville was a complex and multivoiced discourse.[38]

One strategy vaudeville entrepreneurs used to create a cultural middle ground was to appropriate the street, using a formula originally devised by P. T. Barnum in the 1850s. In his effort to create a democratic form of entertainment that combined commercialism, republicanism, "respectability," and mass audiences, Barnum "reassembled a fragmented cultural terrain" by making his museum a "mere extension of the street," "containing on one site as many options as possible." Besides freaks, bearded ladies, the legendary dwarf Tom Thumb, and dioramas of Niagara, Dublin, Paris, and Jerusalem, Barnum's dime museum featured enactments of street types such as the Fulton Market Roarer. Moreover, Barnum invited his audience to become part of the exhibit and perform "clog-dances, breakdowns, glees, and imitations of urban types."[39]

On the one hand, the appropriation of street life by an increasingly commercialized popular culture reflected the "democratic" impulse of mass culture. On the other, it played on a social voyeurism that distanced low life as Other, a spectacle existing for the entertainment of the emerging middle classes.[40] This duality persisted in vaudeville as well. The Opera House of Tony Pastor, which opened in 1865, brought the street to the stage in sketches that often echoed the style of the "lights and shadows" guidebooks, inflected, however, with strong class-conscious accents, as this song about the inequities of New York illustrates:

The Upper Ten Thousand in mansions reside,
With fronts of brown stone, and with stoops high and wide
While the Lower Ten Thousand in poverty deep,
In cellars and garrets, are huddled like sheep.

The Upper Ten Thousand have turkey and wine,
On turtle and ven'son and pastry they dine.[41]

Another sketch, "In the Bowery" (1874), contrasted "your Broadway belles, your Fifth Avenue swells, your exquisitely dressed creatures, with their lavender kids, and their la-de-das" with the rough-edged but honest Bowery people.[42]

The interest in street life continued when vaudeville was at its pinnacle. In 1891, the "Irish Queen" Maggie Cline performed a song, "When Hogan Pays the Rent." The song, about an Irish character who never pays his rent, was acclaimed for the "photographic accuracy" with which it set forth "the excitement in his neighborhood on rent day." Pat Rooney, an Irish comedian, performed a sketch "At the News Stand." "The System," a one-act vaudeville play from 1910, presented a story of intrigue, police corruption, thievery, and low life on the Lower East Side.[43]

It was so-called racial or dialect comedy that most explicitly appropriated the borderlands of city streets for the vaudeville stage. Following the settlement of various immigrant groups in America's metropolitan centers, vaudeville gradually expanded its gallery of "racial" types. To the Irish, "Dutch," French, and minstrelsy acts that were regular features on the stage of Pastor's Opera House, it added Italian, Spanish, Chinese, and Hebrew acts, which became increasingly popular in the last decade of the nineteenth century. In these types, vaudeville relied on what Benjamin characterizes as one of the oldest cognitive apparatuses, the "mimetic faculty," to make the city manifest.[44]

In racial comedy's succinct vocabulary of "type," dialect, clothes, attributes, and even different facial paints (which were marketed especially for that purpose) sufficed to signify different nationalities. According to a contemporary makeup manual, the Italian comedian typically wore a bandanna and used an olive-green powder to achieve an "Italian" pigmentation; the "Hebrew" a shallow white; and the "Chinaman" required a special paint labeled in the catalogue as "Mongolian."[45] In the Irishman, "red in some parts seems essential, red cheeks, sometimes red noses and almost invariably red chin whiskers of some description. A turned up nose, made of putty . . . is usually most effective."[46]

In the popular aesthetic of dialect comedy, type operated in the realm of what Mikhail Bakhtin called "grotesque realism." It hinged on exaggeration, excess, and the uncanny. In its insistence on the mask, gesture, and posture, dialect comedy, like the comedy of Migliaccio, was a comedy of exteriority.

Its physiognomy was a "surface phenomenon" rather than a "topography of
a subjectivity . . . inseparably tied to interiorization." Dialect comedy stayed
on the level of surface, feature, and contour because its humor steadily refused empathy. And it is only through empathy, Georg Lukács argued, that
physiognomy is interiorized and becomes inner depth and drama.[47]

But in the discourse of dialect comedy, the type of grotesque realism overlapped significantly with a different hermeneutics of type, one that enlisted
the "sciences" of physiognomy and phrenology to decipher the body, specifically the face and the head, as the indexical sign of the inner character of the
"Other."[48] This hermeneutical paradigm made its appearance specifically in
conjunction with a trend that sought a further cultural upgrading of vaudeville through the appeal to the aesthetics of representational veritism.

Dialect Comedy and the "Real"

As in all humor, dialect comedy did in fact have a strong ethnographic
component. This was reflected in the evolution and popularity of specific
"racial" stage types, which tended to keep up with the degree of social
mobility and the rate of integration of various national groups into American society. The stage Irishman, who by the 1880s outbilled the popular
minstrelsy act, initially appeared as the greenhorn "Paddy." Paddy was made
up with red whiskers and wig and dressed in rough garments dominated
by the color green, which were either too big or too small, his pants tied
around the waist with a piece of rope. As the Irish established a dominant
presence in the police force, construction, and ward politics, Paddy the
greenhorn was replaced by the East Side "Mike," a contractor, politician, or
policeman, whose speech was characterized by Irish slang and a brogue.

The "Dutch" type was first introduced by Fritz Emmet in the 1880s as the
immigrant character of "Fritz," who was dressed up in wooden sabots, blue
coat, and slouch cap, or, in the Tyrol variant, complete with knee breeches,
laced-jacket, and pointed hat. The Dutch comic of the 1890s, however, represented the middle-class German American, whose nouveau riche status
showed through in his exaggerated dress: his lapels too wide, the checkered
patterns of his dress coat too glaring; his tie and vest beset with heavy gold
chains and showy watches.[49]

At the beginning of the twentieth century, blackface minstrelsy and the
Irish and German comics were rapidly eclipsed by the success of a relative
newcomer in the city and on the vaudeville stage, the Hebrew peddler. The
"Hebrew," according to a contemporary observer, typically "goes on with

shuffling gait, wearing a low-crowned derby hat, speaks with a thick tongue, has a scrubby black beard and gesticulates with horizontal palms."[50]

Adding to the ethnographic aspect of dialect comedy was the fact that its sketches were deeply steeped in the urban milieu. Will D. Saphar, who was of Irish origin, was famous for a dialect/travesty act in which he appeared as a heavy German peasant woman with a "red face, large white cap, fancy shawl, high stomach, large apron, full skirts, woolen stockings, wooden shoes," singing a New York ditty:

Der sveetest ting in life, vat odder peoples say,
Iss Samstag afternoon, a-walkin' down Broadway.
Mein Schwester in der lager beer saloon vill stay.
But I should always make a valk
Right down dot pretty Broadway.
I valk dot Broadway down, I valk dot Broadway down.
Der nicest thing as neffer vas
Iss valk dot Broadway down.
Der fellers vink der eyes,
Und ven I look around,
There ain't no harm I take his arm
Un valk dot Broadway down.[51]

Frank Bush, who was credited with introducing the Hebrew type to the vaudeville stage, would open his performances in grotesque "Jew" makeup, with a "tall, rusty plug hat, long black coat, shabby pants, long beard . . . and large spectacles." He complemented his song, "Solomon Moses," with funny gestures and dance routines:

Oh, my name is Solomon Moses I'm a bully Sheeny man,
I always treat my customers the very best I can.
I keep a clothing store 'way down on Baxter St.,
Where you can get your clothing now I sell so awful cheap.[52]

The sketches of Ben Welch, famous for his Italian and Jewish impersonations, would include such urban burlesques as "A Night and Day in China-town," "Bowery Kick," "The Hebrew and the Dago," and "A Street in Little Italy."[53]

Turn-of-the-century makeup handbooks for actors, influenced by the interest in realism, stressed the need for actors to find real-life models for their impersonations. Young's "practical and exhaustive treatise" on the art of making up, published in 1905, for instance, suggested that actors, "in real life (we must discriminate between real life and the mimic life of the stage) study people as types. Find just what you want, and then reproduce it on the stage."[54]

This advice was reflected in the genealogies racial impersonators constructed for their characters. The "Dutch" comedian Sam Bernard recalled:

> To me, the funniest thing in New York at that time (the late 1870s and early 1880s) was the German American. He was a pompous, weighty, slow-thinking citizen. Through American influence he had fallen under the spell of a prosperous sign peculiar to this period. It was the spell of the two-pound chain attached to a five-pound watch. The chain stretched like a huge cable across the mountainous expanse of his colored vest. He always preferred the outdoors, and was generally found standing on the rear platform of the streetcar. When spread out he became a bulwark for the passengers wedged near him. He was a joy and an inspiration to me. Riding on a car one day, squeezed into an obscure corner, I saw a man snatch a German's watch and hop off the car. The chain hung down straight. I waited leisurely for the climax of the drama. The German emerged slowly from his usual somnolence. He emitted vague guttural sounds, half-finished sentences, slipped words in an effort to articulate his feelings. Obviously his mind was functioning. Anger and explanations were incumbent, but no one could understand what he was saying. Finally, he looked sadly at the chain and said: "Dis ist der zecondt vatch!"
>
> That night in the joke factory I gave an imitation of this perplexed German, inarticulate, yet outraged. With variations, I have been doing the same thing ever since.[55]

Frank Bush had a similar tale of origins for his representations of the "Hebrew drummer" and the Jewish pawnbroker. He presented his Jewish characters with "grotesque make-ups, with derbies or plug hats pulled over their ears, long black coats, long tapering beards, large spectacles, and hands crossed in an obsequious gesture." They were, as he claimed, intended as "a studied mimicry" of an East Side pawnbroker named "Old Man Nelson," whom Bush had watched waiting "on customers day after day for years":

> As people came into the dingy hock shop to pawn their belongings, Bush absorbed every story, every jest, every bit of kindly and witty philosophy, and every

mannerism of the Old Man. . . . Then he brought to the variety stage the pulsat-
ing and kaleidoscopic story of the East Side, taken right from life, with a power of
mimicry that was uncanny. With his perfect delineation of the humorous, kindly,
philosophical old East Side Hebrew, he could stay on Pastor's stage half an hour,
entertain any audience, and leave them applauding for more.[56]

Others relied more on the use of technology to capture their prototypes.
May Robinson, for instance, carried "a kodak—one of those old-fashioned,
snap-shot kind—for the natives of the different towns in France, the little
country villages in England, and the queer-looking people one is apt to
meet in the lower quarters of London will always run if they see you pre-
paring to take a picture. My kodak is hidden under my coat, and I have
become really so expert that I do not have to look into the little peep hole
to see if my subject is in focus, but can successfully 'press the button' while
I am apparently looking in another direction."[57]

As a cultural common ground, then, in grotesque realism dialect comedy brought together two contradictory aesthetic and representational codes:
burlesque and verisimilitude. But within the cultural hierarchy of the late
nineteenth and early twentieth centuries, the representational strategies of
burlesque and verisimilitude were situated very differently. While burlesque
connoted the "low" and the popular, verisimilitude resonated with the growing appeal of realism as the benchmark of "art." Indeed, the apparent "realism" of dialect comedy constituted a significant part of the attraction of
vaudeville for middle-class audiences, for whom it simulated the "scopic
pleasure" of slumming and played on voyeuristic impulses.

Consequently, the burlesque and "realism" within grotesque realism presented two different but overlapping structures of prestige and distinction.
Burlesque, which carried the taint of the vulgar and unrespectable, was a
decidedly lesser source of cultural capital. The interest in the realism of "carefully observed types," however, provided comedians with a strategy for
pitching their performance to the middle classes, and with a potential source
of cultural prestige, which some performers were extremely adept in ex-
ploiting. And as the "alcove realism" of racial comedy mimicked the view
of the city as "theater, not spectacle merely but the potentially revelatory
enactment of meaning," it invited racial comics to step forward to interpret
the racial and moral typologies and categories in which the meaning of the
city was revealed.[58] The careers of Edward Harrigan and David Warfield are
a case in point.

Edward Harrigan and David Warfield

Edward Harrigan was one of the most popular playwrights of the latter part of the nineteenth century. Born in the slums of Gotham Court, one of the most dilapidated sections of New York City, he had started his acting career in the 1860s as part of the Harrigan and Hart team, which specialized in burlesque sketches and impersonations. Although Hart was known for his female impersonations and blackface acts, Harrigan specialized in Irish and Jewish characters. In *Callahan, the Detective,* for instance, he played a Jewish clothing dealer.

Most famous was their Mulligan Guard sketch, which parodied the pseudomilitary marching and target companies manned by immigrants who were banned from the regular militia. On Sundays, companies called the "Cleveland Light Guards, Lafayette Battery, Mustache Fusiliers, or Washington Market Chowder Guard" would assemble at the neighborhood engine house, squeeze into marching formation, and head up first to the home of the leading politician for his support, and then uptown or downtown to the Battery. In the burlesque, Harrigan and Hart stumbled through their drills, hopelessly inept at mastering the marching rhythms and handling their swords and rifles.[59]

The Mulligan Guard act became the basis for a series of full-length plays that Harrigan developed during the last two decades of the century. These plays, with their drafty tenements, rat-bitten people, evictions, seizure and sale of furniture for rent money, coal shutes, coal-gas or "gas-damp," and its language of insult, banter, joking, and immigrant dialects, closely reflected the realities of tenement life seen from a burlesque perspective.[60] The tenements and neighborhoods in *Mulligan Guard Chowder, Dan's Tribulations, The Mulligan Guard Picnic, The Mulligan Guards Nominee, Mulligan's Silver Wedding, Squatter Sovereignty, Waddy Googan, Old Lavender,* and *Reilly and The Four Hundred* were populated by greedy landlords, nouveaux-riches, criminals, and streetwalkers. They featured Irish, African American, German, Italian, and Jewish and, in some in some cases, Chinese, French, and English characters. Brawls, fights, riots, ethnic conflict, ward politics, political corruption, and poverty made up much of the action on stage.[61]

For Harrigan, tenement life presented an unending struggle between have's and have-not's that took place on all levels of society. In general, however, his poor were virtuous, patriotic, good-natured, humorous, and generous; the rich were greedy, self-interested, grim, cynical, and corrupt. In certain respects, Harrigan's plays performed a function similar to much immigrant theater. They introduced immigrant audiences to the intricacies of urban life and the facts of urban politics, ridiculing those who clung to an Old World past as well as those nouveaux-riches who broke the bonds of class solidarity. If his plays often evoked common national and racial stereotypes, they also strove to transcend interethnic barriers. In the moral economy of Harrigan's plays, poverty breeds a common ground: in their shared plight, ethnic groups are more alike than different, and they can cope with the daily struggle of life only through an ethic of mutuality.[62]

The topical nature of the Harrigan and Hart burlesques made the duo a favorite, especially among the newsboys and the Bowery B'hoys.[63] But in an 1886 editorial, William Dean Howells, dean of American realism and influential literary critic for *Harper's Monthly Magazine,* boosted Harrigan's wider reputation as a realist. Reviewing Harrigan's newest production, *Dan's Tribulations,* Howells declared the playwright a member of the literary avant-garde:

> Mr. Harrigan accurately realizes in his scenes what he realizes in his persons; that is, the actual life in this city. . . . It is what we call low life, though whether it is essentially lower than fashionable life is another question. . . . Mr. Harrigan shows us the street cleaners and contractors, the grocerymen, the shysters, the politicians, the washer-women, the servant girls, the truckmen, the police men, the risen Irishmen and Irish woman of contemporary New York. . . . In certain moments . . . the illusion is so perfect that you lose sense of being in the theatre; you are out of that world of conventions and traditions, and in the presence of facts. . . . Consciously or unconsciously, he is part of the great tendency toward faithful presentation of life that is now animating fiction.[64]

It was Harrigan's "realism" that attracted the attention of the more "respectable" audiences. By the end of the nineteenth century, Harrigan, rooted in the immigrant and working-class culture of the Lower East Side, and a fervent proponent of social justice based on traditional republican idealism, had emerged as the mediator of low life for the middle classes. A journalist for the *New York Herald,* on an expedition for an article, "Hunting Types in the Slum with Edward Harrigan," left no doubts about it. Harrigan was an "expert" on the "Other Half":

> These are the common, everyday people—people of the slums and the cross streets, people who may be honest, some of them at a pitch, but who do not wish to be carefully washed or bother to be overscrupulous. They are the class whom we are

over inclined to pity, and about whom we wonder how they make a living, for that matter what they live at all for, why they don't blot themselves off the earth and thus get out of a very disagreeable existence. [Mr. Harrigan] knows our folk. . . . The secret of his success has been that his characters are true to life. It is a secret worth while knowing. Mr. Harrigan has divulged it for the Herald and practically demonstrated how to study the eccentricities in mankind. Come on this trip that I took with Harrigan through the slums.[65]

For Harrigan, whose Irish immigrant characters, by the early 1900s, were gradually becoming outdated and falling out of favor with popular audiences, such publicity presented a welcome boost to a stalled career. As he declared in a 1903 article, "Holding Up the Mirror to Nature," he had steadily grown "in the art of stage realism":

I have sought above all to make my plays like pages from actual life. I have depicted some painful types, I am well aware, and some that have been rather shockingly realistic. . . . My slum and beggar types, my tramps, are not the burlesque caricatures that appeal to the mirth of spectators by absurd and implausible exaggeration of rags and make-up. . . . I examine the general effect of each character with the closest scrutiny, just as I watch the general gestures and movements and "color," so to speak, of the part.[66]

He assiduously proclaimed the truth-value of his representations, stating:

Though I use types and never individuals, I try to be as realistic as possible. Not only must the costuming and accessories be correct, but the speech or dialect, the personal "make-up," the vices and virtues, habits and customs must be equally accurate in their similarity to the facts. Each drama is a series of photographs of life today in the Empire City. As examples, the barroom in one of the Mulligan Series was copied from a saloon in Roosevelt Street, the opium den in Investigation from a "joint" in Pell Street, and the "dive" in Waddy Googan from an establishment in the neighborhood of the Bowery.[67]

Harrigan's cultural mobility was a result of a strategic repositioning of his plays and his capacity as a playwright within what Pierre Bourdieu has termed the "hierarchy of taste and distinction." David Warfield's rise, meanwhile, was the outcome of the more drastic "naturalistic" makeover of his burlesque Jewish-peddler type under the direction of Broadway playwright and stage director David Belasco. Warfield was a veteran Hebrew comic

known for his Jewish-peddler roles in the burlesque revues of Weber and
Fields, where he initially also appeared in Irish and German acts. Appearing in his trademark shabby, ill-fitting coat, derby, and unkempt hair and
beard, his routines depended heavily on a "Jewish" accent, malapropisms, and
mispronunciations. In one revue, he played "Sigmund Cohenski," a wealthy
Jew on vacation in Paris. Confronted with the fact that his daughter has
fallen in love with a U.S. navy captain, whom she considers a "hero," Cohenski tries to dissuade her from pursuing the romance:

> "A hero! Is dot a business? A tailor is a business, a shoemaker is a business, but a
> hero? Better you should marry a bookkeeper."
> "A bookkeeper? I suppose you think the pen is mightier than the sword?" . . .
> "You bet my life. . . . Could you sign checks with a sword?"[68]

Warfield rose to nationwide fame when, in 1901, David Belasco bought
him out of his Weber and Fields contract to play the role of Simon Levi, a
Jewish peddler, in the naturalistic play *The Auctioneer*. In the wake of the
play's success, Warfield became an ardent and articulate advocate of the
realistic portrayal of low life. Countering the Arnoldian concept of culture,
which considered low life to be beyond the bounds of the proper "uplift-
ing" subjects of art, Warfield argued that "there is every reason why the odd
phases of social life should be portrayed. . . . Right here at our door is enough
material for a thousand strong plays, interesting, natural, picturesque, and
full of poetry and fine instructions. . . . Plays based upon these varying types
of humanity in the great Metropolis would be an education to the actors,
and would afford an intellectual and dramatic variety of the highest enjoy-
ability to the people behind as well as those in front of the footlights."[69]

For the next decade, Warfield was the undisputed "professional" Hebrew,
who tirelessly expounded his views on the eccentricities of the race. His
reputation as a ghetto expert also had a literary spin-off. In 1902, Warfield,
in cooperation with social worker Margherita Arlina Hamm, published a
collection of stories under the title *Ghetto Silhouettes*. The stories, according to the book's preface, "are based upon sketches made from the daily life
of the famous East Side of New York City. . . . Here Mr. Warfield gathered
material for his professional work as an actor and playwright and Miss
Hamm spent much time during four years of labor as a Social Settlement
worker."[70]

The volume presented a mélange of highly sentimental stories of little literary merit, some reminiscent of Talmudic parables and shtetl tales, others

projecting a ghetto reconciliation of Christian and Jewish traditions.[71] A series of still photographs of David Warfield, dressed up as Simon Levi in *The Auctioneer,* provided accompanying illustrations.

THE AESTHETIC OF THE COMMON

The cultural mobility of Harrigan and Warfield took place in a context in which, as Edwin Royle observed, the distinction between "art" and "vaudeville" itself was becoming blurred by vaudeville's regular recruitment of "legitimate" stars, a practice dubbed the "Headliner" policy.[72] But the fact that it was William Dean Howells who propelled Ed Harrigan into wider recognition should alert us to the wider contours of the climate in which the "rise" of Harrigan and Warfield could take place. As many critics have argued, one of the dominant impulses of literary realism was rooted in the perception of increasing social divisions within the city. Realism offered to make various social classes knowable to one another through faithful representation of the life of the Other Half. The anticipation of the democratic effects of the "truth"-telling mission of realism was shared by many of its early proponents.[73]

As chief critic for *Harper's Magazine,* William Dean Howells was centrally positioned to envision and formulate the project of realism. In contrast to the exclusivity of "genteel" literature, which considered representation of the lower classes beyond the pale of "art," realist literature would introduce "democracy in literature."[74] As Amy Kaplan has written, Howells expected the realist author to act as educator and guide and lead his genteel audience toward more "democratic" vistas by projecting "a common culture uniting a public of different classes, regions and backgrounds."[75]

In this "aesthetic of the common," social differences would be obliterated by the realization of a "common humanity."[76] It should therefore not come as a surprise that Howells would recognize a kindred spirit in Harrigan's populism.[77] But Howells's affinity with Harrigan stemmed from another source as well. Realism, for all its claims of providing an unmediated transcription of reality, at heart was deeply theatrical. This permeability of theater and literary realism had its foundation, according to Raymond Williams, in the "strain of impersonation" that informed realism's representational strategy.[78]

Williams argues that the expansion of terrain of the novel beyond gentility to "other" classes created a new relation between subject and object. Since there no longer was a continuity between the experiences of the author and his objects, the realist novel was faced with the challenge to represent its various characters as a "knowable community," despite the absence of a shared language or shared traditions, blood relations, and pasts. Ultimately, realism's attempt to reconcile the various social classes centered on the need to find a strategy of representation that would bridge the gap between the material world and literary representation: to make the Other legible while retaining his difference. According to Williams, this turned "the problem of a knowable community" into "a problem of language."[79] The absence of linguistic (and cultural) unity created the need for impersonation: the careful orthographic ventriloquism of the Other.[80]

What Williams refers to is perhaps best illustrated by quoting a passage from Howells's *Hazard of New Fortunes,* a novel that, as Kaplan has observed, is about competing visions of the city.[81] In the novel, Howells relentlessly criticizes the distance the middle-class Marches assume toward the lower classes. Of the Marches strolling around Washington Square and encountering the Italian, French, and Spanish faces around them, Howells remarked: "They met the familiar picturesque raggedness of Southern Europe with the old kindly illusion that somehow it existed for their appreciation, and that it found adequate compensation for poverty in this."[82] Their habit of social voyeurism transforms reality into a picture existing for the amusement of the spectator.[83]

To counter the sense of social distance and alienation occasioned by the mode of the "picturesque," Howells introduces the voice of the German socialist Lindau, who, in his most radical speech, implicitly destroys the Marches' self-complacent perception of reality: "Dere *iss* no Ameriga any more! . . . No man that vorks with his handts among you has the liperty to bursue his habbiness. He iss the slafe of some richer man, some gompany, some gorporation, dat crindt him down to the least he can lif on, and that rops him of the marchin of his earnings that he might be habby on."[84]

The use of dialect, according to Howells, served the political and cognitive goal of introducing different classes and regions to one another in order to make them "know another better, that they may all be humbled and strengthened with a sense of their fraternity."[85] But as staged in Howells's "realistic" rendition, the character of Lindau acquires all the attributes of a dialect comedy act on the vaudeville stage. This affinity with dialect comedy also points to what Williams and Kaplan pinpoint as the danger in realism's use of linguistic mimicry. Rather than serving as a didactic and unifying tool, Howells's ventriloquism evokes the same kind of spectatorship and distance for which he unsparingly rebukes the middle-class Marches. His rendition of Lindau's dialect separates the character from the mostly middle-class, standard English-speaking characters in the novel. It also separates him from the author, who signals his own ironic distance not through direct authorial commentary but through "a whole way of seeing, at a sociologi-cal distance," which according to Williams characterizes the authorial stance in realist novels. With his burlesque accent, this linguistic Other is effect-ively reduced to type and safely contained "within the margins of bourgeois tolerance."[86]

This complementary relationship among impersonation, realism, voyeur-ism, and social distance was central to the new epistemology of the city, which required the mediation of a group of professionals who could trans-gress social and cultural boundaries, and who could translate the results of the intimate observation of social and cultural Others into a more general knowledge of categories and types. Detectives and reporters formed two groups of professionals who combined both standards. Impersonators rep-resented another. Indeed, the racial impersonator joined the urban reporter and the detective as an alternative, modern incarnation of the flâneur.[87]

The Impersonator as Expert on the City

In their rise as "experts" on the ghetto, racial impersonators such as Harri-gan and Warfield catered to the "desire to get hold of an object at very close range by way of its likeness, its reproduction."[88] They capitalized on the interest in the authentic representation of low life by de-emphasizing the burlesque elements in their characterizations, and by rounding out their comic characters through the addition of an element of "pathos." In doing so, they reframed their erstwhile grotesque realist "types" in the terms of an aesthetic of "artificial realism." In artificial realism, Miles Orvell argues, type mediated between realism's dedication to the truth of fact and its search for a more general representation of reality that would reveal the ideal truth that lies behind the infinite variability of (human) nature.[89]

The standard for representational veracity in early realism was repre-sented by photography. The aim of nineteenth-century photography, how-ever, was not the "literal" representation of reality, but the representation of the "truth" of the individual character by finding—as in painting—the pose that captured the individual's distinct personality. The truth of photography was a general, idealized truth, which combined the partial truths of individ-ual observations into a generic ideal image. This concept of truth was per-fectly consistent with the manipulation of reality to make the representation conform to a preconceived "ideal" image. Jacob Riis, for instance, reports how he carefully staged his photographic subjects according to such metonymic typologies as "the poor" or the "beggar."[90]

Playwrights and impersonators such as Harrigan and Warfield drew on the same aesthetic theory. Warfield was quoted as asserting that "the highest art consists not in distorting but in photographing, and it may be idealizing things as they are."[91] Actors, however, could boast a distinct advantage over photography. Photography did not have the capacity to unify different perspectives of an individual and represent, as Oliver Wendell Holmes put it, the many "mental and emotional shapes by which his inner nature made itself known to us in outward appearance."[92] It tried to compensate for the incompleteness of the single portrait, however well composed, by the practice of the "multiple portrait." This showed the subject in an oval circle of smaller portraits that represented different poses and different sides of his character, seconding a single large image—the "whole" of the character—in the center.[93] Another photographic method to obtain a "generic image" was the "composite type." Originally devised by Francis Galton, the founder of eugenics, it projected a number of specimens of a racial or social group into one photographic image in order to arrive at the "purely optical apparition" of the generic criminal or racial type.[94]

Warfield and Harrigan emphasized the fact that the artistry of their impersonations resided not in the closeness of their characters to real life but in their ability to generalize their subjects. In popular magazines, David Warfield was often pictured in the fashion of the multiple portrait, with different grimaces and facial expressions displaying different characteristics of his "Hebrew" type. Warfield himself explained his stage impersonation as a "composite type." As he claimed, "This Jew of mine has no prototype in life. He is a sort of composite character absorbed through general observation." The *Baltimore World* similarly referred to "David Warfield's Jewish peddler" as "a type truly copied from nature—composite, of course."[95]

Galton himself acknowledged the ability of artists to visualize something close to his "composite type." "A composite portrait," he argued, "represents the picture that could rise before the mind's eye of an individual who had the gift of pictorial imagination in an exalted degree."[96] He noted: "It is in the mind of poets and painters generally that we find the artistic power to reside of producing pictures that are not copies of any individual, but represent the characteristics of large classes. Painters and poets create blended portraits in profusion, and we who are not as gifted as they are, can nevertheless understand and appreciate their work."[97] Like the painter in Henry

James's "The Real Thing," who considers it the purpose of art to capture not the individual but the "ideal," Warfield's reference to "generic images" marked him as a genuine artist, able to distill, in his mind's image, the generic "Hebrew."

In their promotion of racial impersonation as a translation of the interior "truth" of "race," actors such as Warfield, Harrigan, and others claimed an expert insight in physiognomy—the reading of character from external appearances. This expertise, they asserted, was based on professionalism: their extensive familiarity with mimicry, the art of making up, their habit of close observation, and their skills of impersonation.

The art of making up, according to a manual on the subject, acquainted the actor with a detailed apparatus of identification. Different types of ears, for instance, to a skilled actor would signal "certain qualities common to distinctive classes. There is the ear of the patrician—small, symmetrical and close to the head; the protruding ear of the bumpkin; the inquisitive ear, and the donkey ear; any of which may be seen in a short walk through a crowded thoroughfare. The Bertillon system of identification and measurement depends as much upon the ear for identification as on any other feature."[98]

Professional knowledge, then, made the actor an expert in the reading of inner character. Declaring, "I believe in studying character all the time," Edward Harrigan demonstrated his proficiency on the street:

> Those dagos selling fruit out there at the crossing I've got in mind just now. They are a good field to work. . . . Do you notice that each one is muttering to himself? An Italian is always muttering. You can never find out what about. I don't believe that they know themselves. It's part of their nature, the expressed note of oppression. Under the right circumstances—revenge or beer—that mutter will swell into a murmur and break into a curse and then there comes murder.[99]

David Warfield attributed his success "to the care and time I have given to studying the quaint Russian types which come to this country from southeastern Europe."[100] "A glance at the Slovak face would tell the whole story to a thoughtful physiognomist," he explained. "The big forehead, often disproportionately large, speaks of untiring mental, moral, and social activities; the small jaw and chin indicate but little sympathy with the pleasures of the flesh and the world; the firm mouth and bony nose symbolize determination and patience."[101]

Impersonators' familiarity with vernaculars and idioms also made them experts in the secret languages and slang of foreign groups and subcultures, which they translated to their audiences in a manner reminiscent of the lexicons of seventeenth-century rogue literature and nineteenth-century metropolitan guidebooks. Ed Harrigan proudly declared: "They call my theatre a 'slang shop,' you know. So it is. I am always looking out for new slang. . . . This 'say' and 'see' so much used just now, are old-timers. They date from the days of the Volunteer Fire Department. 'Not in it' is a gambler's expression. 'Out of sight' comes from the racetrack. 'Boodle' is an old thieves' word similar to the 'swag' of the London crooks."[102]

Warfield advocated the need for actors to "go out and get their dialects by studying the people whom they impersonate."[103] In an article titled "Satire, Wit and Humor of the Russian Jew," he explained the eccentricities of Jewish idiom. Favorite business expressions, Warfield asserts, include "If a man believes you're selling at a loss, he'll buy all you've got"; "A nickel a minute is better than a dollar an hour"; "Make believe you're busy and the banker will give you credit"; and "A man who marries an extravagant woman put two mortgages on his shop." "'Chaser' in their dialect," Warfield continues, "means both a lawyer and an advertising agent, chochem signifies a millionaire and likewise a star boarder in a landlady's boarding house. The practice of dishonest men going into bankruptcy and coming out with a small fortune in their wife's name is summed up in the word 'dalles,' which means a bankrupt's assets and a safe investment."[104]

Based on the professional habit of close observation, David Warfield claimed for actors a unique, intimate knowledge of other cultures. As he explained: "It was an actor who first pointed out that Chinamen walk in single file in New York because it was a necessary habit contracted in China where the sidewalks are two feet wide and often the entire street no more than six feet from wall to wall. It was another actor who hinted at the truth when he said that the Russian Jews talked with their hands and features because in that way they could not be overheard by official spies."[105]

And if the role of the impersonator was that of a popular ethnographer, the stage was a forum for the premiere of many hitherto unknown, quaint customs. "The practice at many family functions of having a bowl or basket filled with coins from which relatives and friends can help themselves . . . is a common custom with the Russian Hebrew," Warfield argued, "and yet, as far as I know, it is unknown in America except where it has been produced on the Broadway stage."[106]

The expertise of the racial impersonator, however, was not based solely on habits of observation—of "detecting." More important, it hinged on the

act of impersonation itself. The centrality of impersonation to the epistemology of the city derived from an understanding of the process of "acting" which held that the act of mimicry itself, in a very real sense, meant a
temporary becoming "Other." This theory of acting, containing a residue of
the thinking in magical correspondences that Benjamin considered to be at
the heart of the mimetic impulse, was itself based on the principles of physiognomy.[107] If, according to the rules of physiognomy, external appearances
corresponded with inner character, the reverse must hold true as well: the
imitation of the external appearance of an Other meant the taking on of an
Other identity.[108]

Impersonation and mimicry, then, provide the key to Otherness, a strategy exploited by detectives going into slums in disguise and journalists and
writers engaging in similar "experiments in reality" by assuming a "low"
identity. From that perspective, actors were professionals in crossing the
boundary between Self and Other. Harrigan, for instance, explained of his
"Old Lavender" persona that he "had found his prototype in real life in a
little East Side restaurant. I drifted into his very spirit, and seemed always
to be seeing him from various points of view."[109]

It is this same theory that underlies the popular fascination with stories
about racial impersonators going into the ghetto in costume and "passing."
In the article "How I Created 'Simon Levi,'" David Warfield recounts his
experience of "going native" on the Lower East Side: "After I had made what
I regarded as a satisfactory study of my involuntary models, I thought one
day that I would attempt to get a verdict upon my work from the very people I was simulating, so I made up as a typical Slovak and went down to the
East Side. . . . I was the cynosure of all eyes and many were the comments,
complimentary and otherwise, made upon my appearance. I treated it all
with Jewish composure."[110]

In another version of the story, "Mr. Warfield not only tramped through
Hester Street, but talked broken Yiddish with the police and postmen;
brought fruit and nuts at the stands; peddled for two blocks; and rummaged
the shops for over two hours. Not once was he suspected or given a question-
ing word or look."[111] Similar stories, which were meant to attest to the professionalism of the actors and the authenticity of their impersonations, were
also told about, among others, the "Dutch"/Jewish impersonator Sam Bernard, the Chinese/Italian impersonator Leo Carillo, the Jewish impersonator Joe Welch and his brother, the Italian/Jewish impersonator Ben Welch.

Joe Welch, famous for acts that typically started with the line, "Meppe
you t'ink I'm a happy man" and concluded, "Und I vished dot I vas dead!"[112]

claimed that his stage Jew, with "unkempt beard and hair, pronounced nose, oversized shoes, derby pulled down far onto his head, dark coat hanging over his ankles," had "its origin in a study from real life, he having given years of close study to the habits and customs of the Jews." As he explained:

> I often mingle with the great congress of nations in New York's East Side, and by conversing with the Hebrew, I get some idea of his point of view and I also discover those peculiarities of inflection and those foreign idioms that result in pidgin English. Really there is more fun to be had in conversing with some of our foreign element than would be had by reading a comic supplement, and I get many a good idea for a joke or story by listening to the guileless remarks of some dealer in second hand clothes.[113]

Welch's trip to Baxter Street in his peddler stage outfit was chronicled by many newspaper columns, one of which reported that Welch "duped many clothing store owners into thinking that he was one of their own."[114] The irony was that Joe Welch, like his brother Ben, grew up in a Jewish immigrant family on the Lower East Side. Warfield, whose original name was Wohlfeld, was of Jewish origin, but he had converted to Christianity after marrying a Roman Catholic woman.[115]

The "Ideal" Cosmopolitan

The ability to "pass" identified the impersonator as socially and culturally distant from his models, and, by negative implication, marked the impersonating subject as essentially nonracial. Thus, it effectively detached those impersonators of relatively recent immigrant origin from the signs of race. For socially ambitious dialect comedians who wanted to be regarded as serious "actors" rather than "low" comedians, this was a crucial act of distancing, for there is no "art" in playing at being the real thing while being the real thing itself. The professional is recognized as such only when he inhabits an identity that is split.

The racial impersonator, then, represented what Robert Park has defined as the "ideal" cosmopolitan, who combines the ability to move undetected through different neighborhoods with a perfect knowledge of its semiotics. But this ability contains a class aspect (as Henri Lefebvre points out) and a racial aspect as well. Although the bourgeois routine of daily life consisted of a journey from suburban home to the workplace in the inner city, localism defined the experience of the immigrant lower classes. The "right to the city" was in fact a white "bourgeois prerogative."[116]

The projection of the bourgeois fantasy of transgressing moral and social boundaries, of "seeing without being seen," the impersonator was the embodiment of an epistemology of the city that depended on the ambivalent movement between inside and outside, closeness and distance, desire and fear.[117]

The knowledge of the Other that he purveyed was a knowledge truly obtained "in passing," in the double meaning of the word. In that sense, dialect comedy represents an example of what Steven Mullaney calls a "rehearsal of culture." A rehearsal of culture is a "temporary movement through 'Otherness,'" "a period of free play during which alternatives can be staged, [and] unfamiliar roles tried out . . . with some license." During such a period, a society in the process of expansion can review what it, conceptually and ideologically, has relegated to the boundaries of its culture. Rehearsals of Otherness, then, engage in a complex negotiation of difference with a variety of outcomes, ranging from symbolic erasure of Otherness to its incorporation.[118]

In the case of dialect comedy, this negotiation involved an intricate exercise in the mapping of social and cultural distance. As Eric Lott has suggested for minstrel shows, racial impersonations depended, in their staging, on the cultural material of racial and ethnic Others, which implied an "uneasy affirmation of cultural exchange."[119] In the accounts of impersonators about the genealogy of their acts, this exchange is acknowledged, but it is consistently depicted in terms of a relation with "involuntary models" in which the impersonator has the upper hand.

In some accounts, the nature of the exchange is characterized as "a find"— free of charge. In response to the question, "And your Jew, where did he come from?" David Warfield replied:

> From the street. I saw him first in Thirtieth Street, when I was at "Weber and Fields." He came along with an old derby hat on his ears and a shabby Prince Albert buttoned tightly about him, and carried a pair of freshly pressed trousers across his arm. There were a great many of that type working in the tailor shops of the neighborhood then, and every time I saw one I had to laugh to myself. Suddenly it occurred to me that this type would be something new on the stage. "Great find!" I said, and began to make a careful study of the peculiarities of the type.[120]

In a similar vein, Harrigan answered to *Leslie's Weekly's* question, "How Edward Harrigan Finds His Types in Real Life," "Find them? . . . I don't have to hunt for them. I have to dodge them. . . . The trouble is, the world is so full of them that it is hard enough to get a mental grasp on just enough of them to weave a little story about. They all want to come in. . . . They all have their own stories written all over them, but they hob-nob together, and live their little lives."[121] In another interview, Harrigan described "both Sixth and Seventh Avenue [as] two favorite places for character picking."[122]

The impersonator tricks the Other out of essential attributes of his identity, the true value of which he himself is unaware, and turns these attributes into capital. This capital could consist of elements of language. Harrigan, accompanied by a reporter, cruises the East Side looking for "types" and engages in a conversation with a street tough. Unbeknown to himself, the uncooperative model imparts to the actor some catchy expressions that the latter can use to fill his "slang shop":

> "Quiet today ain't it," said Harrigan.
> "What's quiet?" replied the damaged looking individual who might be a thief, a tramp, a policy shop stout or a bunco steerer.
> "Business, of course."
> "Rats, what's the matter wid ye?"
> "Looking for a game."
> "Say, look here; what ye tryin' to give one a game o' talk?"
> Harrigan chuckled to himself as we got along down the streets to where the big, bursting bundles of waste paper blocked the side-walk.
> "Twas a good play," said he; "I'm a winner out of that." "A game o' talk." Catchy, isn't it? "A game o' talk." Certainly, that slang is bound to catch on and be popular.[123]

Dialect comedians engaged in similar con games to strip their models of their clothes. Harrigan preferably got his outfits from the backs of immigrants, right off the boat at Ellis Island. Joseph Kline Emmett got hold of the perfect costume for his German impersonation by getting his model drunk.[124] Ben Welch, who specialized in Italian/Jewish impersonations and was referred to as the "Warfield of Vaudeville" because of naturalness of imitations, recounted his conversation with the Italian donor of a hat Welch had set his eyes on:

> Yesterday afternoon Ben Welch was standing in front of Hammerstein's when he noticed an Italian walking by with the worst apology of a hat ever seen on the streets of New York. "Ah," said Welch . . . "that's just the hat for me to use in the Italian character in my act." Welch called to the man and he came over. "I'll give you fifty cents for that hat," began Welch. . . . "All righta; puta de mon in de hand and I giva you da hat." Welch dropped the coin in the fellow's hand and turned

away. The Italian went up to Hammerstein's roof, for that's where he was working, and in a few minutes came down with another hat on his head and strode
majestically up and down in front of Welch. "Go on," called out Welch. "I ain't
going to buy any more hats." "This a da nice hat," exclaimed the Italian. "I'll sell
you fifty cents." "Nope," exclaimed Welch. "I don't want anymore."[125]

What stands out in these accounts is the inherent theatrical nature of the
exchange. In such acts of stripping, the body and speech of the immigrant
subject are commodified instantaneously and replaced by their representation: immigrants do not wear clothes, but as Harrigan points out, "they
wear striking costumes."[126]

THE AUCTIONEER

At the level of "realism," dialect comedy implicitly constructed a social and
cultural hierarchy. It presented culture as biological and racial in nature,
and constructed a racial Other whose identity is fixed through an immutable
correspondence between physiognomy, locale, class, language, morality,
and customs. This construction of social and racial distance is the hidden
subtext of the play *The Auctioneer*, which, in 1901, jolted David Warfield into
a Broadway career. Produced by David Belasco, an early advocate of theatrical naturalism, *The Auctioneer* transplanted Warfield's burlesque Jew
into the realm of "high" culture.[127] As Warfield stated, "The play 'The Auctioneer' was simply a transplanting of my stage Jewish peddler into new
and expanded surroundings. . . . He stepped out of the burlesque, laugh
exciting character I had made him, and became an all around human being,
with pathos as well as comedy in his make-up."[128] In doing so, the play
attempted not only to interiorize physiognomy by suggesting emotional
depth and (racial) character, but to invite empathy as well.[129]

In the play, Warfield played Simon Levi, an auctioneer on Hester Street.
Levi, portrayed as a fundamentally sympathetic character but with a stereotypical shrewd sense of business, amasses a considerable fortune and moves
"uptown" into a Lexington Avenue mansion. This brings him into sudden
proximity to his brother and sister-in-law, Isaac and Rose "Leavitt," who do
not welcome this visible reminder of their lowly roots. Isaac, harassed by
his ambitious wife, devises a scheme to swindle Levi out of his money. Penniless, Levi is forced to return to the slums and takes up peddling, a fate he
carries with considerable grace. When Isaac, whom Levi thought had died
in South America, shows up and begs his brother's forgiveness, Levi and

Esther, his wife, pardon Isaac and Rose for their sins. Levi, in the end, returns to his occupation as an auctioneer and eventually is restored to his wealth.[130]

Despite its pretensions of presenting the Jew Simon Levi as an "all around human being," *The Auctioneer* derives its comedy fundamentally from caricature: the play, in particular, pokes fun at the inability of Jews to "pass" in upper-class society. In one scene, Simon Levi, residing in his uptown mansion, hires a butler and decides to give a ball. He is so enamored with his new dress suit that he decides to wear the overcoat that goes with it, while the butler tries to convince him that wearing it is correct only for the street. Moreover, when the wine is brought in, wrapped in towels, as genteel etiquette dictates, Levi insists that the "rags" be removed so that the guests can see the labels.[131]

To the reviewer of the *New York Times*, however, the play's projection of Levi as an upper-middle-class Jew represented an unfortunate erasure of social distance. Instead of a real picture of slum life, the audience was presented with the image of a life of luxury, which too closely mirrored its own:

> On our first acquaintance with him he is an East Side auctioneer, honestly and kindly.... This is a worthy scene after the fashion of Harrigan's famous sketches which, as studies of low life in New York, were incomparable. Like Harrigan, too, the authors of this work have made the mistake of carrying their characters into scenes of unaccustomed, therefore awkward and unhappy, luxury. Levy inherits a fortune, abandons his auctionship, deserts his picturesque and entertaining friends in the ghetto, rents a house in the fashionable district and becomes dull in prosperity.... It was the error of Harrigan, and it will be the error of all Harrigan's imitators who apparently cannot understand that when people go slumming they do not desire to see themselves, or other people who resemble themselves, however clumsily.[132]

But this erasure of social distance is counterbalanced by the fact that, in the play, the Jew Simon Levi cannot affect the genteel codes of self-representation. His brother, a social climber who parades as a gentleman, moreover, is exposed as a fraud and forced to acknowledge his "true" Jewish self.[133] The plot, then, also played on a discussion about the (im)possibility of social and cultural change.

In the intellectual climate of the turn of the century, which habitually understood culture in terms of "race," the debate about the potential for immigrant acculturation was framed as a discussion about the relative influence of nature and nurture, or innate tendencies and the environment, on the shaping of social identities. Although some sociologists conceded that immediate environmental influences might have a modifying effect on the "racial habits" of non-Caucasian races, others considered non-Caucasians, in particular the African and Semitic races, impermeable to such influences. According to the sociologist Charles Ellwood, the display of etiquette and genteel manners in other races was no more than a superficial layer masking deeper "racial instincts."[134] This conflation of race and class was the flipside of an ideology of middle-class identity that pivoted around the concept of taste. In the context of the increasing prospects of social mobility, civility and gentility emerged as a measurable standard of whiteness.[135]

The Auctioneer confirms this construction of the "Hebrew" race as fundamentally immutable, unable to transcend the limitations of body, physiognomy, age-old habits, mannerisms, and sentiments, even when experiencing social mobility. True gentility was racially unattainable for Jews. The actor David Warfield, however, knew the "codes" of Jewishness to such a degree that his acting substituted for the "real thing." What the audience was presented with was an "authentic" Jew. According to one review,

> Mr. Warfield was perfect not just because of such physical characteristics as the sallow complexion, the thin, wispy hair, the awkward gestures and the shambling gait, the perfect dialect and the almost photographic reproduction of race traits in manner, vocal inflections and facial expressions, but because of the genuine humor underlying the mere comicality, and the constant suggestion of something better below the surface—a generous, loving, patient nature beneath the professional guise of the petty, unscrupulous huckster.[136]

As racial type, Warfield's representation of the "East Side Hebrew" was to be seen as more "real" than reality itself. "This play, I hope, will take the place of a slumming expedition," Belasco is reputed to have commented to a reporter in the early stages of the production.[137] And according to the press, he succeeded. As one reviewer commented, "The picture is absolutely true to life. Its atmosphere is the real thing, down to the very stock of cheap goods, and the giggling girls dressed in Hester Street finery, and the women who run into the store with their shawls over their heads. It is as good as a slumming expedition for the curious."[138]

The perceived authenticity of David Warfield's Jewish interpretations prompted incessant rumors about Warfield's supposed Jewish origins. While one newspaper claimed that Warfield "was born in San Francisco about twenty five years ago, his parents being Jewish," another quoted him as saying, "I'm not a Jew."[139] Warfield himself, however, tended to attribute the confusion between his "real" identity and his stage identity to his artistic skills as an impersonator: "So many people tell me it [the dialect] is just the thing that I presume it must be. I have a gift that way. . . . People always presume I am of the nationality of the part I play.[140]

Paradoxically, then, by virtue of the ability to take on an "Other" (supposedly) purely "fictional" identity and "pass" as Jews, Jewish actors such as Warfield "whitened" themselves for their American, non-Jewish audiences. For these actors, some of whom grew up in the slums and were second-generation immigrants, success on the "legitimate" stage presented just the strategy of social and cultural mobility that plays such as *The Auctioneer* denied its racial Other.

Such cultural distinction was not easy to achieve. In the hope of emulating Warfield's success, Joe Welch appeared in the Broadway play *The Peddler*. His peddler type, however, relied too much on the grotesque realism of his vaudeville characterizations, and Welch failed to receive critical acclaim. He returned to the vaudeville stage, where a few years later he became a casualty of the boycotts of his performances that were instigated by the Anti-Stage Jew Ridicule Committee.[141]

Warfield, however, consolidated his foothold in the world of "high" theater in the whitest role of his career: that of a German musician modeled after Beethoven, in Belasco's play *The Music Master*. In the wake of his success in that role, Warfield assumed distance even from his famous character of a ghetto Jew. Asked whether he felt his "ambition gratified when the Manhattan public acclaimed you as Simon Levi?" he answered, "Frankly, no. I felt encouraged and grateful, but I hankered after a higher, more legitimate kind of success." In response to the question, "But surely, your famous Yid was studied from life?" he retracted his earlier statements: "Not at all. I may absorb, but I never study from life, if you mean in the cold-blooded, literal, photographic way. No doubt I remember actual impressions by the thousand, but when it comes to evolving a character, making him walk and talk on the stage, that's all done from the imagination. . . . Yes, there have been stories printed about my trips to Hester or Bayard Street in search of local color, and even photographs of me in character disguise riding a wheel unrecognized in those slummy localities. All bosh and make-believe."

Warfield's quest for artistic legitimacy, respectability, and whiteness also meant renouncing his former career in burlesque. In response to requests for permission to imitate Herr Anton van Barwig, his character in *The Music Master*, Warfield announced that "he does not care to have 'impersonators' burlesquing what is a very serious character."[142] It was as Shylock in *The Merchant of Venice* that Warfield ultimately won the "higher" acclaim to which he aspired.

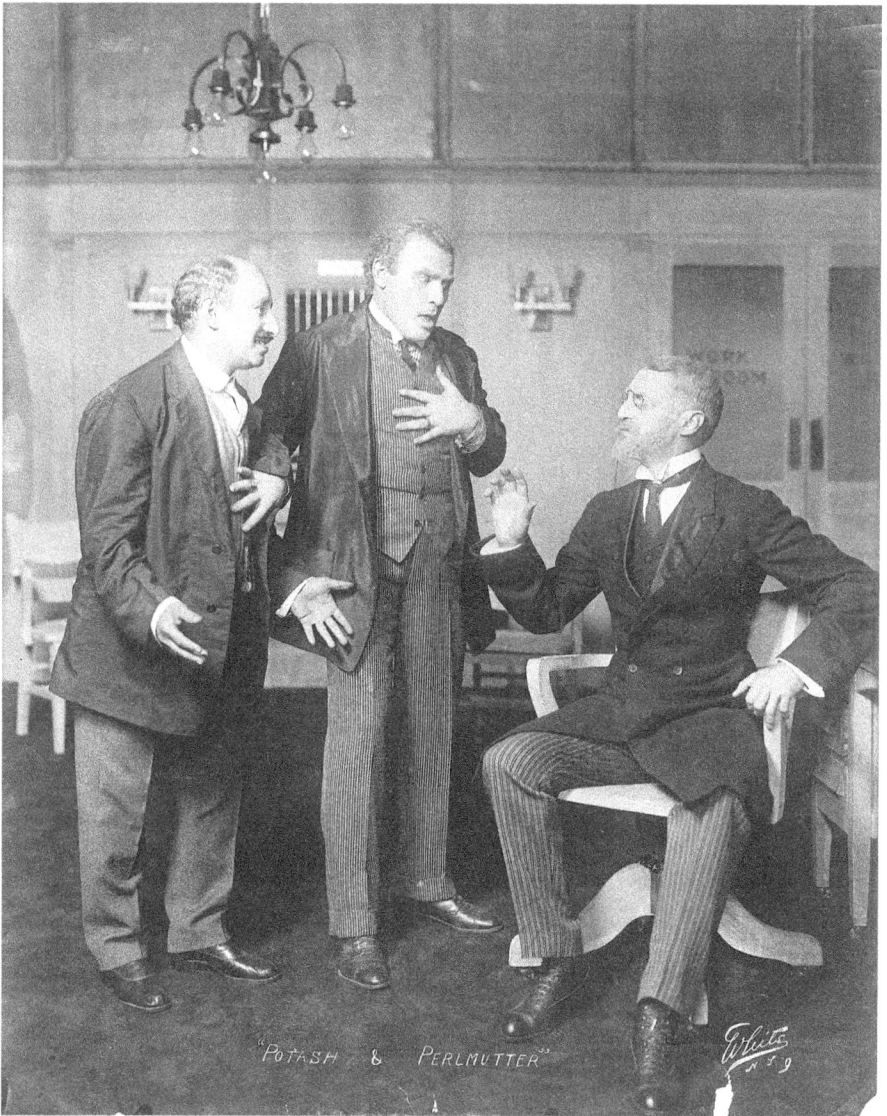

Civilizing the Jewish comic: Alexander Carr and Barney Bernard as Potash and Perlmutter. Stanley Jessup, Alexander Carr, and Barney Bernard, *Potash and Perlmutter,* n.d. Billy Rose Theatre Division, The New York Library for the Performing Arts; Astor, Lenox and Tilden Foundations.

Chapter 7

The Truth of Racial Signs

Civilizing the Jewish Comic

FOR A CASUAL OBSERVER LIKE EDWIN ROYLE, WHAT WAS REMARKABLE (and a little melancholy) about vaudeville was the seriousness with which it banned seriousness. The program, in his words, was "from the artist who balances a set of parlor furniture on his nose to the academic baboon . . . one concentrated, strenuous struggle for a laugh. No artist can do without it. It hangs like a solid and awful obligation over everything."[1]

The formula for a successful vaudeville lineup was simple. The vaudeville bill required one or two headliners, some attention grabbers, some dramatic contrast, and a "climax." As George M. Cohan and George J. Nathan explained in an article in *McClure's* (1913), it all boiled down to a simple "Mechanics of Emotion." The audience "comes to the theater for one definite purpose, to have its emotions played upon," they postulated. The "emotion germs" come in three kinds: tears, laughs, thrills. It is up to the performer to trigger the audience's emotional "reflexes," which, as Cohan and Nathan explained, mechanistically respond to a concise number of formulaic stimuli, well known in the trade.[2]

In vaudeville it was, above all, the laugh that counted. But its "laugh-getters" were of a different nature than the "high-class" ones of the legitimate stage. The vaudeville audience would invariably laugh at the following:

Open your coat and show a green vest, or pull out your shirt-front and expose a red undershirt. Another excellent thing to do is to wear a shirt without sleeves and pull off your coat repeatedly.

Ask the orchestra leader if he is married.

Have the drummer put in an extra beat with the cymbals, then glare at him.

Always use an expression which ends with the query, "Did he not?" Then say, "He did not."

"A peculiarity of this kind of humor," Cohan and Nathan concluded, "is that it finds its basis in the inflicting of pain. . . . The most successful tricks or jokes are always based on the *idea* of pain or embarrassment."[3] Vaudeville was the medium of incubation, standardization, and diffusion for what critics quickly dubbed the "New Humor." This humor replaced "the casual improvisations of the story-teller, as well as the droll whimsy of the minstrel comic," their "flights of fantasy" and their "tolerant recital of the inanities of human beings," with the well-placed "jab to the solar plexus."[4]

This particular morphology was informed by the contraction of time and space characteristic of modern metropolitan life. This meant that, as Cohan and Nathan explained, "Nothing counts in the theatre but the impression of the time being. All the 'mechanics of emotion' are based, from the theatrical craftsman's point of view, on this one solid fact."[5] The modern urban audience lived for the "impression of the moment." It had no patience for "the development of character, setting and atmosphere," and required a more intense, fast-paced, shock-oriented form of comedy.[6]

Not surprisingly, the foundation of the New Humor was the joke. What once was common fare mostly in the masculine culture of saloons and on the streets of the Jewish ghetto exploded onto the mass market. Between 1890 and 1907, the number of joke books published yearly in the United States grew from 11 to 104. The Jewish entrepreneur Henry J. Wehman published the bulk of these books, coming out with sixty titles and sales that ran to more than two million copies. The joke industry, stimulated by an increase in leisure time and family budgets, was fed by professional "jokesmiths," writers who could churn out an average of fifty jokes a day.[7]

The structure of the joke was ruled by a strict economy. Conciseness, incisiveness, and directness were the main ingredients. As Brett Page, advising would-be vaudeville writers, explained, "The first line introduces the situation and invites a slight grin; the second intensifies the situation and provokes a chuckle; the final segment delivers the punch that pushes the laugh over the top."[8] Aiming for the punch line, the new joke eliminated all exposition:

"Every man should take a wife. But he should be careful whose wife he takes."
"I saw you outside the Biltmore Hotel."
"That's where I live."

"At the Biltmore?"

"No, outside the Biltmore."

Neither did the joke mince words when it came to debunking the powerful and privileged. A favorite joke of comedian Cliff Gordon, "The German Senator," was the following: "The rich people say that the poor are getting prosperous. They say look at our streets. You see nothing but automobiles. You don't see half the poor people now that you used to. Certainly you don't. Half of them have already been run over and the other half is afraid to come out."[9]

On the vaudeville stage, the joke was most often packaged in the form of the monologue, or the two-act. Many of these fell into the category of racial comedy, which, by the early 1900s, has become a thriving industry that was not limited to the vaudeville stage. Sheet music with such titles as "When Mose with His Nose Leads the Band" and "Under the Matzos Tree" found eager customers. The brand-new recording industry made the routines and ditties of well-known comedians, like the Welch brothers, Barney Bernard, Julian Rose, and others, available to the public. Publishers I. & M. Ottenheimer and the Wehman Brothers kept business going by providing "new" editions of the latest Irish, Coon, Dutch, Hebrew, or Tramp jokes. Dialect-comedy kits for amateur use, consisting, for instance, of a "Hebrew" mask with matching wig, mustache, and facial paints, a popular item in minstrel catalogues, indicate the extent to which dialect comedy brought its understanding of race into the American home.

In keeping with the general rule that the New Humor derived its punch from "the *idea* of pain or embarrassment," dialect humor made the most of the embarrassments and incongruities of immigrant existence. This was true for the physically oriented humor of Weber and Fields, the favorite comic team of the turn of the century. Their two-act played off the comic contrast between the tall, lanky Fields playing Myer, the slick confidence man, and the short, stout Weber as Mike, the beleaguered plump and dumb man. Children of Jewish immigrants from eastern Europe and reared on the streets of the Lower East Side, Joe Weber and Lew Fields had made their debut in 1879 at the age of twelve as "Irish comedians," appearing on stage singing, "Here we are, an Irish pair," while covering their (Jewish) noses. They elaborated a signature act known for its slapstick humor and its aggressive verbal dialogues, which they performed in a comic language made up of a bastardization of Yiddish, German, and English:

MIKE: "I am delightfulness to meet you."
MYER: "Der disgust is all mine."[10]

By the end of the century, Cohan and Nathan observed, "Mr. Fields' favorite trick of poking his forefinger in Mr. Weber's eye" had become "worth a large fortune in itself," and Weber and Fields had their own music hall on Broadway, where they staged elaborate burlesques of Broadway plays.[11]

Embarrassment and pain also provided the underpinnings for the more philosophical style of Joe Welch, one of the most famous Hebrew monologists. His acts consisted of his typical Jewish schlemiel character recounting his woes:

> Maybe you think I'm happy. I got the bad luck. . . . De oder day I vent to de Grand Central Depot and I lay me a fife-dollar bill on the shelf and say, "I vant a ticket for Yonkers." He say, "Excursion?" I say, "No, funeral." Ven I got to Yonkers, I went to the cemetery to visit my brother's dead grave. I kneel down on de grave and pray and cry for two hours. Den I look at de names on de grave and I see me de mistake. I was crying two hours for nothing. When I find de right grave I shall cry all over again. I vent to de janitor of de cemetery and I ask him, "Vere is my brother buried?" He say, "How long has he been dead?" I say, "Six months." He say, "Vat is his name?" I say, "Nathan Jacobson." He say, "Vat did he look like?" I say, "He is de picture of me." He say, "Impossible! Anybody that looks like you ought to be dead longer than six months."
>
> De other day I thought I could take a Turkish bath, but the man was going to charge me a dollar. I said, "That's too much." So he said, "I'll sell you twelve tickets for ten dollars." I said, "Vat do you take me for? How do I know I'm going to live twelve years more."[12]

The winning formula of dialect humor on the stage, in song, or in print was the theme of immigrants' cultural mistranslation. A standard example was the popular routine "Levinsky at the Wedding": "One thing I didn't like about Abe's wedding was right away it said at the top, 'Your presents is requested.' They can't wait to let you know you must help pay the expenses. And down at the bottom was 'please come in evening dress.' Ikey Blatt wore his pajamas."[13]

Another favorite was "Cohen on the Telephone," routines in which cultural ineptness and linguistic misunderstanding are amplified by new technologies, such as the telephone: "Hullo! Hullo! Are you dere? Hullo! Vot number do I want? Vell, vot numbers have you got? Oh, excuse me, my mistook.

I vant Central 248, please, yes, dot's right, 248. I say, miss, am I supposed to keep saying 'Hullo!' and 'Are you there?' until you come back again?"[14]

In Monroe Silver's "Cohen Becomes a Citizen," Cohen fails at his citizenship exam because he responds to the question, "Do you promise to support the Constitution?" with the answer: "How can I do it? I got a vife and tree children now to support." When asked "Where was the Declaration of Independence signed," Cohen points out the obvious: "At the bottom."[15]

A variation on this theme was the scenario of the immigrant parvenu who blunders his way through genteel society. An example comes from *McNally's Bulletin*—which, in addition to an Irish monologue, "Clay Pipe Mike," an Italian monologue, "My Big-a Brother, Joe," a Hebrew monologue "My Daughter, Rebecca," and a blackface monologue, "Bill Bailey's Son"—includes a typical comic Irish/Straight act:

> STRAIGHT: "By the way, do you know what I mean by the guests?"
> IRISH: "Yes. No."
> STRAIGHT: "Now suppose if you were at home and your wife would set a place for each one in the family at the dinner table and then set another place, that place would be for a guest, see?"
> IRISH: "Sure Oi see. She guessed one too many."[16]

The newfound popularity of the joke lent comedians and gag writers a degree of cultural respectability they had not enjoyed before. In popular magazines and newspapers, they appeared alongside leading figures in politics, industry, and letters. As "experts," they were granted with a "vision" that stemmed from their comic sensibility, and in interviews they were frequently asked to expound on their views on current affairs.[17]

For dialect comedians, many of whom had turned to the stage to escape a poverty-filled childhood in the ghetto, this success was often won in a battle of endurance, against fierce competition, and after years of humiliation in low-end theaters and sideshows. For them, the "laughter of the moment represented the fulfillment of their lives."[18] Some advocates of the New Humor took the joke almost as seriously. The joke, according to Paul W. Goldsbury, provided a nerve tonic for an urban audience overstimulated and inured by the shocks of the urban environment, where, as he explained, "Foul odors greet the nostrils, harsh cries and quarreling voices strike the ear; too often the roar and rumble of elevated trains add to the din. Food is stale and unpalatable; the body touches hard surfaces and coarse fabrics, and the eyes see dull, grimy colors, straight lines, and sharp angles."[19]

As Henry Jenkins points out, however, for others the explosion of "purposeless laughter" had more ominous overtones. The New Humor represented everything they found morally questionable, if not outright reprehensible, about mass entertainment in general, and even more so. Genteel society regarded "refined" laughter as evidence of good breeding. As Richard Burton suggested, "One's sense of the fit time to laugh and the kind of laughter to indulge in on occasion is one of the sure tests of culture in the individual and civilization in a people. . . . The coarse guffaw is a mark of ill-breeding."[20]

The onslaught of the latter had grave consequences for the moral caliber and the social cohesion of the nation. "Society is right in her intuitive feeling that an unbridled laughter threatens her order and her laws," James Sully warned. "The laughing impulse, when unchecked, has taken on ugly and deadly forms." Rampant laughter undermined the basic American values of self-restraint, thrift, and discipline, setting the nation on a course toward lawlessness and anarchy. As one article in the *Atlantic Monthly* asserted in 1903: "[Joking] carried to excess must mean the sacrifice of serious consideration of life and duty, would do away with reverential thought, and replace fervency with flippancy. There is a national tendency to overdo the funny side, to make a joke at any cost. Every joke has its price and some are too expensive. Their payment means a lessening of respect for sacred institutions, a lowering of the standard of morality, a dulling of the sensibility to coarseness and vulgarity."[21]

Underlying the vehement rhetoric on the part of the detractors of the New Humor was the sense that mass entertainment in general, and mass comedy in particular, represented a fundamental threat to the social and cultural hierarchy. At stake was the position of the genteel, Anglo-Saxon Protestant elite as arbiters of national "good taste." Over the source of this attack there was little dispute. It came from the urban environment, where "the rapid pace of things, the possibility of swift advancement to the uncultivated, combined with the theoretical ideal of equality, tends to induce superficiality." And it was the masses of immigrants who were responsible for the decline of "respectable" humor. In Katherine Roof's words:

> We seem to have acquired a class of individuals whose so-called sense of humor takes the form of uncouth flippancy, a type of mind that stares blankly in the face of the real article, and laughs noisily at the things that should command respect. . . . The tremendous influx of Continental foreigners—the raw and often the waste material of the countries they come from—into a democracy, English-speaking

and founded upon Anglo-Saxon morality, is a powerful factor in the creation of a new type. . . . Among other changes a perversion of the idea of humor occurs when the American mental habit is grafted upon minds of a different color."[22]

The New Humor, with its visceral appeal to the emotions, was of course the direct opposite of a bourgeois aesthetic that valued distance, emotional control, and "refined" laughter, and proudly so.[23] As the jokesmith Tom P. Morgan boasted: "We do not get our material by inspiration but by theft, assault and battery and otherwise. A solemn, honest, peace-loving commonality is grabbed, thrown down, turned inside out, and reconstructed into an absurdity. A feeble, hoary-headed idea is ruthlessly set upon, crippled, torn to pieces, put together backwards with a new head or tail on it; the King's English is deliberately murdered—all for a joke!"[24]

What Gilbert Seldes described as the "daemonic" aspect of the New Humor was undoubtedly informed by the intense, neurotic energy of metropolitan life. But with its celebration of the low and the vulgar, its language of abuse, insults, and curses, and its attack on "official culture," it also borrowed from what Mikhail Bakhtin analyzes as the tradition of the carnivalesque and its aesthetic of grotesque realism. The aesthetic of grotesque realism left its mark on the New Humor not only in its "low" subjects, its excessive, absurd, and grotesque imagery and its language of humiliation and insult, but also in its celebration of the tearing apart of the established world order and its fantastic recombination of "heterogeneous elements of reality" as part of a natural process of renewal.[25]

Naturally, this comic language, characterized by its ambivalent, but festive rather than melancholy attitude toward destruction and regeneration, bespoke the hopes and fears of the millions of immigrants who had made the metropolis their home. But the New Humor often also contained a sharp edge and tended to exploit ingrained racial stereotypes. A collection of jokes published by Henry Wehman, for instance, illustrates the dominant formula of "Hebrew" humor at the beginning of the century:

ISAACS: "Nopody can dell how dot lasd fire uf Levy's originated."
ABRAMS: "Ach, no! Dot Levy was an original genius!"

Or the following:

LEVI, JR.: "Fadder, de shentlemans vat puys te tiamond engagement ring yesterday comes py te store to-day ant pawned it."

LEVI, SR.: "How vos he look?"

LEVI, JR.: "All proke up."

LEVI, SR.: "Vill you nefer learn to take interest in te bizness? Vy didn't you try to sell te shentlemans a pistol."[26]

Eventually, the fact that the grotesque and vulgar comic body exploited in the New Humor belonged to an immigrant, and not infrequently to a Jew, was a cause for alarm among immigrant groups. In its opposition to the New Humor, puritanical America found some strange bedfellows.

CIVILIZING THE COMIC JEW

In an intellectual context that interpreted "culture" in quasi-biological terms, behaviors and predilections associated with social class (what Bourdieu terms "habitus") tended to be seen as racially determined. Accordingly, taste and etiquette, as Karen Halttunen, Shawn Michelle Smith, and others have argued, codified bourgeois status through an elaborate system of manners and mores, which it presented as the *outward* manifestation of *inner* (moral) distinction. Taste, or the lack thereof, served as an important marker of class.[27] But since the lower classes were to a significant degree made up of immigrants and their offspring, the discourse of "taste" and "civility" acquired a definite racial component. The appeal to an "inborn superiority" in effect sanctified "(white) middle-class identities in opposition to its cultural Others."[28]

Not surprisingly, for many socially ambitious immigrants, the mastery of etiquette provided the finishing touch to a relentless process of self-fashioning through style. Commodity culture and the installment plan brought at least the outer vestiges of genteel status, as expressed through luxury, style, and abundance, within the reach of the middle and lower-middle classes.[29] Etiquette, the newly established *New York Society for the Cultivation of the Self* promised in 1914, would not only complement that process, it would ultimately transform one into a "true" gentleman. Advertising one of its publications, it promised: "No more valuable aid in the acquiring of familiarity with accepted social forms and customs was ever conceived or planned. . . . If it has not been gathered in from life environment, [this knowledge] . . . can be acquired—and acquired rapidly by those who are willing to learn." Moreover, with the help of "this valuable book of reference," these habits will not be "put on and put off with formal evening dress and dainty reception gowns." Genteel behavior will become innate, "the habitual clothing . . . of true courtesy."[30]

Intellectuals influenced by neo-Lamarckian ideas, however, typically discussed "questions of cultural change and stability" in the biocultural terms of "racial instinct," and seriously questioned the long-term effect of social conditions such as poverty or persecution on the "new" immigrants' "civilizing" potential."[31] From their perspective, "genteel" behavior on the part of immigrants, in matters of taste, manners, or etiquette, could only be a superficial imitation, barely covering "race traits," which, initially shaped as an adaptive response to environmental conditions, had long since become virtually instinctive.[32] And such race traits encompassed such varied characteristics as propensity toward beauty, passion, business acumen, competitiveness, work ethos, shrewdness, civility, manners, and mannerisms.[33]

As immigrant groups like the Irish and the Jews began to experience significant social mobility, "racial comics," with their lower-class antecedents and antics, confirmed boundaries of race and class that the socially mobile desperately sought to erase. With their exploitation of accents, malapropisms, cultural confusion, and breach of etiquette, they became a thorn in the side of those already more established in American society. Their collective self-image was taken hostage by a lower-class, burlesque stage persona, who not only did not conform to the codes of gentility, but seemed to throw the civilizing potential of the group as a whole into doubt.

As a result, the late nineteenth century and the first decade of the twentieth century experienced a growing opposition from Italian, Irish, and Jewish groups to the low, burlesque, and, in the view of critics, demeaning stage representations of racial comedy. The "Society for the Prevention of Ridiculous and Pervasive Misrepresentation of the Irish Character" was one of the first watchdog groups to rally successfully against the "disgrace of the race." Composed of ninety-one Irish societies, it resorted to such tactics as "flooding the theatre and drowning out offensive acts by catcalls, boos, hisses, and the singing of Irish songs while throwing objects such as eggs, potatoes and bricks" to force performers deemed objectionable from the stage.[34]

Among the professional casualties of such raids were the Russell Brothers, who were accused of ridiculing "the honest, hard-working Irish servant girl." Some on the committee found offense that the brothers "raised their dresses on the stage"; others objected to the backside kicks that were a standard feature of the performance and appealed to Oscar Hammerstein, with whom they were under contract, to censure their act.[35] The brothers eliminated some of the "offensive" material and responded to the uproar with a curtain speech, in which they stressed their own Hibernian ancestry and their support for Irish causes as a sign of their good faith. When the riots that had become a standard accompaniment to their performances continued, Hammerstein gave in and terminated the brothers' contract.

In an attempt to renew their act, the Russell Brothers renamed it the "Stage-Struck Maids," and even tried to transform it into a Swedish-dialect act, but they slipped from fame in the first decade of the twentieth century. At the trial of a number of suspected rioters, neither the (Irish) police, nor the (Irish) theater manager, nor members of the audience could be persuaded to testify. The (Irish) Judge Keary, dismissing the charges, publicly supported the defendants' actions, stating: "My impression of the Russell show . . . is very bad. The public should not encourage or patronize such acts. No men of blood, particularly of Irish blood, could sit and listen to anyone who would thus disgrace the women of his race. I am satisfied from the testimony that this act was indecent, shocking and vulgar."[36]

In the first decade of the twentieth century, however, the most vocal opposition rallied around the "Hebrew comic," who had started to overtake in popularity all other forms of racial comedy. A wide-open field, it attracted a wealth of new talent. A review of the 1906 play *Bizzy Izzy's Vacation* mentioned of its star, George Sidney, that "since Mr. Sidney began to assume this style of character, his popularity has grown steadily."[37] The same was true for many other performers who were looking for fresh opportunities.

The rising star of the Hebrew comics was fueled by and in turn stimulated the notion that humor was a particular characteristic of the Jewish people. This concept, a radical departure from previously held ideas of Jews as a humorless, tradition-bound, and oppressed people, was developed in the late nineteenth century in the context of the rise of nationalism, when humor came to be regarded not only as indicative of a people's relative degree of civilization but also as capturing the people's "spirit." Humor was "a form of mental alertness and moral wisdom," and wit, above all, was the highest expression of a comic perception that arose only in a state of philosophical distance, when events reveal their contradictions and incongruities.[38]

Jewish authors and folklorists, eager to identify the "Hebrew spirit," set out to record a tradition of Jewish humor that stretched from the Talmud and the Midrash to the German poet Heinrich Heine. Jewish humor, they claimed, forged as it was in response to millennia of oppression, was marked by its intellectuality, excessive self-mockery, and a particularly philosophical bent, in contrast to the aggressive and physically oriented humor of other peoples.

Even rabbis got involved. Herman Adler, the chief rabbi of London, for instance, wrote in 1893:

The Hebrews . . . at a comparatively early stage in their history, attained that ripe and strong mental development which the elaboration of wit and the comprehension of humour demand. . . . Crushed as he has been to the dust by the iron hand of bigotry, cowed by the soul-chilling venom of contempt that "makest a wise man mad," he could not have survived, had not benign nature mercifully endowed him with extraordinary elasticity, with a wonderful power of resilience which enabled him to elude effectually all the attempts made at every age, and in every clime, to lay him down.[39]

The marketing of "Hebrew" humor relied heavily on the idea that Hebrew joke books, songs, and vaudeville routines represented authentic Jewish humor. But what was being advertised as "Jewish humor" often was less than elevated or intellectual. Not only did Hebrew humor exhibit the coarse directness characteristic of the New Humor, but it frequently exploited ingrained anti-Semitic concepts, such as Jews' "corrupt language," their supposed pinching for money, fraudulent business practices, lack of cleanliness, and hypersexuality.[40]

Not surprisingly, then, the figure of the grotesquely comic Jew, as the supposed embodiment of the "Hebrew," and the Hebrew comic, as the leading exponent of Hebrew "wit," became the subjects of great controversy. This was all the more so because by 1905 the lucrative field of Hebrew comedy had been "almost appropriated by the irrepressible Hebrew behind the footlights."[41]

David Warfield's *The Auctioneer* perhaps best exemplifies the complexities of the early twentieth-century stage Jew. The play was presented to the public as "upgraded" Hebrew comedy. Its comic Jew, in the words of Warfield, was transplanted from the ghetto to "new and expanded surroundings," and, with that, transformed from a "burlesque, laugh exciting character" to "an all around human being, with pathos as well as comedy in his make-up."[42] Such a carefully designed blend of comedy and pathos, according to James Sully, a leading child psychologist and critic of the vulgarity of the New Humor, would "exhibit the intimate connections between that which amuses and that which touches the serious sentiments, respect and pity" and elicit empathy and "thoughtful laughter."[43]

Warfield furthermore contributed to the cultural mobility of the comic Jew from a vehicle for "low" burlesque into an appropriate subject for "art" by talking up the profile of Hebrew comedy. He placed the play squarely within the tradition of the "Satire, Wisdom, and Humor of the Russian Jew." "It is only of late years that the American people have begun to appreciate

the unfailing fountain of humor that is possessed by the Russian and Ruman-
ian Jews," he explained. "Jewish humor . . . is intellectual, rather than physical, and is the utterance of a mature man recognizing grim or laughable
incongruity in things about him. . . . From the most unpromising topics
he extracts some quaint merriment. . . . They are masters in that variety
of humor which springs from negative incongruity."[44]

The play's portrayal of Levi as a devoted family man and its many indoor
family scenes (typically suggestive of emotional depth and bourgeois interiority) were promoted to American Jewish audiences as a corrective to the
stereotypical ghetto Jew. Moreover, in an attempt to preempt criticism, director David Belasco invited a group of clergy from different faiths to attend
a performance of *The Auctioneer* to review "Mr. Warfield's acting and its
moral effect" for the *Chicago American*. Rabbi Schanfarber, of Temple
K'Neseth Anshe Maariv, enthusiastically embraced the play for showing the
"true character of the Jew," evident in "his devotion to his family, his hope-
ful optimism even when all is lost, his desire to spare his kith and kin all
pain and sorrow, his persistence in the face of all untoward circumstances."[45]

The Auctioneer's strategy of cultural upgrading certainly had its rewards
for David Warfield, who was transformed from a vaudeville comedian into
an actor with star status, commanding one of the highest salaries in the
business. (In his first year on Broadway, he was offered, and rejected, a sum
of a million dollars by producer Felix Isman, to be paid over a ten-year
period.)[46] But the play certainly did not lack in stereotypical Jewish representations. The *Chicago Journal* considered "Mr. Warfield's characterization
of Simon Levi . . . genuinely artistic." But what it considered "artistic" were
his "facial expressions of various emotions. Not the smallest detail was
neglected, from the persuasive yet betraying smile, the shambling gait, and
the unwieldy feet—all characteristics of Jewish difference."[47]

Alan Dale, one of the play's few critics, faulted the performance, despite
all its claims to realism, for relying on essentially the same unflattering
stereotypes as the vaudeville stage: "Just a few minutes before . . . old Levi
had sold a rancid overcoat for $20 by making the purchaser believe that a full
pocket book had been left in its pocket by mistake. Just preceding that you
had seen the old Hester Street fellow watering the clothes, and stick up a
'damaged by fire' legend over them. All these tricks . . . cling to the Hebrew
as frogs hover around the Frenchman or frankfurters around the German."[48]

The *Toledo Blade* also failed to be persuaded by the play's supposed realism, pathos, and depth. "Here and there is a moment of intensity which
stirs the emotions of the spectator and makes him for the instant feel that,

after all, perhaps, he is looking at real men and women, suffering real sorrows," it declared. "Such moments, however, are few, and for the most part Mr. Warfield and the other players depend upon broad humor to make their effects. Indeed, the house was roaring with laughter almost from the beginning to the end." But in these characterizations, it continued, Warfield "does nothing to offend, for he characterizes the lowest class, one that cannot be offended." And the paper added, "The very persons who enjoyed it most thoroughly were the members of Toledo's Jewish aristocracy who were at the Valentine in numbers. They recognized in him the lower class Jew, just as others have recognized the stage Bowery Boy and have enjoyed his little mannerisms."[49]

Undoubtedly, the play's delicate balancing act between burlesque and realism, or comedy of manners and tragedy, and the alternate representations of Simon Levi as "comic ghetto Jew" and respectable middle-class family man, provided the key to the play's widespread appeal among Jewish and non-Jewish audiences. Asked "how many enemies [he] had made among the Jews because of his caricatures," Warfield responded: "They like it . . . and people say Jews haven't a sense of humor. Why, in all the time I've been impersonating in Yiddish—and I wore a hooked nose too,—they've been the biggest part of my audience."[50]

A little more than a decade later, however, a rerun of *The Auctioneer* encountered considerably more opposition. When an editorial in the *Chicago Tribune* exempted Warfield's play from the Jewish caricatures objected to by Jewish groups, Rabbi Hirschberg felt compelled to respond. In a public letter to the *Chicago Sunday Tribune*, on January 11, 1914, he took the editor in question to task:

> Sir: When you say: "In 'The Auctioneer' he enters his Hester Street second hand clothing store, smiling the beatific Warfield smile and while radiating tenderness and generosity, pours water on the merchandise and marks it 'Damaged by Fire.' At once we begin to like him; we suspect he is one of us, and when he tells the clerk to put the cotton umbrellas among his silk we are sure of it." You most emphatically call attention to what the majority of stage portrayals of the Jew and the unthinking public have identified as distinctively and peculiarly Jewish characteristics. . . . I am sure that the impression made upon the non-Jewish portion of the audience is a most unfavorable one and that it only serves to confirm the belief—fostered by centuries of the most despicable caricatures—that the Jew is a dishonorable tradesman, a petty scump whose contaminating society ought to be avoided.[51]

By the time of Rabbi Hirschberg's letter, opposition to "the stage travesty of Abraham's descendants" had evolved into an organized campaign to rid the American stage of offensive Jewish characterizations. Most vocal in its opposition against what it described as the "buffoonery of the Jew" was the Chicago Anti-Stage Jew Ridicule Committee, headed by Judge Pam and Miss Mollie Eda Osherman.

The immediate incentive for this "crusade" was a review of a performance of the Hebrew comic Barney Bernard, written by James Bennett for the *Chicago Herald.* In it, Bennett concluded that "Barney Bernard, impersonating not unskillfully an Old Jew, made the Jewish race the butt of much vulgar allusion." And he added, "A gentile can never cease to marvel why the Jews, who are such loyal patrons of the theater, permit the outrageous black-guarding of their race which is the feature of so much current fooling in the playhouse."[52]

The review prompted a decisive reaction from Miss Osherman:

If Mr. Bennett, a non Jew, finds these caricatures and distorted presentations of the Jews unpalatable, both visually and orally, it is no difficult matter to imagine the obnoxious effect they produce on a member of the race so grossly maligned. . . . Not only have these brazen, audacious burlesques nothing to recommend or extenuate them from an artistic standpoint, but this evil has a more serious aspect. Through the power of consistent suggestion, these vulgar types continuously portrayed on the stage implant in the mind of the thoughtless theater-goer the idea that they are in fact representative types of the nationalities they depict, and that their vulgarities are mere traits of the race.[53]

Other reviewers soon followed suit. Ripley Saunders, of the *St. Louis Post-Dispatch,* declared "Mr. Barney's gesticulations and coarse jokes as the dress-suited Jewish roué seeing Paris incredibly offensive." For Osherman, these criticisms were sufficient reason to conclude: "When two well-known critics stigmatize a Jewish characterization as outrageous and incredibly offensive, it seems that there is a clanging call for action." This action culminated in a circular letter, issued by the Chicago Anti-Stage Jew Ridicule Committee on September 1, 1913, which called on Jews to be vigilant: "If, inadvertently, you should attend a playhouse where the Jew is the target of the comedian's vulgar horse-play for the gusto of the audience, register at once a vigorous protest to the management. The Jew has submitted long enough to public slurs and insults on the stage."

A second letter asked that Jews "refrain from attending theatres and nickel

shows where allusions to the Jews are made by coarse and stupid jokes, gesticulations, songs, stories, and obnoxious moving pictures, which cause us
to be despised and humiliated."[54] The Chicago campaign soon was supported
by other American Jewish institutions. In its annual meeting of July 1914,
the Associated Rabbis of America adopted a resolution designed to force
Hebrew comedians from the stage by appealing to their congregants. As the
New York Star reported,

> The rabbis said . . . that it had been their pleasure to preach from the pulpit exactly
> what they saw and to advise to their congregation to shun certain theatres where
> something was said and done to reflect on the Jew and which would incur hatred.
> They said that their congregations had neglected the playhouses mentioned in their
> sermons, and that the box office had suffered all on account of silly and ridicu-
> lous business that could do absolutely no good, and a great deal of social harm.[55]

William Hammerstein, manager of the Victoria Theatre, one of the vaudeville houses targeted by the Chicago Anti-Stage Jew Ridicule Committee,
soon bowed under the pressure and bad publicity and decided that "in the
future no act containing a caricature of the Jew shall be played at the Victoria
Theatre."[56] In August, another major vaudeville theater followed suit. The
Chicago Record Herald announced that the management of the Majestic Theater intended to part company with "all comic roundabouts whose stock in
trade is gibes at the Jewish race," unless they promised to "be very circumspect in word, deed, and make-up." One of the performers under contract,
who the management named as a representative offender, was Joe Welch.[57]

An editorial in the *New York Dramatic Mirror,* however, astutely observed
the contradiction of these "crusades":

> There is a touch of paradox in the agitation among the Jews of Chicago over the
> burlesque Hebrew types seen on stage and their demand for the suppression of
> the stage Jew. There is eminent justification for their disgust. Such distortions, how-
> ever, appeal less to a Genteel audience than to members of the race themselves,
> judging by local standards, at least. Moreover, nearly all the Jew impersonators are
> Hebrews themselves, and they get their engagements in most cases from Hebrew
> managers.[58]

For the supporters of the boycott, this observation struck at the heart of the
problem. Accusing Jewish Hebrew impersonators of self-hatred, the *New
York Clipper* responded:

Fundamentally, there is more than a grain of truth in the deplorable fact that it is usually a co-religionist who slurs his race and his nationality in his presentation of a dubious Jewish type. It is high time to look with unglazed eyes at this condition and resolutely recast our attitude of urbane acceptance of these caricatures as an unprootable evil. These Jewish parasites, who live by brutally and contemptuously slurring their own people, should be dealt with in summary fashion. By boycotting these so-called Jewish impersonators who slimily distort the clean-cut wit and humor of the Jew into offensive "take-offs," this undesirable species should be driven out of existence.[59]

Forced on the defensive, Jewish Hebrew impersonators were at pains to legitimize their characterizations by distinguishing them from those targeted by the critics. Willie and Eugene Howard went so far as to claim rabbinical supervision of their performances, asserting that "every gag we have ever used we have submitted to a rabbi who is a friend of ours and who must approve it before we use it."[60] Belle Baker vouched for the authenticity of her impersonations by pointing to her own Jewish working-class background. Working in a shirtwaist factory was one of the things to which Belle Baker attributed her vaudeville success. "You see," she explained,

a comic song to be truly comic ought to have a true-to-nature touch. If you don't understand the people you are characterizing your impersonation is not a burlesque and not real at all. Well, I don't have to make a sightseeing tour to get my types. I was born in New York right among them. . . . All my impersonations are real. When I sing an Italian or Irish or Yiddish song, I have a definite character in mind that I've known for years. I present the character from that point of view,— not the outsider's.[61]

Presenting himself as "one of the foremost crusaders against the presentation on the stage of disagreeable burlesque types of foreigners," Ben Welch commented on the criticism of Hebrew impersonators:

You are probably aware that I am of the Hebraic persuasion, and while I cannot sympathise with the intolerant spirit of some of my people who would insist on eliminating Jewish characters from the stage, I do, to a certain extent, agree with them in their protests against certain forms of ridicule to which the Hebrew has been subjected. . . . But if we were to remove from the stage the Hebrew character in comedy roles, the stage would lose much. The Irish, or some of the Irish . . . are loudly demanding the effacement of the Irish comedian. We have not yet heard from the Germans, and if any race has been offensively caricatured, it is certainly the Germans. Maybe the Kaiser will file his protest, and after that, we shall expect Booker T. Washington to ask that the negro cease to be impersonated. If this thing keeps up, the stage will be without characters and without comedy.[62]

Nicknamed "The Warfield of Vaudeville" for the "the delicate touch" he gave his "Hebrew and Italian types," Ben Welch successfully branched out into other racial types, and was eager to point out the support for his Italian impressions among Italian American audiences, claiming that "wherever I go delegations call upon me, and sometimes they make me gifts."[63] Joe Welch was less fortunate. Lacking the versatility of his brother, the boycotts instigated by the Chicago Anti-Stage Jew Ridicule Committee effectively ended his career. He died in a mental institution in 1918 at the age of forty-nine.[64]

Others found inspiration in David Warfield's mix of pathos and comedy and his transplantation of the ghetto Jew into a life of luxury and emotional depth. Leo Carillo, who specialized in Chinese, Italian, and Spanish impersonations, staged a "high class of Italian" named Tito Lombardi, whom he characterized as an "extremely temperamental Italian who makes love and dresses indiscriminately."[65] As he explained, it was "no longer necessary to burlesque foreigners in order to bring out their idiosyncrasies":

> Time was when the theatergoers' idea of an Italian was that of an organ grinder, having as his most conspicuous companion article of apparel a red bandana handkerchief. In fact, the public seemed to regard with considerable contempt any attempt on the part of a serious actor to represent anything else. David Warfield, who brought out all the kindly tenderness of the Jew in "The Auctioneer" was the forerunner in this new school. So ably did he succeed in showing that there was a side to the Jew which up to that point had been overlooked, that I was encouraged to make the same attempt in characterizing Tito, the artistic, but impractical designer of fashionable clothes.[66]

Sam Bernard, however, concluded that David Warfield's "old-time Hebrew" had become offensive "not because people have grown tired of this humor, but because a new race of American Jews have sprang from him. They have surpassed him in manners, style, and ways of living." His own Jewish impersonation, he claimed, was "not offensive, because in spite of the racial fact, I am representing the modern Jew, whose attitude toward the Christian race is a revelation of the sentiment and the character of his kind."[67]

Hebrew dialect comedians, many of whom harbored aspirations toward more legitimate and respectable roles themselves, saw the writing on the wall. The result was a gradual cultural upgrading of the comic Jew, from burlesque to realistic, peddler to family man, backward to modern, eastern European to American, lower to middle class, and vulgarity to respectability.

POTASH AND PERLMUTTER

At the heart of the controversy surrounding the Hebrew comic was, as Miss Osherman pointed out in her letter, the suggestion that his vulgarities were "mere traits of the race."[68] The comic Jew resonated strongly with perceptions of Jews as quintessentially "uncivilized" and "vulgar," which had gained widespread currency in America's middle- and upper-class circles around the 1870s, in pace with the social mobility of German Jewry. In 1877, for instance, *The Nation* observed a Jewish tendency toward "gaudiness in dress or ornament," which, it suspected, "has deeper roots than modern history goes, and testifies the purity of the race and the freshness with which the eye still retains the Oriental passion for brilliancy of costume."[69] When eastern European Jews began to move up the social ladder and tried to gain access to cultural domains previously reserved for Gentile social elites, genteel America anew cited Jews' "vulgar ostentation" and "lack of civility" as a legitimate basis for their social exclusion.[70]

The American Jewish elite, made up largely of Jews of German and Sephardic ancestry, was keenly aware of the racial stigma attached to "uncivilized behavior." The German Jewish Walter Lippmann, in a 1922 article in the *American Hebrew,* identified ostentatious bourgeois Jewry as "the fountain of anti-Semitism" and "the greatest misfortune that has ever befallen the Jewish people." Jews, he complained, "dissipate awkwardly." "When they rush about in super-automobiles, bejeweled and befurred and painted and overbarbered, when they build themselves French chateaus and Italian palazzi, they stir up the latent hatred against crude wealth in the hands of shallow people."[71]

The mission of the Anti-Stage Jew Ridicule Committee, then, was decidedly two-pronged: to elevate the caliber of humor presented on the popular stage under the cover of "Hebrew comedy" in accordance with the Jewish tradition of "clean wit and humor," and to upgrade the tastes of the audiences patronizing such performances. The crusade of the Anti-Stage Jew Ridicule Committee confronted Hebrew comedians with the difficult, if not impossible, task of making Jewish humor respectable, and at the same time funny. The play *Potash and Perlmutter,* which saw its premiere in 1913 in the midst of boycotts and vigilantism, was the first to position itself squarely in terms of the "Rehabilitation of the Stage Jew" and successfully circumnavigate the pitfalls of the trade.

Loosely based on sketches written by the English-born Jewish author Montague Glass, the play featured the Polish Jewish comedian Barney Bernard and the Russian-born Alexander Carr in the leading roles. The choice of Barney Bernard as Potash was, to say the least, a risky one. Barney Bernard, who made his first breakthrough after taking over Warfield's peddler role in the Weber and Fields production *Fiddle-Dee-Dee* after Warfield left to play the lead in Belasco's play, was one of the main targets of the vigilance committee.

The committee felt insulted by Bernard's characterization of the wigmaker "Schmaltz" in the production *Rollicking Girl* and his portrayal of "Mr. Cohen from Bridgeport," a "small town Jew with overly thrifty ways."[72] The production *From Across the Pond,* which dealt with the efforts of a German alderman to get elected and included scenes at Ellis Island, a Bowery Dime Museum, Coney Island, and Chatham Square, in which Bernard played Moses Reschitsky, an "East Side Hebrew," also was criticized. In particular, Reschitsky's song "Oy, Oy, Oy, Shicker Is the Goy," relating to his experiences on shipboard, was deemed "objectionable."[73] Bernard's "coarse jokes" and gesticulations as a Jewish American upstart visiting Paris set off a storm of protest. Sensitive to these criticisms, Bernard responded: "It is pleasant to play Jewish parts; but there are difficulties that must be avoided. No nation should be ridiculed or held up to criticism. . . . We must bring out the humor without the malice. The Jewish race has been so persecuted that it is often a trifle over sensitive, and we must be careful to avoid anything that will hurt. It is business as much as anything . . . seven tenths of the audience is Jewish; besides that, the business side of the theater is in the hands of the Jew."[74]

Bernard, in fact, harbored aspirations that went far beyond the burlesque Jewish comedy roles he was known for. "I don't like to be confined in the public's estimation by the term comedian. That has come to be associated with the term 'clown,'" he revealed. "I'd rather be called an actor or an artist or even a thespian."[75] In 1908, his role as Louisiana Lou in the Ziegfeld Follies first opened up the legitimate stage for him. But Bernard's real opportunity came in the form of the role of Abe Potash.

The original Potash and Perlmutter sketches featured the trials and tribulations of Abe Potash and Mawruss (Morris) Perlmutter, two *allrightnik,* upwardly-mobile clothing merchants. The humor of these stories resides

mostly in the plots, which detail the tricks of the trade in the cut-throat, inces-
tuous wholesale cloak and suit trade. In one sketch Potash and Perlmutter
set out to lure a successful designer from another firm, only to discover that
the designer in question is a lemon, whom the firm had been trying to get
rid of without breaking contract. They manage to sell the designer back to
the original firm, by marketing some of Perlmutter's successful designs as
the designer's.

In other sketches, the partners barely escape financial disaster through
the more than unscrupulous practices of shady business associates. A buyer,
who has bought up large amounts of stock on advance credit, is a gambler
who invests the money he has earned on his sales in his pinochle game.
Other buyers are just about to file for bankruptcy, or are planning to flee
the country after pocketing the earnings. Other shady Jewish characters
include the real estate agent Sam Slotkin, who also is the walking trade-
union delegate who orders Potash and Perlmutter's operators to strike for
a "proper place to work in," notably the uptown loft he has been trying to
sell them (243). The sketches also feature the disreputable shyster lawyer
Henry Feigenbaum, who plays the partners against their competitors (whom
he also represents) in order to get commissions from both sides, and the
corrupt salesman Mark Pasinsky, who turns out to be employed by various
concerns at the same time, a ploy that is discovered when he gets his clothing samples from the various firms mixed up.

Potash and Perlmutter, however, are essentially shrewd, but honest, businessmen. Sometimes their commercial insight is clouded by the lure of
various get-rich-quick schemes, which invariably turn sour: Potash's real
estate investment scheme turns out to be a money pit from which he can
barely escape. Fortunately, Potash recognizes a deal when he sees one, and
spends a thousand dollars he had intended to invest into copper mine stock
on silk foulards. The copper stock first soars, then collapses, and the foulards turn out to be the best investment, after all.

Of the two partners, Morris is the "modern" of the two. He and his wife,
Minnie, have ambitions to move to the suburbs. When Abe cannot remember the name of the bookkeeper, Ralph, Morris scorns him:

> "Ralph ain't no harder than Moe or Jake, Abe . . . and anyhow . . . why should an
> up-to-date family like the Tuchman's give their boys such back-number names like
> Jake or Moe?"
>
> "Jacob and Moses was decent, respectable people in the old country, Mawruss,"
> Abe corrected solemnly.

"I know it, Abe," Morris rejoined, "but that was long since many years ago already. Now is another time entirely in New York City." (196)

The up-to-date Perlmutter whistles tunes from "Travvy-ater," which begets him the patronage of a buyer who had been taken to a prizefight by a competing firm, much to his chagrin. Recognizing in Perlmutter a fellow gentleman, the buyer lays out the structures of prestige to be followed by the socially ambitious: "For anybody else but a loafer . . . prize fighting is a nix. Opera, Mr. Perlmutter, that's an amusement for a gentleman."

In the play *Potash and Perlmutter,* the differences between Abe and Morris are accentuated to the degree that they become foils for each other. The racialized body belonged definitely to Bernard. Whereas Mawruss, described as a fortyish "rather good-looking, dynamic Jewish merchant" was played by the tall, lanky, blond Alexander Carr, the short and stocky Barney Bernard played the "rather stout, kindly, whimsical" Abe Potash, who was presented as a generation older than Mawruss.

As partners in business, Potash and Perlmutter trade in cloaks and suits as well as in good-natured insults. One-liners, such as Abe's declaration, "Business is business and charity is charity, y' understand; but even in charity, Mawruss, it don't do no harm to keep the expenses down," establish their shrewd business sense. Their social and cultural profile is filled in by peculiarities of speech and body language, and well-worn jokes about their unfamiliarity with rules of etiquette: "R.S.V.P.," according to a gesticulating Morris, "means, 'remember to send vedding present.'"[76]

Potash and Perlmutter's Jewishness is connoted through food (dill pickles and liver sandwiches), their mangled English (Abe: "If I could sell all to my Landsleute [countrymen] what is in the cloak and suit business . . . we would be doing a million-dollar business), their jokes (upon discovering traveling salesman Manny Immerglick's expense account, Potash exclaims: "Twenty-two dollars for sleeping cars—and he was recommended as a wide-awake salesman!"), and such Yiddishisms as "Oi Vai," "Nu," and "das fehlt nur noch" (lit. "only that is missing").[77]

Yet these traits are offset by their generous impulses and their love for their family and the Jewish people.[78] Whereas the sketches focused exclusively on the business dealings of the two, the play domesticates Abe by giving him a loving wife (a "stout, hearty woman") with a weakness for pinochle and a tendency toward jealousy, and a "beautiful and charming daughter," Irma. Mawruss, in the sketches married to Minnie, in the play is a bachelor, who develops a romantic interest in the young "tall, blonde and beautiful" Ruth Snyder, a successful, ambitious, and financially savvy designer.

Abe's and Mawruss's business sense is not so sharp as to prevent them from being taken advantage of by swindlers and frauds. Mozart Rabiner talks the partners into advancing him three weeks' expenses for his job as a salesman with the reasoning that "I go out with your sample line . . . then if you don't owe me a thousand dollars commissions at the end of the time, why, I don't want to work for you."[79] It also does not preclude the hiring of Boris Andrieff, a young, poetic composer ill-fitted for his bookkeeping job:

> "Abe," says Mawruss, "That feller Andrieff makes music and Chopin better than he makes it bookkeeping. Didn't he send it last week alretty a bill to Perlstein, Gimmelheim and Company for eighty dollars when it should have been eight hundred, yes!"
>
> "Mawruss, can I help it he loves it his music? From Travayater and Travatory backwards all the operas he knows it to Palliatsky. You make me mad, Mawruss. Is it I should let him starve when he knows it languages—German und French und English—which he speaks it even perfecter than you speak it. Bah!"[80]

In spite of their "mercantile shrewdness," Potash and Perlmutter risk financial ruin to save Andrieff, who has developed a romantic liaison with Abe's daughter, Irma, from being deported to Russia. Andrieff, whose father and brother were killed in the "massacre at Kiev," is accused by the Russian police of throwing a bomb and killing the chief of police of Kiev.[81] When he is arrested, Potash mortgages the business to bail him out of jail, then encourages him to jump bail and escape to Canada. Eventually, with the intervention of a Jewish millionaire and philanthropist, Henri Steuerman, the case against Boris is revealed as instigated by "race prejudice."[82] His innocence proven, Boris marries Irma.

Barney Bernard saw his character's "bigheartedness . . . , his love for his own people, and his devotion to his family" as a sign of what he characterized as the "Rehabilitation of the Stage Jew." "I think the day of the ultra comic Jew on the stage, the Jew with the exaggerated nose and splay feet, 't is gone, and I hope that my Potash has helped along with his good work of giving people an idea of the real Hebrew as he lives, breathes and exists today."[83]

"I regard 'Potash and Perlmutter' as true comedy," he explained on another occasion, "and it is the first real play of the Jewish race. . . . With the delicacy and refinement of a true master's hand it sets out the bad as well as the good. . . . Hitherto the principal feature of the humor expected from a Jew character on the stage has been a mean pinching for money. That had to be backed by general buffoonery. In 'Potash and Perlmutter' there is no clowning, and the Jew's love for money is shown in its proper light. . . . Examine into the real meaning and purpose of his love for making money, and you will see that the sole object is his home. . . . [It] is a wonderful lesson, both to Jews and Gentiles. It ought to go a long way to bring the two races together and make them understand and love each other."[84]

The play also contained a moral lesson for "the weaker Jews," represented in the play by the "scathing types of the shyster lawyer and . . . the Pasinsky's who will sink every trick in the trade and ever attempt to seduce their friends' morals." "The classes they represent should take the lesson to heart," Bernard warned. "And many will. None are quicker to learn than the Jew."[85]

According to the actors, the play exemplified the development of the "Jewish character." The difference between Abe Potash and Mawruss Perlmutter in particular illustrated the influence of the American environment on the race. Abe Potash, Barney Bernard explained, "is typical of the present day Jew whose mind and ideas have broadened under the genial influence of American liberty after a boyhood spent in the ghetto of some Russian town where contumely [sic] and abuse have been his early portion." "The character of Abe is supposed to be at least ten years, or nearly a generation, behind that of Mawruss," he continued. "Abe is an immigrant Jew . . . whose spirit was once all but crushed, and you see the effect . . . in an occasional touch of servility, an outburst of something akin to rebellion, and especially in the pathetic caution that makes him suspect in everything some trick to catch and do him."

"Mawruss," Alexander Carr pontificated, "is a fine type of the Jew born and educated in America. There is not the slightest touch of the buffoon about him. . . . He has traveled and mixed with people. He uses words correctly, and the only difference in speech is a slight burring accent which he cannot get rid of. The contrast between him and Abe Potash marks the rapid progress of the Jew in advancing himself in culture as well as wealth."[86]

Yet many reviewers were not so discerning and interpreted the play as manifesting the immutability of the Jewish character in spite of the influences of the American environment. According to the London *Spectator*, the play exhibited the Jewish type "as conditioned by the commercial system of a great American city. It shows us the Jew as 'hustler,' yet at every turn governed or affected by the abiding characteristics of the race. The chief interest of the play is in the conflict between the acquisitive instinct and generous domestic impulses. . . . It is interesting as a psychological study of the mingled enterprise and caution, astuteness and rashness, of the Semitic temperament."[87]

These conflicting readings point to a fundamental ambiguity in the play's interpretation of the "Jewish character." Since Jews, too, understood themselves to be a "race," the play struggled to locate a Jewish racial essence that steered clear of demeaning stereotypes, was susceptible to cultural change, and showed "civilization" to boot. Jews' "innate" comic sensibility provided such a locus. It could connect Jewish characters across the ages and across a diverse social and cultural spectrum.

Barney Bernard and Alexander Carr expounded this view on the Jew's comic essence in their commentaries on the play. They argued that the Jew embodied comedy, and that this was transparent in the Jewish body, as well as in the Jewish mind. As Carr explained, the Jew "has only to be himself and he is excruciatingly funny. The way he raises an eyebrow, the natural expressions that play upon his face, are irresistibly comical without the need of exaggeration." Moreover, in an effort to preempt allegations of racial slurring, Carr emphasized the self-denigrating aspect of Jewish humor. "The awkward part of a Jew's humor is that he is almost invariably the butt of it himself," Carr suggested. "He can therefore, get himself into absurd and laughable situations far more naturally than any other race."

Indeed, Carr continued, it is humor, this "curious bent in the mind of every Jew which gives a twist of its own to everything," which connects the Jewish race across generations and classes. "Take Mawruss, for example," he suggested. "Mawruss has few or no mannerisms except in instants of excitement, and at all times he endeavors to live up to the highest ideals of a gentleman. And yet, far from having to be a mere foil to bring out the humor of Abe, he is equally a source of laughter himself. I doubt if this could be so were the characters other than those of Jews. For Mawruss, despite all his polish, is still a Jew."[88]

Bernard emphasized the respectability of the play's humor by placing it squarely within what he described as an age-old tradition of Jewish humor. *Potash and Perlmutter*, he claimed, stood in a direct line with the "A-number-One humorists" from the days of the Talmud. He continued to attribute the humorousness of Abe's character to "his cautiousness, the fact that [he] has never been able perfectly to learn the language of his new land, [and . . . his] natural wit." Mawruss, Bernard claimed, "is no less amusing, for, though supposed to be a higher and more educated type, the Jew is always shining through."

But the difference between the respectable, innately witty, naturally humorous Jew and the stereotypical commercial, vulgar, and grotesque comic Jew was not easy to maintain. Indeed, it collapses when Bernard illustrates Mawruss's ontological comic quality by recounting a scene from the play. In the scene, Mawruss, "with the utmost polish and grace," insists that Mrs. Potash accept a model gown she has admired in the store's showroom as a present from him. The next instant, however, he remembers the cost, and orders the price of the gown to be charged to Potash. "Little touches like that," Bernard concludes, "make him humorous in a way which could not be given to any other than a Hebrew character."[89]

This scene contrasts Perlmutter's "gentlemanliness," his "polish and grace," with his "baser" commercial instincts. By doing so, it unwittingly evokes long-standing stereotypes of Jewish gentility as superficial, a sign of the uncanny Jewish ability to mimic the manners and mores of their host societies.[90] Underneath a surface polish of gentility, the "false" Jewish gentleman hid an "authentic" identity that was indelibly marked by class and race. The main reason for Perlmutter's failure as a "true" gentleman lies in the fact that he has not mastered the distance from "the realism of necessity"—the realm of bodies, materials, and production—which, according to Pierre Bourdieu, serves as the real mark of social distinction (and of racial difference).

Not surprisingly, many reviewers tended to miss the "respectable" aspects of *Potash and Perlmutter*'s comic Jew as well. The comic appeal of the play, one critic suggested, lay in the fact that it was "so frankly vulgar and commercial." The "dollar mark [was] stamped upon everything," on the "garish home of Perlmutter" as well as on the face of Abe Potash, which was as "a map of commercial expressions."[91]

The comic "Jew shining through" in the Americanized, middle-class, educated, and polished Perlmutter, then, not surprisingly, is still the same stereotypically shrewd Jewish businessman. And by the same token, the comic Jew continues to be the Other of genteel etiquette.[92] Yet this split, comic Jew is simultaneously the hero of the play. When the new designer (who in the later runs of the play is renamed Ruth Goldman, rather than the ethnically more neutral Ruth Snyder) remarks that the philanthropist Henri Steuerman is just the kind of man that makes the Jewish people what they are, Mawruss responds, "Yes, he makes up for the ignorant, the uncouth ones, like me." "I don't think of you as ignorant and uncouth, Mr. Perlmutter," Ruth objects. "A man who can build up a business like this has something fine in him, especially after what you have done for Mr. Andrieff."[93]

This sentence signals the transfer of Ruth's affections from the sensitive artist Andrieff to the sensible Perlmutter. Simultaneously, the play switches from comedy to pathos. "You started in with nothing but brains and energy and you built up a business," Ruth tells Perlmutter, who believes himself bankrupt. "You still have the brains and the energy and knowledge and experience as well. You mustn't give up." And she continues: "I thought I cared for Andrieff . . . but it was his loneliness, his artistic helplessness, that I pitied. . . . But you, Morris, you are a man that needs no pity—a real man, a business man."[94]

Given this wholehearted endorsement of the manhood of the struggling Jewish merchant, it should come as no surprise that *Potash and Perlmutter* struck a chord with Jewish audiences, particularly with members of the cloak and suit trade, and became the longest-running play of 1913. Nor is it surprising that critics of Abraham Cahan's scathing portrayal of the character of the "business Jew" in *The Rise of David Levinsky* advised "recourse to our lovable, amiable and human friends, Abraham Potash and Morris Perlmutter."[95]

Blackface and the laws of nature. "The Wedding of the Chinee and the Coon." Words by Billy Johnson, music by Bob Cole, 1897. Music Division, The New York Public Library for the Performing Arts; Astor, Lenox and Tilden Foundations.

Chapter 8

Blackface, Jewface, Whiteface

Racial Impersonation Revisited

O N April 22, 1922, a month after the death of Bert Williams, Eddie Cantor paid tribute to the colleague with whom he had shared the stage of the Ziegfeld Follies. "He had the advantage of belonging to the race which we all more or less imitate when we put on burnt cork," Cantor began. "He knew each mental attitude of his own race and its humorous reaction to every situation. He had the ability to stand off and affectionately analyze the attributes of his race. As a natural blackface comedian he was far superior to any of us who put on burnt cork. But as an actor Williams was far more than this. . . . [J. J. Shubert] made a phrase which I heartily endorse of Williams both as an actor and a man. 'Bert Williams was one of the whitest actors I have ever known.'"

Cantor's choice of words, which were echoed by the impresario Florenz Ziegfeld, who pronounced Williams "one of the greatest [comedians] of the world, and the whitest man I ever had the honor to deal with," is curious, to say the least.[1] Whiteness, of course, was what Bert Williams, of West Indian origin, was emphatically barred from, as a man *and* as an actor. By all accounts one of the greatest comedians of the early twentieth century, and one of the first black entertainers to wholeheartedly win over white audiences and receive star billing on Broadway, the entertainment industry never let Williams venture far beyond the limitations of blackface comedy. While Eddie Cantor openly burlesqued his "sissified," bespectacled blackface character by letting him do an imitation of the Irish tenor John McCormick, the color line in the theater inevitably bound Williams to a convention of grotesque caricature, requiring him to hide his light complexion beneath paint and a pair of white gloves.

For Cantor, Williams's "racial" qualifications as a "natural" blackface

187

comedian mark his performances as "authentic." But within the contours of this discourse of racial authenticity, Williams suddenly emerges as "more than this": an honorary "white" man and actor. Within what structures of (racial) signification, then, did Bert Williams's posthumously acquired whiteness resonate?[2]

Williams's honorary whiteness calls attention to the ways in which symbolic whiteness structured the hierarchies of prestige within the society at large, as well as within the social field of acting. This value, I have argued, was inherent in a racialized discourse that postulated that the ability to "transcend" (racial) type and innate character was a characteristic of racial whiteness. Other races could "transgress but not transcend the boundaries of race."[3] On the basis of this conceptualization, mutability and "unmarked self-abstraction" became what Patricia McKee, following Michael Warner, calls a "differential resource" of whiteness: a "normative" category that "makes its possible to produce and order differences between various racial and cultural identities." In theory universally accessible, in practice this resource could be manipulated to "discriminatory as well as assimilatory effects."[4] Precisely because it played with the boundaries of selfhood and evoked the ambiguities of self-representation, the theater was a natural staging ground for the investigation and manipulation of identity and the capacity for self-abstraction and self-transformation, and, hence, the nature and boundaries of race and culture.

In the previous chapters, I have tried to show how these issues inserted themselves in particular in racial or dialect comedy, and outlined how the cultural hierarchies within the social field of the performing arts were themselves racially inflected. I have furthermore tried to demonstrate how various performers tried to access "acting" as a "differential resource" in order to manipulate the racial hierarchy, or at least their own social and cultural positioning within it. My argument focused mostly on Jewish actors, who, more than any other ethnic group, turned to the American vaudeville theater as a route to social and cultural mobility, mostly because it was easily accessible to aspiring, predominantly metropolitan, Jewish youth and required little investment.

On the stage, European immigrants, including Jews, appropriated a model of identity that loosened the hold of racial character and its presumed connection between external appearance and internal character. While in the musings of David Levinsky, the resulting split was the cause of melancholia and mourning for the loss of a unified, authentic (racial) self, the masks of Eduardo Migliaccio externalized and rearticulated reality itself as mimicry, in a carnivalesque celebration of the inauthentic, ambivalent, immigrant self. The mask of "Hebrew" comedy, meanwhile, lent itself, in the performances of David Warfield (though unsuccessfully in the case of Joe Welch), to the disavowal of a "racial" self, which was articulated in the split identity of the stage Hebrew and the "actor," a split underwritten by a discourse that pitted racial "authenticity" and "passing" against self-abstraction and professionalism. In *Potash and Perlmutter*, this split between inner and outer is initially displaced onto the difference between the characters of Potash, the immigrant, and Perlmutter, the American. It is ultimately resolved through the trope of "humor," interpreted not, as in the performances of Migliaccio, as the carnivalesque consequence of disjunction and displacement, but as constituting an essence, a Jewish racial core. This core unites, and lends authenticity to, the immigrant Jew (Potash) as well as the Americanized Jew (Perlmutter)—reconciling inner and outer, Jewish mutability and immutability, racial difference and Americanness.

For African Americans, the mask was a well-established figure that invoked the split subjectivity, self-alienation, and thwarted self-expression resulting from living within the shadow cast by the specular image of the "darky." A classic expression of this sentiment is Paul Laurence Dunbar's poem "We Wear the Mask," written at the turn of the century:

> We wear the mask that grins and lies
> It hides our cheeks and shades our eyes,—
> This debt we pay to human guile;
> With torn and bleeding hearts we smile,
> And mouth with myriad subtleties. . . .[5]

Houston A. Baker explains this psychological split, the costs of which W. E. B. Du Bois described in terms of a "veil" that had been imposed on the lives of African Americans as the result of the extraordinary hold of the minstrel mask. As form, the minstrel mask "is a space of habitation not only for repressed spirits of sexuality, ludic play, id satisfaction, castration anxiety, and a mirror stage of development, but also for that deep-seated denial of the indisputable humanity of inhabitants of and descendants from the continent of Africa." Mastery of the minstrel mask by African Americans, Baker argues, "constitutes a primary move in Afro-American discursive modernism."[6]

The function of blackface minstrelsy as a theater of whitening has been well established in recent scholarship. Pre–Civil War minstrelsy, a broad consensus in scholarship suggests, consolidated race- over class-consciousness and firmed up the disputed whiteness of recent immigrants, in particular the Irish.[7] In the twentieth century, meanwhile, "Blackface was the preeminent theatrical vehicle of identity manufacture" for the similarly racially in-between Jews, according to Michael Rogin, because it symbolically evoked the "myth of self-making" and the process of identity change so central to the construction of an "American" identity. As Rogin writes, "Facing nativist pressure that would assign them to the dark side of the racial divide, immigrants Americanized themselves by crossing and recrossing the racial line."[8]

Exploring minstrelsy's connection to the rhetoric of racial "authenticity," Michael North suggests that in minstrelsy the "black mask is less important than the process of masking." The "modern American personality ... is free precisely to the extent that it is inauthentic, free to don and change masks at will," North continues. Indeed, this inauthenticity and mutability measures itself against the presence of the authentic, ignorant, comic, premodern "darky." Or, as North puts it, whereas "blackface declares itself openly as a mask, unfixes identity, and frees the author in a world of self-creation," "the black persona carries all the connotations of natural, unspoiled authenticity."[9]

The tension that opens up between Houston Baker's argument about the meaning of the mask for African American modernism and the emphasis North places on the "inauthenticity" of blackface minstrelsy as point of access to a "modern American personality"—defined by a mutability that is offset against the immutability of a natural and "authentic" black persona—can serve as a point of departure to explore further the posthumous designation of Bert Williams as one of "the whitest actors" in the context of a comparative analysis of black-on-black blackface, Jewish blackface, and intraracial and cross-racial impersonation.

African American Blackface

The whitening potential of acting drew heavily on the belief in self-abstraction and self-transformation as a badge of Americanness. This belief, however, was "backgrounded" by what Toni Morrison calls the "Africanist" presence, the dark, enslaved Other in relation to whom the quintessential American experiences his or her self-transformation, and with it, whiteness, freedom, and newness.[10] The fact that African Americans and racial Others could "transgress but not transcend the boundaries of race" meant that African American role-playing was haunted by the "passing" discourse. On the stage, meanwhile, the (written and unwritten) conventions of the

American entertainment industry actively policed and curtailed the access of African Americans to the symbolics of self-transformation.

African American performers were keenly aware of the ways in which the boundary separating the realm of "reality" or "authenticity" from "theatricality" functioned as a structure of racial difference, shadowing the color line in American society.[11] To safeguard what Amy Robinson calls the "false promise of the visible as an epistemological guarantee," African Americans appearing before white audiences had to wear the yoke of blackface—in the white imagination the evocation of the "authentic" darky.[12] Moreover, the industry rigorously held African American actors and comedians to the ingrained stereotype that, because the African "genius was imitative," African Americans were "naturally" comic but failed as "actors."[13] As one reviewer wrote in response to a performance of George Walker and Bert Williams, perhaps the best-known African American comic pair of the turn of the century: "Nobody will deny that a negro can be one of the most amusing persons possible as long as he remains a negro. He is the most natural dancer in the world, he can sing simple melodies to perfection. He is a happy-go-lucky fellow who can rattle a pair of bones, pick a banjo, and laugh so heartily that everyone must laugh too. He is a capital entertainer—while he is a negro. . . . It is when he tries to speak, do, look like a white man that he is at his worst."[14]

Trying to "speak, do, look like a white man" included the ambition to be recognized as a legitimate actor. For an African American to be anything more than an "entertainer" encroached on the province of whiteness because it suggested mutability, self-distance, and the ability to transcend "type"—a "white" prerogative. "The result of these constraints, George Walker commented, was that

> [s]trictly speaking, the colored performer is to day more an entertainer than an actor, and naturally so. The white population, upon whom all shows must depend for success, refuse to take him seriously. Our poets must stick to dialect to make themselves heard, or to sell their wares, and our composers must write ragtime for the same reason, until the white man's serious consideration has been earned. . . . Can you imagine a love scene between two colored people that would not bring a laugh? No. . . . No matter how carefully written, they must not be otherwise but amusing."[15]

For Bob Cole and Billy Johnson, talented musicians and actors, the solution to the color line in theater lay in freeing themselves, and their company,

from all white control. After withdrawing his music from Black Patti's Trou-
badours (playing at Proctor's Fifty-eighth Street Theater in New York)
because of a conflict with management, Cole issued the "Colored Actor's
Declaration of Independence of 1898," which declared: "We are going to
have our own shows. We are going to write them ourselves, we are going to
have our own stage manager, our own orchestra leader, and our own manager. . . . No divided houses."[16]

In response, Cole's previous managers threatened to blacklist any theater
company that would sign Bob Cole and Billy Johnson's new production, *A
Trip to Coontown*, the first musical comedy entirely written, produced, and
managed by African Americans. Undaunted, Cole took the production to
Canada, where it received rave reviews. When news of the comedy's success
reached the United States, Klaw and Erlanger defied the blacklist threat and
signed the company for a New York premiere in Jacob's Third Avenue Theater. Despite its opening during the week of Rosh Hashanah, crowds were
turned away at every performance.[17]

A Trip to Coontown, a spoof of the popular play *A Trip to Chinatown*,
featured Bob Cole as the tramp "Willy Wayside." Cole's tramp persona evoked
minstrel stereotypes in his "chicken-grabbing" tendencies. Yet he played
the role in a white makeup that, according to one review, made it "almost
impossible to guess his particular tint."[18] The tramp type, well established
in vaudeville, represented the "lowest strata of humankind." He was typically grimed in a "dark sunburn color" simulating a skin "tanned by exposure" and outfitted with a craggy beard, unshaven face, shaggy eyebrows,
and unkempt hair.[19] Given the low station and down-and-out eccentricity
of the tramp, then, Bob Cole's "Willie Wayside" was extremely well chosen:
categorically, he was close enough to "blackness" to cancel out Cole's (sub-
dued) appropriation of whiteness on the stage.

Bob Cole's subversion of stage convention registered in reviews, which
stated that Cole "showed last night that he is capable of playing any white
part far better than most Negro comedians play black ones."[20] Another conceded that Cole was "as good as any white comedians whose specialty is
this style of eccentricity" and considered his "speeches . . . as the tramp . . .
uniformly rich, with touches of nature which lies deeper than pigment."[21]

Similar infractions of the conventions of blackface occurred throughout
the play. Billy Binkerton used his role as a license to demonstrate his skills
of impersonation, which included "an Italian act which is capital." Tom
Brown appeared as a "Chinaman" singing an Oriental parody of Ernest
Hogan's well-known coon song "All Coons Look Alike to Me," entitled "All

Chinks Look Alike to Me."[22] And Lloyd Gibbs, billed as the "black De Reszke" (the most famous tenor of the era), demonstrated a command of Italian idiom and high culture, including operatic arias from Verdi, that challenged the stereotype of the "simple" and crude "coon."

The use of racial-ethnic burlesque was a well-established feature of blackface comedy. As Eric Lott has argued, before the development of ethnic stage types, "blackface was actually used to represent *all* ethnicities on the antebellum stage," incorporating "Irish brogues and other ethnic dialects with absolutely no sense of contradiction."[23] Indeed, in its conjoining of two or more cultural terrains normally considered distinct, or even antithetical, such *cultural pastiche* developed into a favorite comic conceit, which migrated from blackface minstrelsy to racial comedy in general.[24]

The "Hebrew" comic Frank Bush, for instance, accompanied his "Solomon Moses" routine with a "Scottish" dance movement. The team of Morris and Allen specialized in Irish songs, which they performed in Scotch kilts and Hebrew makeup.[25] Jim David, known for his "Dutch" acts, would close with "An Imitation of a Scot Doing a Highland Fling" while still dressed in his Dutch costume. The Weber and Fields production "The Geezer," a takeoff of the popular drama "The Geisha," featured John Kelly, a famous Irish comedian, as Li Hung Chang, a Chinese viceroy and minister of foreign affairs who spoke with a peat-bog brogue. In the same production, the "Dutch" comedian Sam Bernard played "Two Hi," owner of a teahouse, whose Chinese costume was complemented by a low-comedy German chin piece and such Chinese American expressions as "Velly good, by gollies" and "One piece beer mit pretzels." A concert of two Chinese impersonators, Tony Cheong, baritone, and Fooh Long, pianist, consisted of a "spectacle of one Chinaman singing the Pagliacci prologue in Italian and another ragging the scale and his shoulders."[26]

Cultural pastiche abandoned all pretenses to realism, deliberately highlighting the disjunction between the performer and the mask. To some degree, these performances can be interpreted as playing with what Marjorie Garber has called a "category mistake," an unnatural and thus burlesque transgression of "natural" racial identities.[27] But cultural pastiche also detached the codes signifying an "authentic" racial identity (manners, dialect, customs) from their incarnation in body and history. In its play with the imitability and impurity of culture in the urban borderlands, it questioned the idea of inherent racial character. For African American performers, then, cultural pastiche was one comic strategy that could be used to gain mastery over the minstrel mask.

With the inclusion of Ernest Hogan's popular double-edged song "No Coons Allowed" just before the finale, Cole's defiance of the strictures of blackface minstrelsy was just about as blatant as it could be. The refrain, in which Cole, in whiteface, mouths off the racist rhetoric with which, in *Plessy vs. Ferguson,* the Supreme Court in 1896 upheld the legality of segregation ("No coons allowed / This place is meant for white folks that's all / So move on darky down the line / We don't want no kinky-head kind / No coons allow'd in here at all") amplifies once more that this performance was anything but simple "darky" entertainment.[28]

After dissolving his stage relationship with Billy Johnson in 1901, Cole found a new partner in J. R. Johnson, the brother of James Weldon Johnson, author, poet, lyricist, and future head of the National Association for the Advancement of Colored People (NAACP). Subsequent Cole and Johnson productions included *Under the Bamboo Tree* (with lyrics by James Weldon Johnson), *The Shoo-Fly Regiment,* and *The Red Moon,* billed as a "comedy sensation in red and black" about "Minehaha, the offspring of an Indian father and a Negro mother."[29] In these musical comedies, Cole and Johnson impersonated con artists, Indians and Arabs, but they remained haunted by the mark of the "coon" and by critics who regarded their productions "Not Up to Broadway standards."[30] Bob Cole eventually dropped his "coon" persona completely and performed on the vaudeville stage "in white tie and tails, with neither whiteface nor blackface make-up."[31] His career ended after a nervous breakdown in 1910; on August 3, 1911, he drowned in a lake in the Catskills.[32]

George Walker similarly sought recourse in racial solidarity, taking steps to organize the four hundred or so African American entertainers then before the public in what he planned to call the "Williams and Walker International and Interracial Ethiopian Theatre in New York City," a club designed to legitimate African American dramatic talent and emphasize their status as professionals. As the *New Jersey Telegraph* reported, "Mr. Walker thinks a permanent club might result in the development of real dramatic talent and that in the future colored tragedians and romantic actors would come to the front."[33]

In interviews, George Walker repeatedly stated his resistance to the limits blackface imposed on black artistic talent, insisting, "There is no reason why we should be forced to do these slap-stick bandanna acts. It's all rot, this slap-stick bandanna bladder in the face act, with which negro acting is associated. It ought to die out and we are trying hard to kill it."[34] Deeply frustrated with the limitations of stage convention, George Walker and Bert

Williams attempted to subvert the racial order of representation by consciously co-opting the rhetoric of racial "authenticity" and billing themselves as the "real coons." As there seemed to be a great demand for black faces on the stage, Walker explained, "We thought that we would do all we could to get what we felt belonged to us by the laws of nature."[35]

In their appeal to racial authenticity, Williams and Walker played on the cultural capital the "real thing" had acquired with the vogue of realism. At the same time, their rhetoric of "natural" minstrelsy must be seen in the context of a cultural politics that aimed to "claim a self-motivated racial representation."[36] The aim of Williams and Walker was to culturally upgrade their vaudeville comedy routine, in which Williams, in blackface, played the awkward, naive, clown against Walker's arrogant, flamboyant, huckster dandy, and transform it into legitimate art. This ambition resonated with those of a number of young, talented African American performers, writers, and musicians, who were equally intent on dismantling "Negro" stage stereotypes.

Prominent in this group were the poet Paul Laurence Dunbar (who first gained public recognition through the sympathetic reviews of his work by William Dean Howells, the influential editor of the *Atlantic Monthly* and critic for *Harper's Monthly*), Jesse Ship, a theatrical genius with a long experience in minstrelsy, and Will Marion Cook, a composer who had studied with Antonín Dvořák and had developed an interest in popular black musical expression. For these artists, as for Williams and Walker, the rhetoric of authenticity was meant as an adjustment and reappropriation of the (minstrel) mask and the stereotypes and assumptions embedded within it.

But the "real" was also inflected by a racial hierarchy of culture that placed the African American at the primitive stages of cultural evolution and expected him to be a childish, credulous, naturally funny, happy-go-lucky "mis-speakers."[37] Williams and Walker's reclamation of African American humor and blackface minstrelsy as natural, authentic self-expression easily collapsed into the discourse of the "Negro" as a "born entertainer." This is exactly the discursive association that shadows Williams's professional explanation of African American humor in a 1908 interview for the *Age*, where he declared: "The American Negro is a natural minstrel. He is the one in whom humor is native, often unconscious, but nevertheless keen and laughcompelling. He dances from the cradle almost, for his feet have been educated pre-natally, it would seem. He usually has a voice, and there is not much necessity for schools of voice to tamper with a natural voice. There is soul in the Negro music: There is simplicity and an entire lack of artificiality."[38]

As Williams's commentary demonstrates, the rhetoric of authentic self-expression did not negate the assumption of the "biocultural reality" of the "darky" as the "realistic" prototype of the mask, nor did it enhance the status of African American actors as "professionals."[39] Other efforts by African American writers and artists to develop an "authentic" expression of racial selfhood through the use of an African American vernacular speech and music were similarly burdened by the reification of the "coon" as the "touchstone" of authenticity.

Thus, as Michael A. Elliott has argued in reference to the dialect poetry of Paul Laurence Dunbar, author of many of the song lyrics of the shows of Williams and Walker, the discourse of authenticity "circumscribed the range of expression available to African Americans connected to the realist network of writers and editors."[40] African American artists who employed the claim of "authenticity" in order to compete for an audience also had to contend with the fact that their cultural expressions could be said to "emanate" from their "inborn" racial identity. This effectively excluded them from the realm of "art," defined by the capacity for artistic transformation.[41] In addition, as Karen Sotiropulos points out, the commodification of the low— black vernacular, music, and dance styles—that was evident in the era's "coon" craze and in the popularity of "rag" music and the "cakewalk" made cultural "authenticity" by and large a chimera.[42]

The first collaboration of Dunbar, Cook, and Williams and Walker resulted in 1898 in *Clorindy, or the Origin of the Cake Walk,* an operetta that opened at the Casino Roof Garden on Broadway. Designed to serve as a showcase for black talent, the operetta also demonstrates the pitfalls of escaping the stronghold of racial stereotypes through cultural upgrading and authentic "Negro" dialect and music. Cook had intended *Clorindy* to be an operetta featuring "real Negro melodies," but he found that managers would accept a show only if it could be marketed as "variety" and its songs as "coon songs"—the popular term for songs using syncopation, dialect, and black stereotypes.[43] The show featured Ernest Hogan, a famed African American blackface comedian whose "All Coons Look Alike to Me" had inspired the popular craze for "coon" songs that overtook America at the end of the nineteenth century, and Williams and Walker in their cakewalk, which by then had established the couple's fame. It was hailed for its original choral music and syncopated (ragtime) melodies. Yet its plot, a southern plantation romance featuring "dusky belles" and dialect songs like "Who Dat Say Chicken in Dis Crowd" and "Hottest Coon in Dixie," also seamlessly overlapped with the conventions of standard blackface vaudeville fare and its contorted understanding of black "authenticity."[44]

Clorindy highlights the fact that for African American performers who saw their own roles as that of cultural brokers, the aspiration to elevate black theater conflicted with the harsh reality that financial success required the tailoring of performances to the expectations of whites.[45] African American actors inevitably found themselves caught between the demands of its black middle-class audience that performers distance themselves from imagery that was considered "too black," and white audiences, who would respond only to images that fell within the semiotic codes of minstrelsy. As Williams and Walker commented: "The colored theater 'goer,' taken collectively, only wants to see when he attends a Negro show such characters as remind him of 'white folks,' while on the other hand white patrons only want to see him portray the antebellum 'darkey.'"[46]

After *Clorindy*, Williams and Walker attempted to avail themselves of a critical distance from what Walker called "the American 'darky' ragtime limitations," by shifting the locus of the "real" from the "plantation darky" to Africa. In 1900, they experimented with a sketch in a musical farce entitled *The Sons of Ham*, which, according to the *Dramatic Mirror*, seemed designed to "get as far away as possible from the conventional Sixth Avenue coon type, and in this act they have gone to the limit, geographically." The skit closed with "a moonlight African jungle scene, as Walker, dressed in the negligee costume of a dusky female savage, and his partner, attired after the fashion of a male warrior, hop about the stage in a realistic aboriginal manner."[47]

These supposedly "authentic" African materials, Walker claimed, were based on their "study" of a group of native Dahomeans, whom Williams and Walker had briefly impersonated at the San Francisco Midwinter Fair of 1894, when the original natives scheduled to perform were late in arriving. This exhibition of "real African life in a real African village" was meant to stage the superiority of white civilization over "savage" races that legitimated American imperialist expansion. One critic of the Dahomean exhibit wrote of the inhabitants of the village: "Sixty-nine of them are here in all their barbaric ugliness, blacker than buried midnight and as degraded as the animals which prowl the jungles of their dark land. . . . In these wild people we can easily detect many characteristics of the American negro."[48] But for Williams and Walker, the experience proved a source of creative inspiration. As Walker explained, "It was there that we were brought into close touch with native Africans, and the study of those natives interested us very much. We were not long in deciding that, if we ever reached the point of having a show of our own, we would delineate and feature African characters as far as we could, and still remain American, and make our acting and entertaining interesting to American audiences."[49]

Walker's appeal to the cultural capital of the "close" observation and realistic representation of an exotic African tribe resonates with the strategies other dialect comedy performers used to boost their status. The use of "native" African prototypes would provide the team with a model that, in its ambiguous relationship to "African American"—simultaneously different and similar—did not too obviously upset the racial order of representation. At the same time, it did open up a gap between subject and object that allowed for cultural distance, and thus for "acting."

Williams and Walker's most ambitious productions, the musical comedies *In Dahomey* (1902) and *Abyssinia* (1906), transported the pair to Africa in service of the (fraudulent) imperialistic missions of a "Colonization Society" seeking a haven for oppressed African Americans *(In Dahomey)*, and as the ad hoc additions of a southern church group *(Abyssinia)*.[50] Yet this "native" element served mostly as a pretext for the display of the colorful costumes, the spectacular exotic background scenery, and the large groups of singers and dancers on the stage that characterized the ambitious scope of these productions. The bulk of the action featured Williams and Walker in their typical roles as naive simpleton and scam artist in the more conventional locales of Florida and the South, and parodied the pretensions of the "colored aristocracy" and its imitations of white "gentility."[51]

In Dahomey, the more successful of the two musicals, starred George Walker as Rareback Pinkerton, a hustler sent to Florida by a group of scheming investors in order to persuade African Americans to seek refuge in his African colony. Williams played Shylock Homestead, Rareback's simple, happy-go-lucky travel companion. In this scheme, concocted primarily in order to separate a wealthy, senile African American from his riches, Rareback masquerades as a prince of Dahomey, and dispenses dreams of status and black economic autonomy in such songs as "My Castle on the Nile":

> In my castle on the river Nile
> I am gwinter live in elegant style
> Inlaid diaminds onde flo'
> A baboon butler at my do' . . .[52]

Both musicals received great popular acclaim. Their complex musical scores, with melodies by Cook and lyrics by Dunbar, included syncopated rhythms, operatic recitative, and ragtime "coon" songs with a twist, such as "No Coons Allowed" and "Evah Dahkey Is a King," which ridiculed white aristocratic pretensions and African American longing for power through a precolonial, African noble pedigree:

Dar's mighty curious circumstance
Dat's botherin' all de nation.
All de Yankees is dissatisfied wit a deir untitled station.
Dey is huntin' after titles wid a golden net to snare 'em,
an' de democratic people dey's mos' mightily glad to wear 'em. Ho!
But they ain't got all de title.
Fur it is a 'culiar thing,
When a dahkey starts to huntin',
He is sho' to prove a King.
Evah Dahkey is a King!
Royalty is jes' de ting.
Ef yo' social life's a bungle,
Jes you go back to yo' jungle,
An remember dat a yo' daddy was a King.

The song "On Emancipation Day" meanwhile poignantly poked fun at the infatuation of whites with blackness:

On Emancipation day,
All you White Fo'ks clear de way. . . .
When dey hear dem ragtime tunes
White fo'ks try to pass for coons.[53]

The musical comedies featured a panoply of characters, including members of black society, "Dahomean" and "Ethiopian" warriors, and "Falasha" maids (played by Ada Overton Walker and her group of dancers), and offered ample opportunity for experiments in racial cross-dressing. There was even a Chinese cook, named "Me Sing" and played by the African American actor George Catlin, who did a "singsong" recitation of Chinese foods and spoke in "Chinese" dialect. "Think of the amount of powder necessary to bleach the actor to the appropriate hue!" marveled one reviewer at the sight.[54] Only Bert Williams wore burnt-cork blackface in the productions, in a concession to stage convention that freed the other actors from the overt strictures of the "coon" stereotype.

Walker credited the popular success of both shows to their departure from the "American darky ragtime limitations." The introduction of "native African characteristics," he volunteered, "has helped greatly to increase the value of the black performer on the stage. Managers gave but little credit to the ability of black people on the stage before the native African element was introduced. All that was expected of a colored performer was singing and dancing and a little story telling, but as for acting, no one credited a black person with the ability to act."[55]

Critics, indeed, quickly recognized this assault on the color line in theater for what it was. *Abyssinia,* in particular, contained little dialect or imagery that was directly recognizable as conforming to the minstrel stereotype, and consequently it received praise from black critics for its "progressive merits."[56] For the same reason, it came under attack from white critics. A lone voice regarded *Abyssinia* as "a practical illustration that none of the tricks of the theatrical trade can be considered the exclusive property of the white man."[57] Another was confounded by Williams's departure from stereotype, conceding that "so subtle is his humor and so devoid of anything that resembles racial characteristics that it is difficult to believe he is of Ethiopian descent."[58] Yet the predominant white critical response, in particular to *Abyssinia,* was that it failed because it strayed from "what is typical of the American Negro" and attempted to be "too white."[59]

Abyssinia's attempt to transcend the limits of blackface comedy not surprisingly was seen as an encroachment on the province of whiteness. "There is too much of it that is merely bad imitation of the way the white folks do and not enough that is characteristic of the American colored man," one critic complained. He continued, "Certainly whatever hope the colored man has of artistic accomplishment must be in the development of his native tendencies."[60] "Instead of bringing to the foreground the barbaric splendor of middle Africa, the simple melodies and characteristic dances of the colored race, the laughing, rollicking humor of the black man of all time, and the peculiar abilities of Williams and Walker, they constructed a loose-jointed copy of a Broadway musical comedy," another criticized.[61]

White critics overwhelmingly summoned Williams and Walker back to the domain of the "real," the "droll darky." African Americans were "naturally" funny, one critic ventured. "If he could be himself and not try to act he might succeed in getting away with the laugh, but instead of that he tries to be funny and in nine to ten cases he makes a dismal failure of it."[62] "It seems a waste of effort," another pontificated, "that they should try for such effects and meanwhile deprive us of so much that is both true and amusing and which only they can portray—we mean the real American Negro, who sings from the heart out, dances with his whole soul and voices his droll and leisurely philosophy of life with such unction."[63]

For the critic Alan Dale, the biggest affront of the show was that it was too "uppity." *Abyssinia* was a "Negro Show of Too Exalted Ambitions," and the actors in it felt themselves to be "above" blackface. "It was not until the amiably colored Mr. Bert Williams deliberately wrenched himself away from the grandiosely operatic melodrama called 'Abyssinia' at the Majestic Theatre, and condescended to sing to us in his de luxe 'darky' way that the ice was broken," he wrote. "Possibly Bert Williams, noting the uproar and ovation accorded to him when he deigned to be a colored comedian, will inject a little more of this into Abyssinia."[64]

After the death of George Walker, his partner, Bert Williams appeared in 1909 in *Mr. Lode of Koal,* a musical fantasy, in which Tom Brown, in his Chinese impersonation, performed "Chink Chink Chinaman."[65] In the following decade, Williams took his blackface persona to the Ziegfeld Follies, where he played in productions alongside Will Rogers and Eddie Cantor.

His most popular persona was the wistful "Mr. Nobody," a character first introduced in 1905, whose signature song evoked the "self-negation" that, as Frantz Fanon argues, living within the minstrel mask evokes:

I ain't never done nothin' to nobody,
I ain't never got nothin' from nobody, no time.
Until I get somethin' from somebody, sometime,
I'll never do nothin' for nobody, no time.[66]

Houston Baker Jr. has argued that any African American spokesperson "who wished to engage in a masterful and empowering play within the minstrel spirit house needed the uncanny ability to manipulate bizarre phonic legacies. For he or she had the task of transforming the mask and its sounds into negotiable discursive currency. In effect, the task was the production of a manual of black speaking, a book of speaking *back and black.*"[67]

Bert Williams's mastery of the minstrel mask falls within the range of what Homi Bhabha calls "colonial mimicry." Colonial mimicry is a form of repetition and self-doubling that produces a "virtual subject" who incorporates the "narcissistic demand of colonial authority" for a self-same Other, but only partially, as a presence that at the same time is an absence, a "difference that is itself a process of disavowal." Thus, such mimicry "is constructed around an ambivalence." It "continually produces its slippage, its excess, its difference." It is, then, a discourse produced "at the crossroads," which is also a "site of interdiction": uttered between "what is known and permissible and that which though known must be kept concealed," "between the lines, and as such both against the rules and within them."[68]

The disavowal within Williams's mimicry articulated itself within his performances in myriad ways: in his carefully studied reluctance to comply with demands, whether in character, as a black porter, from his white customer, or as a performer, from his audience, when it would ask Williams to sing his signature song, "Nobody"; or in public, in the introductory question, "Is we all good niggers here?" with which Williams, entertaining at private white parties, liked to break the ice.[69]

It was also explicit in Williams's efforts to publicize the fact that his mask was a conscious artifact, and that "the dialect of the southern 'darky'" for Williams "was as much a foreign dialect as that of the Italian," which he had acquired through careful study.[70] "I try to portray the shiftless darky to the fullest extent; his fun, his philosophy," he explained. "There is nothing about this fellow I don't know. I must study his movements. I have to. He is not in me. The way he walks; the way he leans up against a wall, one foot forward. I find much material by knocking around in out of the way places and just listening. Eavesdropping on human nature is one of the most important parts of a comedian's work."[71]

African American observers, not surprisingly, tended to draw attention to the distinction between the "real thing" and the artifice of comedy when commenting on Williams's artistry. The African American writer Jessie Fauset, for instance, explained:

> Without the slightest knowledge of the dialect of the American Negro, he set to work to acquire it. He watched, he listened, he visited various Negro districts North and South, he studied phonetics. He could make the listener distinguish between variations of different localities. He affected, his admirers will remember, a shambling, shuffling gait which at intervals in his act would change into a grotesque sliding and gliding—the essence of awkward naturalness. But awkward or graceful, it was not natural to him, but simply the evolution of a walk and dance which he had worked out by long and patient observation of Negro prototypes.[72]

Booker T. Washington similarly recalled that Williams would get the "material for some of those quaint songs and stories in which he reproduces the natural humor and philosophy of the Negro people" while "standing about in a barber shop or among a crowd of ordinary colored people."[73]

But in the dominant discourse, this difference was consistently overwritten. According to the rhetoric of racial authenticity, Williams's studied racial physiognomy was not an acquired externality, but rather coincided with racial interiority.

This naturalizing move returns in Cantor's description of Williams as a "natural blackface comedian," who as such was "far superior to any of us who put on burnt cork." The consequence of Williams's acquired "natural-ness" was that the editor of the *New York Herald,* by the time of Williams's death, could wonder if his audience "realized that his work was a conscious artifice."[74] Williams's career, as Fanny Brice remarked upon his death, was seriously marred by a lack of material befitting his talent, and was narrowly circumscribed by the color line in theater.[75] Jessie Fauset agreed with this perception, writing in *The Crisis* in the year of Williams's death:

> But does anyone who realizes that the foibles of the American Negro were pains-takingly acquired by this artist, doubt not that Williams might just as well have portrayed the Irishman, the Jew, the Englishman abroad, the Scotchman or any other of the vividly etched types which for one reason or another lend themselves so steadily to caricature? Can anyone presume to say that a man who traveled north, east, south and west and even abroad in order to acquire accent and jargon, aspect and characteristic of a people to which he was bound by ties of blood but from whom he was natively separated by training and tradition, would not have been able to portray with equal affection what, for lack of a better term, we must call universal roles?[76]

Urban Borderlands and Jewish Blackface

For Eddie Cantor, an uneducated, street-smart, Yiddish-speaking urchin from the Lower East Side, the light-skinned Williams, with his impeccable manners and his flawless English, was "a true gentleman."[77] Indeed, within the context of a racial discourse that had elevated respectability, gentility, and good manners as standards of whiteness, Williams's legendary gentle-ness, dignity, manners, and politesse were attributes that would have marked him as "white" in Cantor's eyes.

The whiteness Cantor attributed to Bert Williams as an actor was, of neces-sity, measured in relation to the mask of blackness. His posthumous tribute highlights the fact that this mask, too, was the scene of a curious reversal. On the stage of the Follies, Bert Williams was "an aristocrat of comedy," who played his roles with genteel understatement and an impeccable sense of comic timing, evacuated his blackface character from its stereotypical lewd and ludic characteristics to the degree that he could, and carefully avoided any suggestion of impropriety. By contrast, other blackface comedians such as Al Jolson and Eddie Cantor, with whom Williams performed a father-son blackface act on the stage of the Follies, cracked jokes that were, as one reviewer complained, "more highly colored than their faces," and seasoned their blackface with excessive burlesque.[78]

Fanny Brice, Al Jolson, and Eddie Cantor belonged to a new generation of Jewish performers—which included George Jessel, George Burns, and the Marx Brothers—who significantly reshaped the contours of racial comedy. Instead of "upgrading" the lowly Hebrew stock character by playing him "realistically" (as David Warfield had done) or adapting him to the middle-class norms of respectability and gentility (as in the case of *Potash and Perlmutter*), these performers deliberately downgraded him, performing him with exaggerated Jewish accents and mannerisms. Moreover, they inflected their other roles, including blackface, with Jewish speech and body language as well.

The career of Fanny Brice is illustrative of this shift in performance style. Brice, who was born as Fanny Borach, grew up in a middle-class, English-speaking Jewish household knowing only a few Yiddish words. She honed her mimic talents by imitating the Yiddish, Polish, Hungarian, and German she heard the immigrant servant girls in her household speak, by listening to the dialect comedy routines of Joe Welch, and by picking up her "nigger talk" from her black neighbors and from black entertainers.[79] Her first hit in vaudeville came in 1909, when she premiered "Sadie Salome," a song about a stage-struck Jewish girl and her boyfriend Mose:

When his Sadie came to sight,
He stood up and yelled with all his might
Don't do that dance, I tell you Sadie,
That's not a bus'ness for a lady!
Most e'rybody knows
That I'm your loving Mose
Oy oy oy—where's your clothes?[80]

The author of the song, Irving Berlin, was born in 1888 in Russia as Israel Baline to a Jewish cantor. After the family emigrated to America, Berlin escaped the poverty and overcrowding of his parents' home on the Lower East Side by singing in the Bowery saloons for an audience of prostitutes, pimps, and German and Irish immigrant workers. Furiously ambitious, he absorbed every musical style possible, and, employed as a singing waiter at "Nigger Mike's" on Pell Street in Chinatown—a saloon set up as a slummers' hangout and owned by a Russian Jew—would move effortlessly between the musical styles and dialects of an Italian, Irishman, Jew, or "nigger." By 1909, he had made a career out of musical impersonation, composing songs with a "Jewish" motif such as "Sadie Salome" or "Yiddle on Your Fiddle, Play Some Ragtime," Irish dialect songs ("I Wish You Was My Gal, Molly"), German dialect songs ("Oh! How that German Could Love"), and "coon" songs ("Colored Romeo"), in which he inflected different musical vernaculars with his signature syncopated or "raggedy" style.[81]

On the advice of the musical iconoclast Berlin, Fanny performed "Sadie Salome" with an exaggerated Jewish accent. A smash hit, the success of "Sadie Salome" brought her to the attention of Florenz Ziegfeld, who engaged her for the Ziegfeld Follies, one of Broadway's new attractions. There her Jewish inflections became her trademark. Thus, for the Ziegfeld Follies of 1910, Fanny Brice performed an Irving Berlin "Yiddishe" song, "Goodbye, Becky Cohen," and a "coon" song, "Lovey Joe," slipping an exaggerated Yiddish into her already-over-the-top southern accent; in another performance, she impersonated a black housewife with a Yiddish dialect.[82]

She frequently adopted the persona of a "spunky, poor Jewish girl longing for love and fame," imbuing her performance with "the spirit of Loscha of the Coney Island popcorn counter and Marta of the cheeses at Brodsky's delicatessen, and the Sadies and Rachel's and the Birdies with the turnover heels at the Second Avenue dance halls."[83] But her "Indian squaw" Rosie Rosenstein, her silent-screen vamp Theda Bara, and her royal *maitresse* Madame Pompadour ("I may be a bad voman, but demm good company") also came with the "vocal inflections of the Lower East Side."[84]

Cultural pastiche also characterized the performances of Eddie Cantor. Three hours of his show, Cantor, according to one review, "was white." "In whiteface Eddie Cantor looks like a woe-begone, undernourished youth from the east side. Consequently, when he sidles on in one scene and applies for a job on the police force his mere presence gives the situation a keen farcical quality. . . . For the last fifteen minutes of the show he was in blackface, and he made that feature funnier than usual with an imitation of John McCormack."[85] Cantor, whose stage personality was the opposite of the "manly male," won great acclaim for his "sissified" (and Jewified) rendition of his blackface character, who wore a pair of wire-rimmed glasses.[86] In another sketch, he combined gender and racial travesty by playing "Salome" in blackface.

Al Jolson, who would become world famous for his role in the film *The Jazz Singer* (1927), where he played a Jewish son who abandons family and tradition by choosing to become a blackface singer instead of a cantor, in the first decade of the twentieth century alternated on the vaudeville stage between the act "The Hebrew and His Cadet," in which he teamed up with his brother Harry, and the comic "coon" song "Where Did Robinson Crusoe Go with Friday on Saturday Night."[87] As Robinson Crusoe's "dusky companion," Al Jolson "begs the cannibals not to eat meat on Friday." He speaks excellent French, and "when the pirates allow him to select his form of death, he selects 'old age.'"[88]

Jolson situated his own performances in the context of a modern, refurbished minstrel style. As he explained, "There are a number of points in which the modern minstrel differs greatly from the men who made the word famous. Perhaps the most striking point is that the negro dialect is seldom used, and it is possible to hear a man in blackface telling a story in Jewish or Italian dialect."[89] Even when Jolson, later on, steered his career in a more "respectable" direction, appealing to the rhetoric of racial authenticity and claiming to have "acquired the dialect that has since won him fame and fortune by camping around the wharves and railroad yards watching the negro stevedores at work," his blackface was far removed from the traditional stereotypical southern "darky," something that did grate on the nerves of some critics.[90]

"That minstrelsy of the blackface variety is supposed to represent a certain type of life and portray the characteristics of a race seems to have been forgotten by the modern dabblers in this amusement," one reviewer complained.[91] "While Mr. Marion gives a counterfeit presentment of the antebellum darky servitor in an aristocratic family with such fidelity that one feels one is looking upon and hearing an original, Mr. Jolson makes no attempt whatever to imitate a negro of any period or station in life," another reviewer wrote. "He is merely Al Jolson with burnt cork on his face and into his songs puts every ounce of energy he possesses."[92]

The success of Brice and Jolson, the cultural critic Gilbert Seldes argued in 1924, had to be attributed to the fact that both were racial outsiders. Commenting on the "daemonic" quality of Al Jolson and Fanny Brice, he wrote: "It is noteworthy that these two stars bring something to America which America lacks and loves . . . and that both are racially outside of the dominant caste. Possibly this accounts for their fine carelessness about our superstitions of politeness and gentility. . . . Jolson and Brice go farther, go with more contempt for artificial notions of propriety, than anyone else."[93]

It can be argued that the performances of Eddie Cantor, Fanny Brice, George Jessel, Al Jolson, and the Marx Brothers, for all their internal differences, reshaped "Hebrew comedy" into a Jewish "minor language." Their travesties represented an "apotheosis of the low," a "de-centering" of the "superior" cultural norm of Anglo-Saxondom and its hierarchies of taste, race, and caste. By inflecting this norm with their own low (Jewish) vernacular, these comedians not only assaulted the standards of the majority culture. Exerting their own claims of cultural ownership, they transformed the conventional racial stock types of vaudeville into vehicles for a distinctly modern, Jewish voice.[94]

Indeed, that, in the context of the dominance of the New Humor and the New Jewish Humor, with its "carelessness about our superstitions of politeness and gentility" and its "contempt for artificial notions of propriety," Bert Williams, with his art of understatement and his philosophy of humor derived from the classics, may very well have been the "whitest" actor, according to the standard that linked respectability and whiteness, is an argument that can be made.[95]

Williams's comedy at the Ziegfeld Follies expressed a different ideal of assimilation, and reflected the different social reality of African American performers struggling for legitimacy onstage and off. It also highlights the limits of the counter-discursive strategies embedded in the new Jewish comic voice, which were curbed by the fact that it operated within a cultural system in which "modern" inauthenticity, the ability to "act" and "transcend" type, were tethered to whiteness.

The "low" comic Jewish voice, of course, was not without its detractors. Indeed, the fact that this "crude" style of comedy might be interpreted by the majority culture as the expression of the "quintessential Jew shining through," and seen as evidence of an atavistic Jewish "vulgarity" continued to be a concern among established American Jews. Fanny Brice, however, addressed these concerns by arguing that if her imitations expressed a quintessential Jewishness, that Jewish essence was not the atavistic presence of the lowly ghetto Jew, but a distinctively Jewish capacity for mutability.

The success of Jews as actors, she argued, stemmed from their Jewishness, and served as a testament to their adaptability. "I believe it's because I'm Jewish that I have been a steady climber on the stage," she stated. "Not that my success has been brought by my imitations of Jewish types, but the versatility with which I have been credited, is peculiar to the Jews. There is no need of my giving historical justification for my statement, as scholars have long determined that a variety of experiences, and a constantly changing environment have produced an adaptability in the Jew, rarely possessed by other people."[96]

Brice's comment reprises a distinctive understanding of the Jew as the incarnation of the protean, indefinable, modern self. That perception, Zygmunt Bauman argues, was informed by the fact that Jews "had entered modern times as ambivalence incarnate. . . . In the mobile world, the Jews were the most mobile of all; in the world of boundary-breaking, they broke the most boundaries; in the world of melting solids, they made everything, including themselves, into a formless plasma in which any form could be born only to dissolve again. . . . They embodied incongruence, artificiality, sham and the frailty of the social order and the most earnestly drawn boundaries."[97]

As "ambivalence incarnate," Jews evoked the dominant fear of modern life, the fear of "that which stands outside of, and subverts, the cognitive categories by which the world is organized and hence by which even the category of otherness itself is established." This fear of "under-determination, unclarity, uncertainty," which Bauman dubs "proteophobia," in Europe produced the sinister version of the Jew as "insidiously protean," who masked the immutable racial Other with an uncanny ability for mimicry. For Fanny Brice, by contrast, the particular Jewish protean quality constituted the key to her success on the stage and, by extension, to Jewish success in American culture. Moreover, Jewish mutability presented a formula that enabled Jews to be Jewish *and* white American. In this version, the Jew, as "ambivalence incarnate," is, as Jonathan Freedman puts it, "also that border or boundary figure that calls into question the viability of any model of racial, national, or cultural identity." Hence, Jews could be imagined, and imagine themselves, as a "kind of figure of bounded boundlessness, one who can image the very possibility of existing within a social or a national or an ethnic identity without being completely subsumed by it."[98]

It was this conception of Jewish identity that Bourne took as a model for a "transnational America," a pluralistic nation characterized by unity in diversity, in his essay "The Jew and Trans-National America" (1916). Stating that "Jews can put on and take off cultures without losing their racial identity," and that the Jew "has proven himself perhaps the most assimilable of all races to other and quite alien cultures," Bourne inserted Jews at the heart of modern, pluralistic American culture.[99]

The performances of Brice, Cantor, Jolson, and the Marx Brothers, replicated this gesture. Their comedy can be seen as acts of "reterritorialization," which redefined the terrain of American culture as modern, inauthentic, and free, and reinscribed the Jew, the quintessential actor, protean, urban

and modern, from the margin to its core.[100] And it was precisely this protean quality that made Jews, according to the nativist author Lothrop Stod-
dard, "about as thoroughly 'alien' to America as it is possible to conceive"—
a widely shared sentiment that contributed to a groundswell of public
xenophobia and anti-Semitism in the 1920s, and culminated in the restrictive immigration legislation of the Johnson Act of 1924.[101]

That this modern, excessive, Jewish voice owed much to the mimicry of
African American vernacular styles, as transmitted (however problemati-
cally) through blackface comedy and ragtime, and that it therefore must be
seen as an expression of the mongrelization of culture in New York's urban
borderlands (as Ann Douglas has argued), is undeniable.

It may be that Jewish American comedians broke the codes of the stage
"Hebrew," the "Wop," and the blackface minstrel, successfully detached Jewish mutability from the shadows of "passing" and "imposture" that initially
trailed it, and linked it to a propensity for self-transformation deemed essential "American." But this move was played out against the backdrop of African American actors who remained captive to the specular image of the
"real" darky, and to the investment in keeping the fiction of a fixed relation
between inner racial character and physiognomy intact. As a consequence,
James Weldon Johnson wrote in *Black Manhattan* that it remained "quite
seemly for a white person to represent a Negro on stage, but a violation of
some inner code for a Negro to represent a white person."[102]

Thus, when, in response to the actor Louis Mann's refusal to cave in to
the demands of show business and black up ("I've worn whiskers and fallen
off tables. But I wouldn't black up for any manager"), another actor commented: "Well, I guess I'll go over and see how Bert Williams feels," he did
hit the nail on the head. [103]

The same decade that saw the arrival of Jewish vaudeville stars on Broadway, the heart of modern, metropolitan American culture, also witnessed
the disappearance of black performers. The absence of black talent on Broadway between 1914 and 1921 can be attributed only partly to the death of some
of the leading stars of black musical comedy. The more important factor
was the "colorphobia" that, according to the critic Lester Walton, "hit the
stage." While blacked-up, coon-shouting whites and Jews were making it
big, talented African American performers could no longer attract the interest of the mainstream circuits. "There is no colored star in a white theater
except Mr. Bert Williams," a critic wrote in the *Freeman* in 1914, "and now
the white man is saying that he is not a Negro."[104]

The construction of race as "inherent and incontrovertible difference" depended heavily on the epistemological guarantee of the visual and the legal guarantee of Jim Crow.[105] The suggestion of African American mutability and the transcendence of racial type by African American actors on the stage evoked the possibility of a disjunction between appearance and "real" identity, and of a destabilization of the locus of the "real"—innate identity itself. Given the (il)logic of race and the one-drop rule, and the legacy of racial mixing in America, this destabilization would have struck at the shaky epistemological foundation of the color line.

In a peculiar arrangement, the combination of the isomorphism of the stage and the metropolis—both sites of exchange, of individuals crossing social and cultural boundaries—and theater's paradoxical but ideologically mandated marginality has conspired to grant the stage an important metacritical function. Theater's power to "transcend, criticize or at least self-consciously comment on the structure of those social conditions" under which it was produced has tended to extend itself to the self-reflexive interrogation of the place of the stage in the production of meaning and identity.[106]

In line with that metacritical tradition, the performances of Fanny Brice, Eddie Cantor, and others of their generation transformed the understanding of racial selfhood. From a category of identity which made many native-born Americans and immigrants suspect that beneath the mask of "new" Americanized identities immigrants hid "deeply engrained identities" that were impervious to change, it inched closer to a concept which allowed for a split subjectivity, which did not brand the public, Americanized, mutable, role-playing self as "inauthentic," and which relinquished the idiom of realism and deep interiority for a language of the performative—the stage as metaphor of selfhood.[107]

This language contained the understanding that theater, in the Western world synonymous with "illusion," is not "a site of radical contrast with the world outside of it." Indeed, in the world of modern consumer capitalism in particular, the individual is held enthralled by "the things which s/he does not have, the identities s/he cannot act or put on," and, fueled by that dynamic of desire and lack, aspires to a self-transformation that is mediated by images and illusions which constitute, from the beginning, "what goes to make a human subject, and . . . what he or she apprehends as real."[108]

The ideological imperative of maintaining a separation between stage and reality, however, continued to rely on blackness as the "touchstone" of the real—a level of base existence in which the means to "act" are simply not at hand, or, if they are, do not substantially change who one is. For the time being, the centrality of African American performance in the creation of a modern, inauthentic, role-playing self could be acknowledged only in racial ventriloquism, through erasure.

Al Jolson: Jewish blackface as the face of modernity. "Where Did Robinson Crusoe Go with Friday on Saturday Night" (Waterson, Berlin & Snyder, 1916). From the Romeyn and Kugelmass Collection.

NOTES

Introduction

1. Claude Lévi-Strauss, *The View from Afar* (New York: Basic Books, 1984), 258.

2. Ibid., 259, 262.

3. Ibid., 259, 266–67.

4. James Clifford, *The Predicament of Culture: Twentieth-Century Ethnography, Literature, and Art* (Cambridge, Mass.: Harvard University Press, 1988), 244, 245, 273.

5. Ibid., 244; Lévi-Strauss, *The View from Afar*, 265–66.

6. The discourse of theatricality here links up with that of aesthetics, in particular the opposition of symbol and allegory. This important connection, explored extensively by Walter Benjamin and after him by literary critics such as Jacques Derrida and Paul de Man, will be referred to below. See Rainer Nägele, *Reading after Freud: Essays on Goethe, Hölderlin, Habermas, Nietzsche, Brecht, Celan, and Freud* (New York: Columbia University Press, 1987), 8. The urban exploration narrative is analyzed extensively in chapter 1, "The Epistemology of the City."

7. Clifford, *The Predicament of Culture*, 274–75; Rainer Nägele, *Theater, Theory, Speculation: Walter Benjamin and the Scenes of Modernity* (Baltimore: Johns Hopkins University Press, 1991), 107.

8. Kevin McLaughlin, "Virtual Paris: Benjamin's 'Arcades Project,'" in *Benjamin's Ghosts: Interventions in Contemporary Literary and Cultural Theory*, ed. Gerhard Richter (Stanford: Stanford University Press, 2002), 213.

9. Nägele, *Theater, Theory, Speculation*, 106. Tom McCall, "The Dynamite of a Tenth of a Second: Benjamin's Revolutionary Messianism in Silent Film Comedy," in *Benjamin's Ghost*, ed. Gerhard Richter, 86.

10. Nägele, *Theater, Theory, Speculation*, 107, 71–72.

11. Clifford, *The Predicament of Culture*, 264.

12. Werner Sollors, "Comments," in *Pluralism and the Limits of Authenticity in North American Literatures*, ed. Winfried Siemerling and Katrin Schwenk (Iowa City: University of Iowa Press), 155. Renato Rosaldo, *Culture as Truth: The Remaking of Social Analysis* (Boston: Beacon Press, 1989), 208.

13. This perspective on "performance" and "culture" has continued to hold sway in cultural anthropology until its "deconstructive" turn in the 1990s. See George Marcus

and Michel Fischer, *Anthropology as Cultural Critique: An Experimental Moment in the Human Sciences* (Chicago: University of Chicago Press, 1986).

14. The term is taken from Jonas Barish, *The Anti-Theatrical Prejudice* (Berkeley and Los Angeles: University of California Press, 1981), an incisive overview of the history of Western antitheatricality.

15. Key postmodern analyses of commodity capitalism such as Jean Baudrillard's concept of an "order of the simulacra" and Guy Debord's "order of the spectacle," however incisive they may be, are informed by a barely hidden nostalgia for "authenticity." See Jean Baudrillard, "Simulacra and Simulations," in *Selected Writings*, ed. Mark Poster (Stanford: Stanford University Press, 1988), 166–84; Guy Debord, *Society of the Spectacle* (Detroit: Black and Red, 1983).

16. McLaughlin, "Virtual Paris," 213, 215–16.

17. Nägele, *Theater, Theory, Speculation*, 15.

18. Samuel Weber, *Theatricality as Medium* (New York: Fordham University Press, 2004), 21.

19. William Boelhower, *Through a Glass Darkly: Ethnic Semiosis in American Literature* (New York: Oxford University Press, 1987), 275.

20. Slavoj Žižek, "Eastern European Republics of Gilead," in *Dimensions of Radical Democracy: Pluralism, Citizenship, Community*, ed. Chantal Mouffe (New York: Verso, 1992), 20.

21. Warren I. Susman, "'Personality' and Twentieth-Century Culture," in John Higham and Paul K. Conkin, eds., *New Directions in American Intellectual History* (Baltimore: Johns Hopkins University Press 1979), 212–26; Stuart Ewen, *All Consuming Images: The Politics of Style in Contemporary Culture* (New York: Basic Books, 1988), 74.

22. Samira Kawash, *Dislocating the Color Line: Identity, Hybridity, and Singularity in African-American Literature* (Stanford: Stanford University Press, 1997), 12–13; David Theo Goldberg, *Racial Identities: Writing on Race in America* (New York: Routledge, 1997), 78–108.

23. Weber, *Theatricality as Medium*, 34, 37.

24. Steven Mullaney, *The Place of the Stage* (Chicago: University of Chicago Press, 1988), viii.

25. Weber, *Theatricality as Medium*, 36.

26. See Stephen Greenblatt, "Loudon and London," *Critical Inquiry* 12, no. 2 (1986): 328.

27. Jean-Christophe Agnew, *Worlds Apart: The Market and the Theater in Anglo-American Thought, 1550–1750* (Cambridge: Cambridge University Press, 1986), 9. Michael Rogin acknowledges the "unacknowledged genealogy" of postmodern performance in "the mobile, protean, modernizing self." Michael Rogin, *Blackface, White Noise: Jewish Immigrants in the Hollywood Melting Pot* (Berkeley and Los Angeles: University of California Press, 1996), 51.

28. Agnew, *Worlds Apart*, 60, 61.

29. Ibid., 51, 141.

30. Steven Mullaney, "Strange Things, Gross Terms, Curious Customs: The Rehearsal of Cultures in the Late Renaissance," *Representations* 1, no. 3 (Summer 1983): 53.

31. Nägele, *Theater, Theory, Speculation*, 26.

32. See Jacqueline Lichtenstein, "Making Up Representation: The Dangers of Femininity," in *Representations* 20, no. 4 (Fall 1987): 77–86.

33. Nägele, *Theater, Theory, Speculation,* 26. Benjamin considered the removal of the abyss of the orchestra pit the most radical act in Brecht's epic theater. Ibid., 26.

34. Ibid., 50.

35. Ibid., 26–27; Shawn Michelle Smith, *American Archives: Gender, Race, and Class in Visual Culture* (Princeton: Princeton University Press, 1999), 62.

36. Nägele, *Theater, Theory, Speculation,* 40, 27, 71–72.

37. Susan Buck-Morss, *The Dialectics of Seeing: Walter Benjamin and the Arcades Project* (Cambridge, Mass.: MIT Press, 1991), 347, 305, 306.

38. Laura Bowder, *Slippery Characters: Ethnic Impersonators and American Identities* (Chapel Hill: University of North Carolina Press, 2000).

39. Neil Harris, *Humbug: The Art of P. T. Barnum* (Boston: Little, Brown, 1973). See also Bowder, *Slippery Characters,* 53–58.

40. Karen Halttunen, *Confidence Men and Painted Women: A Study of Middle-Class Culture, 1830–1870* (New Haven: Yale University Press, 1982), 101; John F. Kasson, *Rudeness and Civility: Manners in Nineteenth-Century Urban America* (New York: Hill and Wang, 1990), 46–55; Smith, *American Archives.*

41. Yet that acceptance was "neither complete nor irreversible" because the anxiety about false appearances is a "problem endemic to a society of men and women on the make, of geographical and social movers, of men and women constantly assuming new identities and struggling to be convincing in new social roles." Halttunen, *Confidence Men and Painted Women,* 90.

42. Zygmunt Bauman, *Modernity and the Holocaust* (Ithaca: Cornell University Press, 1989), 59, 58.

43. Bauman, *Modernity and the Holocaust,* 61–62, 59.

44. Warren I. Susman, "Personality and the Making of Twentieth-Century Culture," in John Higham and Paul K. Conkin, eds., *New Directions in American Intellectual History* (Baltimore: Johns Hopkins University Press, 1979).

45. Werner Sollors, *Beyond Ethnicity: Descent and Consent in American Culture* (New York: Oxford University Press, 1982), 38.

46. George Stocking, *Race, Culture, and Evolution: Essays in the History of Anthropology* (New York: Free Press, 1968), 238–39, 251, 253.

47. Ibid., 263. Matthew Frye Jacobson, *Whiteness of a Different Color: European Immigrants and the Alchemy of Race* (Cambridge, Mass.: Harvard University Press, 1998).

48. Mark Pittenger, "A World of Difference: Constructing the 'Underclass' in Progressive America," *American Quarterly* 49, no. 1 (March 1997): 48–49.

49. The discourse of "race traits," which were thought to affect every aspect of human behavior, including temperament, character, intelligence, aesthetic talent, physiognomy, and even political inclinations, demonstrates the degree to which, in the absence of an independent culture concept, race was the dominant lens and provided the dominant idiom for analyzing and discussing what we now call "culture." See Jacobson, *Whiteness of a Different Color,* 39–90.

50. Ibid., 9.

51. Jerome Dowd, "The Racial Element in Social Assimilation," *American Journal of Sociology* (March 1911): 633–35; Charles A. Ellwood, "The Theory of Imitation in Social Psychology," *American Journal of Sociology* (May 1901): 734–36.

52. Dowd, "The Racial Element in Social Assimilation," 633–34; Charles Ellwood argued

that the "the process of growth by imitation" was limited and conditioned by "instinct" and innate tendencies. Ellwood, "The Theory of Imitation," 733–35.

53. Kawash, *Dislocating the Color Line,* 12.

54. Ibid., 3.

55. Patricia McKee, *Producing American Races: Henry James, William Faulkner, Toni Morrison* (Durham: Duke University Press, 1999), 3–4; Richard Dyer, *White* (New York: Routledge, 1997), 38–39.

56. McKee, *Producing American Races,* 7.

57. David Roediger and Eric Lott, working within different interpretive paradigms, argue that pre–Civil War minstrelsy united immigrant workers in a shared white, American, working-class identity. Immigrants like the Irish, who in antebellum America occupied roughly the same social position as free blacks, and shared many of the same stereotypical attributes, became "white" in opposition to the reified blackness of minstrelsy. David Roediger, *The Wages of Whiteness: Race and the Making of the American Working Class* (London: Verso, 1991); Eric Lott, *Love and Theft: Blackface Minstrelsy and the American Working Class* (New York: Oxford University Press, 1993).

For immigrants who started to arrive on America's shores in the 1880s, according to Michael Rogin, blackface, "in turning white to black and back again, . . . played with the process of identity change that transformed poor into rich, daughters into wives and mothers, and immigrants into Americans." The symbolic significance of minstrelsy lay both in the black mask and in the act of masking. Reified blackness allowed for the mutation of the disputed whiteness of the "new" immigrants, specifically Jews, who by this time dominated this style of comedy, into a certified whiteness. Moreover, it allowed Jewish immigrants to consolidate their status while maintaining a subliminal connection to a discarded identity imagined as excessive and black. Michael Rogin, *Blackface, White Noise: Jewish Immigrants in the Hollywood Melting Pot* (Berkeley and Los Angeles: University of California Press, 1996), 49. But the ability of disputed whites to successfully manipulate their identities had a symbolic charge of its own. As Michael North suggests in his analysis of the movie *The Jazz Singer,* "The alternative to Old World tradition with all its rigidity is not blackface per se but the ability to change identities that blackface implies." Modernity implies the cultivation of the surface and the conception of self as actor. The "modern American personality Jakie acquired is free precisely to the extent that it is inauthentic, free to don and change masks at will," North continues. While "the black persona carries all the connotations of natural, unspoiled authenticity. . . , blackface declares itself openly as a mask, unfixes identity, and frees the author in a world of self-creation." Michael North, *The Dialectic of Modernism: Race, Language, and Twentieth-Century Literature* (New York: Oxford University Press, 1994), 6–7. The interpretations of Lott and Rogin in particular give weight to the excess and ambivalences encoded in and enacted through blackface minstrelsy. For Lott, the minstrel show was traversed by libidinal desire as well as fear, a movement he characterized as a dialectic of "love and theft," which involved transgressive, "'unraced' moments of ego-loss" as well as "ego-preserving feeling of racial mastery." Lott, *Love and Theft,* 184.

Rogin reworks the excess and ambivalence of minstrelsy into a split between "racial masquerade" and "racial passing." "While racial masquerade freed [immigrants] from their communities of origin," racial passing "trapped immigrants in . . . unalterable identities," and condemned them to a "sham existence," always fearing exposure. Rogin, *Blackface, White Noise*, 124.

58. Andrew Parker and Eve Kosofsky Sedgwick, "Introduction: Performativity and Performance," in Parker and Sedgwick, eds., *Performativity and Performance* (New York: Routledge, 1995), 3, 6.

59. Seeking to sidestep what he called "descriptive fallacy," which assumes that "statements merely describe some state of affairs," Austin called statements "happy" or "unhappy," more or less conforming to the "humanly comprehensible wish for the appropriateness of our speech" and its desired effects. Timothy Gould, "The Unhappy Performative," in Parker and Sedgwick, eds., *Performativity and Performance*, 31.

60. Parker and Sedgwick, "Introduction," *Performativity and Performance*, 3.

61. Derrida's question was: "Is not what Austin excludes as anomalous, exceptional, 'nonserious,' that is, citation (on the stage, in a poem, or in a soliloquy), the determined modification of a general citationality—or rather, a general iterability—without which there would not even be a 'successful' performative?" Quoted in ibid., 4.

62. Elin Diamond, "Introduction," in *Performance and Cultural Politics,* ed. Elin Diamond (New York: Routledge, 1996), 4.

63. Judith Butler, *Gender Trouble: Feminism and the Subversion of Identity* (New York: Routledge, 1990), 141 (revised edition, 1999: 172–73, 179).

64. Lois McNay, "Subject, Psyche, and Agency: The Work of Judith Butler," in *Performativity and Belonging,* ed. Vikki Bell (London: Russell Sage Foundation, 1999), 176–77; Butler as quoted in ibid.

65. Moya Lloyd, "Performativity, Parody, Politics," in *Performativity and Belonging,* ed. Vikki Bell, 201.

66. Ibid.

67. For a different phrasing of this issue, see Weber, *Theatricality as Medium*, 9, 120.

68. Ibid., 120.

69. Butler, *Gender Trouble,* 179.

70. McNay, "Subject, Psyche, and Agency," 189.

71. Ibid., 177. For instance, for Eric Lott, the excess of the stage cannot completely be contained by the binary structures of self and Other. Performance always threatens to spill over into reality, exposing the histrionic aspects of all social and cultural identities. Thus, the inherent "ideological and psychological instability" of staged structures of difference "regularly exceeds the dominant culture's capacity to fix such boundaries." See Lott, *Love and Theft*, 27.

72. Lloyd, "Performativity, Parody, Politics," 198–211.

73. Butler, *Gender Trouble,* 187.

74. Ibid., 186.

75. Steven Mullaney, "Brothers and Others, or the Art of Alienation," in *Cannibals, Witches, and Divorce: Estranging the Renaissance,* ed. Majorie Garber (Baltimore: Johns Hopkins University Press, 1982), 72. This continues to apply even under the conditions of postmodernity—which according to some (Debord, Baudrillard) extend the range of the theatrical by abolishing the distinction between the "real" and the theater by creating a "Society of the Spectacle" or an "order of the 'hyper-real.'" See also Weber, *Theatricality as Medium.*

76. McNay, "Subject, Psyche, and Agency," 188.

77. Hayden White as quoted in Mullaney, *The Place of the Stage,* 56.
78. Weber, *Theatricality as Medium,* 13.
79. Nägele, *Theater, Theory, Speculation,* 106.
80. McLaughlin, "Virtual Paris: Benjamin's 'Arcades Project,'" 216–17.
81. See, for instance, Amy Kaplan, *The Social Construction of American Realism* (Chicago: University of Chicago Press, 1988); Michael North, *The Dialect of Modernism: Race, Language, and Twentieth-Century Literature* (New York: Oxford University Press, 1994); Cathy Boeckman, *A Question of Character: Scientific Racism and the Genres of American Fiction, 1892–1912* (Tuscaloosa: University of Alabama Press, 2000); Elsa Nettels, *Language, Race, and Social Class in Howell's America* (Lexington: University Press of Kentucky, 1988); Shawn Michelle Smith, *American Archives.*
82. Kaplan, *The Social Construction of American Realism,* 44.
83. As cited in Donald Weber, "Reconsidering the Hansen Thesis: Generational Metaphors and American Ethnic Studies," *American Quarterly* 43, no. 2 (June 1991): 326.
84. For this development, see Jacobson, *Whiteness of a Different Color,* 7–8, 91–135. This tension was inherent in the fact that romantic racialism, for many European immigrant groups as for many African Americans, presented the conceptual basis for a continued peoplehood while at the same time presenting a "limit" to assimilation and universalism. According to Werner Sollors and George Hutchinson, this led to the conceptualization of cultural pluralism and the reconceptualization of race as culture. See Sollors's chapter, "The Ethics of Wholesome Provincialism," in his *Beyond Ethnicity,* 174–207; see also George Hutchinson, *The Harlem Renaissance in Black and White* (Cambridge, Mass.: Harvard University Press, 1995), 62–93.
85. See Jacobson, *Whiteness of a Different Color,* 12 and 274–80.
86. Roediger, *The Wages of Whiteness,* 125.
87. Eric J. Sundquist, *To Wake the Nations: Race in the Making of American Literature* (Cambridge, Mass.: Harvard University Press, 1999), 229, 249.

1. The Epistemology of the City

1. See Paul Boyer, *Urban Masses and Moral Order in America, 1820–1920* (Cambridge, Mass.: Harvard University Press, 1978); Alan Trachtenberg, *The Incorporation of America: Culture and Society in the Gilded Age* (New York: Hill and Wang, 1982); Robert Wiebe, *The Search for Order, 1877–1920* (New York: Hill and Wang, 1967); David Harvey, *The Urban Experience* (Baltimore: Johns Hopkins University Press, 1989).
2. Stuart Blumin, "Explaining the New Metropolis: Perception, Depiction, and Analysis in Mid-Nineteenth-Century New York City," *Journal of Urban History* 11, no. 1 (November 1984): 9.
3. Peter Stallybrass and Allon White, *The Politics and Poetics of Transgression* (Ithaca: Cornell University Press, 1986), 125; Theodore Dreiser, in Boyer, *Urban Masses and Moral Order in America,* 128.
4. Col. Thomas Knox, in Helen Campbell, *Darkness and Daylight, or the Lights and Shadows of New York Life. A Woman's Story of Gospel, Temperance, Mission, and Rescue Work . . . Supplemented by a journalist's description of little known phases of New York life; and a famous detective's years' experiences and observations. By Col. Thomas W. Knox and Inspector Thomas Byrnes* (Hartford, Conn.: A. D. Worthington and Co., 1892), 461; Max

Silverman, *Facing Postmodernity: Contemporary French Thought on Culture and Society* (New York: Routledge, 1999), 67–68.

5. Christopher Prendergast as cited in Silverman, *Facing Postmodernity,* 67.

6. Ibid. Robert Park, "The City: Suggestions for the Investigation of Human Behavior in the Urban Environment," in *Classic Essays on the Culture of Cities,* ed. Richard Sennett (New York: Appleton-Century-Crofts, 1969), 126; Raymond Williams, *The Country and the City* (New York: Oxford University Press, 1973), 154–55.

7. Silverman, *Facing Postmodernity,* 68. As early as 1868 an observer commented that "the social relation of the foreign to the native population has . . . materially changed. They no longer as formerly melt away, or so blend with the native stocks as to become incorporated with it. So large are the aggregations of different nationalities, that they no longer conform to our habits, opinions, and manners, but, on the contrary, create for themselves distinct communities, almost as impervious to American sentiments as are the inhabitants of Dublin or New York." David Ward, *Poverty, Ethnicity, and the American City, 1840–1925: Changing Conceptions of the Slum and the Ghetto* (Cambridge: Cambridge University Press, 1989), 8, 44.

8. Campbell, *Darkness and Daylight,* 39–40.

9. Silverman, *Facing Postmodernity,* 67.

10. Katherine Hoffman, "In the New York Ghetto," *Munsey's Magazine* 23 (1900): 608.

11. See Trachtenberg, *The Incorporation of America,* 101–39; John F. Kasson, *Rudeness and Civility: Manners in Nineteenth-Century Urban America* (New York: Hill and Wang, 1990), 70–107; Marcus Klein, *Easterns, Westerns, and Private Eyes: American Matters, 1870–1900* (Madison: University of Wisconsin Press, 1994), 13–64; Judith R. Walkowitz, *City of Dreadful Delight: Narratives of Sexual Danger in Late-Victorian London* (Chicago: University of Chicago Press, 1992); Maren Stange, "Jacob Riis and Urban Visual Culture: The Lantern Slide Exhibition as Entertainment and Ideology," *Journal of Urban History* 15, no. 3 (May 1989): 274–303; Silverman, *Facing Postmodernity,* 65–69.

12. Following the popular successes of European antecedents of the genre, such as Henry Mayhew's *Lives of the Poor* (1851), Pierce Egan's *Life in London* (1821), and most significantly, Eugène Sue's *Les Mystères de Paris* (1842) (which, in its English translation, sold more than 80,000 copies in the first months of its publication), literary delvings into the urban underworld developed into what amounted to a real vogue. See William R. Taylor, *In Pursuit of Gotham: Culture and Commerce in New York* (New York: Oxford University Press, 1992), 78–88; Werner Sollors, *Beyond Ethnicity: Consent and Descent in America Culture* (New York: Oxford University Press, 1982), 142; George Rogers Taylor, "Gaslight Foster: A New York 'Journeyman Journalist' at Mid-Century," *New York History* 58 (July 1977): 297–312; Janis P. Stout, *Sodoms in Eden: The City in American Fiction Before 1860* (Westport, Conn.: Greenwood Press, 1976), 40–41; Adrienne Siegel, *The Image of the American City in Popular Literature, 1820–1870* (Port Washington, N.Y.: Kennikat Press, 1981); Blumin, "Explaining the New Metropolis": 9–38; George G. Foster, *New York by Gas-Light and Other Urban Sketches,* ed. and intro. Stuart M. Blumin (Berkeley and Los Angeles: University of California Press, 1990).

13. Matthew Hale Smith, Henry L. Williams, and Ralph Bayard, eds., *Wonders of a Great City; or the Sights, Secrets and Sins of New York: Being a wonderful portrayal of the varied phases of life in the greatest city of America* . . . (Chicago: People's Publishing Co.,

1887); Edward Winslow Martin (pseudonym of James D. McCabe), *The Secrets of the Great City. A Work descriptive of the virtues and the vices, the mysteries, miseries and crimes of New York City* (Philadelphia: Jones Brothers and Co., 1868); James D. McCabe, *Lights and Shadows of New York Life, or, the Sights and Sensations of the Great City* . . . (Philadelphia: National Publishing Co., 1872); James D. McCabe, *New York by Sunlight and Gaslight. A work descriptive of the Great American Metropolis* . . . (Philadelphia: Douglas Bros., 1882); J. W. Buel, *Mysteries and Miseries of America's Great Cities, embracing New York, Washington City, San Francisco, Salt Lake City, and New Orleans* (St. Louis: Historical Publishing Co., 1883); Junius Henri Browne, *The Great Metropolis, or a Mirror of New York. A Complete History of Metropolitan Life and Society, with Sketches of Prominent Places, Persons, and Things in the City, as They Actually Exist* (Hartford, Conn.: American Publishing Co., 1869); Campbell, *Darkness and Daylight, or the Lights and Shadows of New York Life*. Campbell's book was republished in 1895 as *Darkness and Daylight; or Lights and Shadows of New York Life. A Pictorial Record of Personal Experiences by Day and Night in the Great Metropolis with Hundreds of Thrilling Anecdotes and Incidents, Sketches of Life and Character, Humorous Stories, Touching Home Scenes, And Tales of Tender Pathos, Drawn from the Bright and Shady Sides of the Great Under World of New York.*

14. See Blumin, "Explaining the New Metropolis," 25; Blumin, "Introduction," in George F. Foster, *New York by Gas-Light*, 58–60; Trachtenberg, *The Incorporation of America*, 103–8.

15. See Trachtenberg, *The Incorporation of America*, 101–8; Alan Trachtenberg, "Experiments in a Foreign Country: Stephen Crane's City Sketches," in *American Realism: New Essays*, ed. Eric J. Sundquist, 139–54; Peter Brooks, "The Text of the City," *Oppositions* 8 (Spring 1977): 7–11; Blumin, "Explaining the New Metropolis"; Philip Fisher, "City Matters: City Minds," in *The Worlds of Victorian Fiction*, ed. Jerome H. Buckley (Cambridge, Mass.: Harvard University Press, 1975), 371–89.

16. See Dana Brand, *The Spectator and the City in Nineteenth-Century American Literature* (Cambridge: Cambridge University Press, 1991); Silverman, *Facing Postmodernity*, 72–95.

17. Alan Trachtenberg, "Experiments in a Foreign Country," 140; see also Deborah Epstein Nord, "The City as Theater: From Georgian to Early Victorian London," *Victorian Studies* 31, no. 2 (Winter 1988): 177.

18. Stallybrass and White, *The Politics and Poetics of Transgression*, 139.

19. McCabe, *Lights and Shadows of New York Life*, 15. Junius Henri Browne exhorts his reader that "the carriage is at the door, my friend. Shut up the shadow-book, and step into the light of the outer world . . . for we will go into the under-ground haunts, as well as the upper abodes of amusement and pleasure. Through and into New York we will look with a calm, yea, philosophic eye; see its open and hidden mysteries at every angle; observe the places we enter, and analyse the people we encounter." Professedly "detached" attitudes toward the urban scene, such as the above, were rare among a genre in which the majority of the specimens were written by members of the clergy. See Browne, *The Great Metropolis*, 30.

20. As quoted in Karen Halttunen, *Confidence Men and Painted Women: A Study of Middle-Class Culture, 1830–1870* (New Haven: Yale University Press, 1982), 39.

21. James D. McCabe, *New York by Sunlight and Gaslight*, iii.

22. James D. McCabe, *Lights and Shadows of New York Life, or, the Sights and Sensations of the Great City*, 55.

23. See Peter Stallybrass, "Marx and Heterogeneity: Thinking the Lumpen Proletariat," *Representations* 31 (Summer 1990): 69–95; see Epstein Nord, "The City as Theater," 164–65.

24. See Rosemary Jann, "Sherlock Holmes Codes the Social Body," *ELH* 57 (1990): 685–708; Brand, *The Spectator and the City*, 22–23.

25. Campbell, *Darkness and Daylight*, vii.

26. Ibid., viii, ix.

27. Trachtenberg, *The Incorporation of America*, 101–39.

28. Allan Sekula, "The Body and the Archive," in *The Contest of Meaning*, ed. Richard Bolton (Cambridge, Mass.: MIT Press, 1992), 343–79. The criminologists Alphonse Bertillon and Cesare Lombroso created "scientific" methods that would allow criminals to be identified through indexes of physical measurements. The English scientist Francis Galton, founder of eugenics, developed his method of the composite portrait in order to replace the vague impression of foreign groups who were seen as a health and criminal threat to the national body. From these easily comparable pictures, a skilled physiognomist could deduce information about their generic character.

29. Miles Orvell, *The Real Thing: Imitation and Authenticity in American Culture, 1880–1940* (Chapel Hill: University of North Carolina Press, 1989), 85–94.

30. As quoted in Matthew Frye Jacobson, *Whiteness of a Different Color: European Immigrants and the Alchemy of Race* (Cambridge, Mass.: Harvard University Press, 1999), 141.

31. Campbell, *Darkness and Daylight*, 697.

32. Ibid., 318. As Campbell comments, however, "One discovers that even under its most foreign aspect these new arrivals grouped in picturesque confusion are not by any means the same as when at home. . . . The races have not yet blended, but the mere presence and contact of all these dissimilar atoms results in an amalgam which is itself American" (319).

33. Ibid., 474.

34. Ibid., 319–20.

35. Ibid., 401, 400, 406.

36. Ibid., 110, 481–82.

37. Ibid., 462, 47–471.

38. Ibid., 459.

39. Jann, "Sherlock Holmes Codes the Social Body," 686.

40. Campbell, *Darkness and Daylight*, 461.

41. Brooks, "The Text of the City," 9. The metaphor of the city as theater, according to Epstein Nord, structures most nineteenth-century Victorian writing on the city, and was rooted in the experience of urban heterogeneity. Epstein Nord, "The City as Theater," 159–60. Otherness, as Kirshenblatt-Gimblett has remarked, is always constructed as inherently dramatic. Barbara Kirshenblatt-Gimblett, "Objects of Ethnography," in *Exhibiting Cultures: The Politics and Poetics of Museum Display*, ed. Ivan Karp and Steven Levine (Washington, D.C.: Smithsonian Institution Press, 1990), 406.

42. Jean-Christophe Agnew, *Worlds Apart: The Market and the Theater in Anglo-American Thought, 1550–1750* (Cambridge: Cambridge University Press, 1986), 59.

43. See Dan Schiller, *Objectivity and the News* (Philadelphia: University of Pennsylvania Press, 1981).

44. As quoted in Kristin Ross, *The Emergence of Social Space: Rimbaud and the Paris Commune* (Minneapolis: University of Minnesota Press, 1988), 82. "Quaint occupations," such as the Saur Kraut Cutter, the Cat Meat Man, and the "sandwich perambulators," have their own distinctive peddling cries. Wall Street, McCabe explains, is obscure to strangers because of its "cabbalistic occupational idiom" sprinkled with such terms as "corner," "margins," "settlements," "rings," "to be short," or "crippled." Criminal urban subcultures also "form a distinct community . . . and have signs by which they recognize each other, and a language, or argot, peculiar to themselves." But even these codes can be broken. For the benefit of the inquisitive reader, McCabe provides a vocabulary of thieves' argot, replicating other popular compendia of thieves' language, such as George W. Matsell's *Vocabulum, or The Rogue's Lexicon* (1859). See McCabe, *Lights and Shadows of New York Life*, 523–24.

45. In *Darkness and Daylight*, the upper classes do not receive the spotlight, in contrast to McCabe's earlier guidebook, which ridicules the linguistic affectations of the upper crust of society. McCabe, for instance, gives a verbatim report of part of a conversation between a young lady of high position in society and an equally "high-toned" young man (221):

HE: "Aw, Miss Jay, saw you 'joying the races to-day."
SHE: "Yeth; they're awfully jawly, ain't they? Right fun to bet, ain't it?"
HE: "Ya-as, rawther jawly to bet when you win you know; but beastly, awfully beastly, to bet and losem you know."

Browne includes a similar "Hebrew" scene: "Our Hebrew friend is engaged in filing a gold coin, and won't perceive us, so intent is he upon his little fraud. No grief in this showy, coarse woman's face as she enters. She is gaily and expensively attired. She is painted like a new signboard and redolent of musk. Her voice is unpleasant and her syntax blunders.

"What'll you lend me on this 'ere? (She offers a large gold miniature.) You see it's purty."

"Vell, madam, ve can't shell dese ting. Osher beeble pichers ishn't vorsh much vid us. Only goot for ole golt, dat ish all, madam. I pledges you mine vort of honor. I geeve you fife tollars—dash ish more dan it ish vorsh, I shvear." Browne, *The Great Metropolis* (477).

46. Campbell, *Darkness and Daylight*, 608.

47. Agnew, *Worlds Apart*, 67; Schiller, *Objectivity and the News*, 110.

48. Mark Seltzer, "The Princess Casamassima: Realism and the Phantasy of Surveillance," in *American Realism: New Essays*, ed. Eric J. Sundquist (Baltimore: Johns Hopkins University Press, 1982), 99.

49. Sekula, "The Body and the Archive"; Stallybrass and White, *The Politics and Poetics of Transgression*.

50. See Patricia McKee, *Producing American Races: Henry James, William Faulkner, Toni Morrison* (Durham: Duke University Press, 1999), 7; Richard Dyer, *White* (London: Routledge, 1997).

51. Agnew, *Worlds Apart*, 161. See also Epstein Nord, "The City as Theater," 174; Seltzer, "The Princess Casamassima," 105. Such texts, as Stallybrass and White argue, were central

in constructing the "urban geography of the bourgeois Imaginary": "It was in the re-forming text as much as in the novel that the nineteenth-century city was produced as a locus of fear, disgust and fascination." "In countless Victorian reformers, the slum, the labouring poor, the prostitute, the sewer, were recreated for the bourgeois study and drawing room. . . . As the bourgeoisie produced new forms of regulation and prohibition governing their own bodies, they wrote even more loquaciously of the body of the Other—of the city's 'scum'." Stallybrass and White, *The Politics and Poetics of Transgression,* 125–26.

52. Stallybrass and White, *The Politics and Poetics of Transgression,* 42. The middle-class spectator surveys places that are invariably dangerous, unpleasant, smelly, poison-ous, hazardous, and ugly, and "even the air of respectability is an element of personal danger" (Campbell, *Darkness and Daylight,* x).

53. See Miles Orvell, "Almost Nature: The Typology of Late Nineteenth-Century American Photography," *Views* (1986), 14–15; Orvell, *The Real Thing: Imitation and Authenticity in American Culture, 1880–1940* (Chapel Hill: University of North Carolina Press, 1989), 35.

54. Epstein Nord, "The City as Theater," 170.

55. Kirshenblatt-Gimblett, "Objects of Ethnography," 413. In their ethnographic real-ism, these exhibitions imposed upon the exotic world a "picture-like" and "legible" quality. Timothy Mitchell, *Colonising Egypt* (Cambridge: Cambridge University Press, 1988), 28.

56. See Kirschenblatt-Gimblett, "Objects of Ethnography," 411; Stallybrass, "Marx and Heterogeneity," 74; Seltzer, "The Princess Casamassima," 101.

57. As cited in Boyer, *Urban Masses and Moral Order in America,* 128.

58. Miles Orvell, *The Real Thing,* 35; see also Deborah Epstein Nord, "The Social Explorer as Anthropologist: Victorian Travellers among the Urban Poor," in *Visions of the Modern City: Essay in History, Art, and Literature,* ed. William Sharpe and Leonard Wallock (Baltimore: Johns Hopkins University Press, 1987), 122–34.

59. See Seltzer, "The Princess Casamassima," 99–100; see also Epstein Nord, "The City as Theater," 160.

60. As cited in Sanford E. Marovitz, "Howells and the Ghetto: 'The Mystery of Mis-ery'" *Modern Fiction Studies* 16 (1970–71): 359.

61. See Orvell, *The Real Thing;* Halttunen, *Confidence Men and Painted Women;* John F. Kasson, *Rudeness and Civility: Manners in Nineteenth-Century Urban America* (New York: Hill and Wang, 1990), 70–111.

62. Browne, *The Great Metropolis,* 582.

63. Byrnes, in Campbell, *Darkness and Daylight,* 695.

64. Campbell, *Darkness and Daylight,* 593–94. A similar, scarcely concealed admira-tion for the mimetic genius and professional skill with which impostors act out various social roles also informs Junius Henri Browne's description of the bag of tricks of pro-fessional con men in *The Great Metropolis* (463):

> The impostors might be termed the intellectual class of the criminals, for they require invention, expedience, originality and tact. They, more than any of the oth-ers, are born into their calling, and are artists after a certain fashion. . . . They have much more of the dramatic element in them, playing parts often more skillfully

than the actors on Broadway. They represent blind men one day, cripples the next, wounded soldiers the third, robbed immigrants the fourth, southern Union refugees the fifth, discharged laborers the sixth, and victims of a railway incident the seventh. They make up admirably; hide one eye, conceal an arm or a leg, create a cicatrice, simulate a sore, counterfeit an agony, imitate a grief, in a manner that would yield them histrionic laurels.

65. Halttunen, *Confidence Men and Painted Women*, 190–98; Kasson, *Rudeness and Civility*, 109–10; for a prehistory of this relationship between antitheatricality and social mobility, see Agnew, *Worlds Apart*, 40, 61. The same concern was played out in various other cultural forums, such as Barnum's dime museum, and informed the late nineteenth-century fascination with magic and forgeries.

66. Terdiman, *Discourse/Counter-Discourse*, 93–95.

67. Ibid., 97–98.

68. Halttunen, *Confidence Men and Painted Women*.

69. Fisher, "City Matters: City Minds," 375, 377.

70. This paradox was repressed in the ideal of bourgeois self-control, which brought virtually all dimensions of personal life, from facial expressions and management of emotions to interaction with strangers, under the range of rules of etiquette. Kasson, *Rudeness and Civility*, 40.

71. Knox, in Campbell, *Darkness and Daylight*, 585–86.

72. Orvell, *The Real Thing*, 52.

73. Audrey Jaffe, "Detecting the Beggar: Arthur Conan Doyle, Henry Mayhew, and 'The Man with the Twisted Lip,'" *Representations* 31 (Summer 1990): 100–101.

74. Moreover, by framing the city as theater, and assuming a distant stance, the middle-class spectator might, rather than penetrating into the secrets of the city, add to its mysteries. By framing urban low life as a series of enacted scenes, such a stance inadvertently turns its low subjects into actors, who might just take on the social roles that the spectator has implicitly assigned to them, thus transforming unproductive bodies into productive bodies, social identity into profit, and the transparency of the urban scene into a mere mirage. See Philip Fisher, "Acting, Reading, Fortune's Wheel: *Sister Carrie* and the Life History of Objects," in *American Realism: New Essays*, ed. Eric J. Sundquist, 259–77.

75. Warren I. Susman, "'Personality' and the Making of Twentieth-Century Culture," in *New Directions in American Intellectual History*, ed. John Higham and Paul K. Conkin (Baltimore: Johns Hopkins University Press, 1979), 220.

76. As quoted in Richard Terdiman, *Present Past: Modernity and the Memory Crisis* (Ithaca: Cornell University Press, 1983), 6 n. 6.

77. Halttunen, *Confidence Men and Painted Women*, 39.

78. Elsa Nettels, *Language, Race, and Social Class in Howell's America* (Lexington: University of Kentucky Press, 1988), 11.

79. Fine, *The City, the Immigrant, and American Fiction*, 145–46.

80. Robert Park, in Halttunen, *Confidence Men and Painted Women*, 39.

81. Bernardino Ciambelli, *I Misteri di Mulberry Stritto* (New York: Frugone and Balletto, 1893); Bernardino Ciambelli, *Il Mistero di Bleecker Street* (New York: Frugone and Balletto, 1899), and John Paley, *Di Shvartse Khevre, oder Nuyork bay tog un nakht: an*

origineler roman fun der Nuyork geto (New York: Hebrew Publishing Co, 1900). Ciambelli, *Il Mistero di Bleecker Street,* 12.

82. Terdiman, *Discourse/Counter-Discourse,* 94.

83. Trachtenberg, *The Incorporation of America,* 103–6.

84. On the relationship between the flâneur and the "flâneur-become-detective," see Susan Buck-Morss, *The Dialectics of Seeing: Walter Benjamin and the Arcades Project* (Cambridge, Mass.: MIT Press, 1991), 305–6.

85. "Es iz a roman fun reyaln leben, es iz a roman fun der wirklikhlkayt, fun der velt vi zi iz. Es iz a roman vos beshraybt zikh ales vos men tut "nekst dor" bay undzer stuben in hoys, es iz a roman fun di gasn un hoysn in velkhn mir leben." Paley, *Di Shvartse Khevre,* 2.

86. Williams, *The Country and the City,* 165.

87. Silverman, *Facing Postmodernity,* 80, 83. Postmodern urban critics such as Paul Virilio and Jean Baudrillard, for whom the postmodern city has become a virtual space of surfaces, ruled by flows of circulation and consumption, appear to have inherited some of this quintessential modern urban angst.

88. Trachtenberg, "Experiments in a Foreign Country," 139.

89. As quoted in ibid. Emphasis in original.

90. In Silverman, *Facing Postmodernity,* 87.

91. Weber, *Theatricality,* 300, 341.

2. DETECTING, ACTING, AND THE HIERARCHY OF THE SOCIAL BODY

1. John F. Kasson, *Rudeness and Civility: Manners in Nineteenth-Century Urban America* (New York: Hill and Wang, 1990), 99–111; Mark Seltzer, "The Princess Casamassima: Realism and the Phantasy of Surveillance," in *American Realism: New Essays,* ed. Eric Sundquist (Baltimore: Johns Hopkins University Press, 1982), 102; Alan Trachtenberg, *The Incorporation of America: Culture and Society in the Gilded Age* (New York: Hill and Wang, 1982), 101–39.

2. Allan Sekula, "The Body and the Archive," in *The Contest of Meaning,* ed. Richard Bolton (Cambridge: MIT Press, 1989), 351, 352–53, Shawn Michelle Smith, *American Archives: Gender, Race, and Class in Visual Culture* (Princeton: Princeton University Press, 1999), 69–93.

3. Smith, *American Archives,* 70–71.

4. Rainer Nägele, *Theater, Theory, Speculation: Walter Benjamin and the Scenes of Modernity* (Baltimore: Johns Hopkins University Press, 1991), 47.

5. Cited in Michael Denning, *Mechanic Accents: Dime Novels and Working-Class Culture in America* (New York: Verso, 1987), 147.

6. Phil Farley, *Criminals of America; or, Tales of Thieves. Enabling Every One To Be His Own Detective. With Portraits, Making a Complete Rogues' Gallery* (New York: Author's Edition, 1876); see Kasson, *Rudeness and Civility,* 105–11.

7. See Philip Fisher, "City Matters: City Minds," in *The Worlds of Victorian Fiction,* ed. Jerome H. Buckley (Cambridge, Mass.: Harvard University Press, 1975), 383.

8. Helen Campbell, *Darkness and Daylight, or the Lights and Shadows of New York Life. A Woman's Story of Gospel, Temperance, Mission, and Rescue Work . . . Supplemented*

by a journalist's description of little known phases of New York life; and a famous detective's years' experiences and observations. By Col. Thomas W. Knox and Inspector Thomas Byrnes (Hartford, Conn.: A. D. Worthington and Co., 1892), 524.

9. Peter Stallybrass, "Marxism and Heterogeneity: Thinking the Lumpen Proletariat," *Representations* 31 (Summer 1990): 69–95.

10. Alan Pinkerton, *Thirty Years a Detective* (New York: G. W. Carleton, 1884), 18–19; Kasson, *Rudeness and Civility*, 111.

11. As cited in Denning, *Mechanic Accents: Dime Novels and Working-Class Culture in America*, 147.

12. Edward Crapsey, *The Nether Side of New York; or the Vice, Crime and Poverty of the Great Metropolis* (1872; reprint, Montclair, N.J.: Patterson Smith, 1969), 56.

13. Sekula, "American Archives," 350.

14. See Kasson, *Rudeness and Civility*, 110–11.

15. As cited in Marcus Klein, *Easterns, Westerns, and Private Eyes: American Matters, 1870–1900* (Madison: University of Wisconsin Press, 1994), 158.

16. As cited in Kasson, *Rudeness and Civility*, 110.

17. As cited in ibid., 111 n. 66.

18. Allan Pinkerton, *The Mollie Maguires and the Detectives* (1877; reprint, New York: Dover Publications, 1973), 16.

19. Ibid., 17, 24, 20, 19.

20. Ibid., 24, 25.

21. Ibid., 25, 28–29.

22. Ibid., 26, 372, 172.

23. Ibid., 60.

24. Ibid., x; see also Klein, *Easterns, Westerns, and Private Eyes*, 134.

25. Pinkerton, *The Mollie Maguires and the Detectives*, 60–61, 172.

26. Ibid., 186, 226–27. As cited in Klein, *Easterns, Westerns, and Private Eyes*, 148.

27. Pinkerton, *The Mollie Maguires*, 228.

28. Mark Pittenger, "A World of Difference: Constructing the "Underclass" in Progressive America," *American Quarterly* 49, no. 1 (1997): 31.

29. Pinkerton, *The Mollie Maguires*, 332, 227.

30. Ibid., 380.

31. Ibid., 502, 505. Klein, *Easterns, Westerns, and Private Eyes*, 152.

32. My argument is informed by Audrey Jaffe, "Detecting the Beggar: Arthur Conan Doyle, Henry Mayhew, and 'The Man with the Twisted Lip,'" *Representations* 31 (Summer 1990): 96–117.

33. Smith, *American Archives*, 62.

34. In Campbell, *Darkness and Daylight*, 695. As I have argued, the culture of personality itself implicitly served as the basis of a social and cultural hierarchy, in which the ability to assume different social and cultural identities became a key marker of a white, middle-class identity. This fact is presaged by the transformation of the figure of the detective, who assumed a pivotal symbolic role in this hierarchy. Not only did the detective gradually lose his disreputable aura, which had been connected to his assumption of false identities and his immersion in low life, but the role of detective, which, as Michael Denning has pointed out, in the 1870s and 1880s popular fiction was frequently taken up by lower-class heroes, but in the 1890s gradually became restricted to

a white Anglo-Saxon male character. The upper-class Nick Carter appears as "a Chinese boy; a dandy, a woman, a farmer, an Irish political boss, and a black boy." Black Tom, The Negro Detective, who solves the mystery of a white woman's body found in the "negro quarters of the city," ultimately turns out to be a white detective in disguise. See Denning, *Mechanic Accents: Dime Novels and Working-Class Culture in America,* 210. Implied in this figurative act of containment (which had its analogue in the 1909 New York legislation which barred "unnaturalized foreigners" from various white-collar jobs, including, significantly, the detective profession) is the idea that the ability to escape type and maintain an authentic, stable self-identity while impersonating various identities is a white, middle- and upper-class prerogative. See John Higham, *Strangers in the Land: Patterns of American Nativism, 1860–1925* (New Brunswick: Rutgers University Press, 1988), 161.

35. Smith, *American Archives,* 62.

36. Pinkerton, *The Mollie Maguires,* 20, 19.

37. Matthew Frye Jacobson, *Whiteness of a Different Color: European Immigrants and the Alchemy of Race* (Cambridge, Mass.: Harvard University Press, 1998), 5.

38. Catherine M. Eagan, "The Invention of the White Races," *American Quarterly* 51, no. 4 (Fall 1999): 926.

39. Pinkerton, *The Mollie Maguires,* 520–21.

40. Ibid., 524–25. This unlinking of race and culture, which found systematic expression in the work of W. E. B. Du Bois, ultimately would provide the basis for a new concept of identity, captured much later by the term ethnicity, which drastically reduced the determinative power of race by containing its influence within an inner, private core. Significantly, this was the model of identity espoused by many national groups as they first gained a collective foothold in middle-class American culture in the 1930s.

41. Neil Harris, "Introduction," in *The Land of Contrasts, 1880–1901,* ed. Neil Harris (New York: George Braziller, 1970), 14.

42. Nellie Bly, *Ten Days in a Mad-house* (New York: Munro, 1900); Philip Fisher, "City Matters: City Minds," in *The Worlds of Victorian Fiction,* ed. Jerome H. Buckley (Cambridge, Mass.: Harvard University Press, 1975), 376.

43. See Harris, "Introduction," 14.

44. Walter Benjamin, "On Some Motifs in Baudelaire," in *Illuminations: Essays and Reflections,* edited and with an introduction by Hannah Arendt (New York: Schocken Books, 1985), 158–59; Amy Kaplan, *The Social Construction of American Realism* (Chicago: University of Chicago Press, 1988), 6–13; Miles Orvell, *The Real Thing: Imitation and Authenticity in American Culture, 1880–1940* (Chapel Hill: University of North Carolina Press, 1989), xv–xx.

45. T. J. Jackson-Lears, "From Salvation to Self-Realization: Advertising and the Therapeutic Roots of the Consumer Culture, 1880–1930," in *The Culture of Consumption: Critical Essays in American History, 1880–1980,* ed. Richard Wrightman Fox and T. J. Jackson Lears (New York: Pantheon, 1983), 7.

46. Ibid., 6. See also Alan Trachtenberg, *The Incorporation of America: Culture and Society in the Gilded Age* (New York: Hill and Wang, 1982), 182–207.

47. Hutchins Hapgood, *Types from City Streets* (New York: Funk and Wagnalls Company, 1910), 15, 18, 17.

48. Judith R. Walkowitz, *City of Dreadful Delight: Narratives of Sexual Danger in Late-Victorian London* (Chicago: University of Chicago Press, 1992), 33.

49. "Experience" was a keyword in the philosophies of John Dewey and William James, who, as Frank Lentricchia has written, advocated a philosophy open to "the barbarities of immediate experience." Lentricchia as cited in Mark Pittenger, "A World of Difference," 36. As Pittenger has written, their influence not only steered much of Progressive thought but also influenced the particular brand of sociology practiced at the University of Chicago School of Sociology, whose graduates (like Wyckoff) displayed a particular fondness for social masquerade.

50. Walter Wyckoff, *The Workers: An Experiment in Reality* (New York: Charles Scribner's Sons, 1898); Lillian Pettengill, *Toilers of the Home: The Record of a College Woman's Experience as a Domestic Servant* (New York: Doubleday, Page and Co., 1905); Alvan Francis Sanborn, *Moody's Lodging House and Other Tenement Sketches* (Boston: Copeland and Day, 1895).

51. Samuel R. Wells, *New Physiognomy, or, the Signs of Character* (1866; reprint, New York: Fowler and Wells, 1894), preface.

52. Ibid., 321.

53. Ibid., 482–83. As Jann has observed, underlying these ideas was the Victorian belief in the deterministic order of the "Great Chain of Being," which held that every element of life was interconnected and fixed in position to support the whole. Rosemary Jann, "Sherlock Holmes Codes the Social Body," *ELH* 57, no. 3 (1990): 689.

54. Wells, *New Physiognomy*, 482.

55. Ibid., 483; preface.

56. Sanborn, *Moody's Lodging House and Other Tenement Sketches*, 1–2.

57. Mrs. John Van Vorst and Marie Van Vorst, *The Woman Who Toils: Being the Experiences of Two Ladies as Factory Girls* (New York: Doubleday, Page and Co., 1904), 11–12.

58. Ibid., 173–74; Mark Pittenger, "A World of Difference, " 40–41.

59. Bly, *Ten Days in a Mad-house*, 5, 9.

60. As cited in Kasson, *Rudeness and Civility*, 46–47.

61. As cited in Pittenger, "A World of Difference," 41.

62. Ibid.

63. Walkowitz, *City of Dreadful Delight*, 36.

64. In his *Experiment in Misery*, a fictional(ized) account of the sampling of tramp life, the author Stephen Crane mockingly evokes the air of superiority that informed some of these social masquerades. His story is framed by the conversation of two friends who are "regarding a tramp" and wondering "how he feels." "You can tell nothing of it unless you are in that condition yourself. It is idle to speculate about it from this distance," is the comment of the older one. "I think I'll try it," the protagonist of Crane's experiment decides. "Rags and tatters, you know, a couple of dimes, and hungry too, if possible. Perhaps I could discover his point of view or something near it." Stephen Crane, "An Experiment in Misery," in *The New York Sketches of Stephen Crane and Related Pieces*, ed. R. W. Stallman and E. R. Wyckoff Hageman (New York: New York University Press, 1996), 33–34. Walter Wyckoff, *The Workers: An Experiment in Reality*, 2.

65. Sanborn, *Moody's Lodging House and Other Tenement Sketches*, 2.

66. Wyckoff, *The Workers: An Experiment in Reality*, 5, 77.

67. Ibid., 124.

68. Pittenger, "A World of Difference," 53–54. Not surprisingly, most narratives lacked

any self-reflection on their self-misrepresentation or on the temporary nature of their boundary-crossing adventure and the limitations this imposed on their perspective.

69. Sanborn, *Moody's Lodging House and Other Tenement Sketches*, 2.

70. Amy Tanner, "Glimpses at the Mind of a Waitress," *American Journal of Sociology* 13 (1908): 50–51.

71. Pittenger, "A World of Difference," 44.

72. Van Vorst and Van Vorst, *The Woman Who Toils*, 22.

73. Pittenger, "A World of Difference," 48, 49.

74. Van Vorst and Van Vorst, *The Woman Who Toils*, 191–92.

75. Wyckoff, *The Workers: An Experiment in Reality*, 241.

76. Pettengill, *Toilers of the Home*, vii.

77. My argument has been significantly shaped by Amy Kaplan, *The Social Construction of American Realism* (Chicago: University of Chicago Press, 1988), 132–39.

78. Theodore Dreiser, *An Amateur Laborer*, ed. Richard W. Dowell (Philadelphia: University of Pennsylvania Press, 1983), 18.

79. Kaplan, *The Social Construction of American Realism*, 132–39.

80. Dreiser, *An Amateur Laborer*, 20.

81. Ibid., 162.

82. Pittenger, "A World of Difference," 31.

83. Philip Fisher, "Acting, Reading, Fortune's Wheel: *Sister Carrie* and the Life History of Objects," in *American Realism: New Essays*, ed. Eric J. Sundquist (Baltimore: Johns Hopkins University Press, 1982), 265, 264.

84. Ibid., 268–69.

85. See Jann, "Sherlock Holmes Codes the Social Body," 685–708; see also Peter Stallybrass, "Marx and Heterogeneity: Thinking the Lumpen Proletariat," *Representations* 31 (Summer 1990): 73; Audrey Jaffe, "Detecting the Beggar: Arthur Conan Doyle, Henry Mayhew, and the 'The Man with the Twisted Lip,'" *Representations* 31 (Summer 1990): 96–117.

86. See Esther Romeyn, "The Home Is Where the Heart Is: The Construction of Ethnicity in the Festival of Nations," manuscript.

87. Henry James, "The Real Thing," *Collected Stories 2 (1892–1910)*, selected and introduced by John Bayley (New York: Alfred A. Knopf, 1999), 39–65.

88. For a discussion of bourgeois aesthetics, see Rainer Nägele, *Theater, Theory, Speculation: Walter Benjamin and the Scenes of Modernity* (Baltimore: Johns Hopkins University Press, 1991), 119–20. For James's aesthetic philosophy as expressed in "The Real Thing," see Orvell, *The Real Thing*, 122–23.

89. Smith, *American Archives*, 66.

90. Ibid.

91. Ibid., 69.

3. Crossing the Bowery

1. E. S. Martin, "East-Side Considerations," *Harper's Weekly* 96 (1897–98): 855.

2. Amy Kaplan, *The Social Construction of Reality* (Chicago: University of Chicago Press, 1988), 44; Eric Sundquist, ed., *American Realism: New Essays* (Baltimore: Johns Hopkins University Press, 1982); Miles Orvell, *The Real Thing: Imitation and Authenticity*

in American Culture, 1880–1940 (Chapel Hill: University of North Carolina Press, 1989); Maren Stange, *Symbols of Ideal Life: Social Documentary Photography in America, 1890–1950* (Cambridge: Cambridge University Press, 1989); Stange, "Jacob Riis and Urban Visual Culture: The Lantern Slide Exhibition as Entertainment and Ideology," *Journal of Urban History* 15, no. 3 (May 1989): 274–303.

3. Hutchins Hapgood, *Types from City Streets* (New York: Funk and Wagnalls, 1910), 17–18, 22, 24.

4. Walter Benjamin, "Über Einige Motive bei Baudelaire," *Gesammelte Schriften,* I.2, ed. Rolf Tiedemann and Hermann Schweppenhauser (Frankfurt am Main: Suhrkamp, 1974), 636, 613–15.

5. Abraham Cahan, "Not One Honest Shudder to Carry Home," in *Grandma Never Lived in America: The New Journalism of Abraham Cahan,* ed. Moses Rischin (Bloomington: Indiana University Press, 1985), 279.

6. "The Bowery at Night," *Harper's Weekly* 35 (1891): 710.

7. Daniel Czitrom, "The Politics of Performance: From Theater Licensing to Movie Censorship in Turn-of-the-Century New York," *American Quarterly* 4, no. 44 (December 1992): 541.

8. Alvin F. Harlow, *Old Bowery Days: Chronicles of a Famous Street* (New York: Appleton and Company, 1931), 427–28.

9. Jacob Riis, *How the Other Half Lives* (1890; reprint, New York: Dover Publications, 1971), 66–67.

10. Harlow, *Old Bowery Days,* 418. On Steve Brodie, "Chuck" Connors, and Bowery culture, see Luc Sante, *Low Life: Lures and Snares of Old New York* (New York, Vintage, 1992), 121–31.

11. Louis Beck, *New York's Chinatown: A Historical Presentation of Its People and Places* (New York: Bohemia Publishing Co., 1898), 317–18.

12. Harlow, *Old Bowery Days,* 424.

13. Hapgood, *Types from City Streets,* 33.

14. Harlow, *Old Bowery Days,* 432.

15. Hapgood, *Types from City Streets,* 34.

16. Harlow, *Old Bowery Days,* 432.

17. Cahan, "Not One Honest Shudder," 280–81.

18. On the performance of "low" identities, see Audrey Jaffe, "Detecting the Beggar: Arthur Conan Doyle, Henry Mayhew, and 'The Man with the Twisted Lip,'" *Representations* 31 (Summer 1990): 96–97.

19. This mechanism of immigrant (self) objectification, Miriam Hansen suggests, is also explored in Charlie Chaplin's *The Immigrant* (1917), in which the future and survival of an immigrant and his companion depend on their discovery by a painter, in other words, on "turning the immigrant image into an aethetic/commerical value." Miriam Hansen, "Early Silent Cinema: Whose Public Sphere?" *New German Critique* 29 (Spring/Summer 1983): 154 n. 15. In these and other performances, the crimes, poverty and depravities of low life were literally turned into theater, and, as such, were effectively displaced and neutralized. Mark Seltzer makes a similar argument about the 1871 novel *The Palace and the Hovel* in "The Princess Casamassima: Realism and the Phantasy of Surveillance," in *American Realism: New Essays,* ed. Eric J. Sundquist.

20. Czitrom, "The Politics of Performance," 541.

21. William Brown Meloney, "The Slumming in New York's Chinatown," *Munsey's Magazine* 41, no. 9 (September 1909): 819; Mary Ting Li Lui, *The Chinatown Trunk Mystery: Murder, Miscegenation, and Other Dangerous Encounters in Turn-of-the-Century New York City* (Princeton: Princeton University Press, 2005). This book on Chinatown and the murder of Elsie Sigel provides detailed historical details about the degree of intermarriage and missionary involvement in Chinatown at the beginning of the twentieth century.

22. Jim Moy, *Marginal Sights* (Iowa City: University of Iowa Press, 1993), 76.

23. Riis, *How the Other Half Lives,* 78.

24. Ibid.; Meloney, "The Slumming in New York's Chinatown," 819.

25. *New York World,* June 19, 1909.

26. *New York World,* June 20,1909.

27. Ibid.

28. Ibid.

29. *New York World,* June 21, 1909.

30. *New York World,* June 20, 1909.

31. Ibid.

32. "Arrest Friend of Miss Sigel," *New York Times,* June 20, 1909.

33. Riis, *How the Other Half Lives,* 77.

34. *New York World,* June 20, 1909.

35. "Arrest Friend of Miss Sigel," *New York Times,* June 20, 1909; "Plot Against White Women," *New York Times,* June 21, 1909.

36. *New York World,* June 20, 1909; "Chong Saw Ling Kill Sigel Girl," *New York Times,* June 23, 1909.

37. Judith R. Walkowitz, *City of Dreadful Delight: Narratives of Sexual Danger in Late Victorian London* (Chicago: University of Chicago Press, 1992), 46–47.

38. A classic account of the relationship between the construction of modern "consumer subjectivity," gender distinction, and the public sphere is Rachel Bowlby's *Just Looking: Consumer Culture in Dreiser, Gissing, and Zola* (New York: Methuen, 1985). See also Janet Wolff, "The Invisible Flâneuse: Women and the Literature of Modernity," *Theory, Culture & Society* 2, no. 3 (1985): 37–46.

39. Walkowitz, *City of Dreadful Delight,* 50.

40. Indeed, Walkowitz argues, "Some respectable women treated shopping and charity work as roughly equivalent recreational activities appropriate to their station." Ibid, 53.

41. The subsequent expedition of the two girls to a seedy bar gives the journalist the opportunity to practice her newly acquired knowledge. As she recounts, "In one room, a fat and merry gentleman came gaily clog-dancing down the floor toward me, arms outstretched, begging me to marry him 'on shpot.' In another room, as I held up my paper at one table, the man nearest gripped my hand and tried to pull me down to him, while his companions laughed. Following instructions, I 'pulled away.'" *New York World,* June 27, 1909.

42. *New York World,* June 20, 1909. These reports were reprints from responses to a similar moral panic in the late 1890s.

43. Jim Moy, *Marginal Sights* (Iowa City: University of Iowa Press, 1993), 81.

44. "Defends Chinese," *New York Times,* June 28, 1909.

45. "Tracking a Murderer," *New York Times*, June 27, 1909.

46. *New York World*, June 22, 1909; see also "White Woman in Opium Den," *New York Times*, June 22, 1909.

47. *New York World*, June 22, 1909.

48. Lawrence Burt, "Women's Love of the Exotic," *Munsey's Magazine* 41, no. 6 (September 1909): 831.

49. Ibid.; "Topics of the Times," *New York Times*, June 23, 1909.

50. *New York World*, June 23, 1909.

51. Burt, "Women's Love of the Exotic," 832.

52. Ibid., 832–33. This comparative analogy between women and the "lower" races, which was based on the mind/body split that subgirded the construction of racial hierarchy and patriarchy, was a staple of nineteenth-century racial science. Phrenology and craniology, which measured the size and shape of the brain as an index of intelligence and racial difference, proved that natural linkage, and proved decisively that the "lower races represented the 'female' type of the human species, and females the 'lower race' of gender." As Nancy Stepan writes, "Women's low brain weights and deficient brain structures were analogous to that of lower races. . . . Similarly, women of higher races tended to have slightly protruding jaws, analogous to, if not as exaggerated as, the apelike jutting jaws of lower races." In Robyn Wiegman, *American Anatomies: Theorizing Race and Gender* (Durham: Duke University Press, 1995), 60, 33.

53. Jacqueline Lichtenstein, "Making Up Representation: The Risks of Femininity," *Representations* 20 (Fall 1987): 78. The basic outlines of this discourse on femininity were transferred to theories of representation and aesthetics. Aristotle, for instance, described the virtues of colors in terms of such feminine attributes as seduction, momentary pleasure, surface, appearance, treachery, obscurity, and ephemerality, whereas line, the complement of color, took on the masculine characteristics of stability, deep understanding, truth, reality, and depth. The same "aesthetic-moral categories" were also linked to specific cultures. While Aristotle used the adjective "Asiatic" to describe an overabundant, excessive, and deceptive use of coloring and ornamentation, he described "Atticism" in terms of simplicity of style, rationality, truthfulness, transparency, and honesty. Ibid., 83.

54. Ibid., 78–79.

55. Burt, "Women's Love of the Exotic," 833.

56. Ibid., 834.

57. William Leach, *Land of Desire: Merchants, Power, and the Rise of a New American Culture* (New York: Vintage Books, 1993), 235.

58. Ibid., 107.

59. Ibid., 105. See also *Visions of the East: Orientalism in Film*, ed. Matthew Bernstein and Gaylayn Studlar (New Brunswick: Rutgers University Press, 1997).

60. Lise-lone Marker, *David Belasco: Naturalism in the American Theatre* (Princeton: Princeton University Press, 1975), 63–64.

61. Lui, *The Chinatown Trunk Mystery*, 82–83.

62. Rosalind Williams, "The Dream World of Mass Consumption," in *Rethinking Popular Culture: Contemporary Perspectives in Cultural Studies*, ed. Chandra Mukerji and Michael Schudson (Berkeley and Los Angeles: University of California Press, 1991), 204.

63. Leach, *Land of Desire*, 83, 102.

64. Ibid., 110. Other fashion shows introduced "ethnographic" displays in the mode of the World's Fairs. A 1917 fashion show based on "Mayan motifs" used glass display cases to exhibit "garments modeled after Indian designs-purses with Mayan embroidery, sports hats bound with Mayan scarfs; cushions made from Indian blankets; and parasols copied from Indian ponchos." In Leach, *Land of Desire,* 103.

65. See Chantal Georgel, "The Museum as Metaphor in Nineteenth-Century France," in *Museum Culture: Histories, Discourses, Spectacles,* ed. Daniel Sherman and Irit Rogoff (Minneapolis: University of Minnesota Press, 1994). According to Georgel, these institutions not only shared the same visual codes, but were complementary parts of the same ideological "fashion machine" of capitalism.

66. Leach, *Land of Desire,* 81, 83.

67. Henry Tyrrell, "The Theatre of New York's Chinatown," *The Theatre Magazine* 3, no. 29 (July 1903), 170.

68. Ibid., 170. But the photographer Arnold Ghente, who visited San Francisco's Chinatown in 1912, was unpleasantly surprised by the inroads made by modern-day commercialism. "Costly silk embroideries in gaudy colors, porcelains of florid design, bronzes with hand-made patina, and a host of gay Chinese and Japanese wares . . . tempt the tourist to enter," he wrote disapprovingly, "while inside cash-registers and department-store manners, replacing abacus and old-time courtesy, indicate up-to-date methods." Irwin, in Arnold Ghente, *Old Chinatown Pictures* (Norwood, Mass.: Plimpton Press, 1912), 206.

69. Williams, "The Dream World of Mass Consumption," 204.

70. *New York World,* June 20, 1909.

71. Meloney, "The Slumming in New York's Chinatown," 820.

72. Ibid., 821–22.

73. Ibid., 823.

74. *New York World,* June 21, 1909.

75. Ibid.

76. "Tracking a Murderer," *New York Times,* June 27, 1909.

77. "First Vice Attack Made on Chinatown," *New York Times,* October 24, 1910.

78. "Sight-Seeing Autos to Shun Chinatown," *New York Times,* October 25, 1910.

79. Ibid.

80. Bowlby, *Just Looking,* 34.

81. Quoted in Lui, *The Chinatown Trunk Mystery,* 218. Barely ten days after the murder, the Elsie Sigel tragedy and Ching Sing's undergoing the "3rd degree" were the subject of a life "exhibit" at the Eden Museum. See *New York Times,* June 27, 1909.

4. Eros and Americanization

1. Katherine Hoffman, "In the New York Ghetto," *Munsey's Magazine* 23 (1900): 608. On the emergence of the Jewish Lower East Side, see Moses Rischin, *The Promised City: New York's Jews, 1870–1914* (New York: Harper, 1962), 76–94.

2. Hoffman, "In the New York Ghetto," 608–19.

3. "Of a Friday in the Jewish Quarter of New York," *Harper's Weekly* 34, no. 17 (1890): 306.

4. Gerald Sorin, *Tradition Transformed: The Jewish Experience in America* (Baltimore: Johns Hopkins University Press 1997), 162. At the turn of the century, 60 percent of the

Jewish working force was employed in manufacturing jobs and 25 percent in trade or clerical jobs. Three decades later, the figures were 57 percent for trade and clerical work, whereas 40 percent had become proprietors of commercial enterprises. By 1937, the children of Jewish immigrants owned two-thirds of New York's 34,000 factories, as well as 104,000 wholesale and retail businesses. Jews also had moved into white-collar and sales jobs, as well as commercial services such as dry-cleaning and private transportation.

5. Irving Howe, *World of Our Fathers: The Journey of the East European Jews to America and the Life They Found and Made* (New York: Harcourt Brace Jovanovich, 1976), 139.

6. Henry James and Burton J. Hendrick, as quoted in Rischin, *The Promised City*, 260.

7. In a book entitled *The Jews in America* (1923), Hendrick propagated the idea that because of their inalienable racial difference, eastern European Jewry should be barred from entering the United States. See Chametzky, "Introduction," in Abraham Cahan, *The Rise of David Levinsky* (New York: Penguin Books, 1993), xvi.

8. Burton J. Hendrick, "The Jewish Invasion of America," *McClure's Magazine* 40 (March 1913): 125–65. A more comical incarnation of the Jewish businessman was presented in the same year in Montague Glass's *Potash and Perlmutter,* a play based on Glass's popular sketches. The play, which scored a record as the longest-running Broadway production of the season, featured the trials and tribulations of two lovable, upwardly mobile Jewish clothing merchants, played by famous Jewish comedians Barney Bernard and Alexander Carr.

9. Ibid., 165. See also Chametzky, "Introduction," xv–xvi.

10. Bernard G. Richards, "Introduction," Abraham Cahan, *Yekl and The Imported Bridegroom and Other Stories of Yiddish New York* (New York: Dover Publications, 1970), vii.

11. Kristin Ross, *The Emergence of Social Space: Rimbaud and the Paris Commune* (Minneapolis: University of Minnesota Press, 1988), 82.

12. Indeed, the lower-class Jake/Yekl, whose Americanizing ambitions are encapsulated in his use of a bungled English, which is visually rendered in the text through the use of italics, speaks an idiom that is virtually indistinguishable from that of the comic Jew of the vaudeville stage. This similarity suggests that the common ground of literary realism and vaudeville burlesque lay in what Raymond Williams has called the "careful orthographic simulation" of the Other. See Raymond Williams, *The Country and the City* (New York: Oxford University Press, 1973), 225.

13. Cahan, *Yekl,* 3.

14. Richards, "Introduction," viii.

15. Sanford E. Marovitz, "Introduction," xiv. The *Bookman* considered Cahan's novella a portrait of the Yiddish immigrant's "racial weakness." Matthew Frye Jacobson, *Whiteness of a Different Color: European Immigrants and the Alchemy of Race* (Cambridge, Mass.: Harvard University Press, 1998), 183.

16. For a detailed account of the publication history of the novel, see Chametzky's introduction to the 1993 Penguin edition.

17. Jacobson, *Whiteness of a Different Color,* 164, 179–84.

18. The review continued: "If Levinsky is a triumphant failure, he is so because of American business, which shaped him to its ends, is *[sic]* viewed from any decent regard for humanity, a miserable monster of success." *The Dial,* November 22, 1917.

19. Kate Holladay Klaghorn, *Survey* 39, December 11, 1917.

20. See Amy Kaplan, *The Social Construction of American Realism* (Chicago: University of Chicago Press, 1988), 44.

21. "Sometimes, when I think of my past, the metamorphosis I have gone through strikes me as nothing short of a miracle. I was born and reared in the lowest depths of poverty and arrived in America—in 1885—with four cents in my pocket. I am now worth more than two million dollars and recognized as one of the two or three leading men in the cloak-and-suit-trade in the United States. And yet, my inner identity . . . impresses me as being precisely the same as it was thirty or forty years ago." Abraham Cahan, *The Rise of David Levinsky,* introduction by John Higham (New York: Harper and Row, 1966), 3.

22. For an incisive reading of *David Levinsky* in terms of Pierre Bourdieu's concepts of "distinction" and "cultural capital," which includes David's observation on the disjunction between labor and appearance in the butcher/gentleman, see Phillip Barrish, "The Genuine Article": Ethnicity, Capital, and *The Rise of David Levinsky,*" *American Literary History* 5, no. 4 (Winter 1993): 643–62.

23. Tashrak, with A. Tannenboym and D. M. Hermelin et al., *Etikete: A veg veyzer fun laytishe oiffirung, heflikhkayt un sheyne manyern far mener un froyen, tsuzamengestelt loyt di beste oyteritetn* (New York: Hebrew Publishing Company, 1912). Chapters on synagogue attendance identified religion as an important aspect of the life of a Jewish gentleman, which was as much subject to the requirements of etiquette as more leisurely pursuits, such as theater or park visits.

Donald Weber points to the centrality of etiquette in *The Rise of David Levinsky* as indicative of David's social and cultural ambitions, in "Outsiders and Greenhorns: Christopher Newman in the Old World, David Levinsky in the New," *American Literature* 67, no. 4 (December 1995): 734–39.

24. Tashrak, *Etikete,* 48.

25. Ibid., 82.

26. Ibid., 81.

27. Edward Alsworth Ross, *The Old World in the New: The Significance of Past and Present Immigration to the American People* (New York: The Century Co., 1914), 165.

28. "The Gentile's Attitude Toward the Jew As a Jew Sees It," *The Menorah Journal* 11, no. 3 (December 1916): 274.

29. In John Murray Cuddihy, *The Ordeal of Civility: Freud, Marx, Lévi-Strauss, and the Jewish Struggle with Modernity* (New York: Basic Books, 1974), 142–44.

30. Abraham Cahan, "Derekh Eretz Beim Esen," *Forverts,* July 21, 1903.

31. On the conflation of whiteness and etiquette, see Valerie Babb, *Whiteness Visible: The Meaning of Whiteness in American Literature and Culture* (New York: New York University Press, 1998), 158–65; on the ambiguous place of Jews within the configuration of whiteness, see Daniel Itzkovitz, "Secret Temples," in *Jews and Other Differences: The New Jewish Cultural Studies,* ed. Jonathan Boyarin and Daniel Boyarin (Minneapolis: University of Minnesota Press, 1997), 181–85.

32. See David Engel, "The 'Discrepancies' of the Modern: Towards a Revaluation of Abraham Cahan's *The Rise of David Levinsky.*" *Studies in American Jewish Literature* 2 (1982): 54.

33. See Susan Sachs, "A New American Dream in Immigrants' Literature," *New York Times,* January 9, 2000, 38.

34. See Dan Vogel, "Cahan's 'Rise of David Levinsky': Archetype of American Jewish Fiction," *Judaism* 23, no. 87 (1973): 281–82.

35. Indeed, Rosenfeld extrapolates, it is precisely because of this correspondence that Jews were "outwardly" able to achieve a "flawless Americanization" without compromising an essential (internal and spiritual) Jewishness. Indeed, Rosenfeld implies, Jewish spiritual striving remains uncorrupted, even if it is transferred onto material striving: it continues to exist under the sign of a deeper, permanent yearning, which is, in essence, the metaphysical yearning of the Diaspora Man. Isaac Rosenfeld, "David Levinsky: The Jew as Millionaire," in Isaac Rosenfeld, *The Age of Enormity,* ed. Theodore Solotaroff (Cleveland and New York: World Publishing Co., 1962), 278. Rosenfeld's essay exhibits an ethnic "boosterism" that, according to Emily Miller Budick and Daniel Itzkovits, was common to Jewish authors in the 1950s who "celebrated the Jewish conquest of America" while maintaining the idea of a Jewish spiritual difference that was the source of a superior moral vision. See Itzkovitz, "Secret Temples," 177, 196; Emily Miller Budick, *Blacks and Jews in Literary Conversation* (Cambridge: Cambridge University Press, 1998). My argument about Jewish "moral knowledge" as a source of Jewish difference has been significantly influenced by Emily Miller Budick's discussion of the writings of Rosenfeld and other American Jewish authors. On Rosenfeld, see Budick, *Blacks and Jews,* 139–42.

36. Rosenfeld, "David Levinsky: The Jew as Millionaire," 287.

37. Abraham Cahan, "The Autobiography of an American Jew: The Rise of David Levinsky," *McClure's Magazine* 41 (July 1913): 117. See also Chametzky, "Introduction," xvii.

38. Barrish, "'The Genuine Article,'" 650.

39. To name but a few of these: Naphtali, the sensitive and passionately religious Talmud student whom David slavishly imitates and misses as a "lover" when he moves out of town; Matilda, the sophisticated, Russianized, and radicalized daughter of a wealthy Jewish benefactress, with whom David falls hopelessly in love; Gitelson, his ship brother, who, dressed as a "dandy," "in spite of himself" adopts a "respectfully contemptuous tone" with David, who is still an educated peddler; Mr. Bender, his shy and "girlish" English teacher, whose perfect "th" makes David "pant with hatred," but whose special attention he comes to "relish dearly"; Jake Mindels, with his "manly exterior and effeminate psychology," whose refined manners, sophisticated English, and style of dress David tries to imitate; and Dora, whose desire for self-improvement matches David's own.

40. This part of my reading of David Levinsky is much indebted to Renata Salecl, *(Per)versions of Love and Hate* (New York: Verso, 1998), in particular 6–33.

41. Walter Benn Michaels, *The Gold Standard and the Logic of Naturalism: American Literature at the Turn of the Century* (Berkeley and Los Angeles: University of California Press, 1987), 41–42, 35.

42. Rachel Bowlby, *Just Looking: Consumer Culture in Dreiser, Gissing, and Zola* (New York: Methuen, 1985), 65, 63.

43. Charles A. Ellwood, "The Theory of Imitation in Social Psychology," *American Journal of Sociology* 6 (May 1901): 722.

44. Ibid: 733, 735.

45. Jerome Dowd, "Discussion," *American Journal of Sociology* (March 1911): 633–34.

46. Ibid., 634–35.

47. Rainer Nägele, *Theater, Theory, Speculation: Walter Benjamin and the Scenes of Modernity* (Baltimore: Johns Hopkins University Press, 1991), 27.

48. Zygmunt Bauman, *Modernity and the Holocaust* (Ithaca: Cornell University Press, 1909), 60.

49. Leslie Fiedler and, more recently, Emily Miller Budick have recognized in *The Rise of David Levinsky* the first in a line of Jewish American novels, including Lewissohn's *Don Juan* and Ben Hecht's *A Jew in Love,* and the oeuvre of Philip Roth, with erotically charged Jewish male protagonists. These novels, according to Budick, take Jewish sexuality as "marker of Jewish difference and as vehicle of authenticity and procreative power."

Yet a too reductive reading of *David Levinsky,* which focuses on sexuality rather than desire as the marker of Jewish difference, runs the risk of misreading Cahan's rhetorical strategy as one that naturalizes Jewish difference as innate, lodged in the body or a "natural" sexuality. See Budick, *Blacks and Jews,* 146; and Fiedler, "The Jew in the American Novel," *The Collected Essays of Leslie Fiedler,* vol. 2 (New York: Stein and Day, 1961).

50. Bourdieu's concepts of "distinction" and "cultural capital" are central to Barrish's perceptive analysis of the novel. Barrish, however, does not explore the racial connotations of the structures of distinction in the United States. See Barrish, "'The Genuine Article.'"

51. See David Biale, *Eros and the Jews: From Biblical Israel to Contemporary America* (New York: Basic Books, 1992).

52. Chametzky writes of Cahan's socialism: "In Cahan's early conversion to socialism and his way of regarding it, there was surely an element of messianic longing in the experience, a hope for self-transcendence and a world better and broader than the narrow one they had been born into. At the root was a deep spiritual longing and hunger." Jules Chametzky, *From the Ghetto: The Fiction of Abraham Cahan* (Amherst: University of Massachusetts Press, 1977), 5.

5. Juggling Identities

1. Carl Van Vechten, "A Night With Farfariello: Popular Bowery Entertainer Who Impersonates Local Italian Types," *Theatre Magazine* 39 (January 1919): 32, Migliaccio Collection, Box 1, Immigration History Research Center.

2. Emelise Francesca Aleandri, "A History of Italian-American Theater, 1900–1905," (Ph.D. diss., New York University, 1983), 149.

3. Kevin McLaughlin, "Virtual Paris: Benjamin's 'Arcades Project,'" in *Benjamin's Ghosts: Interventions in Contemporary Literary and Cultural Theory,* ed. Gerhard Richter (Stanford: Stanford University Press, 2002), 213.

4. *Il Progresso Italo-Americano,* 1934, Migliaccio Collection, Box 1.

5. See Walter Benjamin's observation about Brecht: "There is no better starting point for thought than laughter," in Peter Jelavich, *Berlin Cabaret* (Cambridge, Mass.: Harvard University Press, 1993), 33.

6. Dymphie Verdiessen, "De Commedia dell'Arte tussen Sottie and Bienseance," *Skript* 8, no. 2 (1986): 88–90.

7. Louis Estevan, ed., "The Italian Theater in San Francisco," manuscript (San Francisco: WPA San Francisco Research Monographs 10, 1933), 51; Emelise Aleandri and Maxine Schwartz-Seller, "Italian-American Theater," in *Ethnic Theater in the United States,* ed. Maxine Schwartz-Seller (Westport, Conn.: Greenwood Press, 1993); Deanna Paoli

Gumina, "Connazionali, Stenterello, and Farfariello: Italian Variety Theater in San Francisco," *California Historical Quarterly* 54 (Spring 1975): 26–36.

8. Gumina, "Connazionali, Stenterello, and Farfariello": 31; Estevan, *The Italian Theater in San Francisco,* 49–50.

9. Aleandri, "A History of Italian-American Theater," 150.

10. Farfariello appears in Dante's *Divina Commedia* in canto 4, verse 124. William Ricciardi, *Atlantica,* May 1936, Migliaccio Collection, Box 1.

11. Unidentified clipping, Migliaccio Collection, Box 1.

12. *Gazetta del Massachussetts,* July 29, 1916, Migliaccio Collection, Box 1.

13. Migliaccio Collection, Box 1. The translation is by Estevan, "The Italian Theater in San Francisco," 52–53.

14. Joseph Lopreato, *Italian Americans* (New York: Random House, 1970), 38.

15. Rudolph J. Vecoli, "Contadini in Chicago," *Journal of American History* 51 (December 1964): 410.

16. Thomas Kessner, *The Golden Door: Italian and Jewish Immigrant Mobility in New York City* (New York: Oxford University Press, 1983), 53.

17. Mikhail Bakhtin, *Rabelais and His World* (Bloomington: Indiana University Press, 1984), 37, 53, 40, 44, 41.

18. Migliaccio Collection, Box 5.

19. Migliaccio Collection, Box 7.

20. Ibid..

21. Migliaccio Collection, Box 1.

22. Migliaccio Collection, Box 2.

23. Lopreato, *Italian Americans,* 39–40, 42.

24. Orsi, *Madonna of 115th Street: Faith and Community in Italian Harlem, 1880–1950* (New Haven: Yale University Press, 1985), 20.

25. Ibid., 82.

26. Ibid., 108.

27. See Stuart Ewen, *All Consuming Images: The Politics of Style in Contemporary Culture* (New York: Basic Books, 1988), 72–74. The younger generation often resented this watchful eye, which they felt as an intrusion upon their privacy and a constraint upon their freedom. In *Blood of My Blood,* an autobiography of an Italian American childhood, Gambino recounts a family story that illustrates the conflict that often surrounded the dating practices of the second generation:

One summer evening when [my mother] and her two sisters were young women in their twenties, they strolled with their mother on the boardwalk of Coney Island. . . . By chance they spied at some distance the oldest of their brothers, then a boy in his late teens. He was headed in their direction with a girl, hand in hand. My grandmother was outraged at his brazen public behavior and started toward him. To prevent her from making a scene, the daughters surrounded and blocked her. Meanwhile my uncle had seen them and prudently and quickly steered his unknowing date away from his family. Frustrated by her restraining daughters, my grandmother watched her son retreat with a girl that by her standard could only be svergognata (shameless), sfacciata (brazen), and perhaps even puttana (whore).

Richard Gambino, *Blood of My Blood: The Dilemma of Italian-Americans* (New York: Doubleday, 1974), 168.

28. Orsi, *Madonna of 115th Street,* 122.
29. Migliaccio Collection, Box 3.
30. Sheet music, "Portame a Casa Mia," Migliaccio Collection, Box 1.
31. Migliaccio Collection, Box 7.
32. Aleandri, "A History of Italian-American Theater," 455–56.
33. Migliaccio Collection, Box 3.
34. Orsi, *Madonna of 115th Street,* 154.
35. Migliaccio Collection, Box 9.
36. Migliaccio Collection, Box 5, translation by Aleandri, "A History of Italian-American Theater," 474–75.
37. Orsi, *Madonna of 115th Street,* 87.
38. Ibid., 87.
39. The title of the sketch puns on two connotations of the word "sciammeria," which literally means "to swarm," but also, in the Neapolitan dialect, refers to someone who wears a jacket that is too large and whose clothes do not fit the man.

I like this country, America
Because here we are all equal . . .
I know that in America
I do away with morals
I go with the principle that
no one is better than me.
 In my country, to make love,
You need to stick a knife in your pocket.
Just in case the father or the brother, in defense of honor,
Decides to cut off the point of your nose.
But here love is "ollraite," ["all right"]
Truly it is beautiful,
The father only thinks of "dollare,"
The brother only of "ghelle," ["girls"]
And the coast is clear,
The doors are wide open,
You call: "Come daune." ["Come down."] . . .
Dezze bicose Franci
Mi laiche dis contri.
 And if you marry among us,
Comes trouble, there's nothing that you can do,
Any way, and you will have to pay dearly
Whether she is good or very bad.
But here, in America,
If you have had enough,
you just break off the marriage
And you trade her in
You say: Misto no laiche. ["Mister, I don't like her"]

He gives you a receipt
And after this quick judgment
You get yourself another,
Dezze bicose Franci'
Migliaccio Collection, Box 1.

40. Migliaccio Collection, Box 1.
41. Quoted in *L'Italo Americano de Los Angeles,* Migliaccio Collection, Box 1. Translation by Aleandri and Schwartz-Seller, "Italian-American Theater," 266.
42. Aleandri, "A History of Italian-American Theater," 470.
43. Ibid.
44. Ibid., 468–69.
45. "Quel' umorismo che a sempre per basse classica il grottesco della vita." Migliaccio Collection, Box 1.
46. One Italian-language newspaper, for instance, concluded: "The figures he presents on the stage are no artificial manifestations of the typical life in the colony, but they contain an intense sense of reality, they have an intense psychological expressiveness, and herein lies the secret of his success, because the spectators want to see real figures on the stage, palpitating with life, and they applaud when they are moved, by vibrant emotions." *Il Popolo,* February 25, 1918, Migliaccio Collection, Box 1.
47. Aleandri, "A History of Italian-American Theater," 150.
48. *L'Americolo,* March 28, 1926, Migliaccio Collection, Box 1.
49. Migliaccio Collection, Box 5.
50. *Il Progresso Italo-Americano,* Tuesday, February 20 [year missing], Migliaccio Collection, Box 1.
51. John J. MacAloon, "Introduction: Cultural Performances, Culture Theory," in *Rite, Drama, Festival, Spectacle: Rehearsals Toward a Theory of Cultural Performance,* ed. John J. MacAloon (Philadelphia: Institute for the Study of Human Issues, 1984), 1.
52. Richard Terdiman, *Discourse/Counter-Discourse: The Theory and Practice of Symbolic Resistance in Nineteenth-Century France* (Ithaca: Cornell University Press, 1985), 76; Edmund Burke, *On Symbols and Society* (Chicago: University of Chicago Press, 1989), 26. See also Mikhail Bakhtin, *The Dialogic Imagination* (Austin: University of Texas Press, 1981).
53. Michael Fischer, "Ethnicity and the Postmodern Arts of Memory," in *Writing Culture: The Poetics and Politics of Ethnography,* ed. James Clifford and George E. Marcus (Berkeley and Los Angeles: University of California Press), 196.
54. Judith Butler, *Gender Trouble: Feminism and the Subversion of Identity* (New York: Routledge, 1999), 173.
55. Walter Benjamin, in *Reflections: Essays, Aphorisms, Autobiographical Writings,* ed. Peter Demetz (New York: Schocken Books, 1986), 333–36.
56. Aleandri, "A History of Italian-American Theater," 169.
57. Ibid., 170.
58. Quoted in the *Stockton Daily,* undated clipping, Migliaccio Collection, Box 1.
59. *Il Progresso Italo-Americano,* November 29, 1930, Migliaccio Collection, Box 1.
60. James C. Scott, *Weapons of the Weak: Everyday Forms of Peasant Resistance* (New Haven: Yale University Press, 1986), 185.

61. Drama or ritual drama is a major form of public reflexivity. Taking its "raw stuff" out of what Victor Turner has called "social drama," the conflict or transformation of norms, principles, and conceptions of self, all performance is in a sense a metaperformance—a performance about the performance of social roles. The stripping of status, the unmasking and inversion of roles, however, according to Turner, are particularly characteristic of liminal phases or liminoid states in rituals of transition. During such phases of marginality, in which a group is secluded from the larger society and finds itself "betwixt and between fixed points of classification," this genre of performance typically unveils the structures of the order the liminars are leaving behind and of the one they are about to enter. Liminality, a time when daily reality is suspended, can be the occasion of ambiguity and skepticism, marked by the satirizing of self, others, and political, social, and cultural structures. Through ritual humiliation and the stripping of social insignia, it engenders a "communitas," a social bond of "undifferentiated, equalitarian relations" among the liminars. In this fashion, it prepares the way for the ultimate transformation of roles and statuses. Victor Turner, *Drama, Fields, and Metaphors: Symbolic Action in Human Society* (Ithaca: Cornell University Press, 1974), 38, 45, 233–35, 239.

62. Don Handelman, "The Ritual Clown: Attributes and Affinities," *Anthropos* 76, nos. 3–4 (1984): 321–70; Don Handelman and Bruce Kapferer, "Symbolic Types, Mediation, and the Transformation of Ritual Context: Sinhalese Demons and Tewa Clowns," *Semiotica* 30, nos. 1–2 (1980): 41–71.

63. *Gazetta della Massachusetts,* Saturday, July 26, 1916, Migliaccio Collection, Box 1.

64. Steven Mullaney, "Brothers and Others, or the Art of Alienation," in *Cannibals, Witches, and Divorce: Estranging the Renaissance,* ed. Marjorie Garber (Baltimore: Johns Hopkins University Press, 1982), 68; see James Fernandez, "Some Reflections into Mirrors," in *Persuasions and Performances: The Play of Tropes in Culture,* ed. James Fernandez (Bloomington: Indiana University Press, 1986), 158–66.

65. Colonial mimicry, Homi Bhabha has argued, is a cipher of the "opera bouffe" of the New World. It represents "the desire for a reformed, recognizable Other," who is the "subject of a difference that is almost the same, but not quite."

Mimicry, then, is a form of repetition rather than representation, a form of self-doubling that produces a "virtual subject" who incorporates the "narcissistic demand of colonial authority" for a self-same Other, but only partially, as a presence that at the same time is an absence, a "difference that is itself a process of disavowal." As such, mimicry "is constructed around an ambivalence." It "continually produces its slippage, its excess, its difference." It is, then, a discourse produced "at the crossroads," which is also, simultaneously, a "site of interdiction": uttered between "what is known and permissible and that which though known must be kept concealed," "between the lines, and as such both against the rules and within them." Homi Bhabha, "Of Mimicry and Man: The Ambivalence of Colonial Discourse," *October* 28 (Spring 1984): 126–30.

66. Gabriel Tarde, *The Laws of Imitation,* translated from the 2nd French edition (New York: H. Holt and Co., 1903), 199; Ewen, *All Consuming Images,* 74–75.

67. Charles A. Ellwood, "The Theory of Imitation in Social Psychology," *American Journal of Sociology* 6 (May 1901): 721–41; Jerome Dowd, "The Racial Element in Social Assimilation," *American Journal of Sociology* (March 1911): 633–35.

68. In this role, Farfariello was by no means a unique figure within immigrant communities. One only has to think of Yiddish vaudeville, which emerged in the last years

of the nineteenth century in the saloons of the Lower East Side and was equally sensitive to its urban, immigrant environment. With comic stock types such as the *griner* (the "greenhorn"), the *allrightnik* (who adopts all the customs of the new country), the peddler, the butcher, the cantor, the *schlemiel* husband with his domineering wife, the popular Yiddish stage presented an index of the Jewish immigrants' world in burlesque form.

As in the sketches of Farfariello, one of the distinguishing features of this humor was the importance of dialect. Yiddish vaudeville often exploited Jewish in-group differences. The song "Der Litvak un der Galitsianer" (1914), for instance, evoked the regional differences in Yiddish dialect and the comic misinterpretations that are its result.

> From my wife, I get such aggravation, she's driving me out of my wits,
> She's from a different denomination, I'm a Litvak and she's a Galits.
> We're happily married, I don't want to squawk,
> We understand each other completely, except when we talk.
> I say "mutter"[mother], she says "mitter,"
> Es iz mir bitter [it disturbs me] ikh zog [I say] "putter" [butter], she says "pitter,"
> What's the difference, mutter, mitter, putter, pitter? Oy how I shvits [sweat],
> 'Cause I am a Litvak and she's a Galits.

Differences between Jews from Ukraine, Lithuania, and Poland also received parodic treatment. A sketch by the Yiddish comedian Leo Fuchs, for example, featured a comical interpretation of the different dancing styles of a *Ukrainer,* a *Litvak,* and a *Polak.* The continuous switching between Italian, English, and "Italianese," or Yiddish, English, and "Yinglish," is indicative of the ways in which dialect humor on the immigrant vaudeville stage, as well as in American vaudeville, functioned as a site for reflection on the problems of cultural self-definition. See Esther Romeyn and Jack Kugelmass, *Let There Be Laughter: Jewish Humor in America* (Chicago: Spertus Press, 1997), 22–27.

6. My Other/My Self

1. Edwin Milton Royle, "The Vaudeville Theater," *Scribner's Magazine* 26 (1899): 495.

2. According to a different opinion, it may also have referred to the pastoral ballads from the valley of the river Vire. See Gunther Barth, *City People: The Rise of Modern City Culture in Nineteenth-Century America* (New York: Oxford University Press, 1980), 196; Ronald Snyder, *The Voice of the City: Vaudeville and Popular Culture in New York* (New York: Oxford University Press, 1989), 12.

3. In Peter Jelavich, *Berlin Cabaret* (Cambridge, Mass.: Harvard University Press, 1993), 17.

4. Walter Benjamin, "Über Einige Motive bei Baudelaire," *Gesammelte Schriften,* I.2, ed. Rolf Tiedemann and Hermann Schweppenhauser (Frankfurt am Main: Suhrkamp, 1974), 636, 613–15. Baudelaire made this moment of shock the subject as well as the principle of his poetry. In Baudelaire, the flâneur is a "kaleidoscope endowed with consciousness," who "dives in the urban crowd as if in a reservoir of electric energy." But, Benjamin argues, the "private man can become a flâneur only when he, as such, falls out of the window. In spaces where privatization dominates, there is as little room for the flâneur as in the frenetic traffic of the City." And in the course of time, the flâneur, who would let his "progress" be determined by the pace of the turtle he takes

out for a walk in the Parisian "Passages," is overtaken by Taylor, who, with his mechanization of time exemplified in the assembly line, made "Down with the Flâneur" his motto. Benjamin, "Zentral Park," GS I.2, 671; "Über Einige Motive bei Baudelaire," GS I.2, 630, 627

5. Benjamin, Über Einige Motive bei Baudelaire," GS I.2, 630.

6. See Susan Buck-Morss, *The Dialectics of Seeing: Walter Benjamin and the Arcades Project* (Cambridge, Mass.: MIT Press, 1991), 268.

7. Walter Benjamin, *Illuminations: Essays and Reflections,* intro. by Hannah Arendt, ed. and trans. Harry Zohn (New York: Schocken Books, 1969), 236.

8. See Buck-Morss, *The Dialects of Seeing,* 268–69; Benjamin, GS I.2, 499–500.

9. Barth, *City People,* 193–94.

10. Kevin McLaughlin, "Virtual Paris: Benjamin's 'Arcades Project,'" in *Benjamin's Ghosts: Interventions in Contemporary Literary and Cultural Theory,* ed. Gerhard Richter (Stanford: Stanford University Press, 2002), 215.

11. Henry Jenkins, *What Made Pistachio Nuts: Early Sound Comedy and the Vaudeville Aesthetic* (New York: Columbia University Press, 1992), 62.

12. Jelavich, *Berlin Cabaret,* 25.

13. Jenkins, *What Made Pistachio Nuts,* 63.

14. Ibid., 70.

15. Nägele, *Theater, Theory, Speculation,* 15; Jenkins, *What Made Pistachio Nuts,* 71.

16. Jenkins, *What Made Pistachio Nuts,* 65.

17. Snyder, *The Voice of the City,* 7.

18. Ibid., 4.

19. "Sophie Tucker, songstress, and Amy Leslie with Journal Critic in Pleasant Chat," unidentified clipping, Sophie Tucker File (1923–24), Billy Rose Theatre Division, The New York Public Library for the Performing Arts (hereafter NYPL-PA).

20. Peter G. Buckley, "Culture, Class, and Place in Ante-bellum New York," in *Power, Culture and Place: Essays on New York City,* ed. John Hull Mollenkopf (New York: Russell Sage Foundation, 1988); Lawrence Levine, *Highbrow, Lowbrow: The Emergence of Cultural Hierarchy in America* (Cambridge, Mass.: Harvard University Press, 1988).

21. Snyder, *The Voice of the City,* 5.

22. Ibid., 18.

23. Albert F. McLean, "U.S. Vaudeville and the Urban Comics," *Theatre Quarterly* 1, no. 4 (October–December 1971): 48; Snyder, *The Voice of the City,* 26–41.

24. Rachel Bowlby, *Just Looking: Consumer Culture in Dreiser, Gissing, and Zola* (New York: Methuen, 1985), 63.

25. Royle, "The Vaudeville Theater," 488.

26. Ibid., 487.

27. Snyder, *The Voice of the City,* 85–87.

28. Ibid., 84.

29. Chares R. Sherlock, "Where Vaudeville Holds the Boards," *Cosmopolitan,* vol. 32 (1901–2): 413.

30. I borrow the concept of a "cultural middle ground" from Peter G. Buckley, "Culture, Class, and Place in Ante-bellum New York," 43.

31. Sherlock, "Where Vaudeville Holds the Boards," 412.

32. Snyder, *The Voice of the City,* 34.

33. Royle, "The Vaudeville Theater," 488–89.

34. Snyder, *The Voice of the City*, 89.

35. Ibid., 89.

36. Jenkins, *What Made Pistachio Nuts*, 74–75.

37. Snyder, *The Voice of the City*, 109.

38. Barth, *City People*, 194.

39. Buckley, "Culture, Class, and Place in Ante-bellum New York," 45, 44, 39–40.

40. Ibid., 45.

41. Snyder, *The Voice of the City*, 16.

42. Ibid., 19.

43. Ibid., 114, 23–24.

44. Walter Benjamin, *Reflections: Essays, Aphorisms, Autobiographical Writings*, ed. Peter Demetz (New York: Schocken Books, 1986), 333–36.

45. James Young, *Making Up: A Practical and Exhaustive Treatise on This Art* (New York: M. Witmark and Sons, 1905), 83–130.

46. Ibid., 86.

47. Nägele, *Theater, Theory, Speculation*, 104.

48. Allan Sekula, "The Body and the Archive," in *The Contest of Meaning: Critical Histories of Photography*, ed. Richard Bolton (Cambridge, Mass.: MIT Press, 1989), 347.

49. Paul Antonie Distler, "Ethnic Comedy in Vaudeville and Burlesque," in *American Popular Entertainment: Papers and Proceedings of the Conference*, ed. Myron Matlaw (Westport, Conn.: Greenwood Press, 1977), 75.

50. Sherlock, "Where Vaudeville Holds the Boards," 419. On the "shuffling gait" of the Hebrew, see Sander Gilman, *The Jew's Body* (New York: Routledge, 1991), 38–59.

51. Douglas Gilbert, *American Vaudeville: Its Life and Times* (New York: McGraw-Hill Book Co., 1940), 75.

52. Ibid., 288–89.

53. Unidentified clipping, Ben Welch File, Billy Rose Theatre Division, NYPL-PA.

54. Young, *Making Up*, 32.

55. Paul Anthony Distler, "The Rise and Fall of the Racial Comics in American Vaudeville" (Ph.D. diss., Tulane University, 1963), 65.

56. Edward B. Marks, *They All Sang: From Tony Pastor to Rudy Vallee* (New York: Viking Press 1934), 14–15; Carl Wittke, The Immigrant Theme on the American Stage," *Mississippi Valley Historical Review* 9, no. 2 (September 1952): 227.

57. Young, *Making Up*, 146.

58. Brooks, "The Text of the City," *Oppositions* 8 (Spring 1977), 10; Jean-Christophe Agnew, *Worlds Apart: The Market and the Theater in Anglo-American Thought, 1550–1750* (Cambridge: Cambridge University Press, 1986), 59.

59. Richard Moody, *Ned Harrigan: From Corlear's Hook to Herald Square* (Chicago: Nelson Hall, 1980), 47.

60. Ibid., 173, 175, 183.

61. Ethnic conflicts between the Irish, who occupied the most important political offices, Germans, who occupied minor positions in the judiciary and the police, and Jews and African Americans informed many of his plots.

62. Moody, *Ned Harrigan*, 178.

63. In one Horatio Alger story, the street boy Julius visits a cellar theater in a tenement

on Baxter Street, which is operated by ten newspaper boys. He reports that the spectacle featured a marching band singing "that celebrated local song, the Mulligan Guards," and that according to the stage manager "all acts (which included one in which 'an Irish buddy addicted to the bottle and with a heavy brogue gets pitched out of the window by a German bully [and] a Negro is demolished by the umbrellas of two Hibernians') were copied from Harrigan's performances at the 'Comique.'" Ibid., 73

64. William Dean Howells, "Editors Study," *Harper's Weekly* 37 (July 1886): 316.

65. "Hunting 'Types' in the Slum," with Edward Harrigan," *New York Herald,* July 21, 1891, 21, Harrigan File, Billy Rose Theatre Division, NYPL-PA.

66. Edward Harrigan, "Holding Up the Mirror to Nature," *Pearson's Magazine* (November 1903): 506.

67. Quoted in Warren T. Burns, "The Plays of Edward Green Harrigan: The Theater of Intercultural Communication" (Ph.D. diss., Pennsylvania State University, 1969), 95.

68. Irving Howe, *The World of Our Fathers: The Journey of East European Jews to America and the Life They Found and Made* (New York: Simon and Schuster, 1976), 402.

69. "How the immigrant figures as the playwright's victim. Tendency toward caricature deplored by David Warfield. Wherein the Russian Jew has been maligned," unidentified clipping, December 5, 1901, Warfield File, Billy Rose Theatre Division, NYPL-PA. The introduction of "low" subjects in literature led some to complain that in fiction, "we are hobnobbing with persons with whom we could not in real life bear a moment's interview." Orvell, *The Real Thing,* 106.

70. David Warfield (with Margherita Arlina Hamm), *Ghetto Silhouettes* (New York: James Pott Co., 1902), v.

71. The volume features many stories that Christianize Jewish folklore.

72. Initially, Royle explained, the actor was told that "if he stepped away from the sacred precincts of art, the door of the temple would be forever barred against him. . . . None of the dire suppositions happened. The door of the temple proved to be a swinging door, opening easily both ways, and the actor goes back and forth as there is demand for him and as the dollar dictates." The effect of this "open-door" policy was that legitimate actors were subjected to the demands of the vaudeville aesthetic. But the door also swung the other way, as vaudeville actors crossed over into legitimate drama and infused naturalistic theater with the vaudeville aesthetic. Royle, "The Vaudeville Theater," 490–91; Jenkins, *What Made Pistachio Nuts,* 81.

73. A year before he would defend Eugene Debs in the aftermath of the Pullman Strike, Clarence Darrow connected reform and realism in an article entitled "Realism in Literature and Art," which was published in *Arena* in 1893:

"The true realist cannot worship at the shrine of power nor prostitute his gifts for gold. With an artist's eye he sees the world exactly as it is. . . . You can see and feel the social life, and the gulf that separates the rich and poor. . . . The greatest artists of the world to-day are telling the facts and painting scenes that cause humanity to stop and think, and ask why one shall be master and another a serf—why a portion of the world should toil and spin, should wear away their strength and lives, that the rest may live in idleness and ease. . . . With the vision of the seer they feel the coming dawn, when true equality shall reign upon the earth." Clarence Darrow, "Realism in Literature and Art," *Arena* 9 (1893–94): 107–8.

74. See Elsa Nettels, *Language, Race, and Social Class in Howell's America* (Lexington: University of Kentucky Press, 1988).

75. Amy Kaplan, *The Social Construction of American Realism* (Chicago: University of Chicago Press, 1988), 16–19.

76. Ibid., 21.

77. Ibid., 22.

78. Raymond Williams, *The Country and the City* (New York: Oxford University Press, 1973), 169.

79. Ibid., 171. See also Kaplan, *The Social Construction of American Realism,* 6–13.

80. Williams, *The Country and the City,* 226.

81. Kaplan, *The Social Construction of American Realism,* 44–46.

82. Quoted in Miles Orvell, *The Real Thing: Imitation and Authenticity in American Culture, 1880–1940* (Chapel Hill: University of North Carolina Press, 1989), 110.

83. Williams, *The Country and the City,* 226–27.

84. Quoted in Orvell, *The Real Thing,* 111.

85. Kaplan, *The Social Construction of American Realism,* 22.

86. Williams, *The Country and the City,* 226; Orvell, *The Real Thing,* 112; Kaplan, *The Social Construction of American Realism,* 58.

87. Buck-Morss, *The Dialectics of Seeing,* 306.

88. Benjamin, *Illuminations,* 223.

89. Orvell, *The Real Thing,* 85–94.

90. See Maren Stange, *Symbols of Ideal Life: Social Documentary Photography in America, 1890–1950* (Cambridge: Cambridge University Press, 1989), 24.

91. "How the immigrant figures as the playwright's victim," Warfield File, NYPL-LC.

92. Orvell, *The Real Thing,* 91.

93. Ibid., 91–92.

94. Sekula, "The Body and the Archive," 353; Orvell, *The Real Thing,* 88, 92–94.

95. *Baltimore World,* March 10, 1903. Belasco File, Billy Rose Theatre Division, NYPL-PA.

96. Francis Galton, "Generic Images," *Nineteenth Century* 6 (1879): 166.

97. Ibid., 160.

98. Young, *Making Up,* 72.

99. "Hunting 'Types' in the Slum with Edward Harrigan."

100. David Warfield, "How I Created 'Simon Levi': A Novel Quest for Local Color in the Ghetto," *Theatre Magazine* 2, no. 13 (March 1902): 17.

101. David Warfield, "Jewish Stage Characters," *Jewish Messenger,* March 7 [year missing], Belasco File, Billy Rose Theatre Division, NYPL-PA.

In another interview, Warfield's interpretation was even more detailed: "They are a timid, suspicious, but kindly and affectionate race. They have been crushed and maltreated so long that they instinctively regard a stranger as a foe. Their only defense in those lands from which they come is avoidance, deception and craft. The same qualities appear in New York, but of course are not called into play, yet they leave marks upon the faces, carriage and speech of these immigrants. . . . When you first go among them one of the first things you notice is the expression of the eye and mouth. It is pleading, fearful, intelligent and gentle. The voice corresponds with the face, being seldom loud, hard or indignant. The favorite tone is a piano and often a pianissimo. They use the body, especially the hands, in gesticulation." David Warfield, "How I Created 'Simon Levi,'" 17.

Warfield's physiognomic reading of the "Slovak Jew" resonates strongly with other contemporary efforts to define Jewish expression and the "Jewish type." The response of Joseph Jacobs (who was Jewish) to Galton's Jewish composites, for instance, produced the following interpretation of the typical Jewish face:

> The nose does contribute much towards producing the Jewish expression, but it is not so much the shape of its profile, as the accentuation and flexibility of its nostrils. . . . But it is not alone this "nostrility" which makes a Jewish face so easily recognizable. Cover up every part of composite A but the eyes, and yet I fancy everyone familiar with Jews would say, "Those are Jewish eyes." . . . The fullness of the upper lid, and the protuberance of the lower may be remarked, as well as the scantiness of the eyebrows toward the outer edges. The size, brilliance, and darkness of the iris are also well marked. . . . I fail to see any of the cold calculation which Mr. Galton seems to have noticed in the boys in any of the composites, A, B, and C. There is something more like the dreamer and thinker than the merchant in A. . . . The cold and somewhat hard look in composite D, however, is more confirmatory of Mr. Galton's impression. It is note-worthy that this is seen in a composite of young fellows between 17 and 20, who have had to fight a hard battle of life even by that early age. . . . There remain the forehead, mouth, and chin to add their quota to the Jewish expression. The predominating characteristic of the forehead is breadth. . . . The thickness of the lips, and especially a characteristic pout of the lower one, come out markedly in components and composites. . . . Finally, the heavy chin, especially marked in the profile composites, confirms the popular association of this feature with the quality of perseverance, so ingrained in the Jewish nature. (Joseph Jacobs, "The Jewish Type and Galton's Composite Photographs," *Photographic News,* April 24, 1885, 268)

102. "Hunting 'Types' in the Slum with Edward Harrigan," Harrigan File, NYPL-LC.

103. According to Warfield, "the trouble is that too many actors do just what they see all other actors do, and say just what they hear other actors say. The result is that we have stage dialects." "The trouble with most stage dialects . . . is that they are stage dialects. They are not taken from life. Anyone can roll a few 'r's and ejaculate: 'R-r-r-un so q-wick as you can, alretty,' and have a hand me down stage German dialect. Anyone can say 'Me lik-a da banan,' and set himself up as the dispenser of a Simon pure dago patois. Anyone can shrug his shoulders and, in a piping voice, exclaim: 'Pardong, monsieur, zee gentlemans makes zee grand mistake.' No Frenchman ever talked that way. . . . If a manager says, 'Can you play French parts?' 'Oh, yes,' says the actor. 'And Italian?' 'Certainly.' And that is the way all down the list." Frederick Boyd Stevens, "'Hardest Kind of Work is being Funny' says Dave Warfield—and he ought to know," unidentified clipping, Warfield File, Billy Rose Theatre Division, NYPL-PA.

104. David Warfield, "Satire, Wisdom, and Humor of the Russian Jew," Warfield File, Billy Rose Theatre Division, NYPL-PA.

105. Ibid.

106. David Warfield, "How the immigrant figures as the playwrights' victim," Warfield File, Billy Rose Theatre Division, NYPL-PA.

107. Walter Benjamin, *Reflections: Essays, Aphorisms, Autobiographical Writings,* ed. and intro. Peter Demetz (New York: Schocken Books, 1986), 334.

108. Samuel R. Wells, *New Physiognomy, or, the Signs of Character* (New York: Fowler

and Wells, 1894), 321. As John Kasson and Karen Halttunen explain, the doctrines of physiognomy—which assured the legibility of the urban landscape—also promoted a sense of insecurity: not only might one involuntarily betray one's innermost feelings in a particular expression; a perfect reader of character might also use that knowledge to "false" ends and "fake" a certain social identity which might be nigh indistinguishable from the "real" one. This anxiety prompted a fascination with disguise and anonymity. See John F. Kasson, *Rudeness and Civility: Manners in Nineteenth-Century Urban America* (New York: Hill and Wang, 1990), chap. 3; Karen Halttunen, *Confidence Men and Painted Women: A Study of Middle-Class Culture in America, 1830–1870* (New Haven: Yale University Press, 1982).

109. Harrigan, "Holding Up the Mirror to Nature," 504.

110. David Warfield, "How I Created 'Simon Levi,'" 17.

111. "How David Warfield Won a $50 Wager," unidentified clipping, January 27, 1902, Warfield File, Billy Rose Theatre Division, NYPL-PA.

112. See Harley Erdman, *Staging the Jew: The Performance of an American Ethnicity, 1860–1920* (New Brunswick: Rutgers University Press, 1997), 104; for a transcribed monologue, see Brooks McNamara, ed., *American Popular Entertainments: Jokes, Monologues, Bits, and Sketches* (New York City: Performing Arts Journal Publications 1983), 38–40.

113. Distler, "The Rise and Fall of the Racial Comics," 161–64.

114. Ibid.

115. For identifications of Warfield as Jewish, see Erdman, *Staging the Jew,* 110. See also "As I See Myself and Others—Fanny Brice, Famous Character Actress, Declares She Succeeded Because She Is a Jewess," *Jewish Tribune,* June 12, 1925, Brice File, Billy Rose Theatre Division, NYPL-PA; Felix Isman, *Weber and Fields: Their Tribulations, Triumphs, and Their Associates* (New York: Boni and Liveright, 1924), 239. In truth, Warfield, who probably was of German Jewish origin, might, as many other American Jews of German Jewish background have, felt a strong sense of social and cultural distance toward the recent arrivals from eastern Europe. In "How I Created 'Simon Levi,'" David Warfield stresses the fact that "from time immemorial the Israelite people have been split into factions between which the lines of demarcation have been so strongly defined as to equal those between them and other nations. The Portuguese and Spanish Jews, better known as Sephardim, form one community, the English and American Jews a second, the French a third, the Germans a fourth, while the Russian and Slavic Jews constitute a regular series each different from all the rest." *Theatre Magazine* 2, no. 13 (March 1902): 17.

116. In Richard Sennett, *The Fall of Public Man* (New York: Alfred A. Knopf, 1974), 136–37.

117. For an incisive analysis of the construction of bourgeois identity, see Peter Stallybrass and Allon White, *The Politics and Poetics of Transgression* (Ithaca: Cornell University Press, 1986).

118. Steven Mullaney, *The Place of the Stage: License, Play, and Power in Renaissance England* (Chicago: University of Chicago Press, 1988), 69.

119. Eric Lott, "Love and Theft: The Racial Unconscious of Blackface Minstrelsy," *Representations* 39 (Summer 1992): 27. My argument here is significantly influenced by Lott's analysis of the cultural exchange involved in blackface minstrelsy as discussed in this article, as well as in Lott, *Love and Theft: Blackface Minstrelsy and the American Working Class* (New York: Oxford University Press, 1993).

120. Charles Darnton, "David Warfield," unidentified clipping, Warfield File, Billy Rose Theatre Division, NYPL-PA.

121. Eleanor Franklin, "How Edward Harrigan Finds His Types in Real Life," *Leslie's Weekly*, October 22, 1903, 389.

122. "Hunting 'Types' in the Slum with Edward Harrigan."

123. Ibid.

124. "He went into a beer saloon. I followed, and taking the barkeeper aside, told him that I must have that suit of clothes. The upshot was that the German got tipsy, sold the clothes on his back for a few dollars, and exchanged them with some of the cast-off clothes of the man who sold the beer. That night, I went on stage." John M. Callahan, "Fritz Emmet: St. Louis' Favorite German," *Theatre Studies* 24–25 (1977–78): 22.

125. *New York Telegraph*, May 1908, Ben Welch File, Billy Rose Theatre Division, NYPL-PA.

126. "Hunting 'Types' in the Slum with Edward Harrigan." As Lott demonstrates, minstrels used the same rhetoric about the genealogy of their acts and costumes. See Lott, "Love and Theft." Indeed, the stereotypical attributes of the Hebrew comic were what constituted his "individuality," according to one review of a performance of Ben Welch: "Welch comes on with his shuffling gait, beard, big hat, the paraphernalia of his kind.... He has the great gift of being absolutely natural. He is a Yiddisher of the greatest of the American city's East Side. . . . Deprive him of his gait, his beard, his hat, his paraphernalia, and he has lost his individuality." Distler, "The Rise and Fall of the Racial Comics," 162.

127. For an extensive discussion of Warfield's career, see Erdman, *Staging the Jew*.

128. As cited in Distler, "The Rise and Fall of the Racial Comics," 175.

129. Nägele, *Theater, Theory, Speculation*, 104.

130. Absent a surviving copy from the 1901 play, this plot outline is based on various plot summaries in press accounts and the synopsis presented by Harley Erdman, which he bases on his reading of a promptbook for the 1913 revival of the play. See Erdman, *Staging the Jew*, 108–10.

131. Unidentified clipping, September 24, 1901, Warfield File, Billy Rose Theatre Division, NYPL-PA.

132. *New York Times*, September 24, 1901, Belasco File, Billy Rose Theatre Division, NYPL-PA.

133. See Erdman, *Staging the Jew*, 109.

134. Charles A. Ellwood, "The Theory of Imitation in Social Psychology," *American Journal of Sociology* 6, no. 6 (May 1901): 734–36.

135. Valerie Babb, *Whiteness Visible: The Meaning of Whiteness in American Literature and Culture* (New York: New York University Press, 1998), 158–66.

136. Distler, "The Rise and Fall of the Racial Comics," 175.

137. *New York Herald*, September 1901, Belasco File, Billy Rose Theatre Division, NYPL-PA.

138. Dorothy Dix, "The Auctioneer by David Warfield an Artistic Bit of Portraiture," Warfield File, Billy Rose Theatre Division, NYPL-PA.

139. "David Warfield's Career," unidentified clipping, dated March 1, 1903; *Sunday Chicagonian Portland*, January 8, 1903, Warfield File, Billy Rose Theatre Division, NYPL-PA.

140. Unidentified clipping, September 28, 1901. Warfield File, Billy Rose Theatre Division, NYPL-PA.

141. On the Anti-Stage Jew Ridicule Committee, see chapter 7.

142. "David Warfield dislikes 'imitators,'" unidentified clipping, dated February 1906, Warfield File, Billy Rose Theatre Division, NYPL-PA. Henry Tyrrel, "Hard Work Had Nothing to Do with Success in Acting," *NY World,* March 11, 1906, Warfield File, Billy Rose Theatre Division, NYPL-PA.

7. The Truth of Racial Signs

1. Edwin Milton Royle, "The Vaudeville Theater," *Scribner's Magazine* 26 (1899): 489.

2. George M. Cohan and George J. Nathan, "The Mechanics of Emotion," *McClure's Magazine* 42 (November 1913): 70–71.

3. Ibid., 76–77.

4. Albert F. McLean, "U.S. Vaudeville and the Urban Comics," *Theatre Quarterly* 1, no. 4 (October–December 1971): 47.

5. Cohan and Nathan, "the Mechanics of Emotion," 76–77.

6. McLean, "U.S. Vaudeville and the Urban Comics," 47.

7. Ibid., 48.

8. Henry Jenkins, *What Made Pistachio Nuts: Early Sound Comedy and the Vaudeville Aesthetic* (New York: Columbia University Press, 1992), 80; McLean, "U.S. Vaudeville and the Urban Comics," 48.

9. Quoted in McLean, "U.S. Vaudeville and the Urban Comics," 48–49.

10. Esther Romeyn and Jack Kugelmass, *Let There Be Laughter: Jewish Humor in America* (Chicago: Spertus Press, 1997), 30.

11. Ibid.; Cohan and Nathan, "The Mechanics of Emotion," 76.

12. Brooks McNamara, ed., *American Popular Entertainments: Jokes, Monologues, Bits, and Sketches* (New York: Performing Arts Journal Publications, 1983), 38–40.

13. Paul Anthony Distler, *The Rise and Fall of the Racial Comics in American Vaudeville* (Ph.D. diss., Tulane University, 1963), 207.

14. Joe Hayman, *Twenty Different Adventures of Cohen on the Telephone and Other Samples of Jewish Humour* (London: Austin Rogers and Co., 1927), v.

15. Josh Kun, *Audiotopias: Music, Race, and America* (Berkeley and Los Angeles: University of California Press, 2005), 69.

16. *McNally's Bulletin,* no. 2, 1916, Billy Rose Theatre Division, NYPL-PA.

17. Jenkins, *What Made Pistachio Nuts,* 40.

18. McLean, "U.S. Vaudeville and the Urban Comics," 49.

19. Jenkins, *What Made Pistachio Nuts,* 45–46.

20. Ibid., 41, 44.

21. Ibid., 42–43.

22. Ibid., 47.

23. Ibid., 44. On taste as an index of cultural capital, see Pierre Bourdieu, *Distinction: A Social Critique of the Judgment of Taste* (Cambridge, Mass.: Harvard University Press, 1979).

24. Ibid., 40.

25. Gilbert Seldes, *The Seven Lively Arts* (New York: Harper and Brothers, 1924),

200. Mikhail Bakhtin, *Rabelais and His World* (Bloomington: Indiana University Press, 1984), 41.

26. Wehman Bros., *Hebrew Jokes. No. 2* (New York: Wehman Bros., n.d.), 7.

27. Nan Enstad, *Ladies of Labor, Girls of Adventure: Working Women, Popular Culture, and Labor Politics at the Turn of the Twentieth Century* (New York: Columbia University Press, 1999), 26–27; Shawn Michelle Smith, *American Archives: Gender, Race, and Class in Visual Culture* (Princeton: Princeton University Press, 1999); Karen Halttunen, *Confidence Men and Painted Women: A Study of Middle-Class Culture, 1830–1870* (New Haven: Yale University Press, 1982).

28. See Smith, *American Archives,* 54. Indeed, given the permeability of the American middle class, etiquette remained the one secure marker to differentiate gentility from social and racial interlopers. As Smith remarks, "the middle-classes policed the borders between inner and outer in the performance and control of identities" (55).

29. Andrew Heinze, *Adapting to Abundance: Jewish Immigrants, Mass Consumption, and the Search for an American Identity* (New York: Columbia University Press, 1990), 89–104.

30. Quoted in Mike Bazzett, "A Road Map for Social Mobility," manuscript, University of Minnesota, 14.

31. George Stocking, *Race, Culture, and Evolution: Essays in the History of Anthropology* (New York: Free Press, 1968), 263.

32. Ibid., 244–46, 263–65; Charles A. Ellwood, "The Theory of Imitation in Social Psychology," *American Journal of Sociology* 6 (May 1901): 721–41; Jerome Dowd, "Discussion," *American Journal of Sociology* 16 (March 1911): 633–35.

33. See Matthew Frye Jacobson, *Whiteness of a Different Color: European Immigrants and the Alchemy of Race* (Cambridge, Mass.: Harvard University Press, 1998), 176–87.

34. Paul Anthony Distler, "The Rise and Fall of the Racial Comics" (Ph.D. diss., Tulane University, 1963), 191.

35. Geraldine Maschio, "Ethnic Humor and the Demise of the Russel Brothers," *Journal of Popular Culture* 26, no. 1 (Summer 1992): 85.

36. Ibid., 86; Distler, "The Rise and Fall of the Racial Comics," 193.

37. Unidentified clipping, August 1906, Williams and Walker File, Billy Rose Theatre Division, NYPL-PA.

38. Jenkins, *What Made Pistachio Nuts,* 30–31.

39. For a detailed analysis of this development, see Esther Romeyn and Jack Kugelmass, *Let There Be Laughter: Jewish Humor in America* (Chicago: Spertus Press, 1997), 3–4.

40. Sander Gilman, *The Jew's Body* (New York: Routledge, 1991).

41. James Young, *Making Up: A Practical and Exhaustive Treatise on This Art for Professional and Amateur* (New York: M. Witmark and Sons, 1905), 89.

42. As cited in Distler, "The Rise and Fall of the Racial Comics," 175.

43. Jenkins, *What Made Pistachio Nuts,* 32.

44. David Warfield, "Satire, Wisdom, and Humor of the Russian Jew," unidentified clipping, Warfield File, Billy Rose Theatre Division, NYPL-PA.

45. *Chicago American,* February 9, 1902, Belasco File, Billy Rose Theatre Division, NYPL-PA.

Word of the review also spread to the Yiddish press. The *Jewish Daily News* of May 3, 1903, reported on Rabbi Schanfarber's favorable reaction to the play:

When the famous actor David Warfield played in Chicago, at the Illinois Theater, last spring, his manager, Mr. Belasco, invited a number of prominent clergymen to attend the performance. Some of them were so impressed, that they wrote a strong endorsement. . . . One of the inspired followers of Mr. Warfield's performance was Dr. T. Schanfarber, who stated that David Warfield was a great actor, and that his play *The Auctioneer,* for the first time, represented the Jew on the American stage without caricature. (Belasco File, Billy Rose Theatre Division, NYPL-PA)

46. Distler, "The Rise and Fall of the Racial Comics," 178.
47. Undated clipping, Belasco File, Billy Rose Theatre Division, NYPL-PA; Gilman, *The Jew's Body.*
48. *New York Journal,* September 24, 1901, Belasco File, Billy Rose Theatre Division, NYPL-LC. Alan Dale, however, did acknowledge that "the Jew he depicts is in no way a caricature. . . . It is the creation of a new type . . . the first time since Edward Harrigan's pictures of Irish life." Unidentified clipping, Belasco File, Billy Rose Theatre Division, NYPL-PA.
49. *Toledo Blade,* March 11, Belasco File, Billy Rose Theatre Division, NYPL-PA.
50. *The North American,* January 19, 1901, Belasco File, Billy Rose Theatre Division, NYPL-PA.
51. *Chicago Sunday Tribune,* January 11, 1914, Belasco File, Billy Rose Theatre Division, NYPL-PA.
52. James Bennett in the *Chicago Herald,* April 5, 1913, Belasco File, Billy Rose Theatre Division, NYPL-PA.
53. Distler, "The Rise and Fall of the Racial Comics," 189.
54. Esther W. Natkin Collection, Folder 8, Chicago Jewish Historical Society.
55. Distler, "The Rise and Fall of the Racial Comics," 190.
56. *Chicago Record Herald,* May 3, 1913, Esther W. Natkin Collection.
57. Distler, "The Rise and Fall of the Racial Comics," 189.
58. Quoted in the *Chicago Israelite,* May 10, 1913, Esther W. Natkin Collection.
59. Ibid.
60. Howe, *The World of Our Fathers: The Journey of the East European Jews to American and the Life they Found and Made* (New York: Harcourt Brace Jovanovich, 1976,) 405.
61. Unidentified clipping, dated October 24, 1914, Belle Baker File, Billy Rose Theatre Division, NYPL-PA.
62. Unidentified clipping, Ben Welch File, Billy Rose Theatre Division, NYPL-PA.
63. Unidentified clipping, February 12, 1911, Ben Welch File, Billy Rose Theatre Division, NYPL-PA.
64. Harley Erdman, *Staging the Jew: The Performance of an American Ethnicity, 1860–1920* (New Brunswick: Rutgers University Press, 1997), 152.
65. *American Telegraph,* 1918, Leo Carillo File, Billy Rose Theatre Division, NYPL-PA.
66. *Philadelphia Public Ledger,* November 25, 1913, Leo Carillo File, Billy Rose Theatre Division, NYPL-PA.
67. Unidentified clipping, Sam Bernard File, Museum of the City of New York; see also Distler, "The Rise and Fall of the Racial Comics,"187
68. Distler, "The Rise and Fall of the Racial Comics," 189.
69. Jacobson, *Whiteness of a Different Color,* 164.

70. This pattern, according to John Higham, started in the Gilded Age with the exclusion of Joseph Selighman, a wealthy German Jew, from the (Hilton) Grand Union Hotel in Saratoga Springs in 1877. This incident initiated a perceptible rise in what Higham calls "discriminatory," economically based (as opposed to ideological) anti-Semitism. See Jacobson, *Whiteness of a Different Color,* 164–65.

71. Quoted in John Murray Cuddihy, *The Ordeal of Civility: Freud, Marx, Lévi-Strauss, and the Jewish Struggle with Modernity* (New York: Basic Books, 1974), 142–44. Cuddihy characterizes Lippmann's (temporary) socialism as a "prophylaxis for what he takes to be Jewish ostentation" (144).

72. *Philadelphia Record,* October 23, 1906, Barney Bernard File, Billy Rose Theatre Division, NYPL-PA.

73. *New Jersey Mirror,* October 19, 1907, Barney Bernard File, Billy Rose Theatre Division, NYPL-PA.

74. *Chicago Post,* February 17, 1912, Barney Bernard File, Billy Rose Theatre Division, NYPL-PA.

75. Distler, "The Rise and Fall of the Racial Comics," 170.

76. Irving Howe, *The World of Our Fathers,* 405.

77. *Neal's Monthly,* October 1913, Barney Bernard File, Billy Rose Theatre Division, NYPL-LA; Montague Glass, *Potash and Perlmutter: A Play in Three Acts* (New York: Samuel French, 1913), 324. The play includes an interesting version of ethnic impersonation:

> Mawruss recounts his visit to a boxing match, where he was spying on a buyer named James Burke, to Abe Mawruss: "First a fat Eyetalian by the name of Flanagan fights with a young feller, Tom Evans, the Welsh coal-miner. . . .
>
> "Flanagan don't seem much like an Eyetalian, Mawruss," Abe commented.
>
> "I know it," Morris replied; "but that wouldn't surprise you much if you could seen the one what they call Tom Evans, the Welsh coal-miner."
>
> "Why not?" Abe asked.
>
> "Well, you remember Hyman Feinsilver, what worked by us as a shipping clerk while Jake was sick?"
>
> "Sure I do," Abe replied. "Comes from very decent, respectable people in the old country. His father was a rabbi."
>
> "Don't make no difference about his father, Abe," Morris went on. "That Tom Evans, the Welsh coal-miner, is Hyman Feinsilver what worked by us. And the way he treated that poor Eyetalian was a shame for the people." (184–85)

The partners believe they have lost the buyer, James Burke, to Walsh, the competition, until they run into the boss of the drummer Burke, Mr. Small. Mr. Small recognizes Potash. Potash draws a blank, and then gasps "You ain't Scheuer Smolinski, are you?" Small turns out to be his wife Irma's long-lost brother, who had disappeared after failing in the peddler business (189).

Burke complains about having had to spend hours in the boxing match. "For two hours I got to sit and hear him and his friend . . . another lowlife . . . cussing together." He hears Perlmutter whistling "that tune what you are whistling it, ain't that the drinking song from Travvy-ater already?" "For anybody else but a loafer . . . prize fighting is a nix. Opera, Mr. Perlmutter, that's an amusement for a gentleman."

In the end, Small goes with their line: "I'd give them the order if the line wasn't *near* so good." He puts his arm around Abe's shoulder. "It stands in the Talmud, an old saying but a true one, 'Blood is redder than water'" (191–92).

78. Howe, *The World of Our Fathers*, 404.

79. "In the Spotlight: The Story of 'Potash and Perlmutter,' A comedy by A. H. Woods," *Leslie's Illustrated Weekly Newspaper*, October 2, 1913, Barney Bernard File, Billy Rose Theatre Division, NYPL-PA.

80. See "Potash and Perlmutter"—A Dramatization of the Cloak and Suit Trade," *Current Opinion*, September 1914, Barney Bernard File, Billy Rose Theatre Division, NYPL-PA.

81. Montague Glass, *Potash and Perlmutter*, 47. "Potash and Perlmutter"—A Dramatization of the Cloak and Suit Trade."

82. Ibid. Harley Erdman reads the play as a companion piece to Israel Zangwill's *The Melting Pot*, encouraging assimilation through intermarriage. He understands Boris to be "Russian" and Miss Snyder, who eventually will marry Perlmutter, to be a "gentile." See Erdman, *Staging the Jew*, 155–56.

83. Barney Bernard, "The Rehabilitation of the Stage Jew," *Chicago Tribune*, undated, Barney Bernard File, Billy Rose Theatre Division, NYPL-PA.

84. Alex Carr and Barney Bernard, "The Humor of the Jewish Character," *Theater*, March 1914, Barney Bernard File, Billy Rose Theatre Division, NYPL-PA.

85. Unidentified clipping, Barney Bernard File, Billy Rose Theatre Division, NYPL-PA.

86. Carr and Bernard, "The Humor of the Jewish Character." Bernard also claimed that "Abe Potash . . . has all the characteristics of a real modern Jew, honesty, affection, self-denial and a touch of pathos. . . . The trouble with the old time Jewish characters was that they were all much exaggerated. It's the seriousness of Potash and Perlmutter that makes them so funny." Unidentified clipping, Barney Bernard File, Billy Rose Theatre Division, NYPL-PA.

87. London *Spectator*, undated clipping, Barney Bernard File, Billy Rose Theatre Division, NYPL-PA.

88. Carr and Bernard, "The Humor of the Jewish Character," Barney Bernard File, Billy Rose Theatre Division, NYPL-PA.

89. Ibid. The play saw a number of sequels, entitled "Potash and Perlmutter in Wall Street," "Potash and Perlmutter in Society," and "Business Before Pleasure."

90. Daniel Itzkovitz, "Secret Temples," in Jonathan Boyarin and Daniel Boyarin, eds., *Jews and Other Differences: The New Jewish Cultural Studies* (Minneapolis: University of Minnesota Press, 1997), 178; Jay Geller, "The Aromatics of Jewish Difference; or, Benjamin's Allegory of Aura," in Boyarin and Boyarin, 240.

91. "Abe and Mawruss" Is a Hilarious Hit," *The World*, undated clipping, Barney Bernard File, Billy Rose Theatre Division, NYPL-PA.

92. See Phillip Barrish, "'The Genuine Article': Ethnicity, Capital, and the Rise of David Levinsky," *American Literary History* 5, no. 4 (Winter 1993): 643–62.

93. *Leslie's Illustrated Weekly Newspaper*, October 2, 1913, Barney Bernard File, Billy Rose Theatre Division, NYPL-PA.

94. "Potash and Perlmutter," *Current Opinion*, September 1914, Barney Bernard File, Billy Rose Theatre Division, NYPL-PA.

95. Kate Holladay Klaghorn, *Survey* 39, December 11, 1917.

8. Blackface, Jewface, Whiteface

1. Unidentified Clipping, dated April 22, 1922, Bert Williams File, Billy Rose Theatre Collection, NYPL-PA.

2. Karen Sotiropoulos writes that white actors at the Ziegfeld Follies with whom Williams worked had a habit of calling Williams "the whitest black man I know" or "The Black man with the White heart" or a "black white man." Karen Sotiropoulos, *Staging Race: Black Performers in Turn of the Century America* (Cambridge, Mass.: Harvard University Press, 2006), 191–92.

3. Gayle Wald, *Crossing the Line: Racial Passing in Twentieth-Century U.S. Literature and Culture* (Durham: Duke University Press, 1999), 97.

4. Patricia McKee, *Producing American Races: Henry James, William Faulkner, Toni Morrison* (Durham: Duke University Press, 1999), 10, 8.

5. As quoted in Houston A. Baker Jr., *Modernism and the Harlem Renaissance* (Chicago: Chicago University Press, 1987), 39.

6. Ibid., 17.

7. Whereas according to Alexander Saxton, blackface unified a white working class through bigotry and race hatred, in the analysis of David Roediger it did so through a "contaminated racial desire," in which minstrelsy's image of blacks evoked the white workers' pre-wage slavery, libidinal, careless, expressive, free self. Eric Lott interprets the minstrel image as even more ambivalent. The original "theft" of black performance—and speech styles—occurred at relatively egalitarian sites of interracial mixing, and facilitated the development of a working-class, counter-hegemonic discourse deeply critical of the emerging bourgeoisie, the codes of gentility, and the class hierarchies embedded in them. W. T. Lhamon regards blackface as an American vernacular, and an expression of workers and youth rebellion against the pretensions of the genteel upper class and the capitalist spirit of self-discipline. Yet in spite of, or, according to some interpretations, because of the cross-racial desire embedded in minstrelsy, it never led to interracial solidarity. Indeed, minstrelsy developed into a national vernacular in the 1840s precisely because it did not challenge racial boundaries, and it provided a release from the restraints of bourgeois respectability through the invocation of a disowned black body.

Alexander Saxton, *The Rise and Fall of the White Republic: Class and Mass Culture in Nineteenth-Century America* (London: Verso, 1990); David Roediger, *The Wages of Whiteness: Race and the Making of the American Working Class* (London: Verso, 1988), 13–14, 116. Eric Lott, "Love and Theft, The Racial Unconscious of Blackface Minstrelsy," *Representations* 39 (1992); *Love and Theft: Blackface and the American Working Class* (Oxford: Oxford University Press, 1993); W. T. Lhamon Jr., *Raising Cain: Blackface Performance from Jim Crow to Hip-Hop* (Cambridge, Mass.: Harvard University Press, 1998).

8. Michael Rogin, *Black Face, White Noise: Jewish Immigrants in the Hollywood Melting Pot* (Berkeley and Los Angeles: University of California Press, 1996), 50, 56.

9. Michael North, *The Dialect of Modernism: Race, Language, and Twentieth-Century Literature* (New York: Oxford University Press, 1994), 7.

10. Toni Morrison, *Playing in the Dark: Whiteness and the Literary Imagination* (New York: Vintage Books, 1993), 44–45.

11. I borrow from Steven Mullaney's insight in the operation of power in Elizabethan England and its manifestation on the Elizabethan stage. See Steven Mullaney, *The*

Place of the Stage: License, Play, and Power in Renaissance England (Chicago: University of Chicago Press, 1988), 52, 69–72. African American performers confronted the color line head on in the strictures of their own roles on the vaudeville stage, where prejudice confined them to playing up to the comic "coon" stereotype, and audiences and managers carefully policed "transgressions" of these prescribed roles. The famous actress-dancer Aida Overton Walker commented in an article entitled "The Colorline in Musical Comedy" that "you haven't the faintest conception of the difficulties that must be overcome, of the prejudices which must be soothed, of the things we must avoid whenever we write or a sing a piece of music, put on a play or sketch, walk out in the street or land in a new town. Every little thing we do must be thought out and arranged by negroes, because they alone know how easy it is for a colored show to offend a white audience." Unidentified clipping, Williams and Walker File, Locke Collection, NYPL-PA.

12. Amy Robinson, quoted in James Salazar, "A Good Judge of Character?" *American Quarterly* 54, no. 2 (June 2002): 327.

13. Historian U. B. Phillips, quoted in Rogin, *Blackface, White Noise*, 33.

14. Unidentified clipping, January 11, 1907, Williams and Walker File, Locke Collection, 15, NYPL-PA.

15. "George Walker, of Williams and Walker," unidentified clipping, Williams and Walker File, Locke Collection, 3, NYPL-PA. His wife, the actress Aida Overton Walker, echoed George Walker's comments: "In all the ten years that I have appeared and helped produce a great many plays of a musical nature, there has never been the remotest suspicion of a love story in any of them. . . . It's not accident or because we don't want to put on plays as beautiful and as artistic in every way as do white actors, but because there is a popular prejudice against love scenes enacted by negroes." "The Color Line in Musical Comedy," Williams and Walker File.

16. Helen Armstead-Johnson, "Themes and Values in Afro-American Librettos and Book Musicals, 1898–1930," in *Musical Theatre in America: Papers and Proceedings of the Conference*, ed. Glenn Looney (Westport, Conn.: Greenwood Press, 1984), 134.

17. Ibid.

18. Quoted in Thomas L. Riis, *More Than Just Minstrel Shows: The Rise of Black Musical Theatre at the Turn of the Century* (New York: Institute for Studies in American Music, 1992), 12.

19. James Young, *Making Up: A Practical and Exhaustive Treatise on This Art for Professional and Amateur* (New York: M. Witmark and Sons, 1905), 92–93.

20. Riis, *More Than Just Minstrel Shows*, 13.

21. *New York Dramatic Mirror*, April 9, 1901, Cole and Johnson File, Billy Rose Theatre Collection, NYPL-PA; Riis, *More Than Just Minstrel Shows*, 15.

22. Ibid., 15, 12–13.

23. Lott, *Love and Theft*, 95.

24. On cultural pastiche, see Ronald Sanders, "The American Popular Song," in *Next Year in Jerusalem: Portraits of the Jew in the Twentieth Century*, ed. Douglas Villiers (New York: Viking Press, 1976), 202.

25. Harley Erdman, *Staging the Jew: The Performance of an American Ethnicity, 1860–1920* (New Brunswick: Rutgers University Press, 1997), 105.

26. Douglas Gilbert, *Vaudeville: Its Life and Times* (New York: McGraw-Hill, 1940),

75; Felix Isman, *Weber and Fields* (New York: Boni and Liveright, 1924), 51; unidentified newspaper clipping, dated January 2, 1912, Belle Baker File, Billy Rose Theatre Collection, NYPL-PA.

Yiddish vaudeville, meanwhile, found its comic voice in the constant switching between Yiddish, English, and "Yinglish," offering, in comic language, a reflection on the difficulty of cultural self-definition. Yiddish vaudevillians frequently roamed the terrain of American mythology and popular culture, inserting their characters in the West or in the equally foreign immigrant neighborhoods that adjoined the Lower East Side. In sketches and songs such as "Cordova, the Bronx Casanova," "Gallitsianer Caballero," Leo Fuch's "Yiddisher Cowboy" (a travesty of the American popular song "Home on the Range," in which the "Wild West" turns out to be a Catskills resort and the "cowboy" a notorious womanizer), and Menasha Skulnik's "Scotchman from Orchard Street," pastiche created comic texts that were complexly layered musically and linguistically as well as culturally. Romeyn and Kugelmass, *Let There Be Laughter*, 23–25. Josh Kun, *Audiotopia: Music, Race, and America* (Berkeley and Los Angeles: University of California Press, 2005), discusses Yiddish vaudeville and dialect comedy in his chapter on Micky Katz, 48–85.

27. Marjorie Garber, *Vested Interests: Cross-Dressing and Cultural Anxiety* (New York: HarperPerennial, 1993), 6–40.

28. Riis, *More Than Just Minstrel Shows*, 12–15; David Krasner, *Resistance, Parody, and Double Consciousness in African American Theater, 1895–1910* (New York: St. Martin's Press, 1997), 30–34.

29. Michael North mentions that T. S. Eliot's unpublished play "Sweeney Agonistes" finishes with a minstrel-show version of "Under the Bamboo Tree," which Cole and Johnson had performed to great acclaim at the 1904 St. Louis World's Fair, and which Eliot had attended with his family. Michael North, *The Dialect of Modernism*, 10.

30. Cole and Johnson File, Billy Rose Theatre Collection, NYPL-PA.

31. Riis, *More Than Just Minstrel Shows*, 20.

32. For an incisive discussion of the performances of Cole and Johnson, which merit more in-depth analysis than I can provide here, see David Krasner, *Resistance, Parody, and Double Consciousness in African American Theater, 1895–1910*.

33. *N.J. Telegraph*, January 25, 1906, Williams and Walker File, Billy Rose Theatre Collection, NYPL-PA; Louis Chude-Sokei, *The Last "Darkey": Bert Williams, Black-on-Black Minstrelsy, and the African Diaspora* (Durham: Duke University Press, 2006), 27. The initiative in 1908 led to the founding of the Frogs, which, although established by vaudeville artists, extended membership to black professionals as well. Sotiropoulos, *Staging Race*, 197.

34. Williams and Walker File, Locke Collection, 5, NYPL-PA.

35. George Walker, "The Real 'Coon' on the American Stage," *Theatre Magazine*, August 1906. Williams and Walker File, Billy Rose Theatre Collection, NYPL-PA.

36. Chude-Sokei, *The Last "Darkey,"* 31.

37. Houston A. Baker Jr., *Modernism and the Harlem Renaissance* (Chicago: University of Chicago Press, 1987), 21; Michael E. Elliott, *The Culture Concept: Writing and Difference in the Age of Realism* (Minneapolis: University of Minnesota Press, 2002), 74.

38. Chude-Sokei, *The Last "Darkey,"* 31.

39. Ibid., 57.

40. Elliott, *The Culture Concept*, 68.

41. Ibid., 71–72. Williams, Walker, and Dunbar attempted to interrogate the notion of "authentic" dialect by switching linguistic codes and alternating the use of dialect with "straight" English. The African American elite was well aware that speech and dialect served to trans-code cultural differences into social and racial hierarchies, and prided itself on speaking "flawless English." A joke by George Walker illustrates this awareness:

> FIRST BLACK PERFORMER: What's the use of you trying to play Shakespeare; you can't be a white man. Why not be a nigger and a good nigger?
> SECOND BLACK PERFORMER: My dear fellow, I talk English too well to be a Negro. (Quoted in Sotiropoulos, *Staging Race*, 114)

42. Ibid., 105.

43. Ibid., 87–89.

44. Ann Charters, *Nobody: The Story of Bert Williams* (London: Macmillan, 1970), 38. On the complex cultural politics of the cakewalk, and in particular the performances of Aida Overton Walker, which deserve a chapter in their own right, see Krasner, *Resistance, Parody, and Double Consciousness*, 75–98; Daphne A. Brooks, *Bodies in Dissent: Spectacular Performances of Race and Freedom, 1850–1910* (Durham: Duke University Press, 2006), 326–42; on the "coon" craze, see Sotiropoulos, *Staging Race*, 105–22.

45. Krasner, *Resistance, Parody, and Double Consciousness*, 54.

46. Sotiropoulos, *Staging Race*, 192.

47. Charters, *Nobody*, 54.

48. Sotiropoulos, *Staging Race*, 24.

49. George Walker, "The 'Real Coon' on the American Stage," *Theatre Magazine*, August 1906. Williams and Walker File, Billy Rose Theatre Collection, NYPL-PA.

50. Charters, *Nobody*, 70.

51. For detailed synopses of the comedies, see Brooks, *Bodies in Dissent*, 207–80; Sotiropoulos, *Staging Race*, 123–62; Krasner, *Resistance, Parody, and Double Consciousness*, 66–74, 99–114.

52. Chude-Sokei, *The Last "Darkey,"* 177.

53. See Armstead Johnson, "Themes and Values in Afro-American Librettos and Book Musicals, 1898–1930," 136–39; Riis, *More Than Just Minstrel Shows*, 53–54. The song "Vassar Girl," sung by Aida Overton Walker, was about a girl passing as "exotic" to get herself into college: "I am the first dark belle to go to Vassar / I play the part so well I came from Madagascar. / Oh, the paper howled and said it was a shame / And they really thought I was to blame. / They thought that I had played an awful little game / But they had to own that I got there just the same." Johnson, "Themes and Values in Afro-American Librettos and Book Musicals," 138.

54. Unidentified clipping, Williams and Walker File, Locke Collection, 33, NYPL-PA. Daphne A. Brooks interprets this performance primarily as a commentary on imperialism, which the play also projects in its exploitation of Dahomey as a source of "gold and silver." See Brooks, *Bodies in Dissent*, 245–46.

55. George Walker, "The Real 'Coon' on the American Stage," *Theatre Magazine*, August 1906, Williams and Walker File, NYPL-LC. Williams, Walker insisted, "is the first man that I know in our race to attempt to delineate a darky in a perfectly natural way." Charters, *Nobody*, 71. On the complex cultural politics of the representation of Africa in

these shows, see Chude-Sokei, *The Last "Darkey"*; Brooks, *Bodies in Dissent*, 207–80; Sotiropoulos, *Staging Race*, 125–62.

56. Sotiropoulos, *Staging Race*, 158. Sotiropoulos includes a fascinating discussion of the black middle-class "cult of respectability" and its response to African American minstrelsy. See especially 163–96.

57. Unidentified clipping, Williams and Walker File, Locke Collection, 33, NYPL-PA.

58. *Toledo Blade*, January 28, 1907. Williams and Walker File, Billy Rose Theatre Collection, NYPL-PA.

59. *Chicago Record*, n.d., Williams and Walker File, Locke Collection, 23, NYPL-PA.

60. Unidentified clipping, Williams and Walker File, Locke Collection 23, NYPL-PA.

61. Unidentified clipping, Williams and Walker File, Locke Collection, 15, NYPL-PA.

62. "Funny Negro Comedian," unidentified clipping, dated January 11, 1907, Williams and Walker File, Locke Collection, 37, NYPL-PA.

63. *Chicago Record*, n.d., Williams and Walker File, Locke Collection, 23, NYPL-PA.

64. "Alan Dale Says 'Abyssinia'—Negro Show of Too Exalted Ambitions," *New Jersey American*, February 6, 1906. Williams and Walker File, Locke Collection, 24.

65. Chude-Sokei, *The Last "Darkey,"* 38.

66. Ibid. 35; Ann Douglas, *Terrible Honesty: Mongrel Manhattan in the 1920s* (New York: Farrar, Straus and Giroux, 1995), 329.

67. Baker, *Modernism and the Harlem Renaissance*, 24.

68. Homi Bhabha, "Of Mimicry and Man: The Ambivalence of Colonial Discourse," *October* 28 (Spring 1984): 128–29, 126, 130.

69. Douglas, *Terrible Honesty*, 328.

70. Charters, *Nobody*, 19.

71. Bert Williams, "The Comic Side of Trouble," *The American Magazine* 85 (January–June 1918), in Chude-Sokei, *The Last "Darkey,"* 170.

72. Chude-Sokei, *The Last "Darkey,"* 53–54.

73. Ibid., 75.

74. Ibid., 52.

75. Unidentified clipping, Williams and Walker File, Locke Collection, 69, NYPL-PA.

76. Chude-Sokei, *The Last "Darkey,"* 53.

77. Douglas, *Terrible Honesty*, 328.

78. Knowing full well the extent of the racial sensitivities of his audience, Williams went as far as including a clause in his contract that stipulated that he not be onstage in the presence of any female members of the Follies cast. Ibid.; *Pittsburgh Gazette*, undated, Al Jolson File, Billy Rose Theatre Collection, NYPL-PA.

79. Douglas, *Terrible Honesty*, 371.

80. See Romeyn and Kugelmass, *Let There Be Laughter*, 41. "Sadie Salome, Go Home!" Words and music by Edgar Leslie and Irving Berlin (New York: Ted Snyder Co., 1909). See also Stanley Green, *The Great Clowns of Broadway* (New York: Oxford University Press, 1984).

81. Douglas, *Terrible Honesty*, 354–57.

82. Romeyn and Kugelmass, *Let There Be Laughter*, 88; Stanley Green, *The Great Clowns of Broadway*, 7; Henry Jenkins, *What Made Pistachio Nuts: Early Sound Comedy and the Vaudeville Aesthetic* (New York: Columbia University Press, 1992), 71.

83. Romeyn and Kugelmass, *Let There Be Laughter*, 42.

84. Ibid., 43.

85. *Telegraph,* April 14, 1922, Eddie Cantor File, Billy Rose Theatre Collection, NYPL-PA. In *Whoopee,* the movie version of which appeared in 1930, Cantor adopts a series of disguises—genteel hypochondriac, black cook, cowboy-outlaw—and, masquerading as an Indian trying to sell a blanket and doll, lapses eventually into the accent and gestures of a Lower East Side peddler: "Look, if I sell you for $40, I couldn't make a cent. I should live—it costs me alone thirty-five and a half dollars—so I should sell you for $40. Such a *chutzpah! Ir darf zikh shemen* [You should be ashamed of yourself!]."

Michael Rogin has characterized the difference between the Al Jolson of *The Jazz Singer* and the Eddie Cantor of *Whoopee* as a difference between racial passing and racial masquerade. According to Rogin, Jolson's use of the discourse of "racial passing" implied a wish "to replace one's birth parents and genealogy," and "trapped immigrants in . . . unalterable identities," condemning them to a "sham existence." Cantor's "racial masquerade," meanwhile, held the promise of "metamorphosis through role-playing" and "freed immigrants of their communities of origin." Michael Rogin, *Blackface, White Noise,* 124.

86. Jenkins, *What Made Pistachio Nuts,* 71.

87. Romeyn and Kugelmass, *Let There Be Laughter,* 40.

88. Unidentified clipping, Al Jolson File, Billy Rose Theatre Collection, NYPL-PA.

89. Clipping, "The Art of Minstrelsy," undated, Al Jolson File, Billy Rose Theatre Collection, NYPL-PA.

90. Unidentified clipping, Al Jolson File, Billy Rose Theatre Collection, NYPL-PA.

91. *Pittsburgh Gazette,* undated, Al Jolson File, Billy Rose Theatre Collection, NYPL-PA.

92. Unidentified clipping, Al Jolson File, Billy Rose Theatre Collection, NYPL-PA.

93. Gilbert Seldes, *The Seven Lively Arts* (New York: Harper and Brothers, 1924), 200.

94. Romeyn and Kugelmass, *Let There Be Laughter,* 10; Stephen J. Whitfield, "The Distinctiveness of American Jewish Humor," *Modern Judaism* 6, no. 3 (October 1986): 251–52.

95. Once asked by a journalist if he wished he had been born white, Williams answered negatively, but he admitted that he thought being black was an "inconvenience." Questioned by another journalist, who asked Williams if he thought that "all great negroes did not have white blood in their veins," Williams responded with outrage: "White blood make a black man any smarter!" shouted Williams, "I guess not! Why, what kind of white blood do we get! The very worst and lowest and meanest there is. And when a man with some of this in his veins becomes famous you say the bad white blood did it?" Sotiropoulos, *Staging Race,* 192.

96. "As I see myself and Others," *Jewish Tribune,* June 12, 1925, Fanny Brice File, Billy Rose Theatre Collection, NYPL-PA.

97. As quoted in Jonathan Freedman, *The Temple of Culture: Assimilation and Anti-Semitism in Literary Anglo-America* (Oxford: Oxford University Press, 2000), 31.

98. As quoted in Freedman, *The Temple of Culture,* 32, 45; Itzkovitz, "Secret Temples," 178; Jay Geller, "The Aromatics of Jewish Difference; or, Benjamin's Allegory of Aura," in *Jews and Other Differences: The New Jewish Cultural Studies,* ed. Jonathan Boyarin and Daniel Boyarin (Minneapolis: University of Minnesota Press, 1997), 240.

99. Daniel Itzkovitz, "Secret Temples," in *Jews and Other Differences,* ed. Boyarin and Boyarin, 183–84.

100. See Romeyn and Kugelmass, *Let There Be Laughter,* 9–10. Gilles Deleuze and Félix Guattari, *Kafka: Towards a Minor Literature,* Theory and History of Literature, vol. 30 (Minneapolis: University of Minnesota Press, 1986). Minstrelsy, Rogin concludes rather cryptically, "accepted ethnic difference by insisting on racial division." It "helped create New World ethnic identities—Irish American and Jewish American—that were culturally pluralist within the melting pot." Yet on the question of how exactly minstrelsy reinforced "the distinction between race and ethnicity," a distinction it can only have gestured toward, Rogin remains rather vague. The difference between the trajectory of Jewish and African American performers in vaudeville and musical revues from 1900 to 1910 may illuminate some aspects of this process. Rogin, *Blackface, White Noise,* 56–57.

101. Walter Benn Michaels, *Our America: Nativism, Modernism, and Pluralism* (Durham: Duke University Press, 1995), 24.

102. James Weldon Johnson, *Black Manhattan* (New York: Da Capo Press, 1990), 191.

103. Unidentified clipping, Al Jolson File, Billy Rose Theatre Collection, NYPL-PA.

104. Sotiropoulos, *Staging Race,* 226.

105. Robyn Wiegman, *American Anatomies: Theorizing Race and Gender* (Durham: Duke University Press, 1998), 31.

106. Steven Mullaney, *The Place of the Stage: License, Play, and Power in Renaissance England* (Chicago: University of Chicago Press, 1988), 56.

107. Charles Musser, "Ethnicity, Role-Playing, and American Film Comedy: From Chinese Laundry Scene to Whoopee (1984–1930)," in *Unspeakable Images: Ethnicity and the American Cinema,* ed. Lester Friedman (Chicago: University of Illinois Press, 1991), 60.

108. Rachel Bowlby, *Just Looking: Consumer Culture in Dreiser, Gissing, and Zola* (New York: Methuen, 1985), 64–65.

INDEX

Page numbers in italics refer to illustrations

media (*see* by name, e.g., *McClure's*). *See also* photography

Meloney, William Brown, 59

Merriwell, Frank, 28

Michaels, Walter Benn, 94

middle class, 7, 12, 149–50; March family (fictional), 38, 143–44; professionalism, 31–37, 144. *See also* bourgeoisie; slumming; social masquerading

Migliaccio, Eduardo ("Farfariello"), xxix, *100*, 103–4, 188–89, 240n46; grotesque reality in works, 116–22; impersonations, 101–3

Mills, Frederick, 44

mimicry. *See* imitation/mimicry; social masquerading

minstrel mask, 187, 199, 201–2

minstrelsy, xxxi. *See also* blackface comedy; minstrel mask

"Mio Compare, Il" (Farfiello sketch), 106–7

missionary work, 63–64, 65–67

mobility: cultural, 142; downward, 45, 112–13; geographic, 130; upward, 114–15, 163. *See also* social class

modernist architecture, ix

modernity, x, xii, xxii, 3, 126, *211*, 216n57; Broadway and, 109–10; capitalist industrialization and, xvi, 3–4, 15; contradictions of, 90; urban space and, xvii, xxv, 3–4, 24. *See also* camera; city, the; urban space

Monarch, Major (fictional), 49–50

Monarch, Mrs. (fictional), 48–51

moral economy, 22

morality, 181–84

moral superiority, 8, 165

moral transgression, 108–9

Morrison, Toni, 190

Mott and Pell streets, 9

Moy Kee (fictional), 71

mug shot, 2, 8

Mulberry Bend, 9

Mulberry Street, 17, 101. *See also* Little Italy

Mullaney, Steven, xvi, xxv, 255–256n11

Munsey's Magazine, 5, 68, 69, 74, 81

"mystery and misery" genre, xxvi, 17, 24, 24–25

Nägele, Rainer, xvi–xvii

"narratives of exposure," xxvi, 7, 22

naturalization of social differences, xviii

neo-Lamarckianism, xx–xxi, 11, 43, 167

New Humor, 160, 165, 207

New York City, 1880–1920 period, xi, xiv, xxvi, 3, 9. *See also* by neighborhood

New York Clipper, 173–74

New York Democratic Mirror, 173

New York Herald, 139

New York Society for the Cultivation of the Self, 166

New York Times, 153

"Old Man Nelson," 136–37

Opera House, Pastor's, 132, 133

opium dens, 55, 58–59, 67, 71, 74, 77, 140

Orientalism, 70–73, 129

Orvell, Miles, 14, 144

Osherman, Mollie Eda, 172, 176

Other, the, xxvii; having knowledge and experience of, 39, 42, 150, 228n49; racial others, xxvi–xxvii, xxix, 63. *See also* self, the

Otherness, xxix, 13, 148

padroni, 105

Page, Brett, 160

Paley, John, *Di Shvartse Khevre* (*The Black Gang*), 18, 22–25

Panizza, Oskar, 127

Parker, Cornelia Stratton, 42

Parkhurst, Reverend, 38

Pasinksy, Mark (fictional), 178

"Pasquale Passaguai" (Farfiello sketch), 118–19

passing, 148–49, 155, 190, 199, 260n85; inability to pass, 153

Pastor, Tony, 128, 132

peddler, Jewish, 82–83, 134–35, 141, 145. *See also* "Hebrew" type

Pell Street, 9

performance of identity, 87, 89, 94

quest for artistic legitimacy, 155–65;
"Satire, Wit and Humor of the Russian
Jew," 147; in *The Auctioneer*, 141, 142,
169–72; in *The Music Master*, 155–56
Warner, Michael, 188
Water Street area, 9
Wayside, Willie (fictional), 192
Weber, Joe, 193. *See also* Weber and Fields
Weber, Max, xiv, 25
Weber, Samuel, xv, xxv
Weber and Fields, 161–62
Wehman, Henry, 165–66
Wehman Brothers, 161
Welch, Ben, 135, 174–75
Welch Brothers, 161
Welch, Joe, 148–49, 173, 175; "Cohen on
the Telephone," 162–63
Wells, Samuel, *The New Physiognomy*, 39
whiteface, xxix, xxx–xxxi, 187
whiteness, xxx–xxxi, 36; as a bourgeois
prerogative, 149–50, 187–88, 200;
attaining, 89, 155, 190–91; transcending
racial boundaries, 188, 191, 203. *See
also* bourgeoisie

Williams, Bert, *186*, 191, 200–203, 207,
209; *Abyssinia*, 200–201; as a gentle-
man, 203–4, 234n12; as "Mr. Nobody,"
201; on race, 259n78, 260n95
Williams, Raymond, 142–43
Williams, Rosalind, 71
Williams and Walker, 198–200; *Clorindy,
or the Origin of the Cake Walk*, 196–97;
the Interracial Ethiopian Theatre,
New York, 194; *The Sons of Ham*, 197
Willy (fictional), 23–24
Winant, Howard, 9
World War II, xxx
Wyckoff, Walter, 38, 43, 45

Yankel (fictional), 23–24
Yekl (Cahan), 83–84, 234n12
Yiddish, xxvi, 81
Yiddish vaudeville, 241, 242n68, 257n26
Young, James, 136

Ziegfeld, Florenz, 205
Ziegfeld Follies, 177, 187, 207, 255n2

INDEX

Page numbers in italics refer to illustrations

Esther Romeyn is assistant research scholar in the Center for European Studies at the University of Florida and the coauthor of *Let There Be Laughter: Jewish Humor in America.*

www.ingramcontent.com/pod-product-compliance
Lightning Source LLC
Chambersburg PA
CBHW020826270326
41928CB00006B/449